Miller

OCCUPATIONS AND SOCIETY

OCCUPATIONS AND SOCIETY

TOWARD A SOCIOLOGY
OF THE LABOR MARKET

PAUL D. MONTAGNA
BROOKLYN COLLEGE

JOHN WILEY & SONS
NEW YORK, SANTA BARBARA
LONDON, SIDNEY
TORONTO

This book was set by Trotta Composition, Incorporated.

It was printed and bound by Vail-Ballou Press, Incorporated.

Text and cover design by Jerome Wilke.

Production supervised by Theresa A. Harmsen.

Library of Congress Cataloging in Publication Data:

Montagna, Paul D.
   Occupations and society.

   Includes bibliographical references and indexes.
     1. United States—Occupations. 2. Labor and laboring classes—United States. 3. Labor supply—United States. 4. Industrial sociology—United States. 5. Occupational mobility—United States.
I. Title.

HD5724.M63   301.5'5   76-40121
ISBN 0-471-61383-5

Printed in the United States of America

10 9 8 7 6 5 4 3 2 1

IN MEMORY OF
ERWIN O. SMIGEL
SCHOLAR, TEACHER, MENTOR, FRIEND

PREFACE

An increasing number of intellectuals today are predicting that humanity is destined for a period of authoritarian forms of social control. In the words of Lionel Trilling, they feel that "Alienation is to be overcome only by the completeness of alienation,"[1] a point we have not yet reached. Others hope that new methods of operating in the social structure will lead to a new historical stage. One suggestion is that workers must become active and share in the control over production, natural resources, and communications processes, that is, over the entire work process. Another related suggestion is that there is developing a set of common interests among the growing professional class and other highly skilled workers. This "new working class" is counteracting the power of the ruling elites. Still others say, however, that the professional elite will be co-opted by the values and consciousness of those in positions of authority.

These are some of the broader issues being advanced by social scientists as the world of work is explored in greater depth. Occupational sociology plays an important role in these studies by providing analyses of individuals in occupations, of entire occupations, and even of occupational groups and categories (e.g., white-collar, blue-collar, professional).

For the beginning course in the sociology of occupations most textbooks have summarized the research in the field by separating into several chapters the major occupational categories and groups devised by the United States Bureau of the Census and then adding a few chapters on occupational mobility, career choice, occupations and education, and the like. This book does not omit these traditional chapters, but includes them as part of a larger perspective on occupations—that of social stratification. Often, occupations textbooks will relegate stratification theory to part of a chapter on social mobility. I incorporate stratification theory throughout the text, permitting an exploration of the broader questions posed above. Also, personal involvement in work (i.e., alienation or lack of it) and level of technological development (degree of automation) are examined at each level of the occupational structure in relation to these questions.

This book has been designed to interest the instructor as well as the student (therefore, it does not "talk down" to the student) by introducing several areas of new material. For example, Chapter 4 summarizes for the first time in a sociological context a small but important field in economics—labor market stratification. It is used along with stratification theory in sociology as an explanation for occupational structure and change at various points throughout the text. This chapter should be of considerable interest to those concerned with inequality and poverty in American society. It is the opinion of most labor market theorists that these two areas—inequality and poverty and occupations—cannot be separated for analysis but are both part of the structure and dynamics of the labor market. I agree with this interpretation and make it an important part of my analysis of occupations, as the subtitle of this book indicates.

Therefore, Part 1 deals with a description and analysis of the labor force (what the jobs are) and the labor market (how the jobs are apportioned and why). It forms the basis for a critical analysis of work and occupations. It is critical in that it attempts to analyze control systems and structures as well as those who are controlled.[2] It is also critical in that it analyzes ideas about occupations historically and with a view toward demystifying the ideas and social systems that determine the occupational structure.

Part 2 offers an explanation of occupational dynamics by analyzing how people in occupations react to organizational growth and technological development, that is, specifically, the rationalization of the work process. This is accomplished by reviewing (mostly) symbolic interactionist studies covering more than 35 occupations, and Marxist and functionalist interpretations of working-class bourgeoisification and middle-class proletarianization. Labor market stratification theory is used to analyze the labor force in terms of degree of worker autonomy instead of by the usual measurements of skill and prestige. In the process, "objective" Bureau of the Census categories are shown to be as ideological as any other method of analysis and, in fact, tend to conceal the circumstances of labor force dynamics.

Part 3 deals with the relationship between occupations and the family and

occupations and education. This section points to the role of these two institutions in maintaining a "dual labor market" structure of affluent and poor
workers in the American labor force.

Although designed to be used primarily as a textbook in the sociology of
occupations or the sociology of work, this book can also be used as a complement to basic texts in social stratification, organizational sociology, the sociology of industry, bureaucratic organizations, and labor market theory. It is intended as a theoretical statement as well as a summary of the literature. The
more descriptive view of the field of occupational sociology can be gotten by
covering Chapters 1 to 2 and 9 to 16. The remaining chapters will introduce
the reader to both old and new analytical areas of the field. Instructors thus
have the opportunity to assign just the "core" of the field (the descriptive
view) and let those who desire to do so explore other chapters on their own.

A major underlying thread found throughout the book is Max Weber's
idea of the increasing rationalization of society and its work processes. I view
this as an overwhelming feature of modern industrial societies, not yet counter-
ed by beneficial features of industrialism. Yet, although I fear the "iron cage"
of bureaucracy as Weber described it, I am optimistic that the creative potential of human society will ultimately transcend our peculiar secularism, which
removes emotion, art, poetry, and the spiritual from our work.

The idea for a new textbook in the sociology of occupations came from
the late Erwin Smigel, Professor of Sociology at New York University. It was
Professor Smigel's intention to create a book with a more encompassing view
of the field than any had previously managed. He asked two of his former
students, Kenneth Henry and myself, to join him in this project. The book
was never started because of Erwin's untimely death, but our discussion of the
project and the lasting influence on me of his untiring optimism were critical
factors in initiating the present work and carrying it through to completion.
Professor Smigel's kindness and encouragement and his belief in sociology as
a meliorating science have led generations of his students into productive research. The works of many of them are cited herein.

Tom Gay, sociology editor at John Wiley & Sons at the time I began
planning the book, was patient enough to guide me through several partial
drafts and encouraged me to continue with the task. Eliot Freidson, Richard
Hall, and George Ritzer read these drafts and offered their suggestions and
support at this important early stage. Lucile Duberman and George Ritzer
read the entire manuscript. Their comments prompted significant changes in
several chapters. If any clarity of theoretical perspective is experienced by
the reader, it is because of the critical efforts of Peter Manning, who exposed
gaps and inconsistencies in the text. This led to a major revision.

I would also like to thank Ralph Kaminsky, Ron Miller, Dennis Palumbo,
and Catherine Silver for comments on earlier drafts of chapters, and Dawn Day,

Deborah David, Marcia Freedman, Mary Howard, Drew Humphries, and Orlando Rodriguez for their comments on parts of later drafts. Jim Wessel and Bob Cohen of the Center of Human Resources at Columbia University were very helpful in locating sources and contacts in the labor market field. I have incorporated the suggestions of my critics selectively. Any errors of fact or "deviations" from theory are mine alone.

With much perseverence and understanding of an author's idiosyncracies, Richard Baker has carried the editing through to its final stages. The aid of Jacky Lachmann in the myriad of administrative matters was indispensable.

In Chapter 16, I demonstrate that the family affects one's work in many important ways. My own work is no exception. My wife, Doris, read and criticized each chapter as it was written. Joan has given her moral support, and Eve and Lee their patience during the time this book was written. For their aid and support I am grateful.

Paul D. Montagna

FOOTNOTES FOR PREFACE

[1] Lionell Trilling, *Sincerity and Authenticity* (Cambridge, Mass.: Harvard University Press, 1971), p. 171.

[2] Nanette Davis describes her approach in these terms. See her *Sociological Constructions of Deviance* (Dubuque, Iowa: Wm. C. Brown Co., 1975), p. 11.

CONTENTS

1 INTRODUCTION   1

PART 1 OCCUPATIONAL STRUCTURE

2 OCCUPATIONAL CATEGORIES   13

Structural Levels of Occupational Analysis 13
Labor Force Participation 17
Occupational Categories 19
Profile of the American Labor Force: Occupational
    Groups 21
A Look at Some Specific Occupations 25
Occupational Prestige 30
Functionalist and Conflict Theories of Stratification
    36
Occupations and Social Status 37
A Note on the Accuracy of Population Statistics 42

THEORIES OF POST-INDUSTRIAL
3 SOCIETY   49

A Functionalist View 50
A Conflict Theory View 52
A Postcapitalist View 53
The Service Society 55
Stratum Versus Class 57
Conclusion 62

THEORIES OF LABOR MARKET
4 STRATIFICATION   65

Neoclassical Economic Theory 65
Dual Labor Market Theory 67
Radical Theory 71
Multiple-Segment Theory 79
The Dual Labor Market: Occupational Groups 82
Unemployment and the Employed Poor 83
Underemployment (Subemployment) 86
The Need for Research 86
Summary and Conclusions 89

OCCUPATIONAL CHARACTERISTICS
5 BY RACE   97

Where the Jobs Are: Occupational Distribution in
   the United States 97
Employed Persons, by Occupation 99
Occupational Mobility 106
Unemployment and the Employed Poor 107
Some Effects of Inequality 114
Class, Race, and Occupation: The Interest Group
   Approach 115
The Marxist Approach 117
The Interest Group Rebuttal 118
Summary and Conclusions 119

OCCUPATIONAL CHARACTERISTICS
6 BY SEX   125

Occupational Sex Typing **126**
Income Inequality **130**
Sex Typing and Sex Roles **131**
Occupational Choice **134**
Employment Inequality **136**
Men's Liberation: Social Policy for Sexual Equality
    in Occupations **141**
Summary and Conclusions **142**

OCCUPATIONAL CHARACTERISTICS
7 BY AGE   147

Employment and Unemployment **147**
Employment and Education **151**
Other Factors **153**
Entry into the Labor Force **154**
Occupational Mobility **155**
Aspirations and Values **159**
Summary and Conclusions **161**

PART 2 OCCUPATIONAL DYNAMICS

OCCUPATIONS AND
8 ORGANIZATIONS   169

Rationalization **169**
Bureaucratization and Professionalization **172**
Organizational Constraints **174**
Professional Associations and Unions **175**
Professional Bureaucracy **178**
Occupations as Social Control Units **182**
The Role of Technology **185**
Social Effects **187**
Summary and Conclusions **187**

THE PROFESSIONS: APPROACHES

9 TO THEIR STUDY 195

The Structuralist Approach **196**
The Interactionist Approach **202**
The Social Class Approach **209**
Summary and Conclusions **212**

THE PROFESSIONS: LABOR MARKET

10 STRATIFICATION 221

Sex Stratification **221**
The Situation of Blacks **227**
Work Alienation **230**
Professional Change **232**
Summary and Conclusions **236**

EXECUTIVES, SUPERVISORS AND

11 PROPRIETORS 247

Executives **248**
Are Executives a National Upper Class? **255**
Managers **256**
Supervisors **260**
Proprietors **263**
Professionalization and Ideology **265**
Work Alienation **267**
Summary and Conclusions **268**

12 SEMI-PROFESSIONALS AND PROTECTIVE SERVICE WORKERS 279

Nursing 281
Social Work 286
Public School Teaching 288
Public Relations Managers 290
Chiropracty 291
Pharmacy 292
Paraprofessionals 294
Protective Service Workers: The Case of the Police 294
Summary and Conclusions 299

13 CLERICAL AND SALES WORKERS 309

Women in Clerical and Sales Occupations 310
The Modern Office as a Female Ghetto 312
Salespeople 313
Telephone Operators 316
Grocery Clerks: Dirty White Collars 318
Work Alienation 319
Automation and Alienation 325
Summary and Conclusions 329

14 SKILLED AND SEMISKILLED WORKERS: THE WORKING CLASS 337

The Working-Class Subculture 338
The Working Class: An Occupational Profile 339
The Building Industry Trades 341

Railroad Engineers **343**
General Contracting: The Layperson as Entrepreneur **343**
Factory Workers **345**
Assembly-Line Workers **347**
Automation: The American Experience **348**
Taxicab Drivers **350**
Butchers and Truckers: Occupational Culture versus Occupational Community **351**
Is There a Working Class? **353**
Is the Working Class a Social Class? **354**
Work Alienation **356**
Summary and Conclusions **360**

15 UNSKILLED AND SERVICE WORKERS: THE LOWER CLASS

371

Migrant Farm Workers **372**
Waitresses **373**
Janitors **374**
Private Household Workers **375**
Jazz Musicians: A Deviant Occupation **376**
The "New Working Class" **380**
Summary and Conclusions **381**

PART 3 OCCUPATIONS AND INSTITUTIONS

16 OCCUPATIONS THE FAMILY, AND THE INDIVIDUAL

389

The Effect of Family on Occupation **389**
The Effect of Occupation on Family **392**
Careers **396**
Demographic Trends **397**

Bureaucracy and Personality **398**
Occupation and Personality **400**
Work Alienation **401**
Summary and Conclusions **402**

17 OCCUPATIONS AND EDUCATION 409

The Importance of Education **409**
Educational and Occupational Attainment of Non-whites **413**
Educational and Occupational Attainment of Women **413**
Utilization of College Graduates **417**
Social Mobility **418**
The Radical Critique of Education **425**
Summary and Conclusions **430**

AUTHOR INDEX 439

SUBJECT INDEX 449

OCCUPATIONS AND SOCIETY

1 INTRODUCTION

People's occupations are generally regarded as the most important indicator of their positions in the social structure. Occupations provide income, social status, and personal satisfaction. They are the most ubiquitous of all social and sociological factors—used in the measurement of social class, political motivations, leisure-time orientations, and other work and non-work related characteristics. Occupation is used as a category to measure changes in individual life patterns—called occupational careers—as a phenomenon explaining marriage and divorce patterns, and as a political organization to protect workers engaged in similar work tasks and to develop a common consciousness among them.

The task of this book is to examine how this multitude of events, patterns, and forces is related to occupations. Because occupations are the objective indicators of the economic and social forces being played out in the labor market, they are analyzed here from the perspective of labor market stratification. Specifically, the thesis of this book is that the economic relations of production in most societies, as manifested in the cult of individualism[1] (e.g., "professionalism" and "human capital"), lead to a dual labor market of primary occupations and secondary occupations based on distinctions of race, sex, and age. Primary sector occupations are characterized by high job stability, clearly defined career patterns, and a high degree of work involvement. Secondary occupations are highly unstable and alienating. This dual classification system of the organization of occupations in society has become a major tool for the critical analysis of the labor force. It cuts across traditional occupational categories and groups. Some of those occupations normally placed low in the system of stratification are more accurately classified in the primary sector of the labor market (e.g., highly skilled craft workers, some transport equipment operators) and others more highly placed belong in the secondary sector (many clerical and sales workers).

Throughout history occupations have served as an organizing principle for societies. The initial occupational groups were developed in Roman times along the lines of the great Roman families.[2] Since the family structure was the most important social structure, the *collegia* patterned themselves after them, imitating their rites and festivals. As a moral force, these occupations were destroyed by the barbarian invasions, and it was not until the system of guilds developed in the Middle Ages that they again became powerful moral and political forces by regulating commerce and production levels. The guilds were ultimately displaced by the factory system, which organized nationally instead of locally.

It is at this point that our modern-day analysis of occupations begins. Although St. Simon, Toennies, and others discussed the role of occupations in society, it was Karl Marx who integrated the worker into the system of production by making him indispensable to the work process. The human being is *homo faber*—the producer.[3] According to Marx, people create their own social existence by developing tools and organizing work activities to meet their collective needs. The forces of production (occupational knowledge, tools, and skills) and the social relations of production are the economic structure. The superstructure of the state, religion, and educational institutions are forms of social control and serve to legitimate the capitalist world order of class positions within this economic structure. The surplus labor (excess productivity) of workers is used to expand capital (the wealth of the owners) at the expense of the workers. In the process a person's work is transformed into a commodity to be bought and sold on the market as any other piece of merchandise. This exploitation and the resulting alienation ends in the workers' forming a proletariat that becomes a "class for itself," acting consciously in its own interests to overthrow the capitalist or bourgeoisie class by revolutionary action.[4]

Many have modified Marx's theory. Among the more famous early "revisionists" was Eduard Bernstein, who stated that the distribution of wealth was becoming more, not less, equalized. With the further development of democratic institutions, more people would share in decision making at all levels and the workers would improve their economic status. Lenin emphasized the trade union as a key to the revolutionary movement. It was the revolutionary intellectuals outside the proletariat who could develop the necessary consciousness among the workers, "protect" them from capitalist points of view, and develop the new socialist society. They are the vanguard.

Emile Durkheim mounted a major attack on Marxist thought, portraying industrial society as one with the potential for high moral achievements. This would be brought about through a system of occupational associations, working together in individual yet solidary ways. The social division of labor does not automatically bring about societal integration, but neither does it produce, in Durkheim's words, "disperson and incoherence." Alienation is not inevitable. If occupations properly developed society-wide codes of ethics they would act as a moral force to counteract the power of the corporate business economy.[5] R. H. Tawney saw in this the entire reorganization of industrial society.[6] However, in 1939 Talcott Parsons argued that the professions and business are not different—they are both rational, functionally specific, and universalistic in their approaches.[7]

Max Weber expanded Marx's position by viewing the stratification of society on the basis of three factors: class, status, and power. His conceptualization of class is complex, based on three types: (1) property classes, which comprise privileged (the propertied) and unprivileged (the propertyless); (2) the acquisition class, which provides mobility into other classes through one's occupation; and (3) social class, personal associations based on the material conditions of property classes. Property classes, then, are the core on which class is built.[8]

Social status is a measure of prestige derived from one's occupation and "style of life." A social stratum is a group of individuals with the same level of prestige. Often, a property class provides the basis for a social stratum. Indeed, "with some over-simplification, one might say that classes are stratified according to their relations to the production and acquisition of goods; whereas status groups are stratified according to the principles of their *consumption* of goods as represented by special styles of life."[9]

The most important element for Weber in measuring social class is property, followed by occupation (acquisition class), and then by prestige (social status). Property, the economic component, underlies political power as well.[10] Like Marx, Weber sees the economic factor of property as the key variable of class relations in capitalist society.

It is the way in which Weber has been interpreted that provides the deep contrast to the Marxist argument. A number of American sociologists of the traditional liberal perspective have given Weber's three factors of class, status, and power equal weight in their formulations. As a result, occupational prestige measures have been touted as the definitive measure of "social class."[11] This perspective believes that increased labor productivity will improve the worker's living standards and lead to class harmony instead of class conflict.

Workers' income will be determined by their productivity, that is, education and skill, which is the functionalist view of social stratification (to be discussed in Chapter 2). If education is an intervening variable, then poverty (the lack of income) can be reduced and eliminated if workers are educated properly and given equal opportunity to attain that education. Trade unions are the way in which workers can organize to improve their working conditions and to gain some form of industrial democracy and equal opportunity.[12] This, in turn, supports a pluralist view of politics, that several competing interest groups, including the working class, are active in interest-group politics.

In contrast to this is the conflict theory of stratification, which emphasizes power as the most significant factor affecting social stratification. Native ability and education are seen to be dependent on the amount of exercised or potential power of the individual or group. These two theories provide the framework for two major contemporary perspectives that utilize occupational information: postindustrial (Chapter 3) and labor market (Chapter 4) perspectives.

Postindustrial theorists emphasize the switch of the most modernized industrial societies from a goods-producing economy to a service-producing one. The production and control of knowledge is the central focus of these theorists, with the more functionally oriented emphasizing society's affluence and consumption patterns and the conflict oriented examining poverty and the structural control of the production of knowledge.

Labor market theorists, comprising three major "branches," concentrate on the factors determining occupational success. The neoclassical branch is similar to the functionalist model, emphasizing the individual's abilities and effort (vocational training) as measures of ultimate occupational standing. The dual-labor and radical branches depict a "dual" labor market, a segmented system of occupations, in which the upper level, the primary sector, has an economic interest in excluding those who attempt to enter from the lower-level occupations—the secondary sector. The phenomenon is supported by the high degree of occupational discrimination evidenced in the sectors and their subsectors. Chapters 5 to 7 detail this situation on the basis of race, sex, and age. For example, Chapter 5 shows that recent gains by blacks are somewhat deceptive when the kinds of specific jobs within the broader occupational categories are compared. Although there has been an increase of blacks in the professions in proportion to the increase for whites, most of the increase is in the lower paying and less prestigious jobs. Analysis is also completed of this group's occupational mobility, patterns of employed poor and the unemployed, and of the relationship of social class to occupation from the conflict and functionalist perspectives.

The pervasiveness of female-dominated occupations and reasons for their persistence in the labor force is discussed in Chapter 6. The effects of sex role discrimination of occupational choice is explored and a major study of labor market segmentation is examined. The role of education and first jobs in the occupational careers of young people is covered in Chapter 7. Again, discriminatory patterns similar to those of women and nonwhites are found for youth. Thus it is that women, nonwhites, and youth serve as a reserve labor force for the American economy, to be employed during peak periods of economic expansion and unemployed or underemployed at all other times.

A corollary of the thesis of this book is that occupations in the primary labor market are more autonomous[13] than those in the secondary labor market and that the work performed is considered more meaningful and provides considerable wealth, prestige, and power. Empirical support is presented in Part 2, the examination of the dynamics of the occupational structure. Chapter 8 discusses the source of the organization of work, which is either "administrative" (internal, by managers) or "occupational" (external to the organization, by workers' associations). The latter, the more autonomous for occupations as a whole, is characteristic mostly of primary sector occupations, that is, the professions, other highly paid, stable, white-collar occupations, and skilled blue-collar occupations.

Another corollary of the main thesis is that the continual rationalization of occupational knowledge reduces occupational autonomy. Chapters 9 to 15 provide concrete examples of how this process of rationalization works in individual occupations. Those in occupations with a great deal of abstract, theoretical knowledge, or those who claim to have this knowledge, find this the source of their power. They prevent others from access to it in order to maintain power and they either create new knowledge or expropriate available knowledge to increase their power. Women, nonwhites, and the young are confined largely to those occupations characterized by more practical nontheoretical knowledge—those in the secondary labor force. Each of these ethnographic chapters focuses on the issues of alienation and technological change. The two can be viewed as both causes and consequences of the rise and fall of occupations.

Part 2 thus depicts how occupations, through ideology and innovation, compete for power in the social system with other occupations, especially among the more professionalized ones, and how occupations both encourage and discourage rationalization in a dialectic process of change.

In the more descriptive passages of Part 2, the sociological research of a large number of occupations is reviewed, emphasizing the daily life and "subculture" of the people in them. The question of how occupational ideologies are developed and used is covered in analyses of nurses, social workers, public school teachers, butchers, and jazz musicians. Also discussed are the attempts of these and other occupations (e.g., taxicab drivers, factory workers, subcontractors, railroad engineers, and car salespeople) to gain control over the work environment and client transactions.

A major dichotomy in a large number of descriptive studies is between working class and middle class. Traditionally, the former include all blue-collar occupations and the service occupational group (not to be confused with services industries, such as health service, public service, etc.). The middle class includes all white-collar occupations except the very small number of high-income, high-status occupations. Conflict theorists argue for the inclusion of clerical workers in the working class, taking the position that office work has acquired most of the features of working-class jobs.

Most researchers conclude that the working class has a separate subculture and limit its occupational representation to blue-collar workers (craftsmen, operatives, and nonfarm laborers). However, dual labor market theory measures occupations on the basis of degree of worker autonomy instead of the more traditional measure of prestige. It discloses that, contrary to what might be expected, some working-class occupations include primary sector jobs and some middle-class occupations contain secondary sector jobs. Automation and technology are more easily introduced into secondary labor force jobs.

The argument is explored in Chapters 14 and 15, in which the Marxist model concludes that as knowledge becomes more rationalized by means of organizational and technological devices, workers in the secondary labor force become more alienated at the expense of even greater occupational success of those in the primary sector. But although the working class is adding many new occupations to its ranks (e.g., clerical workers, subprofessionals), it does not have awareness as a "class for itself." The functional model, on the other hand, sees technology in the form of automation as the way to integrate formerly discrete tasks into a more meaningful whole. As a result, workers become more involved in their work, and alienation is reduced.

In Part 3, I review and analyze the relationship between occupations and institutions, specifically, the family and education. The role of the family in one's occupational aspiration and occupational attainment is discussed in Chapter 16. Also, the effect of one's occupation on his family life is covered. Topics such as the working mother and the imbalance between income and expenses in the family life cycle are explored. The debate of how one's work affects one's personality also is reviewed. I emphasize how the conflict between family values and occupational values has changed with the continued rationalization of the workplace. Two important factors emerge that contradict the Marxist analysis: that rationalization of the work process also leads to innovation among workers, and that the expanded hierarchy of authority is conducive to further innovation and self-direction. However, these are severely limited by educational tracking, so that those in the secondary labor force find it difficult to achieve mobility into the primary labor force.

In the United States, the belief that education is *the* vehicle for upward social mobility persists even though most research has shown otherwise.

Chapter 17 deals with this issue, again presenting the two opposing views (functionalist and conflict). The structure of the labor market and educational institutions in societies operating under the meritocratic ideology is examined. How the labor market is structured and maintained to support this system is the topic of the radical critique of education.

In sum, the sociology of knowledge approach is largely used in this book. Specifically, the modern age is an age of doubt and suspicion, where intellectual uncertainty is increased by the increase in knowledge. We tend to doubt what we know; there is no "necessity of truth."[14] Reality is demystified. From a Marxist perspective, suspicion encourages the demystifying of knowledge and simultaneously the repression of the demystifying process by those in power. Those without power, the workers in industrial societies, are alienated. They are prohibited from attaining an accurate picture of their economic and psychological repression or are unable to change their position in society even if they are aware of their predicament. The control of knowledge and knowledge change by the leaders of the major societal institutions governs this process. The primary labor market represents those who are in control and their immediate subordinates and advisors. The secondary labor market comprises the largely powerless workers.

Many concrete examples are given in Part 2 of those in the secondary labor market. Secretaries, filers, and other office workers, clerks, telephone workers, waitresses, and assembly-line workers: these and many more are examples of jobs that have poor working conditions, high turnover, and low wages, all characteristic of the secondary labor market.

Work is still a primary institution in society and crucial to the well-being of individuals. Workers still spend a large part of their waking hours at work, many of them at hard physical labor and under severe conditions. Thus, whether or not they experience a false consciousness, workers are obliged to engage in tasks invented by others, directed by others, with tools owned by others, and from which profits are expropriated by others.

However, modern bureaucratic systems do seem to offer a small area of freedom and power in which its members can maneuver. Areas of uncertainty generated by structural changes are quick to be exploited by workers in various occupations, especially those that are more professionalized. But this all happens within the system. There are no concerted efforts by workers to make significant changes in the organization and to control the work process.

FOOTNOTES FOR CHAPTER 1
INTRODUCTION

1. The cult of individualism is not limited to capitalist societies. Socialist countries suffer as well. See Adam Schaff, *Marxism and the Human Individual* (New York: McGraw-Hill Book Co., 1970).

2. Much of this discussion is derived from Emile Durkheim, *Professional Ethics and Civic Morals*, trans. by Cornelia Brookfield (New York: The Free Press, 1958), pp. 23-33.

3. The remainder of this paragraph is summarized, in part, from Bertram Silverman and Murray Yanowitch, "Radical and Liberal Perspectives of the Working Class," *Social Policy, 4* (January-February 1974), 40-41.

4. Actually, Marx portrayed four occupational classes: the bourgeoisie—the factory owners, bankers, financers, and managers; the petit bourgeoisie—the small shopkeepers and store owners; the proletariat—feudal peasants, tenant farmers, and later the skilled and unskilled factory workers; and the lumpenproletariat—the "scum" of society: thieves, criminals, vagabonds, and the unemployed.

5. Emile Durkheim, *The Division of Labor in Society*, trans. by George Simpson (New York: Macmillan, 1933), Preface to the Second Edition. First published in France in 1893.

6. R. H. Tawney, *The Acquisitive Society* (New York: Harcourt, Brace & World, 1920), Chapter 9.

7. Talcott Parsons, "The Professions and Social Structure," *Social Forces, 17* (1939), 457-467.

8. Max Weber, *The Theory of Social and Economic Organization*, trans. by A. M. Henderson and Talcott Parsons (New York: Oxford University Press, 1947), pp. 424-429.

9. Max Weber, *Economy and Society*, ed. by Gunther Roth and Claus Wittich (New York: Bedminster Press, 1968), p. 937. Weber's class concepts are neatly summarized by Charles H. Anderson, *The Political Economy of Social Class* (Englewood Cliffs, N.J.: Prentice-Hall, 1974), pp. 116-121.

10. Anderson, *The Political Economy of Social Class*, p. 120. For another view of the conflict tradition of Weber, see Randall Collins, "Reassessments of Sociological History: The Empirical Validity of the Conflict Tradition," *Theory and Society, 1* (Summer 1974), 160-164, 172.

[11.] Talcott Parsons, "Equality and Inequality in Modern Society, or Social Stratification Revisited," *Sociological Inquiry, 40* (Spring 1970), 24.

[12.] Selig Perlman, *A Theory of the Labor Movement* (New York: Augustus M. Kelley, 1949). Originally published in 1928.

[13.] Autonomy is defined as freedom to determine the knowledge to be used in the occupation and how that knowledge is to be applied in various situations.

[14.] Gunter W. Remmling, *Road to Suspicion: A Study of Modern Mentality and the Sociology of Knowledge* (New York: Appleton-Century-Crofts, 1967), Chapter 1.

PART 1

OCCUPATIONAL STRUCTURE

In examining the occupational structure one must first review the various typologies for categorizing occupations and the rationale behind each typology. This is the task of Chapters 2 to 4. Chapter 2 describes the U.S. government's set of categories and then examines how sociologists of different persuasions have utilized them. Chapter 3 reviews the rearranged perspective on occupational structure of postindustrial theorists. Chapter 4 covers the major theories of occupational structure developed by labor market economists. Chapters 5 to 7 then develop the evidence for the acceptance of the dual labor market explanation as a clear and useful organization of occupational structure. Each of these three chapters is devoted to a discussion of one of the three major explanatory variables: race, sex, and age.

2 OCCUPATIONAL CATEGORIES

The most common source for analyzing occupations is government data, which are arranged into various occupational categories and groups. Utilizing these data, social scientists attempt to rank order occupations on the basis of prestige, income, education, and various other cultural background factors in their own research studies. This chapter deals with the types of data available and how they are interpreted and used by sociologists and other social scientists.

STRUCTURAL LEVELS OF OCCUPATIONAL ANALYSIS

The most abundant source of information on occupations is found in U.S. government statistics collected by the U.S. Department of Labor's Bureau of Labor Statistics and the U.S. Department of Commerce's Bureau of the Census. These agencies present major statistical summaries and special reports on the general social and economic characteristics of the U.S. population. In addition, they supply detailed information on occupations and the work force in a continuous series of publications. From these reports four basic structural levels can be classified for further analysis and interpretation. They are:

1. The national labor force.
2. Occupational categories.
3. Occupational groups.
4. Specific occupations.

The first level, the national labor force, shows all workers of a country as a proportion of its total population. It gives us a "societal perspective"[1] of the size and general institutional characteristics of the working and nonworking population. For example, 38 percent of the total U.S. population comprises its entire employed work force. In other words, slightly more than one in every three persons (one of every two adults—see Table 2.1) supports the population of the country. The second level breaks down the labor force (the 38 percent) into four basic categories: white-collar workers, blue-collar workers, service workers, and farm workers. A further refinement is the third level, occupational groups. White-collar workers, 48 percent of all workers in the United States in 1972, include the occupational groups of professional and technical workers, managers and administrators, sales workers, and clerical workers.

Finally, at the fourth level, specific occupations are found. (See Table 2.2 for a visual breakdown of the four levels.) Professional and technical occupations include, for example: physicians, lawyers, college and university teachers, public school teachers, clergymen, engineers, natural and social scientists, librarians, programmers, draftsmen, other technical occupations, and new sub-professional health occupations such as electrocardiograph technicians, occupational therapy aides, surgical technicians, and optometric assistants. Actually, there is a fifth level of occupational titles, that are, in effect, descriptions of jobs in each occupation. The occupation "engineer" is the generic term covering the multitude of job descriptions in engineering. For example, there are scores of engineering titles listed in the areas of aerospace, agriculture, biomedicine, ceramics, chemical, civil, electrical, industrial, mechanical, metallurgical, and mining.

On the other hand, some occupations are nothing more than job titles or a set of specific skilled tasks (e.g., bus driver, paperhanger, plasterer, deckhand, miner, hospital attendant, usher, and even the skilled trades of carpet installer, tinsmith, or plumber). These jobs have never developed the broad knowledge base and societal acceptance of that base necessary for an expansive division of labor and specialization. Nor in many cases have they, as a collective movement, developed the authority to achieve and maintain a definite career for their members, a series of sequential steps from lower to higher status and income increases to match the steps.

For most purposes, however, we shall use the more common definition of occupation, which defines occupations as social roles and thus includes "jobs" and "skills" as well:

An occupation is the social role performed by adult members of society that directly and/or indirectly yields social and financial consequenses and that constitutes a major focus in the life of an adult.[2]

TABLE 2.1 LABOR STATUS OF THE POPULATION OF THE UNITED STATES, FEBRUARY 1970

	NUMBER (000 OMITTED)	PERCENT OF TOTAL POPULATION	PERCENT OF NONINSTITUTIONAL POPULATION 16 AND OVER
Total noninstitutional population 16 years and over in the labor force:			
Employed	77,489	38	58
Unemployed	3,794	2	3
	81,283	40	61
Total noninstitutional population 16 years and over not in the labor force:			
Homemakers	34,643	17	25
Students	8,920	4	6
Retired, and others	11,110	5	8
	54,673	26	39
			100
Persons under 16 years of age	62,908	32	
Inmates of institutions	2,307	1	
Members of armed forces	3,342	1	
	68,557	34	
Total United States population:	204,513	100	

Source. Adapted from Seymour Wolfbein, *Work in American Society* (Glenview, Ill.: Scott, Foresman & Co., 1971), p. 7.

TABLE 2.2 FOUR LEVELS OF STRUCTURAL ANALYSIS OF THE LABOR FORCE

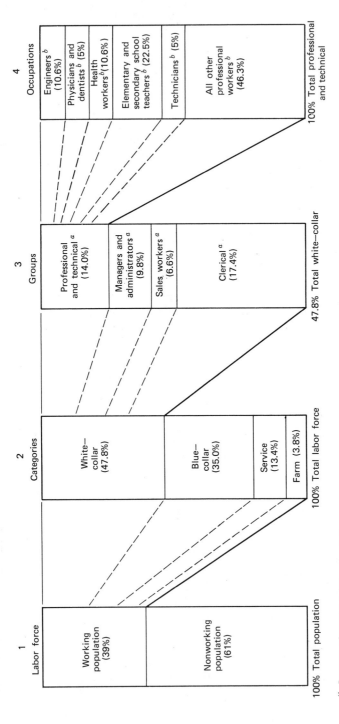

[a] Percent of total working population.

[b] Percent of professional and technical workers.

Sources. Levels 1, 2, and 3: U.S. Department of Labor, Bureau of Manpower Administration, *Manpower Report of the President, 1973* (Washington, D.C.: U.S. Government Printing Office, 1973); Level 4: U.S. Department of Commerce, Bureau of the Census, *General Social and Economic Characteristics: 1970 Census of Population* (Washington, D.C.: U.S. Government Printing Office, 1972).

The generic meaning of the term will be discussed in later chapters that deal with occupational careers and that examine occupational groups in the work force.

LABOR FORCE
PARTICIPATION

Most people are surprised to learn that over 40 percent of the nation's adults do not work in officially recognized occupations (Table 2.1). Almost half this number, more than 34 million women, are housewives. Technically, "homemaking," as the Bureau of Labor Statistics calls it, is not an occupation if we define an occupation as the Bureau of the Census does—"gainful employment."[3] Our definition is totally different from this and has different consequences, as pointed out in Chapter 6.

Of that part of the population counted as workers, the size of the labor force has not changed much over the past 25 years. In 1947, it totaled 59 percent of the adult noninstitutional population; in 1973 it totaled 61 percent. It is when we examine the labor force for differences in age, sex, and race that we begin to see major differences. For example, the proportion of white males in the labor force has decreased from 86 percent in 1950 to 80 percent in 1972, and for nonwhite males it was from 86 to 74 percent. In contrast, that of white females has increased from 33 to 43 percent for the same years. For nonwhite females the rate of increase was much less, from 47 to 49 percent.[4]

In all cases the most obvious difference is in sex distributions. In all age groups, both white and nonwhite, women are less frequently employed than men (Table 2.3). In no age group do they come even close to the employment rate for men. In their highest employed age group, 20 to 24 years, only 58 percent of women are employed, which is two-thirds of the rate for men in the same age grouping. The woman's place is indeed in the home. If homemaking were to be recategorized (and paid), there would obviously be more equalization of labor force participation.

The relationship of age to participation is that which might be expected in our society. Younger people are still in school and so reduce the percentage in the labor force up through age 24. Highest rates of employment are found among the middle groups, at age levels where persons have the greatest family responsibility and are at their peak of productivity. The one exception is white women, ages 25 to 34, whose participation decreases. They temporarily leave full-time employment to raise a family. The same pattern does not prevail for nonwhite women who, more often than not, must continue to work while raising a family.

Racial discrimination is most evident in the younger age groups. For nonwhite men it continues all through work life at a decreasing rate. For

TABLE 2.3 LABOR FORCE PARTICIPATION RATES IN THE UNITED STATES, BY AGE, SEX, AND COLOR, 1971 (IN PERCENT)

AGE AND SEX	WHITE	NONWHITE
Men	80.5	75.9
16-19	59.8	46.6
20-24	85.9	84.0
25-34	96.5	93.2
35-44	97.1	92.4
45-54	94.7	86.9
55-64	82.6	77.8
65+	25.6	24.5
Women	42.6	49.2
16-19	45.5	31.3
20-24	58.0	56.1
25-34	43.6	59.2
35-44	50.2	61.0
45-54	53.7	59.4
55-64	42.5	47.1
65+	9.3	11.5

Source. U.S. Department of Labor, Bureau of Labor Statistics, *Employment and Earnings* (Washington, D.C.: U.S. Government Printing Office, January 1972), pp. 118-119.

nonwhite women, a different pattern emerges in the 25 to 34 age category, where their percentage at work increases, whereas the percentage of white women decreases. One common explanation is that the lack of a male breadwinner requires that the woman take a job in order to keep the family intact. However, an alternative analysis questions this view, stating just the opposite cause-effect relation: that the black woman's handicap in the labor market, not the man's, has added to the instability of the black family.[5] The women are found disproportionately in personal service and household occupations as compared to the men, who are spread more evenly through the occupational groups (see Table 4.1). Because the black woman owes allegience to two households, does she give less emotional support to her own family than she could and should? Wouldn't her efforts at home be found less than satisfactory by her husband? This is not to say that if black males had equal employment opportunities, higher wages, and lower rents, that their wives would not have had to take these domestic jobs. But comparison to other women in domestic occupations (e.g., the Irish in the 1930s) shows different attitudes toward such work following marriage, leading one to speculate that

historical events, in addition to economic ones, are responsible for this phenomenon.[6]

OCCUPATIONAL CATEGORIES

It is generally recognized that occupation is the most significant determinant
of a person's social status, and attempts have continually been made to measure and categorize occupations in some hierarchical order. As far back as
1897, William C. Hunt, working for the Bureau of the Census, separated occupations into four major categories: the proprietor class, the clerical class,
skilled workers, and the laboring class.[7] Years later and after many refine-
ments, Alba Edwards developed a list of six major categories for the Bureau
of the Census. These were later reduced to four: white-collar workers, blue-
collar workers, service workers, and farm workers. These status levels each
contain several occupational groups:

White-collar	Professional and technical Farmers and farm managers Managers, officials, and proprietors Clerical Sales
Blue-collar	Craftsmen and foremen Operatives Laborers
Service	Service workers Private household workers
Farm	Farm laborers and foremen

As Edwards was careful to note, these groups each exhibited distinct life-
styles, economically, intellectually, and socially.[8] Even though subsequent
studies have shown that these occupational groups are not unidimensional
regarding social status (i.e., those higher on the list do not at all times have
higher status than those lower on the list), they still remain the most popular
rough indicator of status in the United States.

There are few data sources for occupational categories on the national
level that can be used for comparison. Table 2.4 gives the most recent data
available for three countries, Australia, Italy, and the United States. As
examples of modernized, industrialized countries, all three show the expected
profile of large white-collar and blue-collar categories and a small farm sector.
Advances in science and technology reduce greatly the number of workers
needed to produce the agricultural needs of a modern society and, at the
same time, create new occupational specialties and new products and services

TABLE 2.4 OCCUPATIONAL STRUCTURE IN AUSTRALIA, ITALY, AND THE UNITED STATES, ADULT MALE LABOR FORCE (AGES 25-64, IN PERCENT)

OCCUPATIONAL CATEGORY	AUSTRALIA 1965	ITALY 1963-1964	UNITED STATES 1962
Nonmanual (professionals, managerial, clerical, sales)	35	22	39
Manual (craftsmen, operatives, laborers)	52	51	54
Farm (farmers, farm managers, farm laborers)	13	26	7

Source. Leonard Broom and F. Lancaster Jones, "Career Mobility in Three Societies," *American Sociological Review, 34* (October 1969), 653.

that require new occupations in the nonmanual category.[9] However, even within this group of three countries, there are significant differences. Studies indicate that the percentage of the labor force in agriculture is an indicator of the degree to which a society is "advanced" economically (i.e., the smaller the proportion of farm workers to the total work force, the more advanced the nation).[10] Moore has shown that at midcentury the average number of workers in agriculture for advanced nations was about 15 percent, in developing countries approximately 45 percent and, in the least developed countries, above 60 percent.[11] In 1954, Italy, at 47 percent, would not be considered an advanced nation. The decrease since then places it in the economically advanced group of countries. However, it is still far behind Australia and the United States. Table 2.4 also reveals that the farm category is displaced largely by nonmanual occupations, the percentage of American or Australian manual workers being no greater than the percentage of Italian manual workers. As it happens, farm workers displaced by industrialization do not jump into nonmanual occupations. Instead, there is a movement of farm workers into manual occupations and, simultaneously, of manual workers into occupations in the nonmanual category.

PROFILE OF THE AMERICAN LABOR FORCE: OCCUPATIONAL GROUPS

Viewed from its various occupational groups over time, the American occupational structure (Table 2.5) reveals rapid fluctuations that indicate the extreme pressures put on the work force in the face of accelerating social and economic changes. The most imposing figures are the totals for white-collar and farm categories. We have already briefly discussed the major reasons for these dramatic changes. What is noteworthy at this point is the occupational groups that experienced the greatest change. The tremendous increase in professional and technical workers (from 4 percent in 1900 to 14 percent in 1970, nearly a 300 percent increase) is exceeded only by clerical workers (from 3 percent in 1900 to 17 percent in 1970). The increasing need for expertise in highly specialized, technically complex work functions has led to the expansion of professional jobs such as physicists and astronomers, college teachers, aeronautical and electronic engineers, social workers, the health service occupations in medical and dental laboratories, hospital administration, physical and occupational therapy, draftsmen and designers in defense industries, and accountants, programmers, and machine technicians in business and government organizations.

It appears that the proportion of jobs in the clerical occupations is begin-

TABLE 2.5 PROFILE OF THE AMERICAN LABOR FORCE, 1900–1980
(IN PERCENT)

MILLIONS OF WORKERS	(29) 1900	(49) 1930	(62) 1950	(67) 1960	(79) 1970	(95) 1980
WHITE-COLLAR						
Professional and technical	4	7	9	11	14	16
Managers and proprietors	6	7	8	11	11	10
Clerical	3	9	12	15	17	18
Sales	5	6	7	6	6	6
Total	18	29	36	43	48	50
BLUE-COLLAR						
Skilled workers	10	13	14	13	13	13
Semiskilled workers	13	16	20	18	18	16
Unskilled workers	13	11	7	6	4	4
Total	36	40	41	37	35	33
SERVICE WORKERS						
Private household workers	5	4	3	3	2	a
Service workers, Other than private household	4	6	8	9	10	a
Total	9	10	11	12	12	14
FARM WORKERS						
Farmers and farm managers	20	12	7	4	2	a
Farm laborers and foremen	18	9	4	4	2	a
Total	38	21	11	8	4	3

a No figures given.

Sources. David L. Kaplan and M. Claire Casey, *Occupational Trends in the United States, 1900 to 1950,* Bureau of the Census, Working Paper No. 5 (Washington, D.C.: U.S. Department of Commerce, 1958); *Statistical Abstract of the United States, 1961,* and *Statistical Abstract of the United States, 1971* (Washington, D.C.: U.S. Government Printing Office); U.S. Department of Labor, Bureau of Manpower Administration, *Manpower Report of the President, 1972* (Washington, D.C.: U.S. Government Printing Office, 1972), p. 259; U.S. Department of Labor, Bureau of Labor Statistics, *The U.S. Economy in 1980* (Washington, D.C.: U.S. Government Printing Office, 1970), Bulletin 1673.

ning to level off. Much of this can be attributed to fully or partially automated secretarial work, from automatic typing from voice recordings to automatic microfilm data retrieval systems. However, there are still large increases in jobs such as office machine operators, teacher aides, telephone operators, library attendants, and mail carriers.

The moderate decline in blue-collar jobs is almost entirely due to the decrease in unskilled jobs. Improved machinery and automated techniques have eliminated many of the tasks of unskilled laborers—ditchdigging, stevedoring, teamstering, lumberjacking, and several unskilled manual jobs in factories. Despite the threat of "total automation" spelling the demise of blue-collar work, these occupational groups, with the exception of the unskilled, have maintained their numbers in proportion to the total work force. Available research does not disclose any clear effect of automation on the blue-collar group as a whole. Although technology has affected workers in goods-producing industries, new blue-collar occupations have developed rapidly in the service-producing industries. For example, the number of truck drivers has increased tenfold since 1940.

The increasing cost of personal service work has led to the rapid decrease in numbers of private household workers, both live-in servants and those who serve many households. This is accounted for by the increase in labor-saving devices around the home and the advent of packaged home services.[12] The increase in service workers is the result primarily of the expansion of the occupations of firefighter, police officer, sanitation worker, hospital attendant, practical nurse, and other community service occupations.

The Department of Labor estimates that there will be an average 25 percent increase in the number of persons in the labor force from 1968 to 1980. The occupational groups that will exceed this increase are led by professional and technical workers with a 50 percent increase, followed by service workers with a 40 percent increase, clerical workers with 35 percent, and sales workers with 29 percent. Groups that will increase at a rate lower than the average are: managers and administrators, 22 percent; skilled workers, 22 percent; and semiskilled workers, 10 percent. The remaining two groups will decrease in size: unskilled workers by 2 percent and farm workers by 33 percent.[13] Those occupations expected to grow most rapidly are primarily within the professional and technical group: systems analysts, 183 percent; programmers, 129 percent; pilots and copilots, 117 percent; and dental hygienists, 109 percent.[14]

However, this gives us only part of the picture of employment because those who qualify for the various jobs vary by occupational group and by occupation. For example, a majority of professional and technical occupations require a college degree and, although only about 15 percent of our work force hold college degrees, the competition for professional jobs is intense. While the total number of unemployed persons increased by 80 percent between

TABLE 2.6 NUMBER OF COLLEGE GRADUATES IN OCCUPATIONAL
GROUPS

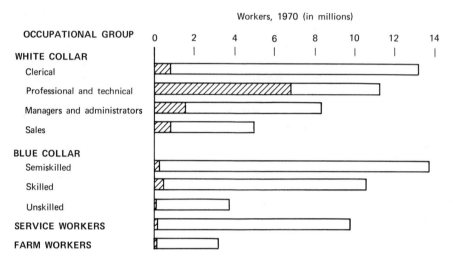

Source. Department of Labor, Bureau of Labor Statistics, *Occupational Outlook for College Graduates: 1972-73 Edition* (Washington, D.C.: U.S. Government Printing Office, 1972), p. 5.

1969 and 1971, unemployment among professionals rose by 125 percent. Although the professionals' unemployment rate is still lower than the national average (2.2 percent compared to 4.9 percent in 1973), this leveling off of employment coincided with a sharp increase in new college graduates seeking employment in the professions.[15] Even more serious, the proportion of college graduates in the work force has increased from 11.5 percent in 1962 to 15 percent in 1973, and it is expected to reach 16.8 percent by 1980, over 15.9 million workers.[16] Between 1968 and 1980 it is estimated by the Bureau of Labor Statistics that 10.5 million college graduates will enter the labor force. During this same time span, the number of jobs available will fall short of the supply of graduates by at least 100,000 jobs.

    3.5 million, through growth of industry.
    4.3 million, through replacement (retirement, death).
    2.6 million, through rising educational requirements (i.e., college degrees
             made a requirement of obtaining the position).
    ——
10.4 million, total.[17]

The Carnegie Commission on Higher Education is much more pessimistic. In its May 1973, report it estimates that during the 1970s there will be a surplus of at least 3 million college graduates who will not be able to find jobs traditionally suitable for a college graduate. Unless rising educational requirements meet the above estimate of the Bureau of Labor Statistics, there will likely be an even higher rate of unemployment among professionals. Add to this the fact that college graduates are primarily in white-collar occupations and are concentrated within the professional and technical group (see Table 2.6) and the conclusion is that the "general scarcity of professional personnel and intense demand for college graduates which prevailed during most of the 1960s have come to an end."[18]   Therefore, although large increases are seen to be occurring within some occupational groups and large decreases within others, care must be taken to interpret these changes in light of other significant social and economic changes in our society. Factors such as education among white-collar workers and horizontal job movement among blue-collar workers are cases in point.

A LOOK AT SOME SPECIFIC OCCUPATIONS

The fourth level of structural analysis, the level of specific occupations, allows us to view an occupation as a social role. It is often said that we get to know people, initially at least, not by what they are but by what they do. A specific occupational role confers on an individual social prestige and personal identity.[19]   These roles have been formalized in most large work organizations by written job descriptions. The most comprehensive list of job descriptions in existence is contained in the *Dictionary of Occupational Titles,*[20] which describes over 20,000 separate occupations. The profession of engineering, for example, contains over 20 subcategories. An example of a page from this book (Illustration 2.1) shows the extent to which labor has been divided by the continued increase in specialization in modern large-scale organization. On a single page the range extends from geophysicists to gherkin picklers.

Illustration 2.1

GEOLOGIST (profess & kin.)-Continued tises on findings for furtherance of scientific study or as an aid to location of natural resources, such as petroleum-bearing formations. May organize scientific expeditions and supervise removal of fossils from deposits and matrix rock formations. May specialize in study of plant fossils and be designated *Paleobotanist.* May specialize in study of fossilized micro-organisms and be designated *Micro-paleontologist.*

PETROLOGIST (profess & kin.). Investi-

gates composition, structure, and history of rock masses forming earth's crust: Applies findings to such fields of investigation as causes of formations, breaking down and weathering, chemical composition and forms of deposition of sedimentary rocks, methods of eruption, and origin and causes of metamorphosis.

PHOTOGEOLOGIST (profess & kin.). Examines and interprets aerial photograph with aid of three-dimensional viewing device to identify rock types, structural

Illustration 2.1 (Continued)

trends, seam and fault alinements indicating subsurface geology, and other topographical features of value in geological surveying or mineral exploration.

STRATIGRAPHER (profess. & kin.). Studies relative position and order of succession of deposits containing or separating archeological material. Studies relation of life of past ages, evolutionary changes as recorded by fossil animals and plants, and successive changes in distribution of land and sea as interpreted from character of fossil content of sedimentary rocks.

GEOLOGIST, ENGINEERING (profess. & kin.). *see* GEOLOGIST.

GEOLOGIST, GROUND WATER (profess. & kin.). *see* GEOLOGIST.

GEOLOGIST HELPER (profess. & kin.). *see* SCIENTIFIC HELPER.

GEOLOGIST, MARINE (profess. & kin.). *see* OCEANOGRAPHER, GEOLOGICAL *under* GEOLOGIST.

GEOLOGIST, MINING (profess. & kin.). *see* GEOLOGIST.

GEOLOGIST, PETROLEUM (petrol. production) *see under* GEOLOGIST.

GEOMAGNETICIAN (profess. & kin.). *see under* GEOLOGIST.

GEOMORPHOLOGIST (profess. & kin.). *see under* GEOLOGIST.

GEOPHYSICAL-LABORATORY SUPERVISOR (petrol. production) 029.168. director, geophysical laboratory; engineer, chief, geophysical laboratory; research engineer, geophysical laboratory; superintendent, geophysical laboratory. Plans and coordinates research activities of geophysical laboratory to develop new or improved instruments and methods for measuring physical characteristics of earth's crust which provide data for petroleum exploration: Consults with management and field and laboratory technical personnel to determine specific phases of geophysical prospecting in which improved processes might be evolved by study and experimentation. Plans research programs and initiates and directs experiments to perfect prospecting procedures, explore possibilities of new theories, and develop improved or new instruments. Supervises workers designing, building, and field testing experimental instruments, such as seismometers, that record sound waves transmitted through earth formations. Supervises workers in repair and maintenance of prospecting instruments. Controls personnel actions, promotes company policies, and performs other administrative duties.

GEOPHYSICAL OPERATOR (petrol. production) *see* OBSERVER, SEISMIC PROSPECTING.

GEOPHYSICAL PROSPECTOR (petrol. production) *see under* GEOPHYSICIST (profess. & kin.).

GEOPHYSICIST (profess. & kin.). 024.081. Studies physical aspects of earth, including its atmosphere and hydrosphere: Investigates and measures seismic, gravitational, electrical, thermal, and magnetic forces affecting earth, utilizing principles of physics, mathematics, and chemistry. Analyzes data obtained to compute shape of earth, estimate composition and structure of earth's interior, determine flow pattern of ocean tides and currents, study physical properties of atmosphere, and help to locate petroleum and mineral deposits. Investigates origin and activity of glaciers, volcanoes, and earthquakes. Compiles data to prepare navigational charts and maps, predict atmospheric conditions, and establish water supply and flood-control programs.

GEODESIST (profess. & kin.). Employs surveying and geodetic instruments, such as transits, theodolites, and other engineering instruments, in setting up and improving network of triangulation over earth's surface in order to provide fixed points for use in making maps. Establishes bench marks (known points of elevation). Performs gravimetric surveying to determine variations in earth's gravitational field, and provides data used in determination of weight, size, and mass of earth.

GEOMAGNETICIAN (profess. & kin.). terrestrial magnetician. Sets up magnetic observatories and stations to chart earth's magnetic field. Applies data obtained to problems in fields of telephony, telegraphy, radio broadcasting, navigation, mapping, and geophysical prospecting.

GEOPHYSICAL PROSPECTOR (petrol. production). Studies structure of subsurface rock formation to locate petroleum deposits, using such physical and electrical testing instruments as seismograph, gravimeter, torsion balance, magnetometer, pendulum devices, and electrical-resistivity apparatus to measure various characteristics of earth. Computes, from instrument readings, variations in physical forces existint at different locations, and interprets data to reveal subsurface structures likely to contain petroleum deposits. Prepares

Illustration 2.1 (Continued)

charts, profiles, or subsurface contour maps. Determines desirable locations for drilling operation. Oversees field crews drilling shallow boreholes in designated terrain and collecting samples of soil for chemical analysis of hydrocarbon content. May be designated according to type of equipment used as *Electrical Prospector; Gravity Prospector; Magnetic Prospector; Seismic Prospector.*

GLACIOLOGIST (profess. & kin.). Studies effects of glaciation in changing surface of earth.

HYDROLOGIST (profess. & kin.). Studies distribution, disposition, and development of waters of land areas, including form and intensity of precipitation, and modes of return to ocean and atmosphere. Maps and charts water flow and disposition of sediment. Measures changes in water volume due to evaporation and melting of snow. Studies storm occurrences and nature and movement of glaciers, and determines rate of ground absorption and ultimate disposition of water. Evaluates data obtained in reference to such problems as flood and drought forecasting, soil and water conservation programs, and planning water supply, water power, flood control, drainage, irrigation, crop production, and inland navigation projects.

OCEANOGRAPHER, PHYSICAL (profess. & kin.). Studies physical aspects of ocean, such as density, temperature, and ability to transmit light and sound; movement of sea, such as waves, tides, and currents; and relationship between sea and atmosphere.

SEISMOLOGIST (profess. & kin.). Works at fixed locations throughout globe and studies courses and phenomena of earthquakes, using special devices and machines, including seismograph. Establishes existence of active fault lines or areas where earthquakes have occurred and near which it would be hazardous to build cities, dams, or lofty structures.

TECTONOPHYSICIST (profess. & kin.). Studies elastic deformation of flow and rupture of constituent materials of earth's crust and makes deductions concerning forces causing these deformations (changes). Studies formation of strata underlying continents and ocean beds, and forces at work in earth's crust, and general structure of coastal layers. Work is mostly research and findings applicable to prospecting.

VOLCANOLOGIST (profess. & kin.). Studies occurrence, origin, and activity of volcanoes; origin of igneous rocks; and ore-forming processes occurring in earth in presence of igneous rock. Performs duties as described under *Geophysical Prospector* (petrol. production) in studying ore bodies that may be commercially exploitable.

GERMANIUM PROCESSOR (electronics) *see* CRYSTAL GROWER.

GERM DRIER (corn prod.) *see* DRIER ATTENDANT (corn prod; grain & feed mill.).

GERMINATION MAN (malt liquors) *see* GERMINATION WORKER.

GERMINATION WORKER (malt liquors) 522.885. compartment man; drum man; germination man; temperature man. Tends equipment that controls temperature and humidity in drums or compartments in which barley is germinated to produce malt: Starts fans that force and circulate moist, heated air into drums and compartments. Moves damper counterweights or lowers handle to adjust and obtain specified temperature and humidity. Adds water to drum, using metered hose, or starts screw type mixing machine equipped with water sprayer to insure uniformity of germination. Removes sample of germinated barley from drum or compartment for laboratory analysis. Records such data concerned with malting cycle as air and water temperature and humidity content.

GERM-SEPARATOR MAN (corn prod.) 521.782. separator operator. Operates flotation machine to remove germs (embryos) from cracked grain, and tests product to insure that plant standards are met: Determines specific gravity of cracked grain suspension, using hydrometer, and turns valves to add grain or water to attain specified density. Starts machine that agitates suspension and permits oil-laden germs to rise to surface. Adds liquid of specified density, that causes germs to float, to test residue for presence of germs. Makes iodine titration on fluid and suspension leaving germ separator, computes sulfur dioxide content from amount of iodine added, and records test findings. May turn valves to regulate flow of materials to other processes, as directed. May operate shakers to remove bran and other fibers from starch suspension.

GET-READY MAN (auto. ser.) *see* NEW-CAR GET-READY MAN.
—(ret. tr.) *see* CAR CHECKER.

GETTERER (elec. equip.) I. 725.887. Applies to stems of lead wires used in making incandescent lamps: Picks stem from tray and applies getter on lead wires with brush.

Illustration 2.1 (Continued)

Replaces stem in tray to dry. Adds thinners to getter and stirs mixture to maintain specified consistency.
—(elec. equip.) II *see* GETTERING-FILA-MENT-MACHINE OPERATOR.

GETTER OPERATOR (elec. equip.) *see* GETTERING-FILAMENT-MACHINE OPERATOR.

GETTER WELDER (electronics) *see* MOUNTER I.

GETTERING-FILAMENT-MACHINE OPERATOR (elec. equip.) 509.885. getterer; getter operator. Tends machine that sprays or dips tungsten wires with chemical (getter) used to burn off residual air and moisture in electric light bulbs: Fills receptacle of machine with getter. Starts machine that sprays or dips getter onto tungsten filaments and observes that getter is applied uniformly and without distortion. May weigh specified quantity of filaments and calculate number, using slide rule and known weight of single unit. May place tray with coated filaments in oven to dry.

GHERKIN PICKLER (can. & preserv.). *see* PICKLER.

GIANT-TIRE REPAIRMAN (auto. ser.) *see* TIRE REPAIRMAN.

GIGGER (textile) *see* GIG TENDER.

GIG TENDER (textile) 585.885. gigger. Tends machine that raises and sets direction of fiber on surface of woolen cloth, giving cloth a soft and lofty hand: Mounts roll of cloth on shaft at feed end of machine, using hoist. Sews end of cloth to leader cloth in machine, using portable sewing machine. Turns handwheels to raise or lower contact rollers that press cloth against gigging cylinder to control amount of nap. Turns valves to admit water into wet-out boxes. Starts machine and processes cloth back and forth through machine until nap has been raised according to specifications. Relaxes pressure on contact rollers and processes cloth through machine to set direction of nap. May tend machine equipped with steaming roller rather than wet-out boxes and be designated as STEAM GIGGER.

GILDER (any ind.). I. 749.781. gold charmer; gold-leaf gilder; metal-leaf gilder; metal-leaf layer. Lays metal leaf, such as aluminum, gold, or silver, on surfaces of items, such as books, furniture, harps, and signs, to decorate them using brushes: Brushes sizing (thin glue) on sections of items which are to be covered with leaf (gilded). Paints sizing according to design. Transfers leaf from supply book onto pallet, rubs camel-hair brush in hair to electrify it, picks up leaf with brush and lays leaf over sizing. Rubs leaf with polished burnishing. . .

A more representative cross section of occupations can be seen by examining Table 2.7, in which occupations are placed in their respective groups by size.

TABLE 2.7 SIZE AND RANK OF SELECTED OCCUPATIONS IN THE UNITED STATES, 1968

OCCUPATIONAL GROUP	OCCUPATION	NUMBER OF PERSONS IN OCCUPATION	RANK OF OCCUPATION BY SIZE[a]
Professional, technical, and kindred workers	Elementary school teachers	1,200,000	4
	High school teachers	900,000	9
	Accountants	525,000	24
	Physicians	285,000	37
	Lawyers	270,000	43

TABLE 2.7 (Continued)

	Chemists	125,000	75
	Dentists	100,000	84
	School counselors	54,000	120[b]
	Astronomers	1,000	225
Managers and administrators	Bank officers	145,000	71
	Construction managers, self-employed	139,000	61[b]
	Industrial traffic managers	16,000	174
	Public administration officials	200,000	53[b]
Clerical and kindred workers	Stenographers and secretaries	2,500,000	2
	Bookkeepers	1,190,000	5
	Receptionists	225,000	49
	Office machine operators	148,000	63[b]
Sales workers	Retail sales workers	3,000,000	1
	Real estate sales workers and brokers	220,000	50
	Secruities sales workers	110,000	83
	Wholesale trade sales workers	608,000	23[b]
Craftsmen, foremen, and kindred workers	Carpenters	875,000	10
	Machine tool operators	525,000	25
	Tool and die makers	150,000	69
	Diesel mechanics	80,000	97
	Locomotive engineers	37,000	131
	Glaziers	6,000	213
	Masons	176,000	64[b]
	Factory foremen	847,000	11[b]
Operatives and kindred workers (semiskilled)	Local truck drivers	1,175,000	6
	Assemblers	800,000	11
	Hospital attendants	710,000	15
	Factory inspectors	580,000	22

TABLE 2.7 (Continued)

OCCUPATIONAL GROUP	OCCUPATION	NUMBER OF PERSONS IN OCCUPATION	RANK OF OCCUPATION BY SIZE[a]
	Railroad brakemen	75,000	98
	Furnacemen, smelterers, and pourers	65,000	125[b]
Laborers, except farm and mine (unskilled)	Construction laborers	725,000	12
	Manufacturing laborers	305,000	38[b]
	Longshoremen and stevedores	46,000	122[b]
	Stock handlers	512,000	27[b]
Service workers, excluding private household workers	Waiters and waitresses	1,000,000	8
	Police	280,000	40
	Barbers	210,000	51
	Firefighters	190,000	54
	Elevator operators	27,000	185[b]
	Hotel housekeepers	20,000	192

[a] The ranking of occupations is based on a cross section of occupations selected by the U.S. Department of Labor's Bureau of Labor Statistics and therefore does not include many occupations with large numbers of people.

[b] In order to broaden the representation of the list, statistics are utilized from the Department of Commerce, Bureau of the Census, *Detailed Characteristics: United States Summary, 1970 Census of the Population* (Washington, D.C.: U.S. Government Printing Office, 1973), pp. 718-724. In many cases the Bureau of Labor Statistics data are far out of line with those of the Bureau of the Census. For example, in 1968, the former lists 6000 glaziers, whereas the latter lists 25,000. However, in the larger occupations, figures generally agree.

Source. Occupational Outlook Quarterly, 12 (May 1968).

OCCUPATIONAL PRESTIGE

Occupational prestige exists in some form in all human societies. Prestige is most simply and broadly defined as societal judgments as to the worth of individuals or groups. It is measured on the basis of taste, birth, and occupation.[21] Three approaches are used to obtain this measure and more than one can be used to obtain a single measure. The first approach is the "reputational," in which judgments are made of one another by members of a community or organization. The most famous example of this approach is W. Lloyd Warner's study of "Yankee City," in which respondents listed six basic strata

of their community, ranging from upper-upper to lower-lower class.[22]   The
second approach is "subjective," where individuals rank themselves into strata.
In this situation, respondents generally list fewer categories.   Robert Lane's
respondents in "Eastport" listed only two basic categories.[23]   Another sub-
jectivist study conducted by *Fortune* magazine in 1940 showed that 80 percent of Americans consider themselves as "middle class."   People want to see
themselves as basically the same as others, unless confronted with reminders
(in this case, categories) of their recognized position in society.   When those
questioned were asked to choose between four categories (lower class, working
class, middle class, upper class), a large percentage (47 percent)chose middle
class and nearly as many (43 percent) chose working class.[24]

In the third approach, the "objective," the researcher stands outside the
group and, after detailed examination, determines the strata.   This usually
results in the most refined set of strata, in one case involving 10 such layers
in a community.

The most common method of measuring occupational prestige in the
United States is the reputational approach, where occupations are rank ordered
on the basis of persons' opinions of their "general standing" in society.   The
first such rating on a national level was conducted in 1947 by the National
Opinion Research Center (NORC) at the University of Chicago, in which 90
occupations were rated by a national sample of 2920 persons.[25]   During the
interviews respondents were handed a card that stated: "For each job mentioned, please pick out the statement that best gives *your own personal opinion* of the *general standing* that such a job has."   The choices were: "excellent," "good," "average," "somewhat below average," "poor," and "don't
know."   The resulting scores showed that people consistently ranked occupations in the same way, regardless of age or geographic location.   (See Table
2.8 for a sample of rankings).

However, since only about one-third of the nearly 300 specific occupations
listed by the Bureau of the Census are included, it was felt that some way of
extrapolating from the known data on occupational prestige should be found
to expand the range of what appeared to be a highly accurate measure of
occupational standing.   Using data from the 1950 census, Otis Dudley Duncan
found that the amount of education and size of income of workers in an occupation correlate highly with the NORC prestige rating of that occupation.
Thus, the subjective dimension of occupational prestige coincides with an
"objective" measure of social standing.[26]

In addition, it was hypothesized that income, education, and occupation
are "functionally" related; that a person qualified for an occupation by obtaining an education and, as a result of pursuing an occupation, he obtains income.
Thus, education is a "cause" of occupation and income an "effect" of occupation.[27]

TABLE 2.8 NORC PRESTIGE RATINGS AND DUNCAN SOCIO-ECONOMIC INDEX FOR 45 SELECTED OCCUPATIONS

NORC TITLE	EQUIVALENT CENSUS OCCUPATION TITLE	IN-COME[a]	EDUCA-TION[b]	NORC PRESTIGE RATING[c]	DUNCAN SOCIO-ECO-NOMIC INDEX	NORC "TRANS-FORMED" BY DUNCAN SOCIO-ECONOMIC INDEX[d]
Physician	Physicians and surgeons	76	97	97	92	89
College professor	College presidents, professors, and instructors (n.e.c.)	64	93	93	84	83
Banker	Manager, banking and other finance	78	82	92	85	84
Dentist	Dentists	80	100	90	96	93
Architect	Architects	75	92	90	90	86
Chemist	Chemists	64	86	90	79	81
Lawyer	Lawyers and judges	76	98	89	93	89
Civil engineer	Engineers, civil	72	86	88	84	83
Minister	Clergymen	21	84	87	52	71
Airline pilot	Airplane pilots and navigators	72	76	83	79	81
Accountant for a large business	Accountants and auditors	62	86	82	78	80
Owner of a Factory that employs about 100 people	Managers, manufacturing	60	56	81	61	81
Building contractor	Managers, construction	53	45	76	51	74
Author of novels	Authors	55	90	76	76	80

Instructor in the public schools	Teachers (n.e.c.)	48	91	73	72	78
Railroad engineer	Locomotive engineers	81	28	67	58	73
Welfare worker for a city government	Social and welfare workers	41	84	59	64	75
Undertaker	Funeral directors and embalmers	42	74	57	59	74
Trained machinist	Machinists	36	32	57	33	65
Electrician	Electricians	47	39	53	44	69
Reporter on a daily newspaper	Editors and reporters	67	87	52	82	82
Manager of a small store in a city	Managers, retail	42	44	45	43	72
Policeman	Policemen and detectives	34	47	41	40	68
Bookkeeper	Bookkeepers	29	72	39	51	71
Railroad conductor	Conductors, railroad	76	34	38	58	64
Mail carrier	Mail carriers	48	55	34	53	71
Carpenter	Carpenters	21	23	33	19	58
Plumber	Plumbers and pipefitters	44	25	29	34	66
Automobile repairman	Mechanics and repairmen, automobile	22	22	26	19	58
Machine operator in a factory	Operatives and kindred workers (n.e.c.), manufacturing	21	20	24	17	56

TABLE 2.8 (Continued)

NORC TITLE	EQUIVALENT CENSUS OCCUPATION TITLE	IN-COME[a]	EDUCA-TION[b]	NORC PRESTIGE RATING[c]	DUNCAN SOCIO-ECO-NOMIC INDEX	NORC "TRANS-FORMED" BY DUNCAN SOCIO-ECONOMIC INDEX[d]
Barber	Barbers, beauticians, and manicurists	16	26	20	17	56
Streetcar motor-man	Motormen, street, sub-way, and elevated railway	42	26	19	34	65
Clerk in a store	Salesmen and sales clerks (n.e.c.) retail trade	29	50	16	39	67
Restaurant cook	Cooks, except private household	14	22	16	15	54
Coal miner	Mine operatives and laborers (n.e.c.), coal mining	7	7	15	2	25
Truck driver	Truck and tractor drivers	21	15	13	15	54
Night watchmen	Guards, watchmen, and doorkeepers	17	25	11	18	57
Filling-station attendant	Attendants, auto service, and parking	15	29	10	19	e
Restaurant waiter	Waiters and waitresses	8	32	10	16	55
Taxi-driver	Taxicab drivers and chauffeurs	9	19	10	10	49

Janitor	Janitors and sextons	7	20	8	9	47
Bartender	Bartenders	16	28	7	19	58
Soda fountain clerk	Counter and fountain workers	12	30	6	17	56
Shoe-shiner	Bootblacks	9	17	3	8	46

[a] Percent of males in the 1950 experienced civilian labor force with incomes of $3500 or more in 1949, based on those reporting income, adjusted for age.

[b] Percent of males in the 1950 experienced labor force having graduated from high school, adjusted for age.

[c] "Average," "somewhat below average," "poor," and "don't know" answers are excluded because it was found that the relationship between the original NORC score ("excellent" to "poor") correlated very highly with the "excellent" or "good" answers alone. Albert J. Reiss, Jr., with Otis Dudley Duncan, Paul K. Hatt, and Cecil C. North, *Occupations and Social Status* (New York: The Free Press, 1961), pp. 117-119.

[d] Scaled to predict the "excellent" or "good" ratings received by the occupation, that is, what the NORC score *should be* on the basis of the Duncan Socio-Economic Index score. Reiss, Duncan, Hatt, and North, *Occupations and Social Status*, Table B-1, Appendix B, contains the "transformed" scores.

[e] No information given.

Source. Albert J. Reiss, Jr., *et al.*, *Occupations and Social Status* Table VI-1, pp. 122-123. Copyright © 1961 by The Free Press of Glencoe, Inc. Reprinted by permission of the publisher.

FUNCTIONALIST AND CONFLICT THEORIES OF STRATIFICATION

From such research the functionalist theory of stratification has been given strong support. This theory states that the distribution of rewards in a society is "a function of" the distribution of system needs. Roles, specifically occupational roles, are rewarded in proportion to their contribution to the common good, that is, those roles that have the greatest importance for society and that require the greatest training and talent.[28] Therefore, a person's social status will depend very much on his or her occupation, the "result" of training and talent. For most functionalists occupation becomes the single most important indicator of social status or social class.

At this point we get into a conceptual muddle because prestige, social status, and social class are often used interchangeably by social scientists to mean the same thing. For some, however, the term social class has a more specific meaning—persons stratified on the basis of wealth. The definition may or may not include other factors such as formal social organization and common ideology. This definition once had real meaning for European society, which was stratified into rigid social groups for many centuries.

The essence of the conflict theory of stratification is that the distribution of rewards in a society is the result of the distribution of power and not the result of the distribution of system needs.[29] Social inequality emerges as the result of domination, exploitation, and constraint of one or more groups by another group or groups. This dominance is initially established through any or all of the following: ownership of property; the unequal control of scarce goods and services; and the unwillingness or inability of the oppressed to organize.[30]

Conflict theorists also use occupations as a measure of social status and, in their examination of social classes, they utilize occupational groups and categories. Some of their more recent analyses deal with the degree of consciousness and potential organization among new white-collar occupations, especially health and education professionals, which may lead to a "new working class."

Social stratification, as a general term, is defined as "structured social inequality" an "arrangement of positions in a graded social hierarchy of socially superior and inferior ranks," on the basis of wealth, prestige, and power,[31] or, as others have defined them, class, status, and power.[32] Functionalists emphasize prestige, while conflict theorists emphasize wealth and power. For functionalists, "a social system is functional when it provides persons with goods or privileges proportionate to their contributions to the welfare of the valu[ing] groups or society."[33] Which goes back to St. Simon's dictum: "From each according to his abilities, to each according to his efforts." These efforts or contributions are rewarded unequally to those persons with superior qualities (of ability and effort), according to what is of value to the society. Physicians will receive higher income, more prestige, and more power than sanitation workers.

Conflict theorists would not necessarily disagree with this formulation, except that persons or entire occupations with superior qualities have not always reached their positions on the basis of ability. All too frequently luck, inheritance, or pressure group tactics result in the accumulation of wealth, power, and prestige. Conflict theorists are more likely to subscribe to Karl Marx's statement: "From each according to his abilities, to each according to his needs." The problems associated with each of these stances and their role in the sociology of occupations is examined more fully in Parts 2 and 3.

OCCUPATIONS AND SOCIAL STATUS

The major assumption underlying the measurement of occupational prestige is that occupations can be rank-ordered on the basis of two measures: first, how people feel about them, that is, the NORC scale of occupational ratings; and second, on the basis of certain "attributes" such as education and income, the Duncan Socio-Economic Index. The overall reliability of both measures was confirmed by repeating the original studies.[34]

There are, however, a few significant differences between the two measures. Table 2.8 summarizes the NORC ratings and the Duncan Socio-Economic Index for the 45 occupations where NORC titles are comparable to census titles. As can easily be seen, there is some discrepancy between the two measures. The difference in scores for clergymen is greatest. At first glance, one might assume that the prestige the public accords this occupation is much greater than that measured by education and income. But to assume that public ranking is the sole cause of the difference is a gross error. Factors such as free housing for the clergy are not counted in the income dimension and would change the Socio-Economic Index rating considerably. Likewise, social prestige is not considered as important as income and education by the NORC respondents when asked what they thought was the "one main thing about such jobs that gives this standing." One out of every three replied that income or education were important, whereas only 14 percent stated that the job carries social prestige. The important point is that the criteria of ranking are many and varied.[35]

Another method of classifying occupations is the Warner seven-point occupational scale, which is incorporated in his Index of Status Characteristics (ISC).[36] The ISC is perhaps the most widely known and most sophisticated short classification available. The respondent is rated on the basis of four scales, each with values ranging from 1 to 7: occupation, source of income, house type, and dwelling area. The scale for rating occupations is two-dimensional. Each of the seven occupational categories (slightly modified versions of the Edwards census categories) is ranked into one of seven possible strata, depending on skill required for the job and the prestige value assigned to the job by the community. The authors testify to the importance of occupation in the measure of social status when they give it a weight higher than the other three indicators in the final version of the ISC scale.[37]

Rank-ordering occupations presents several problems. Although most likely there is an ordinal scale of prestige for occupational groups (see Table 2.8), there is no indication that specific occupations form a unidimensional scale taken as a whole. Several occupations seemed to be evaluated on different continua by the respondents. Researchers have tried to construct categories of occupational positions that would give a picture of these several dimensions. The first such attempt was made by Paul Hatt, using the NORC occupational prestige data, in which eight "situses" and their "families" were scaled.[38] A situs is defined as a number of occupations whose status system may be considered as a unit.[39] Hatt arrived at eight situses, each with several families. It is the families of each situs that are found to be unidimensional; that is, there is strong agreement among the public regarding the rank-ordering of these occupations on a single-dimensional continuum. The situses are:

1. Political.
2. Professional.
3. Business.
4. Recreation and aesthetics.
5. Agriculture.
6. Manual work.
7. Military.
8. Service.

The occupations of the business situs included one or more from each of four families: big business, small business, labor organizations, and white-collar employees. The occupations of the manual work situs included one or more from each of five families: skilled mechanics, construction trades, outdoor work, factory work, and unskilled labor.

Another test of situses was conducted by Morris and Murphy. They constructed 10 unidimensional situses on the basis of the societal functions the occupations perform.[40]

1. *Legal authority.* Formulation, arbitration, interpretation, or enforcement of law.
2. *Finance and records.* Monetary affairs, or processing of records, accounts, and correspondence.

3. *Manufacturing.* Fabrication of articles and processing of raw materials on a production-line basis.
4. *Transportation.* Movement of persons or goods.
5. *Extraction.* Extraction or procurement of raw materials.
6. *Building and maintenance.* Construction of buildings and installation, and repair of equipment and property.
7. *Commerce.* Buying, selling, exchange, or marketing of goods.
8. *Aesthetics and entertainment.* Creation of art forms or provision of entertainment, recreation, and information for the public.
9. *Education and research.* Formal instruction or training.
10. *Health and welfare.* Detection, prevention, or alleviation of illness, hazards, or distress.

Technically, these situses are "equally valued"; that is, each situs provides an equally important function for society and is judged so by members of society. However, in practice this just does not work out. Morris and Murphy noted that people tend to rank the situses. A group of college students ranked them in the following order:

1. Education and research.
2. Health and welfare.
3. Legal authority.
4. Manufacturing.
5. Extraction.
6. Commerce.
7. Building and maintenance.
8. Transportation.
9. Finance.
10. Arts and entertainment.

Since many occupations can occur in more than one situs (e.g., engineer in education and research, manufacturing, or extraction; physician in education, or health and welfare), "equally valued" situses contain supposedly equally valued occupations that are, in fact, unequally valued. Medical school physicians (education and research) are generally ranked higher by the medical profession than practicing physicians (health and welfare). Practicing CPAs (finance and records) are generally ranked higher than CPA faculty (education and research) by members of their profession.

A more recent attempt to scale occupations was made at the University of Michigan.[41] The researchers utilized the method of the "smallest space analysis," developed by Louis Guttman,[42] which measures degree of *occupational similarity,* defined as the likeness of individuals in occupations or of one occupation with another, as measured by factors such as education, income, attitudes, and behavior. Similarity is measured by distinctions made on the basis of the sociological function of occupation and the psychological functions of dealing with things, data, or people. The psychological functions are taken from the "Structure of Worker Functions," an organizing list of the *Dictionary of Occupational Titles,* Vol. II:

STRUCTURE OF WORKER FUNCTIONS

WORKING WITH THINGS	WORKING WITH DATA	WORKING WITH PEOPLE
A. Observing	A. Observing	A. Observing
B. Learning	B. Learning	B. Learning
C. Handling	K. Comparing	R. Taking instructions-helping
D. Feeding–offbearing	L. Copying	S. Serving
E. Tending	M. Computing	T. Speaking–signalling
F. Manipulating	N. Compiling	U. Persuading v. Diverting
G. Operating-Controlling	O. Analyzing	W. Supervising X. Instructing
H. Driving–operating	P. Coordinating	Y. Negotiating
I. Precision Working	Q. Synthesizing	Z. Mentoring

Similarity of worker functions implies status ranking on the basis of some preexisting notion of the value of complex tasks. (Notice that the structure of worker functions is ordered on the basis of degree of complexity of worker task.) Therefore, those occupations found at the upper left corner of Table 2.9 are generally of higher status and those toward the lower right corner are generally of lower status. This measure of occupational similarity goes beyond other measures of occupational ranking by measuring aspects of occupations themselves, particularly occupational functions, and not merely dimensions that relate to occupations such as education or income. The problem remains that people will rank the same occupation on different levels for different reasons. In addition, occupations will be perceived differently in different geographical locations or by different subcultures.

With all these measures the tendency is to view society as stratified on the basis of slight gradations of prestige, wealth, and power, where the individual has the opportunity to move up or down through these strata on the basis of his or her abilities in education and on the job. The family of the individual (specifically, the father's occupation) is regarded as the starting point by which one measures the distance one has moved upward or downward. This is what Nisbet calls "level consciousness,"[43] in contrast to "class consciousness," and

TABLE 2.9 GROUPINGS OF 22 MAJOR OCCUPATIONAL HEADINGS USED IN THE *DICTIONARY OF OCCUPATIONAL TITLES* ON THE BASIS OF DATA, PEOPLE, AND THINGS HIERARCHIES

PEOPLE	THINGS	DATA			
		Very High	High	Medium	Low
High	High		Farming, fishing, etc. Medicine and health		
	Medium				
	Low	Counseling and guidance	Education and teaching Farming, fishing, etc. Legal and law enforcement Medicine and health		
Medium	High	Arts	Crafts	Merchandising	Crafts
	Medium	Managerial and supervisory	Transportation		
	Low	Music Managerial and supervisory Counseling and guidance Writing	Business relations Managerial and supervisory Transportation	Entertainment Merchandising	
Low	High	Engineering Math and science	Farming, fishing, etc. Crafts Medicine and health	Photography, etc. Investigating, etc.	Crafts
	Medium			Clerical	Machine work
	Low	Engineering Math and science	Business relations Medicine and health Farming, fishing, etc. Legal and law enforcement	Clerical Investigating, etc.	Elemental Personal service

Source. John P. Robinson, Robert Athanasiou, and Kendra B. Head, *Measures of Occupational Attitudes and Occupational Characteristics*, p. 435. Copyright © 1969 by Institute of Social Research, University of Michigan Survey Research Center. Reprinted by permission of the author and publisher.

it is representative of the functionalist perspective in sociology. Other theorists have similar views of the system of stratification in our society, but they tend to deemphasize the importance of occupation as a determining factor.

Both the views of functionalists and conflict theorists are examined regarding perspectives on postindustrial society in Chapter 3. In Chapter 4, I examine three different labor market theories in economics that deal with occupational structure. Two of these schools are polar opposites that can roughly be compared to functionalism and conflict theory.

A NOTE ON THE ACCURACY OF POPULATION STATISTICS

In an extensive study commissioned by the National Research Council of the National Academy of Sciences, an advisory committee concluded that there are some serious problems of underenumeration of the 1970 census data. In its summary, *America's Uncounted People*,[44] the committee concludes that just as in the census counts of 1950 and 1960, the 1970 count failed to enumerate all persons in a household. The term "household," or family residence, is seen as a serious stumbling block. For example, in many cases the passage of migrants from rural to urban centers is organized in terms of extended family instead of family residence or household. Thus, when asked, "Who is living or staying here and has no other home?" the respondent does not include, among others, the migrant worker. The Bureau of Labor Statistics logic assumes that "people have one primary household attachment that is more important to them than all others and that those uniquely important attachments are known to the respondents who actually fill out the census form or respond to a census interviewer."[45]

> *Missing people are not inherently missing, or invisible, or anonymous, until they are made so by a lack of fit between the assumptions and procedures that guide the counting operation that attempts to locate them and the subjective, experiential categories, or characteristic behaviors, in which they define their own life situations . . . . Social data are not simply 'out there for the asking,' but rather are structured in terms of purposes, assumptions, instruments, and interactions among people, which to varying degrees, perturb, focus, and depend on the customary ambits of everyday life.*[46]

This social structure is continually being renegotiated by people, and census definitions must also fit these new definitions. Little emphasis is given to the fact that in many cases isolation from conventional social institutions is only a stage in a career (e.g., participation in communes).[47] Thus, not only racial and ethnic minority groups are undercounted, but also moderately wealthy and very mobile whites.[48] There are no data available yet that estimate the undercount of the 1970 census. But taking the 1960 census undercount as a case in point,[49] in the 15 to 19 year age group there were an estimated 233,000 white males (3.8 percent of all white males in the work force) not counted and 144,000 white women (2.4 percent). For nonwhites of the same age group the numbers were: men, 114,000, or 12.5 percent of all nonwhite men in the labor force; and women, 91,000, or 10.1 percent. In the 25 to 29 year age group, nonwhite males were undercounted by 19.7 percent. This high trend continues through to the 50 to 54 age group, where the undercount rate is 17.8 percent.

It is therefore advisable to consider all population and workforce statistics as approximations only and not as exact or, in some cases, even accurate estimates. A Population Health Survey conducted by the City University of New York's Graduate School Center for Social Research used an interview survey instead of the mailed survey used by the Bureau of the Census and found that the 1970 Puerto Rican population of New York City was undercounted by 204,700. Their population count of 1,016,500 increases the Puerto Rican population of the city by 20 percent. That all these persons were actually missed brings into question the analysis on census data of this and other minority groups. The Bureau of the Census places the "Spanish-heritage" population at 9.2 million, whereas Senator Joseph Montoya (D. New Mexico) says that a more accurate estimate would place the number at around 14 million, 50 percent larger than the government figure.

Even the values and biases of those who define and determine census categories and titles will have significant effects on occupations. For example, the male bias in the *Dictionary of Occupational Titles* will seriously affect the classifications, compensations, and potential of jobs. A rest room attendant is rated equal to a foster mother; a newspaper carrier is rated higher tha a nursemaid; a striptease artist higher than a homemaker; a marine mammal handler higher than a nursery school teacher; and a parking lot attendant equal to a child care attendant.[50]

Such biases and error factors must be taken into consideration when evaluating census data, especially where it is suspected that large numbers of the uncounted could be present (e.g., in poverty groups, the unemployed, and ethnic and racial groups).

FOOTNOTES FOR CHAPTER 2
OCCUPATIONAL CATEGORIES

[1] Kenneth Henry, "Occupational Sociology in Perspective," (unpublished paper, 1972).

[2] Richard H. Hall, *Occupations and the Social Structure* 2nd Ed.; (Engle-wood Cliffs, N.J.: Prentice-Hall, 1975), p. 6.

[3] Alba M. Edwards, *Population; Comparative Occupational Statistics for the United States, 1870 to 1940* (Bureau of the Census, Washington, D.C.: U.S. Government Printing Office, 1943).

[4] U.S. Department of Labor, Bureau of Manpower Administration, *Man-power Report of the President, 1973*, (Washington, D.C.: U.S. Government Printing Office, 1973), pp. 131, 132.

[5] Edwin Harwood and Claire C. Hodge, "Jobs and the Negro Family: A Reappraisal," *The Public Interest*, No. 23 (Spring 1971), 125-131.

[6] Harwood and Hodge, "Jobs and the Negro Family: A Reappraisal."

[7] Theodore Caplow, *The Sociology of Work* (Minneapolis: University of Minnesota Press, 1954), p. 31.

[8] Edwards, *Population*, p. 179. See also, Caplow, *The Sociology of Work*, pp. 33-34.

[9] William A. Faunce and William H. From, "The Nature of Industrial Soc-iety," in William A. Faunce and William H. Form (eds.), *Comparative Per-spectives on Industrial Society* (Boston: Little, Brown, & Co., 1969), p. 8.

[10] Wilbert E. Moore, "Changes in Occupational Structures," in Neil Smelser and Seymour Lipset (eds.), *Social Structure and Mobility in Economic Development* (Chicago: Aldine Press, 1966), p. 197.

[11] Moore, "Changes in Occupational Structures," p. 201.

[12] Hall, *Occupations and the Social Structure*, p. 230.

[13] U.S. Department of Labor, Bureau of Labor Statistics, *The U.S. Eco-nomy in 1980*, Bulletin 1773, 1970, p. 58.

[14] *The U.S. Economy in 1980.*

[15] Michael F. Crowley, "Professional Manpower: The Job Market Turn-around," *Monthly Labor Review* (October 1972), 11.

[16] Department of Labor, Bureau of Labor Statistics, *Occupational Outlook for College Graduates: 1972-73 Edition* (Washington, D.C.: U.S. Govern-ment Printing Office, 1972), p. 4.

[17] Department of Labor, Bureau of Labor Statistics, *College Educated Work-ers, 1968-80* (Washington, D.C.: U.S. Government Printing Office, 1970),

p. 3; and Crowley, "Professional Manpower: The Job Market Turn-around," p. 14.

[18] Crowley, "Professional Manpower: The Job Market Turnaround," p. 15.

[19] Everett C. Hughes, *Men and Their Work* (New York: The Free Press, 1958), pp. 23, 44.

[20] *Dictionary of Occupational Titles*, 3rd Ed., 3 Vols. (Washington, D.C.: U.S. Department of Labor, Bureau of Employment Security, U.S. Employment Service, 1965).

[21] Max Weber, *From Max Weber: Essays in Sociology*, ed. and trans. by Hans H. Gerth and C. Wright Mills (New York: Oxford University Press, 1946), pp. 186-194. See also Thomas E. Lasswell, *Class and Stratum* (New York: Houghton-Mifflin Co., 1965), p. 48.

[22] W. Lloyd Warner et al., *Yankee City Series*, 4 Vols. (New Haven: Yale University Press, 1941-1947). All three approaches were used by Warner and his associates in this very thorough analysis of community stratification.

[23] Robert E. Lane, *Political Ideology: Why the American Common Man Believes What He Does* (New York: The Free Press, 1962).

[24] Richard Centers, *The Psychology of Social Classes* (Princeton, N.J.: Princeton University Press, 1949), p. 78.

[25] National Opinion Research Center, "Jobs and Occupations: A Popular Evaluation," *Opinion News*, IX (September 1, 1947), 3-13. Reprinted in Reinhard Bendix and Seymour M. Lipset (eds.), *Class, Status and Power* (New York: The Free Press, 1953), pp. 411-426. For a history and summary of the NORC study and related studies, see Albert J. Reiss, Jr., with Otis Dudley Duncan, Paul K. Hatt, and Cecil C. North, *Occupations and Social Status* (New York: The Free Press, 1961).

[26] Reiss, Duncan, Hatt, and North, *Occupations and Social Status*, pp. 124, 195.

[27] Otis Dudley Duncan, in Reiss, Duncan, Hatt, and North, *Occupations and Social Status*, pp. 116-117.

[28] The original statement of the functionalist position is given by Kingsley Davis and Wilbert E. Moore, "Some Principles of Stratification," *American Sociological Review, 10* (April 1945), 242-249.

[29] Gerhard Lenski, *Power and Privilege: A Theory of Social Stratification* (New York: McGraw-Hill Book Co., 1966), Chapter 1.

[30] Beth VanFossen, "Functionalism and the Justification of Social Inequality." Paper presented at the annual meeting of the American Sociological Association, August 25, 1973, New Orleans, La.

[31] Celia S. Heller (ed.), *Structured Social Inequality* (New York: The Macmillan Company, 1969), p. 4.

[32] Bendix and Lipset (eds.), *Class, Status and Power.*

[33] Lasswell, *Class and Stratum*, p. 61.

[34] Replication of the NORC study is found in Robert W. Hodge, Paul M. Siegel, and Peter H. Rossi, "Occupational Prestige in the United States, 1925-63," *American Journal of Sociology, 70* (November 1964), 256-302; for the Duncan Socio-Economic Index, Charles B. Nam and Mary G. Powers, "Changes in the Relative Status Level of Workers in the United States, 1950-60," *Social Forces, 47* (December 1968), 158-170.

[35] Reiss, Duncan, Hatt, and North, *Occupations and Social Structure*, p. 132.

[36] W. Lloyd Warner, Marchia Meeker, and Kenneth Eells, *Social Class in America: The Evaluation of Status* (New York: Harper & Row, 1960), Chapters 8-11.

[37] Warner, Meeker, and Eells, *Social Class in America*, p. 181.

[38] Paul K. Hatt, "Occupation and Social Stratification," *American Journal of Sociology, 55* (May 1950), 533-543.

[39] Hatt, "Occupation and Social Stratification."

[40] Richard T. Morris and Raymond J. Murphy, "The Situs Dimension in Occupational Structure, *American Sociological Review, 24* (April 1959), 231-239.

[41] John P. Robinson, Robert Athanasiou, and Kendra B. Head, *Measures of Occupational Attitudes and Occupational Characteristics* (Ann Arbor, Mich.: University of Michigan Survey Research Center, Institute for Social Research, 1969).

[42] For an early application, see Edward O. Laumann and Louis Guttman, "The Relative Associational Contiguity of Occupations in an Urban Setting," *American Sociological Review, 31* (April 1966), 169-178.

[43] Robert A. Nisbet, "The Rise and Fall of Social Class," *Pacific Sociological Review, 2* (Spring 1959), 11-17.

[44] Carole W. Parsons (ed.), *America's Uncounted People* (Washington, D.C.: National Academy of Sciences, 1972).

[45] *America's Uncounted People,* p. 62.

[46] *America's Uncounted People,* pp. 57-58.

[47] *America's Uncounted People,* pp. 64-65.

[48] Ann R. Miller and Susan Klepp, in a report to the Advisory Committee on Problems of Census Enumeration, "America's Uncounted People," Department of Labor, 1972.

[49] Jacob S. Siegel, "Completeness of Covering of the Nonwhite Population in the 1960 Census and Current Estimates and Some Implications," in David M. Heer (ed.), *Social Statistics and the City* (Cambridge, Mass.: Harvard University Press, 1968), pp. 42-43. Reprinted in *America's Uncounted People,* p. 28.

[50] "Policy Talk," in *Social Policy,* 2 (March-April 1972), 59.

3 THEORIES OF POSTINDUSTRIAL SOCIETY

Since the early 1960s, a group of social theorists have begun to look at the occupational structure in a different way. Instead of making just the traditional white-collar versus blue-collar distinction, they also dichotomize the labor force into goods-producing workers and service-producing workers. This provides a different picture of the functions of occupations, since both service-producing and goods-producing industries include workers from white-collar, blue-collar, and service categories. As indicated in Table 3.1, the distribution of employment in these two sectors shows dramatic changes in the increase in service-producing and decrease in goods-producing workers over the past three decades.

Because of this significant change in occupational structure and the attendant social consequences, the United States and other technically advanced nations have been called "postindustrial." Daniel Bell defines a society as postindustrial as compared to industrial when it is primarily information-producing instead of goods-producing; when the motivating force is information power instead of machine power.[1]

The occupations of the service-producing sector are found in many industrial groups.

Business services. Banking and finance; real estate; insurance carriers, agents, and brokers; securities dealers and exchanges; credit agencies.
Personal services. Retail trade (including general merchandise stores, food stores,

TABLE 3.1 SECTOR DISTRIBUTION OF EMPLOYMENT IN THE UNITED
STATES (IN PERCENT)

	1947	1968	1980
Goods-producing	51.0	35.9	31.7
Service-producing	49.0	64.1	68.4

Source. Adapted from Daniel Bell, "Labor in the Post-Industrial Society," *Dissent, 19*
(Winter 1972), 169.

apparel and accessories stores, furniture and appliance stores, and eating
and drinking places); laundries; garages; beauty shops; advertising; motion
pictures; hotels and lodging; other recreation.
Transportation, public utilities, and communications. Railroad, air, and
motor freight and passenger transportation operators and technical support
staff; radio, TV, and telephone workers and technical staffs; electrical, gas,
and oil companies and technical support staffs.
Health, education, research, and government. Hospitals and related medical services; colleges and universities; research organizations; autonomous
professionals; federal, state, and local governmental employees.

A FUNCTION-
ALIST VIEW

In *The Coming of Post-Industrial Society,* Bell points out that the United
States is presently the only nation with more than half its labor force engaged
in service-producing occupations (about 60 percent in 1973), and more than
half its gross national product is produced by these services. Whereas in 1900
7 in every 10 workers in the United States engaged in the production of
goods, by 1980 the proportions will be reversed: 7 in every 10 workers will
be engaged in service-producing industries. Bell contends that the occupational
distribution of the postindustrial society is represented in the preeminence of
the professional and technical category. It is this group's development and
control over theoretical knowledge and technology that makes the new society
unique.

The fundamental fact about work in this society is that "individuals now
talk to other individuals, rather than interact with a machine."[2] Whereas
semiskilled work is the occupational counterpart of mass production, for Bell
professional work is the occupational counterpart of the information revolution. Another way of defining a postindustrial society is "through the change
in occupational distributions; i.e., not only *where* people work, but the *kind*
of work they do. In large measure, occupation is the most important determinant of class and stratification in society."[3]

Bell pictures a general decline of the organized working class and the growth of an interest-group society in the postindustrial era. The conflict of the past 100 years and more between management and workers (between the ruling class and the proletariat) will not intensify as Marxists predict because of the strength of what Max Weber called "status groups" —racial, ethnic, and religious—whose ties are stronger than occupationally based ties, and because the labor problem has become "encapsulated." One reason is that methods of labor-management negotiation have become institutionalized. The United Auto Workers meet secretly in advance with the Big Three auto manufacturers to work out a general agreement on what the major issues are and how they will be handled *before* any public announcements are made. "The politics of the next decade is more likely to concern itself, on the national level, with such public-interest issues as health, education, and the environment, and, on the local level, crime, municipal services, and costs." Labor no longer has the power to polarize these issues around its cause.[4]

Another reason is that in the service sector unions must organize. However, they will find it difficult because the service economy is largely a female-centered economy in terms of its occupational groups—especially teachers, technicians, and health services. Seventy-three percent of all women work in services, only 27 percent in goods-producing industries. Also, proportionate to men, more women are found in service occupations than in goods-producing ones. In goods-producing industries 81 percent of all workers are men and 21 percent are women. In service-producing industries 46 percent are women and 54 percent men. Given these figures and the fact that women are traditionally more difficult to organize than men—their jobs are not considered as permanent—the trade union movement will find many difficulties in organizing this sector. Another problem arises with the drag on productivity as the number of service-producing workers increases and the number of goods-producing workers decreases. Services, especially government services, compete for the money produced by the goods-producing sector in the areas concerned with the rights of minorities: children, ethnic groups, students, and women.[5]

Because he initially ties himself to the status group concept, Bell can be placed into the functionalist perspective. He pictures postindustrial society as basically consensual. Organizations and institutions interrelate with a minimum of conflict, and order is best maintained by a system of meritocratic rewards. Through training and talent the individual will get ahead. This view is not much different from that propounded by the President's Commission on Technology and the American Economy, of which Bell was a member and contributor. In its report, the Commission had a vision of the postindustrial society as a technically self-guided system that, once the socio-political controls are set, will handle with dispatch the minor deviations that will occur. There is an "indicative planning," a strong central planning board to control

public and private organizations.[6] This situation actually has occurred in the
United States between the government and corporations in the defense industry, where the public is completely left out of any decision making or control. This state within a state distributes government largesse to favored corporations, which guarantees the latter a market for their products.[7]

A CONFLICT
THEORY VIEW

Perhaps the most comprehensive conflict perspective of postindustrial society
is given by the French sociologist, Alain Touraine.[8] Like Bell, Touraine treats
information as the central factor in the postindustrial society.

However, Touraine sees people as programmed into a highly organized
production system that encompasses and controls the educational process,
scientific research, consumption patterns, and the organization of communications and authority systems.

> The dominated classes are no longer defined by wretchedness but by con-
> sumption and the tasks they carry out, hence by dependence on the forms
> of organization and culture worked out by the ruling groups. They are
> no longer excluded; they are integrated and used.[9]

This overintegrated society creates a new working class of "dependent
participants." People participate in organizations without having authority
over their economic decisions.[10]

The leader of this new working class of dependent participants is the university. Other important areas are the research agencies, technicians in large-
scale organizations such as public health experts, consulting engineers, accountants, jurists, psychologists, labor physicians, instructors, educators, and skilled
workers. These form the core for a new class movement. Essentially, this
constitutes a sizable part of the service sector, excluding most business services. In their varied work situation, being forced to make decisions without
attendant authority robs this class of workers of their personal autonomy.
This is where the new struggle lies: not in the question of domination through
property but in domination through dependence on the "mechanisms of en-
gineered change and hence on the instruments of social and cultural integration." In a society of services, social control over these services now involves
control over members of the working class not only in their occupational roles
but also as consumers and as community members with family, friends, and
life-styles—their culture.[11]

Whereas Bell sees constantly struggling interest groups in a state of near
or complete powerlessness, Touraine believes the common interests of the service sector will provide the basis for a new working-class social movement.
Whereas Bell supports the ideology of meritocracy and liberal individualism,

Touraine sees the development of an antagonistic class of workers in a direct political struggle through occupational organization and cultural action.

A POSTCAPITAL-
IST VIEW

A different view of postindustrial society is provided by Robert Heilbroner. Society is "postcapitalist." There is qualitative, not quantitative, change in growth.[12] The postindustrial society is *not* the result of the decline of the industrial or goods-producing sector. The percentage of people employed by industrial organizations has not changed significantly in our century. The common observation that we have shifted from an industrial society to a service society is not entirely accurate. As Table 3.2 indicates, the major shift has been from agriculture to service. As Heilbroner notes, these statistics must be interpreted with care. For example, those jobs *functionally* related to agriculture are greater in number than those *formally* related to it. The farm machinery and chemical fertilizer industries and the governmental farm agencies (local, state, and federal) are functionally tied to the agricultural sector, although formally they are classified as industrial (goods-producing) and service-producing, respectively. Also, the large increase in service employment is affected by the large number of homemaking jobs not previously categorized that are now categorized as service-producing (e.g., the laundry and restaurant industries, professional care of the aged, and welfare). Also, Heilbroner contends that much of this is responsible for the increase in female employment from 18 percent in 1890 to 37 percent in 1969.[13]

TABLE 3.2 DISTRIBUTION OF EMPLOYED WORKERS IN SELECTED COUNTRIES, 1900-1970 (IN PERCENT)

		AGRICULTURE	INDUSTRY	SERVICE
United States	1900	38	38	24
	1970	4	35	61
France	1950	35	45	20
	1970	17	39	44
West Germany	1950	24	48	28
	1968	10	48	42
United Kingdom	1950	6	56	39
	1970	4	45	50

Source. Robert L. Heilbroner, "Economic Problems of a 'Post-Industrial' Society," *Dissent, 20* (Spring 1973), 164. Copyright © 1973 by Dissent Publishing Corporation. Reprinted by permission of the publisher.

The postindustrial society is postcapitalist to the extent that there is economic consensus that funds should be spent on "socialist" programs such as
guaranteed incomes, family allowances, public health plans, and educational
subsidization. But it remains capitalist politically in terms of its degree of
economic concentration and the linking of political and economic elites. This
is true of all potential postindustrial states: the United States, Japan, France,
and Germany. The postindustrial sector of services is not a countervailing
force; the present political economy is now proceeding to expand its economic
concentration into service industries. Bell states that most retail trade firms,
personal and professional services, finance and real estate firms, and hospitals
employ fewer than 1000 persons.[14] However, Heilbroner correctly points out
that the large firms are predominant in several of the occupational groups of
the service sector. For example, the 50 largest banks in the United States employ one-third of all banking employees. The top 50 insurance companies employ almost one-half of all insurance employees.[15]

Heilbroner concludes that there are some qualititative changes that do indicate we are heading toward a postindustrial society.

- There is an association of work with reading, writing, and calculation
  instead of with handling things.
- There is an expectation of security of the job. Middle-class young
  people are increasingly expecting as a right that they will not work
  until age 21 to 25 and that when they do a position for which they
  were trained will be available.
- There is the acceptance of a planned society, coordinated by an overt
  corporate-government relationship.

However, other factors prevent us from arriving:

- The increase in gross national product has come not from areas dealing with human welfare, but mostly as a result of increased armaments,
  space exploration, gadgetry, style changes, and the like.
- Research and development has increased from $1 billion in 1918 to
  $20 billion in 1966, but the amount invested in basic research in 1966
  was only $1 billion.
- The "knowledge explosion" has been mostly in areas of specialized,
  formalized, abstract knowledge. The development of generalized knowledge has suffered. Consequently, persons become less versatile in performing work outside their trained specialties.[16]

Heilbroner cannot be easily categorized as either a functionalist or conflict theorist, since he rarely gets to describe how society *should* change. But
in one important work he notes how major structural changes will be necessary in order for humanity to hope to live in some kind of minimal peace,

harmony, and democracy. Therefore, he concludes, the idea that a viable postindustrial society will be possible within the present political and economic framework is an absurdity.[17]

THE SERVICE
SOCIETY

An example is presented by Gartner and Riessman in which occupational structure is used to develop a view that we will soon go beyond the postindustrial society to the service society. They suggest that there are five separate analytical sectors that have developed historically, each with its predominant occupational structure, technology, design, and axial principles (see Table 3.3). The industrial phase was predicated on advanced agricultural productivity, just as the services phase is predicated on advanced industrial productivity. Yet, while industrialism has depended primarily on the capitalist mode of production, the service economy must ultimately utilize the socialist mode of production—of active participation in decision making at all levels of work, personal growth, people-oriented planning, decentralization, continuing education, work autonomy, ecological constraints, and demystification (e.g., gynecological self-help and student tutoring).[18]

The service sector is made up primarily of women, the young, and minorities—the groups that have less power and status—sometimes referred to as the secondary labor market. Also included are the older white males of the industrial sector. Gartner and Riessman point to the necessity to the service society of that large group of people who, for the greater part of their lives, remain outside the work force. These people, mostly on welfare, are "dispensable" as far as production of goods or services is concerned, but they are not dispensable as consumers. What is characteristic of the service society is that it is a society of *human* services; that is, it is consumer-focused, and it is relational and interpersonal. Human services are initiated to "produce benefit for the recipient." The consumer is crucial as a *force of production*, that is, as an instrument of production.

> *The student, for example, not only consumes the product of education, that is, his/her own learning, but is a key (perhaps the key) factor in the production of his/her own education. Similarly, the health of the patient is a consequence of how accurate a history he/she gives to the doctor, the extent to which he/she follows the prescribed regimen, etc.*[19]

This creates a multiplier effect—it produces an impact far beyond the number employed. By definition, then, human services include all those employed in education, mental health, welfare services, day care, and the like. These are important consumer goods; they affect a broad consumer population: clients, students, patients. Certain other service occupations are satellite human services (e.g., sales, advertising, and many personal services).[20]

TABLE 3.3 THE FIVE SECTORS OF ECONOMIC DEVELOPMENT

ECONOMIC SECTOR	AGRICULTURAL	INDUSTRIAL	POSTINDUSTRIAL (TERTIARY)	POSTINDUSTRIAL (QUARTERNARY)	QUINARY
Name	Communal society	Industrial society	Postindustrial society	Postindustrial society	Service society
Primary occupations	Farmers and farm laborers	Semiskilled workers, engineers	Transportation, public utilities	Finance, real estate and insurance, wholesale and retail trade	Human services professionals, education, health and social services
Technology	Human and animal labor, water and wind power	Synthetic energy	Information	Information	Relational
Design	People-nature	People-fabricated nature	People-ideas	People-ideas	People-people
Axial principle	Economic growth[a]	Economic growth	Theoretical knowledge	Theoretical knowledge	Consumer values

[a]See Immanual Wallerstein, *The Modern World-System* (New York: Academic Press, 1974), Chapter 1. *Source.* Adapted from Alan Gartner and Frank Riessman, *Social Policy, 4* (November-December 1973), 89. Copyright © 1973 by Social Policy Corporation, New York, New York 10010. Reprinted by permission of the publisher.

STRATUM
VERSUS
CLASS

Social policy writers suggest the specific occupations to be found in the new class structure. They are more explicit than Bell. Bell states that the professional and technical occupational group, rapidly growing to be the single largest occupational category, will be the leading force in the postindustrial society. But do mere numbers make the difference? Which professional and technical workers hold the most influential positions, the goods-producing or the service-producing workers? Is it the outside researcher contracted to analyze some aspect of firm organization or financing or is it the firm's lawyers and accountants? And what about those firm managers and executives who have come from a professional background? There is a great deal of mobility between these two occupational groups.

If so many professionals are found in both sectors of the economy and moving into and out of the professional group itself, then it is unlikely that the unusual situation that Bell predicts will come to pass, that is, "the clash between the professional and the populace, in the organization and in the community is the hallmark of conflict in the post-industrial society."[21] Instead, as Touraine points out, it will be more an ambivalent situation in which professionals will sometimes join the technocrats and other times fight them. In the long run this will irritate both the ruling elite and consumers.[22]

Still another view depicts the technical elite of the corporations (the "technostructure") as being at the core of the decision-making elite, tied in closely with the executive branch of the federal government. Academic professionals are somewhat of a countervailing force to these elites who serve the present military-industrial complex.[23] The implication is that professional and technical workers in the goods-producing sector are more important to the decision-making process than service-producing workers in this category.

Another theorist[24] emphasizes that the rates of growth in the professional and technical category have been large only in the lower-level occupations—clerks and minor public officials, school teachers, technicians, professional auxiliaries—most of whom work in large bureaucracies. These workers most often are not organized into a solidary group but, instead, are co-opted by the elite, which they admire and look to as a reference group—the traditional pattern of embourgeoisement of the lower-middle class. However, with their new, highly trained skills, they may come to see the contradiction between these skills and their lack of autonomy and, in unionization, demand more than just better wages and hours but also more worker control of administration and production. In Birnbaum's view, however, this development is not likely.

Blue-collar workers, as an actual and potential organized power group,

TABLE 3.4   OCCUPATION AS A PERCENTAGE OF INDUSTRY GROUP, 1970

ECONOMIC

| | GOODS-PRODUCING | | | | |
Occupational Category and Group	Agriculture, Forestry, and Fisheries	Mining	Construction	Manufacturing	Total Goods-Producing
WHITE-COLLAR					
Professional and technical	2.9	10.6	4.5	9.9	8.4
Managers and administrators	0.9	6.0	9.5	5.2	5.5
Sales workers	0.4	0.1	0.8	2.7	2.2
Clerical workers	1.8	9.6	6.3	12.5	10.2
Total white-collar	6.0	26.3	21.1	30.3	26.3
BLUE-COLLAR					
Craft workers	1.5	25.0	55.9	19.7	23.9
Operatives	2.0	42.1	8.8	43.1	33.2
Laborers, except farm	6.4	4.1	13.2	4.6	6.2
Total blue-collar	9.9	71.2	77.9	67.4	63.3
SERVICE WORKERS	0.6	1.5	1.0	2.3	1.9
FARM WORKERS	83.5	—	—	—	8.5
Total percent	100.0	100.0	100.0	100.0	100.0
Total number	2,840,488	630,788	4,572,235	19,837,208	27,880,719
Industry group percent	3.7	0.8	6.0	25.9	(36.5)

Sources. Adapted from U.S. Department of Commerce, Bureau of the Census, *Detailed Characteristics: United States Summary, 1970 Census of Population* (Washington, D.C.: U.S. Government Printing Office, (1973), Table 232, pp. 788-797; and Department of Labor, Bureau of Manpower Administration, *Manpower Report of the President, 1973* (Washington, D.C.: U.S. Government Printing Office, 1973), p. 142.

cannot be ignored. Goods-producing workers may continue to decrease dramatically over the next 40 years and thereby decrease the power of unions as a working-class movement, as Bell predicts. But the proportion of blue-collar workers has not decreased over the last 70 years (see Table 2.5). In fact, they are needed in increasing numbers in the service-producing sector of the economy. As of 1970, more than one out of every three blue-collar workers—about 10 million—is located in the service-producing sectors (see Table 3.5).[25] A majority of these workers are the skilled craftsmen and semi-skilled operatives who operate and maintain the machines for the railroad, air,

SECTOR

		SERVICE-PRODUCING			TOTAL OCCUPATIONAL CATEGORY AND GROUP	
Business Services	Personal Services	Transportation, Public Utilities, and Communications	Health, Education, Research, and Government	Total Service-Producing	Percent	Number (000) Omitted
7.5	3.1	7.6	42.2	18.6	14.2	11,351
14.7	12.6	7.3	5.9	10.0	10.5	6,371
19.1	18.0	1.3	0.3	10.0	6.2	5,445
35.7	14.2	24.3	23.5	22.4	17.4	13,748
77.0	47.9	40.5	71.9	61.0	48.3	36,915
5.8	9.9	22.1	3.3	8.1	12.9	10,609
8.7	10.3	26.0	1.8	8.6	17.7	13,456
3.2	4.6	7.3	1.2	3.5	4.7	3,431
17.7	24.8	55.4	6.3	20.2	35.3	27,496
5.3	27.3	3.1	21.8	18.8	12.4	9,773
—	—	—	—	—	4.0	2,367
100.0	100.0	100.0	100.0	100.0	100.0	76,553
8,221,668	17,507,255	5,186,101	17,712,856	48,627,880	—	76,553
10.7	22.9	6.8	23.1	(63.5)	100.0	—

motor freight, and passenger transportation industries, the communications industries, and the public utilities.

If we compare each of the industry groups (i.e., the columns in Table 3.4) to the final column in Table 3.4, "Total Occupational Category and Group," the various concentrations of each group can be seen. In the services-producing sector, professional and technical personnel are overrepresented in the health-education-research-government industries, managers and sales workers in the business and personal services, and clerical workers in all except personal services. For the four service-producing areas as a whole, it is interesting that the transportation-public utilities-communications area is the only one underrepresented in the white-collar category (40.5 percent as compared to the average of 48.3 percent for total white-collar category) and the only one overrepresented in the blue-collar category (55.4 percent as compared to

TABLE 3.5 INDUSTRY GROUP AS A PERCENTAGE OF OCCUPATION, 1970

ECONOMIC

Occupational Category and Group	GOODS-PRODUCING				
	Agriculture, Forestry, and Fisheries	Mining	Construc-tion	Manufac-turing	Total Goods-Producing
WHITE-COLLAR					
Professional and technical	0.7	0.5	1.7	17.4	20.3
Managers and administrators	0.4	0.6	6.6	16.1	24.3
Sales workers	0.2	0.1	0.6	9.7	10.6
Clerical Workers	0.3	0.4	2.1	17.9	20.7
Total white-collar	0.5	0.5	2.6	16.2	19.8
BLUE-COLLAR					
Craft workers	0.4	1.5	24.1	36.8	62.8
Operatives	0.4	2.0	3.0	63.5	68.9
Laborers, except farm	5.2	0.8	17.6	26.7	50.3
Total blue-collar	1.0	1.6	13.0	48.7	64.3
SERVICE WORKERS	0.2	0.1	0.5	4.6	5.4
FARM WORKERS	100.0	—	—	—	100.0
Total percent	3.7	0.8	6.0	25.9	36.5
Total number	2,840,488	630,788	4,572,235	19,837,208	27,880,719

Source. Adapted from U.S. Department of Commerce, Bureau of the Census, *Detailed Characteristics: United States Summary, 1970 Census of Population* (Washington, D.C.: U.S. Government Printing Office, 1973), Table 232, pp. 788-797.

35.3 percent overall). This points out the significant concentration of these operative and technical support workers in blue-collar occupations. In addition, the only overrepresentation among blue-collar groups is to be found in the skilled and semiskilled groups in this transportation-public utilities-communications area (22.1 percent and 26.0 percent, respectively).

It is not so much the goods-producing sector where unions have been effective in organizing as it is blue-collar workers. The largest proportion of workers in the transportation-public utilities-communications area is in the blue-collar occupational groups (Table 3.5; overall 10.6 percent compared to 6.8 percent industrywide). Furthermore, the largest industries in this area are those most highly unionized: trucking, telephone, electricity, and sanitation. People are changing from one industry to another (function) in many

SECTOR

| SERVICE-PRODUCING | | | | | TOTAL OCCUPA-TIONAL CATEGORY AND GROUP | |
Business Services	Personal Services	Transportation, Public Utilities, and Communications	Health, Education, Research, and Government	Total Service-Producing	Percent	Number (000) Omitted
5.4	4.8	3.5	65.9	79.6	100.0	11,351
19.1	34.4	5.9	16.3	75.7	100.0	6,371
29.0	58.0	1.3	1.1	89.4	100.0	5,445
21.5	18.0	9.2	30.6	79.3	100.0	13,748
17.3	22.7	5.7	34.5	80.2	100.0	36,915
4.5	16.5	10.8	5.4	37.2	100.0	10,609
5.3	13.3	10.0	2.5	31.1	100.0	13,456
7.7	23.5	12.1	6.4	49.7	100.0	3,431
5.3	15.8	10.6	4.0	35.7	100.0	27,488
4.5	49.0	1.7	39.4	94.6	100.0	9,773
–	–	–	–	–	100.0	2,367
10.7	22.9	6.8	23.1	63.5	100.0	76,553
8,221,668	17,507,255	5,186,101	17,712,856	48,627,880	–	76,553

cases without changing from one occupational category to another. Personal service operatives become farm equipment operatives. Construction truck drivers become interstate truck drivers. The great migration from blue-collar to white-collar appears to be slowing down now. Thus it is not so much the fact that the professional group is expanding rapidly as that the industry group of health-education-research-government is expanding rapidly—the point made by Gartner and Riessman. This is where the unions must make their effort for new recruits, especially among professional, technical, and clerical workers. This is where an increasing number of white-collar jobs take on working-class characteristics. Computer operators and other office machine operators find that their work tasks are becoming semiautomated. Telephone operators, bookkeepers, and counter salespeople are examples of white-collar occupations equally as alienating as the traditionally alienating blue-collar assembly-line jobs. These are the legions of the secondary labor force, further described in Chapter 4 and Chapters 13 to 15.

CONCLUSION

Theorists of postindustrialism represent both functional and conflict orientations in their formulations. Functional theory is best represented by Daniel
Bell, whose focus on consensus tends to deemphasize conflict among the professional and technical group. This school tends to see the central forces of
Western societies as industrialism and bureaucratization instead of as capitalism and class relations.[26] Most of the postindustrial society literature deals
with the effect of structural changes caused by production on persons as consumers, citizens, and members of the public, but not as workers. Most seem
to find it unnecessary to pay attention to the occupational and productive
processes as such but only to what happens to the larger society when the
occupational and productive forces are affected by these structural changes.
Whether workers might effect change through the productive process is generally not discussed.[27]

There are exceptions, and some of them have been briefly reviewed here.
Touraine sees the development of new aspects of the class struggle (in the
Marxist sense of class) and, although weak on theory, Gartner and Riessman
explain the development of a service society as a result of this social movement. However, others examine the social class phenomenon from a different structural perspective. These are the labor market economists, to whom I
now turn.

FOOTNOTES FOR CHAPTER 3—
THEORIES OF POST-INDUSTRIAL SOCIETY

[1] Daniel Bell, *The Coming of Post-Industrial Society* New York: Basic
Books, 1973), p. 20.

[2] Bell, *The Coming of Post-Industrial Society,* p. 163.

[3] Bell, *The Coming of Post-Industrial Society,* p. 15.

[4] Bell, *The Coming of Post-Industrial Society,* pp. 163-164.

[5] Bell, *The Coming of Post-Industrial Society,* pp. 15-33.

[6] *Technology and the American Economy,* Vol. I of the Report of the National Commission on Technology, Automation, and Economic Progress
(Washington, D.C.: U.S. Government Printing Office, 1966), pp. 103-
113.

[7] For a further discussion, see Benjamin S. Klineberg, *American Society
in the Post-Industrial Age* (Columbus, Ohio: Charles E. Merrill Publishing
Co., 1973), p. 124.

[8] Alain Touraine, *The Post-Industrial Society: Tomorrow's Social History: Classes, Conflicts and Culture in the Programmed Society* (New York: Random House, 1971). First published in 1969 by Editions Denoel S.A.R.L., Paris.

[9] Touraine, *The Post-Industrial Society*, p. 74.

[10] Touraine, *The Post-Industrial Society*, pp. 8-9.

[11] Touraine, *The Post-Industrial Society*, pp. 18, 54-55.

[12] Robert L. Heilbroner, "Economic Problems of a 'Post-Industrial' Society," *Dissent, 20* (Spring 1973), 163-176.

[13] Heilbroner, "Economic Problems of a 'Post-Industrial' Society," 164-165.

[14] Daniel Bell, "Labor in the Post-Industrial Society," *Dissent, 19* (Winter 1972), p. 187.

[15] Heilbroner, "Economic Problems of a 'Post-Industrial' Society," 169.

[16] Heilbroner, "Economic Problems of a 'Post-Industrial' Society," 171, 166-167.

[17] Robert L. Heilbroner, "The Human Prospect," *The New York Review of Books* (January 24, 1974), 21-34.

[18] Summarized from statements by Alan Gartner and Frank Riessman in *Social Policy, 4* (November-December 1973), 87-90, and (January-February 1974), 57-58.

[19] Gartner and Riessman, *Social Policy* (November-December 1973), 88.

[20] Alan Gartner and Frank Riessman, "Notes on the Service Society," *Social Policy, 3* (March-April 1973), 62-69.

[21] Bell, *The Coming of Post-Industrial Society*, p. 129.

[22] Touraine, *The Post-Industrial Society*, p. 65.

[23] John Kenneth Galbraith, *The New Industrial State* (New York: Houghton Mifflin & Co., 1967).

[24] Norman Birnbaum, *Toward A Critical Sociology* (New York: Oxford University Press, 1971), pp. 398-400.

[25] One of every five service-producing workers (20.2 percent) is blue-collar. See Table 3.4

[26] Richard Hill, "The Coming of the Post-Industrial Society," *The Insurgent Sociologist, 4* (Spring 1974), 38.

[27] Birnbaum, *Toward A Critical Sociology*, p. 401.

4 THEORIES OF LABOR MARKET STRATIFICATION

Economists have developed three major theories to deal with the phenomenon of labor market stratification. They are neoclassical economic theory, dual labor market theory, and radical economic theory.[1] All three use wages or earnings as the basic measurement factor distinguishing individuals and categories in the labor market. Wages represent the standard of living of persons, that is, what they can purchase in goods and services, and to some extent the wealth they can accumulate and the prestige they can command. However, each theory analyzes wages in a different way. This chapter provides a basic description for each theory, reviews supporting research, and compares it to related sociological work.

NEOCLASSICAL ECONOMIC THEORY

The basis for neoclassical theory is the principle that the labor market is shaped by economic motivation. The market is fluid and competitive and all in it are rationally in pursuit of their own interests. Employers will adjust their recruitment in response to changes in wages and productivity in order to maximize efficiency in production. Workers will make investments in education, training, and information based on changes in wage scales in order to maximize their return on their productive skills.

Neoclassical theory is often referred to as

the "queue theory" of labor economics, where employees are ranked along a single ordinal scale by their respective marginal productivities, that is, the rate of output of goods and services of each worker in relation to his or her input of labor. Workers at different stages of the queue are located in different although indistinct submarkets.[2] This comes close to functional theory in sociology, which says that people are provided with income according to the value of their contribution to society. Value in this case is the measure of marginal productivity.

The productivity components are *supply,* and the requirements of the market are *demand.* The two "intersect," with the assumption that the status quo market represents a harmony of all economic interests, both employees and employers, for the betterment of all society. Any changes would work against the social welfare. The market is in perfect competition—or, it ultimately will be because competition in one sector will generate competition throughout the system by improving the quality of labor productivity and, therefore wages. Workers' income is thereby maximized.[3]

The theory assumes that with perfect competition and market equilibrium wages will vary with variations in the worker's ability (talent) and work experience. Rational individuals maximizes the accumulation of capital through their institutions. The earned income of each is equal to his or her marginal product. All persons are influenced equally by society's institutions because they have the same effect on different individuals. Therefore, if one's income is low, it is because one's productivity is low. Different degrees of individual success are the result of personality characteristics, for example, motivation to complete education, rationally make decisions on monetary investment, and the like.[4] In a purely competitive labor market a firm is motivated by profit maximization only. Each worker is utilized in the most efficient manner possible. Workers are hired on the basis of their efficiency.

There is an economic incentive in a free market to separate economic efficiency from other characteristics of the individual. A businessman or an entrepreneur who expresses preferences in business activities that are not related to productive efficiency is at a disadvantage compared to other business competitors who do not. Such individuals are, in effect, imposing higher costs on themselves than are other individuals who do not have such preferences. Hence, in a free market, the latter will tend to drive out the former.

Therefore, if employers discriminate, their businesses would ultimately fail because less productive people would be employed. For a business to be successful, it would have to hire blacks roughly in proportion to their numbers in the population. This assumes no difference in innate and acquired abilities between the races and, in addition, it assumes equal occupational information and employment preferences.[5]

A major development of neoclassical theory is the "human capital" theory of labor market economics, which states that wages are the result of invest-ment of individuals in formal education, on-the-job experience, and certain "innate abilities."[6] The less the human capital, the lower a person's wages and the more the human capital, the higher the wages. Strictly speaking, the only barriers to entry into an occupation are the individual ones of education, job skills, and ability. Workers know all there is to know (perfect informa-tion) about availability of jobs on the market. Investment in human capital is the single best way to eliminate poverty. As one critic describes it, this is an orthodoxy that asserts that "poverty is a function of inadequate human capital."[7]

DUAL LABOR MARKET THEORY

During the early 1960s, social scientists began to take a closer look at poverty in America. Books such as Michael Harrington's *The Other America* and Lee Rainwater's *And the Poor Get Children* were well received and widely read. But it was not until the late 1960s that poverty was related to the occupation-al structure by economists in a new paradigm that depicted two largely sepa-rate work forces, the primary labor market and the secondary labor market.

One of the acknowledged early precursors of this model was Clark Kerr, who put forth the idea of the "balkanization" of the work force.[8] In his analysis, Kerr indicated the number of formal barriers that workers faced in a highly structured labor market. Another early writing that emphasized the duality of the labor market viewed the job structure in America as racially dual. The primary market, roughly 85 percent of the market, recruits white workers and has its own occupational distribution, institutions, and procedures for recruitment, promotion, and training. The secondary market performs the same functions for black workers.[9]

The theory took a major developmental step with the work of two econo-mists, Doeringer and Piore. They postulate that in addition to racial discrimi-nation there is discrimination by sex and age. They use the terms "internal labor market" and "external labor market" to elaborate the dichotomy. The internal labor market is "an administrative unit, such as a manufacturing plant, within which the pricing and allocation of labor is governed by a set of ad-ministrative rules and procedures." The rules give certain rights and privileges not available to workers outside the organization or occupation. For example, they give exclusive rights to jobs filled internally, and they give continuity of employment with no direct competition from workers in the external market. It is very similar to "industrial feudalism," or balkanization of the labor mar-ket. The external labor market contains all other workers. The movement of people into and out of this market is governed by the economic variables of supply and demand at points of entry and exit.[10]

The two markets meet where criteria governing the entry to an organization or occupation are responsive to external market conditions. But the internal market arrangements take over once the individual is in the organization or occupation. For example, in the case of skilled construction workers, at rare intervals there will be job openings when demand is high or when pressure is brought to bear by civil rights legislation. But then the doors are shut and only those already within the organization have any upward vertical mobility.[11]

Piore further develops this basic dichotomy in the dual labor market theory, which comprises a primary sector and secondary sector. The primary sector offers "jobs with relatively high wages, good working conditions, chances of advancement, equity and due process in the administration of work rules, and above all, employment stability."[12] In the secondary sector,

Jobs tend to be low-paying, with poorer working conditions, little chance of advancement, a highly personalized relationship between workers and supervisors which leaves wide latitude for favoritism and is conducive to harsh and capricious work discipline; and with considerable instability in jobs and a high turnover among the labor force.[13]

The primary sector is divided into two "tiers." The upper tier is distinguished from the lower tier by the higher pay and status of the occupations and the greater promotion opportunities afforded. There are the better professional and managerial jobs. Their work offers more opportunity for individual creativity, initiative, and occupational security than the lower tier. Their high occupational mobility and large number of job changes tend to be similar to those of the secondary sector but for different reasons—they are advancing in position and not stagnating or declining.[14]

The secondary labor force is made up of persons with the following experiences and characteristics.[15]

1. Persons with stable but low-wage work experience, primarily adults. Black females and recent immigrants from Latin America and the United States South are disproportionately represented in this group.
2. Teenagers with little or no previous work experience. Urban-born blacks are disproportionately represented.
3. Adults with a work history of chronic turnover and poor work habits.
4. Persons with clearly defined obstacles to employment—the aged, mothers with young children, students seeking part-time work, addicts, alcoholics, illiterates, and physically and mentally handicapped persons.
5. Persons not in the labor force who have sources of income—welfare, gambling—that are competitive with productive employment.

These are rank-ordered according to the person's ability to adjust to primary employment openings. The fewer of these experiences and characteristics a person has, the easier it is for that person to enter into and adjust to the primary labor market.

Occupational groups are organized according to these sectors and tiers as follows.

Primary sector
    Upper tier   Professional and technical workers
                      Managers and administrators
    Lower tier   Salespersons
                      Clerical workers
                      Skilled workers (craftsmen)
Secondary sector   Semiskilled workers
                          Operatives, except transport equipment
                          Transport equipment operatives
                      Nonfarm laborers (unskilled)
                      Service workers[16]

Piore makes another important distinction between the upper and lower tiers, that the work of the upper-tier occupations is "deduced from a set of general principles, and mobility chains [career patterns] are constructed ... so as to produce these principles and develop facility in their application."[17] That is, upper-tier occupations maintain a generalized and diffuse body of theoretical knowledge, whereas in the lower-tier occupations the basic learning process is specific, training is mostly on-the-job, and skills are nothing more than an array of *specific* skills. Learning is not logically organized into a set of theories about the nature of reality in the particular area of production.

This produces a different model of occupational structure. Traditional occupational groups are retained, but occupations are viewed according to their knowledge base (specific versus generalizing) and career patterns (stabilizing, long ladders versus shorter, variable ones). Because diverse occupations are included in the occupational groupings, there are obvious exceptions. For example, protective service and clerical occupations in civil service organizations are quite stable. However, in general, the model proves to very useful and is employed throughout this book.

Several social, historical, and economic factors help to maintain labor market duality. Market size and uncertainty affect the division of labor which, in turn, affects the skill distribution of jobs. Work tasks become more specialized and routinized in the secondary sector and the lower tier of the primary sector and broader and more generalized in the upper tier. The two sectors become more interdependent and, at the same time, more anta-

gonistic.[18]   A classic case is the modern hospital, which has an occupational
hierarchy that seems to be purposely designed to promote conflict. In a
study of hospital workers, the Ehrenreichs point out that there are several
score service jobs ranging from nurses aides to porters and kitchen workers,
a like number of clerical jobs such as secretaries, ward clerks, and medical
record librarians, and the same number of professional and technical positions,
from registered nurses, to physical therapists, lab technicians, and the various
physicians' specialties.[19]   These all have a system of ranking by uniforms, pins,
or titles. Racial and sex discrimination are blatant. In New York City hospitals 98 percent of all physicians are white and 93 percent are males, while 98
percent of nurses are females. In New York City municipal hospitals between
80 and 90 percent of service workers (aides, cooks, maids, etc.) are black or
Puerto Rican. Although the production process (the healing of the client)
mixes the two groups (sectors) in intimate daily contact, there is almost a
complete lack of job mobility between them. This remains true even though
there exists a great deal of functional interchangeability between jobs, for example, in the work of registered nurses and practical nurses.[20]

Piore examines federally funded manpower projects and finds them seriously wanting.[21]   Most of the primary sector jobs that program participants
obtained were jobs that they would have gotten on their own. The poor are
still confined to the secondary labor market. The poor participate in the economy and, because they do, it is in the interest of certain groups to keep them
active in the secondary sector. They serve the interests of those who hold
economic and political power. In addition, licensing is used as a barrier to the
primary market. Because licensing policies in the primary sector are controlled by the people in those occupations, the poor find it difficult to obtain
information about occupational entry and find entry limited because of race
and sex discriminatory practices.

Finally, contrary to classical economic theory, employers have tended to
support federal social legislation to encourage employment stability. In this
way they experience less employee turnover and absenteeism, with the resulting higher costs of operation caused by highly specialized on-the-job training.[22]
In line with this theory, American trade unions are supported by management
because each is a decentralized amalgam of units with its own work norms,
values, and customs. The shop is "the basic unit of organization even in industrial unions with highly centralized governmental structures and uniform
national policies." This is maintained by the National Labor Relations Act,
which guarantees union representation in collective bargaining and majority
rule in the bargaining unit.[23]   All these processes tend to solidify the barriers
between the two markets.

Piore emphasizes that it is only in the upper tier that people have any
control over their occupational destinies. He points out that the theoretical

body of knowledge of the professional and managerial groups places them in a different tier.[24] It is because they have control of this functionally important knowledge that they have power, wealth, and prestige. It is not only job stability that is important, but the fact that these occupational groups have *careers.* The concept of career has a limited meaning in this context. A career is "a graduated sequence of ever-increasing responsibilities, within an occupation ... or an organization, with recognized signposts along the way. [It] ... is a minority elite institution in Western society."[25] Only professional and technical workers and managers and administrators fit this description. "Career sequences of jobs are *cumulative,* in that previous experience adds value to the career and the future opportunities."[26] This experience includes colleague control over the knowledge base of the occupation.

Contrary to human capital theorists, who believe that the problem of unemployment resides primarily in faulty individual behavior, dual labor market theorists claim that it is primarily social institutions and patterns that cause the problem. Employment in primary jobs depends to a great extent on the degree of social acceptability of work groups and occupation. This acceptability is determined by factors such as race, sex, and shared social beliefs.[27]

Using dual labor market theory to analyze the occupational structure, one significant finding is that an increasing number of secondary jobs are in the service-producing sector of the economy (i.e., nonindustrial industries). Four out of every five clerical workers and one out of every two unskilled workers are found in the secondary labor force (see Table 3.5). This puts an entirely different light on what is happening in the postindustrial or service society. According to dual labor market analysis, if we are to be a service-producing society, we are also to be a society of mostly secondary jobs.

RADICAL THEORY

More and more questions have been asked over the past decade by writers, both conservative and radical, about the purported abundance and fairness of the American political economy.

> Why is it that although the United States has had one of the highest employment growth rates of nine major industrialized nations that it also has one of the highest unemployment rates?[28]
>
> Why is it that white males are disproportionately represented in greater numbers in the high-income brackets and lesser numbers in the low-income brackets?[29]
>
> Why did 13 percent of all craft workers, 24 percent of all operatives, 37 percent of all service workers, and 39 percent of all laborers earn less than $5000 annually in 1969?[30]

Why is it that 12 percent of the labor force, by Bureau of the Census standards (23 percent by BLS standards), are in poverty?

Why is it that the top 1.6 percent of our adult population owns over 80 percent of corporate stocks? Why does the top 0.5 percent own one-third of the U.S. personal wealth and this share has been increasing since 1949?[31]

Why do the lower 50 percent of adults in the United States hold only 8 percent of the national wealth?[32]

Finally, why is it that U.S. industry does not pay higher wages even though recent (1960-1972) increases in productivity in U.S. manufacturing have nearly offset the rise of hourly compensation, whereas, by contrast, in seven European Economic Community nations, plus Canada, Japan, Sweden, and Switzerland, taken as a whole, productivity increases have offset only about half the rise in unit labor costs?[33]

With a strong emphasis on the work of Karl Marx and Marxist theorists, radical economic theorists have constructed a model to explain these inadequacies and contradictions. The central thesis is that poverty and inequality are necessary functional aspects of capitalism, not merely aberrations that can be remedied by minor adjustments to the system.[34] The mode of production that governs capitalism is wage labor in a class system that is determined by "the way in which the means of production [are] owned and ... the social relations between men which [result] from their connections with the process of production."[35]

This wage labor is functional because, first, the poor are a reserve army of unemployed that can be called on when needed to work for low wages if the nonpoor threaten to strike; second, the poverty underclass serves as a measuring stick of success for those above it; third, wages can be used to induce workers to perform alienating work under poor working conditions instead of changing the job through technology or abolishing it; and fourth, goods and services can be purchased at lower prices by the nonpoor as long as wages are depressed among the underemployed and the working poor. Thus, real income is "substantially increased" for the nonpoor by poverty.[36]

This is accomplished through purposeful organized stratification of the labor market by the capitalist class, the power elite. This class does not necessarily act as a class for itself (i.e., as society-wide political organization and consciousness, but it is a class in itself; it has a common position with regard to the economic mode of production—wage labor). Wage labor is stratified by three major social forces: (1) socialization of the individual; (2) "hierarchy fetishism"; and (3) structural elements.[37] Regarding the first, stratification takes place with the development of personality through public education supported by the capitalist class. The necessary ideology and vocational training is supplied to office and factory workers in industry.[38]

The second major factor of stratification is achieved where the capitalist class develops a stratified (dual) labor market by maintaining a "hierarchy fetishism" among workers. This fetishism is a desire among employees for higher status and better jobs, but not higher income. Employers create an elaborate (and largely unnecessary) hierarchy of authority that creates an "illusion of mobility by creating trees of artificial job positions which workers can climb branch by meaningless branch." They also encourage job specialization to stratify the work force further—it allows for finer distinctions by the employer. Finally, on a broader level, employers encourage the white-collar versus blue-collar distinction, white-collar workers being potentially the most threatening group because of their proximity to management in their work. This balkanizes the labor market, making for level consciousness instead of class consciousness. That is, workers come to see themselves in competition with several classes or strata instead of as being dominated by a power elite. In addition, employers find it easy to discriminate against workers on the basis of age, sex, and race—these are not disguisable characteristics of workers, and there have been implicit and explicit discriminatory practices against them.[39]

The third source of labor market stratification is found in *structural* elements of the society, specifically industrial and local labor market characteristics in which the individual is involved (e.g., the degree of market concentration of an industry, the political power of the trade union, the relation of the industry to the state, the rate of employment of the local labor market, and profit rates). Bluestone sees these structural elements as separable by *industrial* structure into the "tripartite economy": the core economy of powerful national industries found mostly in durable goods, extraction, and heavy construction; the peripheral economy of agriculture, nondurable manufacturing retail trade, and subprofessional services; and the irregular economy of monetary activities, mostly in ghetto areas, not included in national income measurements. It pays for the capitalist class to support this tripartite system, and it does so by recognizing the need for and actively supporting the ever expanding manpower and human resource development programs, income security programs, and housing, health, food, and welfare programs.[40]

This theory of labor market stratification has been summarized as follows:[41]

The acquisition of affective traits through the family and schools (as a function of the parent's class and social status) begins to set the limits on the range of labor-force opportunities which become increasingly narrowed as one enters an occupation (dual labor market theory) and an industry in a particular local labor market (tripartite theory). Two parallel systems of stratification interact—one involving individuals and occupations, the other in other industrial structure.

One observation is immediately apparent: there are very few elements of

*labor-market status that lie within the individual's control, even though
virtually all public policy and social research take as their premise that
low income can be corrected by manipulating some personal attribute
of the individual.*

Another Marxist analysis of the labor force utilizes some of the same data
as postindustrial theorists to make its point.[42] Harry Braverman states that
six occupational groups—craftsmen, operatives, laborers, clerical, sales, and
service—comprise the reserve army of labor in the United States. A few occupations are excluded from this army: foremen, salesmen, agents, and brokers
of advertising, insurance, real estate, and stocks and bonds, manufacturer's
representatives, and salespeople in wholesale trade. This reserve army has
grown from about 50 percent of the labor force in 1900 to about 70 percent
in 1970.

Thus, there has been a continual increase in the proportion of labor devoted
to the increase in capital. These new "working class" occupations tend to
grow with the growth of automation. The most rapidly expanding are the
"female occupations," the clerical and service occupations.

The people of the reserve army are often unemployed or part-time workers. They float from one job to another; they are hired as they are needed
and then laid off as demand decreases. The automobile has greatly facilitated
the growth and flexibility of these workers. The increased physical mobility
permits their availability in a wider geographical area. Industries then have
a larger labor pool from which to select workers. Unemployment insurance
is collected from these workers during periods of employment to cover their
unemployed periods, thus acting as a safeguard mechanism to counter social
and political unrest during periods of high unemployment.

Although the service-producing sector of the economy is growing, the average rates of pay for its occupations are decreasing. The goods-producing sector is shrinking, but its average rates of pay are 17 percent higher than service-
producing occupations and are increasing. About one-half of this difference
is explained by the factors of age, sex, race, and education. Since the earnings of a large number of the service-producing occupations do not support
the average family, there is a growing "poverty in the midst of plenty" or, as
Marx more aptly phrased it, "an accumulation of misery corresponding to an
accumulation of capital." The old conservative belief that if poor people were
willing to work they would rise out of their poverty is contradicted by the
fact that in the average American family in 1970 the equivalent of less than
one worker was able to work full time.

This is further substantiated by analysis of 1970 census data, which indicates that the underemployed comprise at least 6 of every 10 persons in
central city low-income areas. This includes the official unemployed of 5

percent; the discouraged jobless workers and part-timers who want to work full time: 4 percent; and the full-time employed poor (using the $6960 Bureau of Labor Statistics level for a family of four): 52 percent. With the exception of craftsmen and foremen, all occupational groups of the working class had median weekly earnings below the poverty level. Clerical and service, the "female occupations," were the lowest of all.[43]

Working from the 1967 national Survey of Consumer Finances, conducted by the Institute for Social Research at the University of Michigan, two separate empirical studies come to essentially the same conclusions regarding the nature of the dual labor market. The more elaborate of the two indicates the "bilateral" nature of the labor market by analyzing the major difference between the human capital approach and the more radical approach to labor market stratification.[44]

The authors note that in human capital theory all industries and occupations are treated as though they operate in a single labor market. Therefore, a higher wage reflects a higher marginal productivity of the worker, regardless of occupation. Both individuals (the worker) and industries and occupations (the organization) are perfectly homogeneous; that is, neither of the two operates in segmented or balkanized markets.

This theory of the "bilateral labor market" states that both sides of the market are segmented. The individual (supply) is represented by the human capital factors of education, technical skills, and on-the-job performance, and the social factors of race, sex, migration of workers, and amount of information about the labor market. The organizational factors (demand) are the occupation and industry in which the individual is located.[45] The effects of segmentation can be seen by examining Chart 4.1, where H_1, H_2, and H_3 equal the level of human capital for three different segments of the labor force and I_1, I_2, and I_3 equal three different states of the industry or organization in terms of profit, degree of capital intensity, degree of unionization, and degree of demand fluctuation.[46]

Three totally different situations can occur.

1. Differences in human capital: (H_3 to I_1 versus H_1 to I_1 versus H_2 to I_1). A skilled machine operator (H_3) in the automobile industry (I_1) will likely have higher wages than an unskilled janitor (H_1) or semi-skilled assembly-line worker (H_2) in the same industry (I_1).
2. Differences in industry characteristics: (H_2 to I_1 versus H_2 to I_2). A semiskilled machine operator (H_2) in a fabricated steel plant (I_2) earns more than an unskilled worker. The segmentation of industries may be caused by different degrees of unionization, race or sex discrimination, or unwillingness to move because of seniority rights.
3. Differences in *both* (personal characteristics and structural character-

istics): $(H_3$ to I_1 versus H_2 to I_3). A skilled mechinic (H_3) in a clothing factory (I_1) earns less than a semiskilled machine operator (H_2) in a steel fabrication plant (I_3).[47]

**CHART 4.1   POSSIBLE OUTCOMES OF THE RELATION BETWEEN INDI-
VIDUAL AND STRUCTURAL FACTORS IN THE LABOR
MARKET**

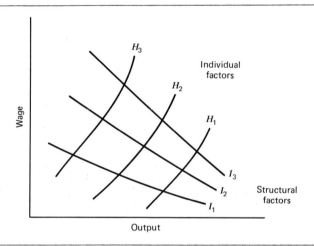

Source. Barry Bluestone, William M. Murphy, and Mary Stevenson, *Low Wages and the Working Poor*, p. 25. Copyright © 1973 by the Institute of Labor and Industrial Relations, The University of Michigan and Wayne State University. Reprinted by permission of the publisher.

Government programs are designed to alleviate only one side of the problem (i.e., the supply side) by training low-skilled workers from minority groups in projects such as the various Manpower Training Programs instituted by the federal government in the 1960s War on Poverty and by HEW and EEOP antidiscriminatory policies. "At best, increased mobility will distribute workers more 'fairly' over the existing jobs." They will not decrease the number of low-skill, low-wage jobs nor increase high-skilled, high-wage jobs.

To summarize briefly the authors' findings, first, personal characteristics (human capital values) of race, sex, education, migration, region of country, and health of individuals are held constant (i.e., the work force is segmented) to measure the effects of industry and occupation on wages. It was found that minority groups are paid lower wages even after education is controlled. About 70 percent of wage differences between black and white men cannot be explained by differences in formal education. Nor can 100 percent of

differences between male and female, nor 86 percent of the differences between white men and black women.

Second, to measure the effects of education, migration, and health on
wages, industries and occupations are segmented and compared. Analysis disclosed that race partly determines the level of education of a worker and the
occupation and industry that worker will enter. Sex also partly determines
occupation and industry, women being found predominantly in the peripheral
economy (see below). Education, too, partly determines occupation and industry. In most cases education actually *increases* the differences in earnings
between races and sexes. That is, in proportion to white males, white and
black females and black males are found in more low-wage jobs the higher
their education (with the exception of blacks with college degrees and white
females with postbaccalaureate work). Finally, not only are there large differences in earnings of low-wage workers between race-sex groups *within* the same
industry, but also there are large differences *between* industries when race, sex,
and education are controlled. For example, a black worker with a high
school degree can make 43 percent more in a position in public administration
than he can in a similar position in retail trade.[48]

The other empirical study, working from the same Survey of Consumer
Finances, constructs a similar model of personal characteristics and structural
variables.[49] Holding constant the effects on wages of personal characteristics
of education, years in present job, race, age, sex, and marital status, Wachtel
and Betsey find a substantial amount of unexplained variance that can be
accounted for by the structural variables of occupation and industry. This
variation in wage earnings extends across industries. "Individuals will earn
varying amounts in the same occupational category depending on the industry
in which they are employed, after adjusting for the personal characteristics
[human capital] on the wage." For example, laborers with the same human
capital earn from $4708 to $6136, depending on the industry in which they
are employed. They conclude that wage earnings of individuals depend on
human capital factors of the individual and the economic structure in which
they work, the latter being much more important in the determination than
the former.

The authors describe how the human capital explanation for unemployment and low wages, utilized through government legislation in the 1960s,
concluded that the problem was that workers made inadequate investment in
themselves. This was caused by either irrationalities in the workers' behavior
(the nineteenth-century view of poverty that the poor have no one to blame
except themselves) or by discrimination in educational markets. This argument concludes that once these irrationalities and discrimination are reduced
through *equality of acquisition of human capital,* the problem of low income
will be solved.

However, as Wachtel and Betsey point out, the problem lies not with personal characteristics but with structural characteristics, that is, how this human capital is used in the labor market. Demand conditions of the market as manipulated by large firms exert tremendous influence. Thus, laborers in areas of transportation, communication, and public utilities will receive lower incomes regardless of the human capital they bring to the job.

Emphasis has been on the characteristics of the poor and not on the causes of poverty. The problem is not simply to provide jobs but to provide jobs with adequate income. If workers are removed from one structural environment only to be placed back into a similar structural environment, we should not except much change in earning ability. In order to effect change, one must study the structure of the labor market.[50]

In an elaborate analysis of prestige accorded to occupations by the general public (see the NORC Scale, Table 2.8), two sociologists come to quite different conclusions from those of radical theory.[51] They state that women hold jobs about equal in *prestige* to men if their education is equal to that of men. Therefore, the process of occupational attainment is "substantially similar" for both men and women. This attainment is mostly the effect of education and is only slightly affected by the social origins of individuals. Women do not have to have higher educational qualifications than men in order to obtain a similar job.

The study does not take into account variations in income and what this income will buy, that is, what it can command in terms of power and further wealth. Prestige (value attached to status) does not bring as much in the way of power and wealth as income does. (Only one question out of the three used to measure occupational prestige on the NORC scale asks the respondent whether he or she *thinks* the occupation pays well.)

As I shall point out in Chapter 6, a woman with a Ph.D. in chemistry or an M.B.A. will receive a job as a chemist or a government agency manager, just as a man will. But the level at which she begins is lower, her upward mobility during her career is slower and, with the exception of government-rated jobs, her salary is much lower for equal work. Another question that comes up is whether one occupation is comparable to another if it happens to have the same prestige rating. For example, are secretaries comparable to construction operatives? The industry or situs of the occupation must also be considered.

Treiman and Terrell also imply that the poor are poor primarily because they have not attained enough education; that once they make adequate investment in themselves in terms of human capital (helped through the increasing equality resulting from their ability to acquire human capital), a true equality of opportunity will prevail in a single labor market of queued jobs. Structural effects on income (e.g., unionization and intensity of capitalization) and how they vary within the labor market to produce segmented work structures are not considered. Nor do they deal with the peculiar and problematic nature of the traditional occupational categories and groups of the Bureau of the Census. The next section of this chapter describes a unique attempt to deal with both these problems.

MULTIPLE—
SEGMENT
THEORY

A major study, which attempts to introduce broad changes in the categorizing of labor markets, has further refined the concept of segmentation. Marcia Freedman introduces the concept of *sheltering mechanisms.*[52] Just as there are trade and tax shelters, there are market shelters in which persons seek attachment to an occupation or an organization that can afford them some measure of shelter through providing stability of employment, protection against risk, and earnings sufficient to support themselves and their dependents according to accepted standards of health and decency.

Shelters take the form of restrictions on entering occupations through control by licensing, unionization, formal educational requirements and, indirectly, through fringe benefits provided by private firms for their employees. This control is further extended in large organizations through stability of employment, civil service regulations, collective bargaining agreements, and the development of internal labor markets.

Freedman's study clearly indicates the weaknesses of the federal government's present system of occupational classification. She realigns occupations within traditional census occupational categories and groups and adds two new major groups. Professionals are separated from semiprofessionals, and technicians and clericals are dichotomized into office clerical and nonoffice clerical. Based on these 10 revised occupational groups and 27 industries, she develops a 270-cell occupation-industry matrix which, in turn, serves as the basis for labor market levels or segments of occupational shelter (16 in 1960 and 14 in 1970), as measured by mean annual earnings. Table 4.1 details these segments.

Seven structural characteristics interact to create these segments.

1. Amount of time worked (full-time or part-time and full-year or part-year).
2. Class of worker (salaried or wage-earning private individual; government employed; self-employed).
3. Degree of industry concentration.
4. Mean establishment size.
5. Promotional possibilities (degree of vertical mobility within the occupation-industry cell).

6. Extent of licensing.

7. Extent of collective bargaining.

TABLE 4.1 SEGMENTS OF THE LABOR MARKET, BASED ON 1970 OC-
CUPATION-INDUSTRY MATRIX[a]

RANK	GROUP COMPOSITION
1	Professionals in health; producer services (accounting, engineering, advertising, legal)
2	Managers in manufacturing, wholesaling, and finance, insurance, and real estate
3	Professionals in some manufacturing and trade; sales workers in finance, insurance, and real estate
4	Managers in construction, utilities, health, education, and restaurants
5	Semiprofessionals and technicians in some durable manufacturing and finance, insurance, and real estate; sales in wholesaleing
6	Professionals and semiprofessionals and technicians in public administration; craft workers in some manufacturing, transportation, utilities, and public administration
7	Professionals in education; craft workers in construction and transportation equipment
8	Managers in agriculture, retail industries, and other consumer services; craft workers in other consumer services
9	Managers and office clericals in public administration; nonoffice clericals in most manufacturing and in public administration; sales in durable retail industries; craft workers in trade industries
10	Operatives, service workers, and laborers in metal manufacturing, transportation equipment, food, trucking, and transportation
11	Semiprofessionals and technicians in producer services; office clericals in most manufacturing and finance, insurance, and real estate; nonoffice clericals in finance, insurance, and real estate
12	Operatives in machinery, textile, other manufacturing, and trade; laborers in construction
13	Semiprofessionals and technicians in health services; office clericals in some service industries; sales in nondurable retail industries; laborers in agriculture
14	Nonoffice clericals in nondurable retail industries; service workers in education, restaurants, and other consumer services (auto repair, barbering, laundering, etc.)

[a] The following are examples of how occupations and industries are distributed. Computer
programmers (technicians) are separated out from computer system analysts (professionals).
Public school teachers are classified as semiprofessionals and college and university teachers

TABLE 4.1 SEGMENTS OF THE LABOR MARKET, BASED ON OCCUPA-TION-INDUSTRY MATRIX[a] (CONTINUED)

as professionals. Foremen (skilled craftsmen) are transferred to managers, as well as sales managers, clerical supervisors, and farm managers. Office clericals include titles such as stenographer, typists, office machine operators, and file clerks. Nonoffice clericals include messengers, bill collectors, shipping clerks, telephone operators, and ticket agents. Some operatives (semiskilled) are moved into craftsmen (skilled): butchers, insulation workers, blasters and powderdermen, and milliners.

In transportation industries, trucking and warehousing is separated from the rail, bus, air, and water transportation category. Business services are split into three sections: (1) finance, insurance, and real estate, (2) wholesale trade, and (3) producers' services, including advertising, engineering, architectural, accounting, law firms, transportation services, and other miscellaneous services. There are additional categories of health (hospitals and other medical services), public administration (federal, state, local, and postal services), and education (including nonprofit organizations and welfare and religious services).

For an example of a "traditional" (U.S. Census) matrix of occupation-industry by percentages, see Tables 3.4 and 3.5.

Source. Marcia Freedman, *Labor Markets: Segments and Shelters* (Montclair, N.J.: Allanheld, Osmun, 1976), see Appendix A. Copyright © 1976 by Allanheld, Osmun & Company. Reprinted with permission of the publisher.

Four personal characteristics are related to the matrix in a separate analysis: age, sex, race, and education. Age is the most significant predictor of membership in sheltered groups. Freedman's analysis shows how young workers (under 25) were located mostly in the lowest segments. Likewise, the 21 occupations in which young workers were highly concentrated were located in the lowest segments. Older workers, especially white males, were found in the highest segments. Women and nonwhites were concentrated in the bottom segments. Nonwhites improved their positions between 1960 and 1970, but remained disadvantaged compared to whites. The extent of isolation of women in the "female occupations" is indicated by the 46 cells of the 270-cell occupation-industry matrix in which at least 60 percent of the employed were women in both 1960 and 1970. Only five of the female-dominated cells were considered to have "moderate" or "considerable" promotion possibilities. Women have few employment shelters, even when they have long job tenure.

All these factors are advantages to employers who, in giving occupational shelters to the organized white males, find very helpful the flexibility provided by a reserve labor force of women, youth, and racial minorities. Without sheltering they can be hired and fired without cause in order to meet the exigencies of consumer demand.

The structural characteristics point to the effects of a segmented market. Licensing tends to prevent the development of career ladders of upward mobility between occupations in the same hierarchy. For example, both practical nurses and registered nurses must be licensed in order to practice in most places, preventing the nonlicensed from obtaining a job and experience by acquiring on-the-job training. Unions tend to artificially stimulate demand for services by controlling the size of the labor force in a given occupation or industry. The result is to increase wages—by about 15 percent, according to most studies. Looking at the industry-occupation cells with the highest frequency of unionization, the analysis recorded an average 16 percent advantage in wages of the unionized. In total, about 60 percent of all jobs are sheltered.[53]

In a study of the socio-economic achievement of American men in the labor force, Hauser and Featherman found an overall drop in occupational prestige from 1962 to 1972, as measured by the Duncan Socio-Economic Index. However, there was at the same time an increase in real income (controlling for inflation) of $1454 for whites and $1900 for blacks. The authors note that 72 percent of this increase was unexplained by increased educational attainment, increased occupational status, changing family size, and changing socio-economic background. They suggest that the major part of the increase is due to "socio-economic opportunity," that is, through schooling and occupational achievement.[54] However, another interpretation would be that increasing labor market segmentation is a major cause of this increase in income and decrease in prestige. Detailed analysis of labor market shelters set up or expanded during this time, especially in construction and semiprofessional occupations, would be important to test this thesis.

THE DUAL LABOR MAR- KET: OCCU- PATIONAL GROUPS

On the basis of the dual labor market studies reviewed here, occupational groups are classified as follows as a working model.

> Primary labor force.
>> Professional and technical workers.
>> Managers and administrators.
>> Sales workers.
>> Craft workers.
>> Transport equipment operatives.
> Secondary labor force.
>> Clerical workers.
>> Operatives, except transport equipment.
>> Laborers (farm and nonfarm).
>> Service workers.

This classification is only a rough outline;[55] a few specific occupations do not fit the model. For example, it will be pointed out that some sales workers, such as dime-store counter salesworkers, are not primary labor force workers. Nor are most large-city police officers secondary labor force workers. However, the model will be used for purposes of broader occupational and labor market analysis.

UNEMPLOY- MENT AND THE EMPLOYED POOR

Unemployment rates vary significantly by occupation. Persons in clerical positions are twice as likely to be unemployed as are professional and technical workers (Table 4.2). The semiskilled (operatives) and unskilled (nonfarm laborers) have the highest rates of any occupational groups—6.9 percent and 10.3 percent, respectively.[56] In the early 1970s the black-to-white ratio of unemployment stayed at about 1.8 to 1; that is, there were 1.8 black workers unemployed for every white worker. However, it has increased to more than 2 to 1 as unemployment rates have gone up during the mid-1970s.[57] The rate for women is higher than for men: in 1970 it was 5.2 versus 3.9 percent for men. For young people (ages 16 to 24) it was one-and-one-half times the national rate (9 percent). For teenagers, it was 12 percent, twice the national average.[58] Thus, if one happens to be female, nonwhite, and young, one's chances of being among the unemployed are very high. In 1972, the jobless rate for young black teenagers was 33.5 percent; for young black teenage girls it was 38.6 percent.[59]

These Department of Labor rates represent those persons who are actively seeking work but cannot find any. However, as an increasing number of analysts are pointing out, this does not include all those who are not working and are able and willing to work either full time or part time. The government's criterion for determining who is unemployed is whether someone has been actively seeking a paid job during the 4 weeks immediately preceding the monthly Current Population Survey.[60] If no limit were put on the length of time a person has been seeking a job, there would be an additional 21 million persons now outside the labor force who would be classified as unemployed (e.g., housewives who cannot find jobs, part-time workers who want full-time jobs, and the chronically unemployed). This would increase the unemployment rate to 25 percent of a labor force of 104 million persons.[61] This does not include those persons who are employed solely because of military spending for the armed forces (3 million) and related defense, civil service, and industrial occupations (11 million).[62] A very large proportion of these undoubtedly would initially become unemployed if the United States changed over to a nonmilitary peacetime economy.

TABLE 4.2 AVERAGE ANNUAL UNEMPLOYMENT RATE, BY OCCU-
PATIONAL CATEGORY AND GROUP, 1958-1973 (IN PER-
CENT)

Total Unemployed	**5.0**
Professional and technical	1.8
Managers and administrator	1.4
Sales workers	3.8
Clerical workers	3.8
Total white-collar	2.8
Craft workers	4.2
Operatives	6.9
Nonfarm laborers	10.3
Total blue-collar	6.4
Private household workers	4.3
Other service workers	5.9
Total Service workers	5.6
Farmers and farm laborers	2.6

Source. Adapted from Department of Labor, Bureau of Manpower Administration, *Manpower Report of the President, 1974* (Washington, D.C.: U.S. Government Printing Office, 1974), p. 275, Table A-17.

Poverty figures are, like unemployment statistics, vastly underestimated. As Table 4.3 indicates, the number of unemployed and *employed* persons who are poor varies significantly, depending on which government bureau's figures one employs. Comparing the basis for each low-income budget, I accept the Bureau of Labor Statistics (1970) $6960 figure for a family of four as more realistic than the Bureau of the Census budget of $3743.[63] This increases the number of employed poor from roughly 1 in every 20 to 1 in every 5 (5.9 percent versus 19.7 percent—see Table 4.3). Calculating from the occupational group figures of Table 4.3, among secondary workers the rate is extremely high, averaging about 4 in every 10 (40 percent), whereas for primary workers it is around 11 percent, or 1 in every 10.

Thus, several questions are posed by the government figures alone. Why is there consistent race, age, and sex discrimination through the years? Is it because, as some social and physical scientists have claimed, that there are real genetic differences (at least by race, if not by sex or age)? Or are there cultural differences created by poverty, that is a low self-image, limited aspirations, impulsiveness, fatalism, social isolationism, and so forth, which are transmitted intergenerationally and result in an alternative set of values, beliefs,

TABLE 4.3 THE EMPLOYED POOR, BY OCCUPATIONAL CATEGORY AND GROUP, 1970 (IN PERCENT)

OCCUPATIONAL CATEGORY AND GROUP	(A) UNEMPLOYED 1969[a]	(B) EMPLOYED AND UNEMPLOYED (FAMILY INCOME LESS THAN $7000)[b]	(A) LESS (B) ESTIMATED BUREAU OF LABOR STATISTICS EMPLOYED POOR	CENSUS BUREAU EMPLOYED POOR[c]
Total labor force	3.5	23.2	19.7	5.9
Professional and technical	1.3	9.9	8.6	2.1
Managers and administrators	0.9	10.4	9.5	2.4
Sales	2.9	16.8	13.9	3.4
Clerical	3.0	25.0	22.0	4.6
Total white collar	2.1	15.5	13.4	3.1
Skilled workers	2.2	18.2	16.0	4.4
Semiskilled workers	4.4	27.8	23.3	5.9
Unskilled workers	6.7	41.0	34.3	12.3
Total blue-collar	3.9	28.7	24.8	7.5
Service worker, except private household	4.3	40.4	36.1	11.2
Private household workers	3.6	83.4	79.8	51.4
Total service	4.2	61.9	57.7	31.3
Farm managers and farmers	–	50.7	–	17.7
Farm laborers and foremen	–	70.7	–	32.3
Total farm	1.9	60.7	58.8	25.0

[a] U.S. Department of Labor, Bureau of Manpower Administration, *Manpower Report of the President, 1974* (Washington, D.C.: U.S. Government Printing Office, 1974), Table A-17, p. 275.

[b] U.S. Department of Commerce, Bureau of the Census, *Detailed Characteristics: United States Summary: 1970 Census of Population* (Washington, D.C.: U.S. Government Printing Office, 1973), Table 255. Includes all income of all persons 14 years and older in a four-person family with heads in the experienced civilian labor force. This includes wages and salaries, public assistance income, social security incomes, and income from dividends, interest on savings, investments, royalties, and other income-producing investments.

[c] *Detailed Characteristics*, calculated from Table 262, p. 998.

and goals different from those of the majority?[64] Or is it because of structural problems in the society? The neoclassical view, most often based on Census Bureau statistics (see Chapter 5), says that people are the way they are because of personal differences such as I.Q., basic personality patterns of motivation, aspirations, and the like. The radical view says people are the way they are because of the structural character of the society and not because of any "culture of poverty" or personality defects.

UNDEREM-PLOYMENT (SUBEMPLOY-MENT)

Radical theorists have given much thought to the concept of underemployment. Underemployment differs from unemployment in that it includes not only persons who are unemployed for long periods of time (the "hard-core unemployed") but also those unemployed for short periods. Thus, underemployment, also called "subemployment," is the broader concept, including the unemployed, full-time workers with several spells of unemployment, part-time workers who want full-time work, all those family income earners whose wage rate is less than $3.50 per hour for a 40-hour week (1970 figures), and "missing persons" in the census undercount.[65] It is estimated that fully one of every four persons is underemployed. Other researchers, working with the mass of statistics from the Bureau of the Census 1970 Census Employment Survey, have concluded that the national rate of underemployment in central city low-income areas amounts to 6 of every 10 persons.[66]

Although there are no statistics for total underemployment by occupation, there are data on the unemployed that include full-time and part-time workers with several spells of unemployment (table 4.4). Most noticeably, the highest rates of unemployment are among the blue-collar group. Also, for these groups the percentage *increases* as the number of spells of unemployment increases. These much higher rates support the suggestions that real unemployment rates are much higher than government unemployment statistics indicate.

THE NEED FOR RESEARCH

Radical economic theory was born out of labor market research in studies conducted in San Francisco, Boston, and Chicago. All three cities showed significant intramarket wage differentials between primary and secondary markets.[67] Also, several studies of racial discrimination not necessarily related to theory bear testimony to the existence of the structures these theorists describe. (These will be further explored in Chapter 5.)

TABLE 4.4 EXTENT OF MALE UNEMPLOYMENT 16 YEARS AND OVER IN 1971 BY OCCUPATIONAL GROUP FOR FULL-TIME AND PART-TIME WORKERS

OCCUPATIONAL GROUP	PERCENT UNEM- PLOYED	PERCENT OF TOTAL WITH UNEMPLOYMENT	
		WITH TWO SPELLS OF UNEMPLOY- MENT	WITH THREE SPELLS OR MORE OF UNEMPLOY- MENT
All occupational groups	15.2	16.9	18.1
Professional and technical	7.8	14.9	11.9
Engineers	5.8	—	—
Medical and other health workers	3.3	—	—
Teachers, except college	4.7	—	—
Engineering and social technicians	13.7	16.4	6.0
Managers and administrators	5.8	15.2	10.3
Sales workers	10.0	16.0	13.6
Clerical workers	12.0	15.6	11.1
Craft workers	17.7	16.9	20.6
Carpenters	29.9	20.6	29.1
Construction crafts, excluding carpenters	27.8	18.5	25.7
Mechanics and repairmen	11.7	13.5	13.5
Other craft workers	12.9	14.6	13.8
Operatives, except transport	23.4	16.2	16.2
Transport equipment operatives	17.0	18.4	18.1
Laborers, except farm and mine	28.7	17.4	23.1
Construction	38.2	19.4	28.4
Manufacturing	31.5	16.1	13.9
Other industries	23.5	16.7	23.9
Service workers	16.6	18.3	18.9
Protective service workers	7.1	13.9	16.5
Waiters, cooks, and bartenders	26.9	21.5	23.4
Other service workers	15.4	16.4	15.3
Farmers and farm managers	1.3	22.7	27.5
Farm laborers and foremen	15.9	23.0	26.5

Source. U.S. Department of Labor, Bureau of Labor Statistics, *Work Experience of the Population in March, 1972* (Washington, D.C.: U.S. Government Printing Office, 1974), Table C-3, p. A-52.

One study, by Howard Wachtel, is a direct test of the radical thesis. He compares two Fiat auto plants, one in Yugoslavia, one in Italy, and shows that with technologically similar plants and rates of productivity, the Yugo-slavian plant had much less hierarchy. The capitalist plant (in Italy) practiced the divide-and-conquer technique of balkanization.[68]

However, of the three theories, radical economic theory has been the least researched. One reason is that it is so new, growing partly out of dual labor market theory. As a leading spokesman for this paradigm comments, dual market theory is sort of a "halfway house" for radical theory, that dual-mar-ket theory can be analyzed in class terms but doesn't itself go that far to link the primary-secondary distinction to other potential class divisions.[69] This is shown in its recommendations to alleviate poverty. Dual labor market people usually suggest that the state must provide higher-paying, stable, public-service employment to secondary workers. There is no hint of the need to change the system in order to get rid of the problem, just more of the same kind of planning and programming as applied in the past.

Radical theorists, on the other hand, agree that only by increased class awareness and class action will workers' shares of surplus value (profits) in-crease significantly. Given the present political system in the United States, it is likely to be a long and intense struggle.[70]

Radical theorists call for more sociology in the testing of labor market stratification. Gordon is most adamant in this direction. He points out the present weaknesses of the theories because of the lack of empirical research. Taking, for example, the measurement of underemployment in a period of rapid economic growth, he notes that two widely different interpretations could easily be produced. The neoclassical argument is that hiring and pro-motion will move quickly down the queue to encompass secondary workers who will leave jobs *en masse* to take better ones. This will cause high job instability as workers move up the ladder. The dual-market and radical argu-ment is that high secondary labor turnover will occur because these people have become discouraged with their inability to move into better jobs or to keep their present jobs and thus work only intermittently at odd jobs. In order to prove one of these hypotheses correct, one would have to make de-tailed analyses of career patterns of specific occupations by age, race, and sex.[71]

Gordon also points out that sociologists have researched the area of con-sumption patterns and have attempted to show that *experiences in consump-tion* (life-style) have changed class definitions to include middle-class and working-class families in addition to those families shaped by their *experi-ences in production*—white-collar and blue-collar. He notes that radical eco-nomists are expanding on this by looking at consumption and production experience simultaneously.[72] The question of whether blue-collar workers have been developing a middle-class subculture is one of the main questions of the functionalist school of stratification in sociology, as we pointed out in

Chapter 2. This emphasis definitely lessens the importance of occupation as a factor in studying social class. It even changes the nature of what social class is. There is a small number of conflict sociologists interested in work-force stratification,[73] but little research has been done in this area.

Radical theory raises many questions that remain unexplored by the more "traditional" paradigms in economics and sociology. For example, do the highest paid blue-collar workers (skilled craftsmen of the primary sector) now throw their allegiance to the middle class, or are they still part of the working-class movement? Are unionizing professionals and technicians part of the capitalist class because of their higher salaries or are they part of the much heralded "new working class?" These are the kinds of questions to which the model of radical economic theory addresses itself. The traditional dichotomy of the work force of mind versus matter, body versus brain, or head versus hands into a simple white-collar versus blue-collar comparison is being questioned.

SUMMARY
AND CONCLU-
SIONS

Labor market economists can be classified into three paradigms: neoclassical, dual labor, and radical. The neoclassical paradigm tends to stress the relationships of individuals to one another in a free market situation. The dual-market approach sees structural impediments to these relationships that do not make for a free market. The radical group agrees with the structural argument and emphasizes the dialectical nature of the process of interaction between the individual and his institutions.[74]

A growing number of labor market economists are using *poverty* as the basis for examining American society, whereas most postindustrial society theorists use *affluence* as their basis. Radical economists emphasize *production experience* in their focus, and sociological functionalists emphasize *consumption experience.* The implications of these emphases have been spelled out briefly in these first four chapters. In the remainder of the book I shall attempt, where possible, to clarify further the effects of these paradigms on research and theory dealing with occupations.

All these paradigms rely heavily on studies and statistics on the occupational structure. Most utilize the present framework of occupational categories and groups. Dual-labor, human capital, and radical economists have suggested that these categories can be modified to provide a better understanding of occupational structure. These models will be used where possible to explore and explain the nature of our occupational structure and dynamics.

One way to explore segments of the labor force is to view its stratification in the manner that the dual-market and radical paradigms approach it—by

race, sex, and age. This is the order of the next three chapters. Some of the
statistics are presented in Table 4.5 as a review and introduction.

TABLE 4.5 MINORITY GROUPS BY PERCENT OF TOTAL POPULATION
AND LABOR FORCE, 1970

MINORITY GROUP	PERCENT OF TOTAL POPULATION	PERCENT OF TOTAL LABOR FORCE
Blacks	11	10
Latinos	5	3
Women	51	43
Youth	20	21
The aged	10	4
The poor		
Official (Bureau of the Census)[a]	13	6
Unofficial (Bureau of Labor Statistics)[b]	33	20
The unemployed		
Official	4	6
Unofficial	13	25

[a] U.S. Department of Commerce, Bureau of the Census, *Detailed Characteristics: United States Summary: 1970 Census of Population* (Washington, D.C.: U.S. Government Printing Office, 1973). Calculated from Table 259, p. 962, and Table 261, p. 988.
[b] See Table 4.3 for labor force poor. The figure of 33 percent is arrived at by multiplying the number of family heads by four, adding 1.2 million unrelated individuals, and dividing the sum by 200 million.

A comment is in order concerning the minority groups[75] selected for analysis. I have selected race, sex, and age aggregates because there is a large body of data available. There are other groups that could be considered except for the dearth of occupational information about them: ethnic groups, homosexuals, bisexuals, ex-convicts, and ex-mental patients. They have been studied by sociologists, mostly in descriptive monographs and articles, but there is very little statistical information dealing with their occupational lives.

FOOTNOTES FOR CHAPTER 4
THEORIES OF LABOR MARKET STRATIFICATION

[1] David M. Gordon, *Theories of Poverty and Underemployment* (Lexington, Mass.: D.C. Heath & Co., 1972), p. 14.

[2] David M. Gordon, "American Poverty: Functions, Mechanisms, and Contradictions," *Monthly Review, 24* (June 1972), 72-79.

[3] Gordon, *Theories of Poverty and Underemployment,* Chapter 3.

[4] Gordon, *Theories of Poverty and Underemployment,* Chapter 3.

[5] The example is given by Ken Gagala, "The Dual Urban Labor Market," *Journal of Black Studies, 3* (March 1973), 350-370. Gagala argues that businesses that do not hire blacks in proportion to their numbers do not always fail. In fact, in many cases they improve their position on the market. This is because whites do not want to hire people whom their clients do not want. Thus, employment and productivity decisions cannot be separated from social factors.

[6] Lester C. Thurow, *Poverty and Discrimination* (Washington, D.C., The Brookings Institution, 1969), pp. 66-69; Gary S. Becker, *Human Capital* (New York: Columbia University Press, 1964), p. 62.

[7] Bennett Harrison, "The Theory of the Dual Economy," in Bertram Silverman and Murray Yanovitch (eds.), *The Worker in "Post-Industrial" Capitalism* (New York: The Free Press, 1974), p. 269.

[8] Clark Kerr, "The Balkanization of Labor Markets," in E. Wight Bakke et al. (eds.), *Labor Mobility and Economic Opportunity* (New York: John Wiley & Sons, 1954).

[9] Harold Baron and Bennet Hymer, "The Negro Worker in the Chicago Job Market," *Employment Service Review* (August 1966), 32-34.

[10] Peter B. Doeringer and Michael J. Piore, *Internal Labor Markets and Manpower Analysis* (Lexington, Mass.: D.C. Heath & Co., 1971), pp. 1-2.

[11] Doeringer and Piore, *Internal Labor Markets...,* pp. 169-171.

[12] Michael J. Piore, "Notes for a Theory of Labor Market Stratification," Working Paper No. 95, Department of Economics, Massachusetts Institute of Technology (October 1972), p. 2.

[13] Piore, "Notes for a Theory of Labor Market Stratification," p. 3.

[14] Piore, "Notes for a Theory of Labor Market Stratification," pp. 3-4.

[15] Doeringer and Piore, *Internal Labor Markets...,* p. 179.

[16] Piore, "Notes for a Theory of Labor Market Stratification."

[17] Piore, "Notes for a Theory of Labor Market Stratification," p. 15.

[18] Michael J. Piore, "On the Technological Foundations of Economic

Dualism," Working Paper in Economics, Massachusetts Institute of Technology.

[19] John and Barbara Ehrenreich, "Hospital Workers: A Case Study in the 'New Working Class,'" *Monthly Review, 24* (January 1973), 15.

[20] Ehrenreich, "Hospital Workers...."

[21] Michael J. Piore, "Jobs and Training," in Samuel H. Beer and Richard E. Barringer (eds.), *The State and the Poor* (Cambridge, Mass.: Winthrop Publishers, Inc., 1970), pp. 53-83.

[22] Michael J. Piore, "Public and Private Responsibilities in On-the-Job Training of Disadvantages Workers," Working Paper No. 23, Department of Economics, Massachusetts Institute of Technology (June 1968).

[23] Michael J. Piore, "Fragments of a 'Sociological' Theory of Wages," Paper presented at the American Economic Association Winter Meeting, December 29, 1972, p. 6.

[24] Piore, "Notes for a Theory of Labor Market Stratification," p. 8.

[25] Elliott A. Krause, *The Sociology of Occupations* (Boston: Little, Brown & Co., 1971), p. 41. See also Harold L. Wilensky, "Work, Careers, and Social Integration," *International Social Science Journal, 12* (1960), 554.

[26] Krause, *The Sociology of Occupations,* p. 41. Piore, "Notes for a Theory of Labor Market Stratification," p. 8, uses the term, "mobility chain," for all jobs that have some regular order of sequence, that is, primary sector jobs.

[27] Peter B. Doeringer and Michael J. Piore, "Unemployment and the 'Dual Labor Market'" *The Public Interest,* No. 38 (Winter 1975), 72.

[28] Constance Sorrentino and Joyanna Moy, "Unemployment in the United States and Eight Foreign Countries," *Monthly Labor Review, 97* (January 1974), 49-51.

[29] Lester Thurow, "Toward a Definition of Economic Justice," *The Public Interest,* No. 31 (Spring 1973), 78.

[30] Eli Ginzberg, "The Long View," in Sar A. Levitan (ed.), *Blue-Collar Workers* (New York: McGraw-Hill Book Co., 1971), p. 22.

[31] G. William Domhoff, *Who Rules America?* (Englewood Cliffs, N.J.: Prentice-Hall, 1967).

[32] Robert J. Lampman, *The Share of the Top Wealth Holders in National Wealth* (Princeton, N.J.: Princeton University Press, 1962).

[33] Patricia Capdeville and Arthur Neef, "Productivity and Unit Labor Costs in 12 Industrial Countries," *Monthly Labor Review, 96* (November 1973), 14-21. This analysis includes the effects of current monetary realignments.

[34] Howard M. Wachtel, "Capitalism and Poverty in America: Paradox or Contradiction?" *Monthly Review, 24* (June 1972), 51.

[35] Maurice Dobb, *Studies in the Development of Capitalism* (New York: New World Paperbacks, 1963), p. 7.

[36] Wachtel, "Capitalism and Poverty ...," p. 52.

[37] They are summarized by Wachtel, "Capitalism and Poverty ...," pp. 56-57.

[38] An excellent summary of theory and research in this area is provided by Samuel Bowles and Herbert Gintis, "I.Q. in the U.S. Class Structure," *Social Policy, 3* (November-February 1973-1974), 65-96.

[39] Gordon, *Theories of Poverty and Underemployment*, pp. 73-79.

[40] Barry Bluestone, "Capitalism and Poverty in America: A Discussion," *Monthly Review, 24* (June 1972), 65-71.

[41] Wachtel, "Capitalism and Poverty ...," p. 58.

[42] Harry Braverman, *Labor and Monopoly Capital: The Degradation of Work in the Twentieth Century*, special issue of *Monthly Review, 26* (July-August 1974).

[43] Braverman, *Labor and Monopoly Capital.* Data on the underemployed used by Braverman are from William Spring, Bennett Harrison, and Thomas Vietorisz, "In Much of the Inner City 60% Don't Earn Enough for a Decent Standard of Living," *New York Times Magazine* (November 5, 1972), 47. The makeup of the underemployed is discussed later in this chapter.

[44] Barry Bluestone, William M. Murphy, and Mary Stevenson, *Low Wages and the Working Poor* (Ann Arbor, Mich.: Institute of Labor and Industrial Relations, The University of Michigan and Wayne State University, 1973).

[45] Bluestone, Murphy, and Stevenson, *Low Wages and the Working Poor.* For a sociological statement dealing with similar factors (limited to theoretical aspects) that match individuals to jobs in organizations, see Arne L. Kalleberg and Aage B. Sørensen, "The Matching of Men to Jobs: Mechanisms and Consequences for Organizations and Individuals," Institute for Research on Poverty, University of Wisconsin, Discussion Paper No. 212-74, August 1974. Theodore Caplow presents many of these factors in

his discussion of types of labor markets. See his *The Sociology of Work* (Minneapolis: University of Minnesota Press, 1954), Chapter 7, "The Sociology of the Labor Market."

[46] Bluestone, Murphy, and Stevenson, *Low Wages and the Working Poor,* p. 25.

[47] Bluestone, Murphy, and Stevenson, *Low Wages and the Working Poor,* pp. 25-26.

[48] Bluestone, Murphy, and Stevenson, *Low Wages and the Working Poor,* pp. 60, 79, 101-104, 137-138.

[49] Howard M. Wachtel and Charles Betsey, "Employment at Low Wages," *Review of Economics and Statistics, 54* (May 1972), 121-129.

[50] Wachtel and Betsey, "Employment at Low Wages."

[51] Donald J. Treiman and Kermit Terrell, "Sex and the Process of Status Attainment: A Comparison of Working Women and Men," *American Sociological Review, 40* (April 1975), 174-200.

[52] Marcia Freedman, *Labor Markets: Segments and Shelters* (Montclair, N.J.: Allanheld, Osmun, 1976).

[53] Freedman, *Labor Markets,* Chapters 6 to 9.

[54] Robert M. Hauser and David L. Featherman, "Socio-economic Achievements of U.S. Men, 1962 to 1972," *Science, 185* (July 26, 1974), 325-331. One example would be to further document Jason Epstein's explanation of the New York City financial debacle; that the construction industry, aided and abetted by the banks, created a metropolitan shelter for itself strong enough to overcome resistance to its building boom and the municipal funding needed to support it. See his article, "The Last Days of New York," in *The New York Review of Books, 23* (February 19, 1976), 17-27.

[55] One of the very few empirical studies of dual-labor markets agrees with this classification. Ruth Fabricant Lowell, *The Dual Labor Market in New York City,* The City of New York Human Resources Administration, Office of Policy Research, December 1973 (revised, October 1975).

[56] The average annual unemployment rate by occupational category and group has not changed significantly over the past 16 years (see Table 4.2), with the exception of operatives, who have almost halved their unemployment rate from 11 to 6 percent.

[57] U.S. Department of Labor, Bureau of Manpower Administration, *Manpower Report of the President, 1973,* and *Manpower Report of the President, 1975* (Washington, D.C.: U.S. Government Printing Office, 1973, 1975).

[58] U.S. Department of Commerce, Bureau of the Census, *Detailed Character-istics: United States Summary, 1970 Census of Population* (Washington, D.C.: U.S. Government Printing Office, 1973), p. 679.

[59] *Manpower Report of the President, 1973*, p. 21.

[60] Technically, unemployment is defined as: "Those who did not work dur-ing the survey week, were available for work, and (1) had engaged in job-seeking activity during the four weeks previous to the survey week, (2) were waiting to be called back to a job from which they had been laid off, (3) were waiting to report to a new job to start within the next 30 days." Everyone else is considered to not be in the work force. Herman P. Miller, "Measuring Subemployment in Poverty Areas of Large U.S. Cities," *Monthly Labor Review, 96* (October 1973), 14.

[61] Bertram Gross and Stanley Moses, "Measuring the Real Work Force: 25 Million Unemployed," *Social Policy, 3* (September-October 1972), 6-8.

[62] Paul M. Sweezy, "On the Theory of Monopoly Capitalism," *Monthly Re-view, 23* (April 1972), 2.

[63] To indicate the effects of inflation in the early 1970s, the BLS rate has increased to an estimated $9200 as of the fall of 1974. Ann Draper, "The Explosion in Family Living Costs," *The American Federationist* (November 1974).

[64] For a review of the "culture of poverty" theories see Charles H. Anderson, *Toward a New Sociology*, Rev. Ed. (Homewood, Ill.: The Dorsey Press, 1974), pp. 162-167.

[65] Gordon, *Theories of Poverty and Underemployment*, p. 6. The term "subemployed" has also been used in a slightly more restricted definition by Miller, "Measuring Subemployment in Poverty Areas...," pp. 10-18.

[66] Spring, Harrison, and Vietorisz, "In Much of the Inner City...," p. 44. Because his definition of underemployment is more restricted, Miller's ratio is halved to only 3 of every 10 workers. See Miller, "Measuring Subemployment in Poverty Areas."

[67] Gordon, *Theories of Poverty and Underemployment*, pp. 113-114.

[68] Howard M. Wachtel, *Workers' Management and Workers' Wages in Yugo-slavia: The Theory and Practice of Participatory Socialism* (Ithaca, N.Y.: Cornell University Press, 1972).

[69] Gordon, *Theories of Poverty and Underemployment*, p. 95.

[70] Bluestone, "Capitalism and Poverty in America ...," notes that "the dual economy is ... the normal and natural outcome of a system based on

private investment decisions." Profits are naturally reinvested more heavily in the more capital-intensive, more concentrated, and more profitable industries. Consequently, there ultimately is a "secular deterioration" of wage terms in the remaining industries—the peripheral and irregular economies. This deterioration also takes place in family and school socialization of the child. The state reinforces this as an adjunct of the capitalist class through tax loopholes in a "mildly progressive" tax structure (e.g., corporate depreciation and depletion allowances, investment tax credits, etc., and through welfare and manpower programs. The incredibly high percentage of income received and wealth owned by the richest sector of the economy indicate that the state has an explicit policy of maintenance of the system. However, in the long run, secular deterioration leads to political instability. Poverty as functional for the capitalist class cannot be maintained indefinitely.

[71] Gordon, *Theories of Poverty and Underemployment*, pp. 100-101.

[72] David M. Gordon, "American Poverty: Functions, Mechanisms, and Contradictions," *Monthly Review, 24* (June 1972), 77.

[73] For example, Martin Oppenheimer, "The Sub-Proletariat: Dark Skins and Dirty Work," *The Insurgent Sociologist, 4* (Winter 1974), 7-20.
Edna Bonacich has developed a theory of the "split labor market," which points to a dual labor market of highly paid protected workers and a large unprotected group of cheap labor. In the United States the latter are mostly nonwhites. However, the primary cause of the split market is not racist but is the effect of a complex history of class struggle. Once blacks received protective legislation in this country they were no longer sought after as cheap labor. As always, business, looking for the cheapest source of labor, went to foreign labor markets and pockets of domestic unprotected labor. Edna Bonacich, "A Theory of Ethnic Antagonism: The Split Labor Market," *American Sociological Review*, 37 (October 1972), 547-559; and Edna Bonacich, "Advanced Capitalism and Black/White Relations in the United States: A Split Labor Market Interpretation, *"American Sociological Review*, 41 (February 1976), 34-51.

[74] Radical economists often cite Marx's statement that "Men develop through the activities they [as individuals] enter into in their social relations, and in particular, in the process of securing their material well-being."

[75] A sociological minority group is defined in terms of its lack of power to control its destiny and not by its numbers. A minority group can therefore comprise a majority of a population being studied (e.g., women as a percent of the total population).

5 OCCUPATIONAL CHARACTERISTICS BY RACE

This chapter deals with patterns of racial discrimination and segregation in the United States labor market. These phenomena are viewed from several perspectives. First, the general occupational distribution is reviewed and comparisons are made between white and nonwhite groups. Employment and unemployment patterns are then analyzed, and the size of the secondary labor force is estimated for each. Studies comparing black and white occupational mobility rates are also reviewed, and an analysis is completed of that portion of the labor force that is employed *and* poor. The chapter concludes with a discussion of various theoretical positions on the relationship between social class and race and the empirical data used to support them.

WHERE THE JOBS ARE: OCCUPATIONAL DISTRIBUTION IN THE UNITED STATES

Just as the number and types of occupations vary by industry, so too do they vary by size of place, that is, whether the location of the person's job is in a rural or urban area.[1] In 1970, three out of every four jobs were in urban locations. One out of every three workers were in central-city jobs. Jobs are also spread in different proportions throughout the occupational spectrum. Naturally, most farm occupations are found in rural areas.

TABLE 5.1 OCCUPATION OF EMPLOYED PERSONS BY SIZE OF PLACE, 1970 (IN PERCENT)

OCCUPATIONAL CATEGORY AND GROUP	TOTAL URBAN	CENTRAL CITY ONLY	RURAL	TOTAL EMPLOYED
WHITE-COLLAR				
Professional and technical	16.2	15.2	10.6	14.2
Managers and administrators	8.7	7.6	7.2	10.5
Sales workers	7.8	7.2	4.9	6.2
Clerical workers	19.5	21.6	11.9	17.4
Total white-collar	52.2	51.6	34.6	48.3
BLUE-COLLAR				
Craft workers	13.2	12.1	16.0	12.9
Operatives	16.2	16.7	21.7	17.7
Laborers, except farm	3.7	4.5	5.4	4.7
Total blue-collar	33.1	33.3	43.1	35.3
SERVICE WORKERS	13.2	14.7	11.5	12.4
FARM WORKERS	0.7	0.4	10.8	4.0
Totals	100.0	100.0	100.0	100.0

Source. U.S. Department of Commerce, Bureau of the Census, *General Social and Economic Characteristics: United States Summary* (Washington, D.C.: U.S. Government Printing Office, 1972), p. 408.

Also, there are more blue-collar jobs (43 percent) and fewer white-collar jobs (34 percent) in rural areas proportionate to urban or central-city areas (see Table 5.1).

With higher city taxes, increased cost of property and construction, and the reduced quality of city transportation, heavy industry is moving out. But it is being replaced by industries with occupations that must be clustered together and do not need as much space. Thus, a larger number of professional, technical, managerial, and administrative personnel work in the administrative offices and executive headquarters in urban areas. This also breeds specialization, so that a diversity of shops are found, shops that smaller cities and suburbs cannot support, such as *nouveau art* shops, specialty clothing stores, publishing houses, and home decoration supply firms. The government sector has also expanded, with most of its service personnel positions locating in the central city.[2]

The high number of rural operatives (see Table 5.1) is due in large part to those who run the machines on the highly mechanized farms and those working in mining and manufacturing plants. The large number of blue-collar workers in urban areas gives a hint of the dramatic movement of jobs from the central city to the suburbs. Long known for its dominant role in attracting manufacturing industries, the central city is now relinquishing this task. In 1958, three-quarters of all metropolitan area manufacturing jobs were in the central cities. By 1967 this had been reduced to less than one-half the jobs.[3] In 1960, the 15 largest metropolitan areas accounted for nearly two out of every three jobs in their central cities. By 1970, this had been reduced to one out of every two.[4] This tremendous shift in jobs from city to suburbs was accompanied by workers who live and work in the suburbs. For the 15 largest SMSAs, 72 percent of workers who live in the suburbs (8.7 million) also work in them. There are now 1.5 million workers in these SMSAs who commute from central city homes to jobs in the suburbs.[5] The market for jobs lies more outside the central city for the first time since farm occupations began to decline rapidly at the turn of the century. In the last 20 years alone the suburbs have added more than 20 million people. This "outward movement" has been compared to the great westward migration of the 1800s.[6]

For the most part, nonwhite workers are not taking part in this migration. For example, the black proportion of the United States population is about 11 percent (23 million). In central cities it is 28 percent. In 1970, three out of every five blacks (58 percent) lived in central cities. In the same year one out of every four whites (28 percent) lived in central cities.[7]

There are well over 2 million Latino families in the United States, 84 percent of whom live in or around major cities. With the notable exception of New York City's Spanish Harlem, they are located outside the central city areas, or in the nearby suburbs.[8] But these are not the usual middle-class enclaves that are customary in this country. They are "barrios," ghetto areas such as the suburban one of East Los Angeles.

EMPLOYED PERSONS, BY OCCUPATION

Over the last two decades there have been some marked changes in the occupational structure of nonwhites in the United States (see Table 5.2). At first glance, the picture looks like one of considerable improvement for nonwhites. However, except for the past decade, the proportion of increase (or decrease)

TABLE 5.2 COMPARISON OF WHITE AND NONWHITE PARTICIPATION RATES IN THE LABOR FORCE BY OCCUPATIONAL CATEGORY AND GROUP, SELECTED YEARS, 1948-1973

MILLIONS OF WORKERS (000) OMITTED:	[a]	[a]	(58,082)	(6,892)	(61,913)	(7,714)	(73,518)	(9,197)	(78,689)	(10,025)
	1948		1955		1960		1970		1973	
OCCUPATIONAL CATEGORY & GROUP	WHITE	NON-WHITE	WHITE	NON-WHITE	WHITE	NON-WHITE	WHITE	NON-WHITE	WHITE	NON-WHITE
WHITE-COLLAR										
Professional and technical	7.2	2.4	9.8	3.5	12.2	4.7	14.8	9.1	14.4	9.9
Managers and proprietors	11.6	2.3	11.1	2.3	11.5	2.3	11.4	3.5	11.0	4.1
Clerical workers	13.6	3.3	14.2	4.9	15.5	6.6	18.0	13.2	17.5	14.9
Sales workers	6.7	1.1	6.9	1.3	7.3	1.8	6.7	2.1	6.9	2.3
Totals	39.1	9.1	41.0	12.0	46.5	15.4	50.8	27.9	49.9	31.1
BLUE-COLLAR										
Skilled workers	14.6	5.3	14.1	5.2	13.8	5.7	13.5	8.2	13.9	8.9
Semiskilled workers	21.0	20.1	20.2	20.9	17.8	20.7	17.0	23.7	16.3	22.2
Unskilled workers	4.9	14.3	4.7	15.8	4.4	14.1	4.1	10.3	4.6	9.7
Totals	40.5	39.7	39.0	41.9	36.0	40.5	34.5	42.2	34.7	40.8

SERVICE WORKERS

Private household	1.5	15.6	1.8	14.8	1.9	14.9	1.3	7.7	1.1	5.7
Other than private household	6.4	14.7	7.2	16.8	8.3	17.9	9.4	18.3	10.6	19.6
Totals	7.9	30.3	9.0	31.6	10.2	32.8	10.7	26.0	11.7	25.3

FARM WORKERS

Farm managers	7.8	8.5	6.0	5.0	4.4	3.7	2.4	1.0	2.1	0.7
Farm laborers	4.6	12.5	3.9	9.5	2.9	7.5	1.6	2.9	1.6	2.1
Totals	12.4	21.0	9.9	14.5	7.3	11.2	4.0	3.9	3.7	2.8

[a]Figures are not available prior to 1954 because population controls by color were not introduced until that year.

Sources. U.S. Department of Commerce, Bureau of the Census, Statistical Abstract of the United States, 1960, and Statistical Abstract of the United States, 1971 (Washington, D.C.: U.S. Government Printing Office, 1960 and 1971); U.S. Department of Labor, Bureau of Manpower Administration, Manpower Report of the President, 1974 (Washington, D.C.: U.S. Government Printing Office, 1974), pp. 256, 269.

TABLE 5.3   NONWHITES AS A PERCENTAGE OF ALL WORKERS IN SELECTED OCCUPATIONS: 1960, 1970, 1972 (IN PERCENT)

OCCUPATION	1960	1970	1972
Total employed	11	11	11
Professional and technical	4	7	7
medical and other health	4	8	8
Teachers, except college	7	10	9
Managers and administrators	3	4	4
Clerical	5	8	9
Sales	2	4	4
Craft workers and foremen	5	7	7
Construction craft workers	7	7	9
Machinists and other metal craft workers	4	6	6
Foremen	2	5	6
Operatives	12	14	13
Durable goods	10	14	a
Nondurable goods	9	5	a
Nonfarm laborers	27	23	20
Private household workers	50	42	41
Other service workers	20	19	19
Protective services	5	8	10
Waiters, cooks, and bartenders	15	13	14
Farmers and farm workers	16	11	9

aFigures not available.

Sources. U.S. Department of Labor, Bureau of Labor Statistics, *The Social and Economic Status of Negroes in the United States, 1970* (Washington, D.C.: U.S. Government Printing Office, 1971), p. 61; U.S. Department of Commerce, Bureau of the Census, *The Social and Economic Status of the Black Population in the United States, 1972*, Current Population Reports, Series P-23, No. 46 (July 1973), p. 51.

for nonwhites was less than for whites in most categories and groups. During the 1960s, some real gains were made, especially by blacks. For example, the number of black workers in higher-paying occupations increased sharply [109 percent over that of whites (31 percent)] . However, the proportion of white to black workers continues to be large in this area.[9] The proportion of nonwhites in lower-paying, lower-status occupations (farm and nonfarm laborers and service workers) is about double that of the comparable group of whites— about 40 percent as compared to 20 percent in the 1970s[10]—another indicator of the existence of a dual-labor market based on racial lines (see Table 5.3). A general conclusion of a major study of the United States occupational structure emphasizes that occupational discrimination against blacks still predominates, that the more highly educated blacks are not hired at the same occupational levels as whites with the same education.[11]

Nevertheless, there have been improvements in the nonwhite-to-white ratio, which does attest to some success, however little, in equalizing job opportunities in the labor market over the past two decades. As Table 5.2 indicates, as a percentage of their respective total numbers, whites were ahead of nonwhites 4 to 1 in white-collar jobs in 1948 (39.1 percent compared to 9.1 percent). In 1970 that ratio had been reduced to 2 to 1. Another way of looking at the increase is by comparing the percent of nonwhites in various occupational groups to their size in the labor force (Table 5.3). However, even these figures are deceptive, since the gains of nonwhites have been primarily in the less prestigious and lower-paying occupations and positions within those occupations. In 1970, black male social workers represented 1 of every 20 black professionals (4.6 percent—see Table 5.4), Latino male social workers 1 of every 50 Latino professionals, and white male social workers 1 of every 100 white professionals. For physicians, engineers, and lawyers, the figures run in the opposite direction, whites holding a larger percentage of their professional jobs in these more prestigious occupations.

In all occupations salary levels are lower for nonwhites and for women. Even with education held constant, there is a discrepancy in income.[12] For example, Latino men with a college background earn about $2750 less per year than those in the general population with the same education. The fact that Latino men with a low amount of education earn *more* than the total population is because a high proportion of those in this low-education category are blacks, whose average earnings are even lower than that of Latinos.

Many reasons are given for these discrepancies in income, including the inability of recent immigrants to compete for jobs compatible with their educational attainments because they were trained in another culture and thus are not vocationally as well suited to practice their trade or profession in this country, that language is sometimes a barrier,[13] and that apprenticeship rules are an obstruction. Undoubtedly, these are obstacles to employment, but many times they are used as excuses for the important factor of discrimination.

The discriminatory barrier shows up again when comparing Table 6.4 to Table 6.5, minority group employment by sex. The overall conclusion is that except for women in clerical occupations and men in sales occupations, in the largest U.S. organizations there are fewer black and Latino workers in white-collar jobs in proportion to their numbers in the total labor force, and more in proportion to their numbers in blue-collar jobs. What this signifies is that minority group members of the U.S. labor force are increasing their numbers in professional and other white-collar occupational groups, but they are being relegated to the less prestigious occupations in these groups and to those jobs in smaller organizations (or they are self-employed). These are the jobs that are less stable because of the large failing rate of small businesses. Occupa-

TABLE 5.4 SELECTED OCCUPATIONS AND EARNINGS OF EMPLOYED OCCUPATIONAL GROUP

	BLACK					
Numbers: (000) Omitted	4,312 MEN			3,577 WOMEN		
OCCUPATIONAL GROUP	Number (000) Omitted	Percent in Occupational Group, 1970	1969 Earnings	Number (000) Omitted	Percent in Occupational Group, 1970	1969 Earnings
Professional and technical						
Physicians	5	2.1	$21,985	0.8	2.8	$ 5,547
Engineers	14	5.5	10,494	0.7	0.02	7,713
Lawyers	3	0.1	12,033	0.4	0.02	c
Social workers	11	4.6	8,397	23.0	6.1	6,098
Teachers, college and university	9	0.4	8,867	7.0	0.2	5,637
Teachers, elementary	19	9.2	7,432	114.0	30.4	6,828
Managers						
Bank officers and managers	3	0.3	$ 8,284	1.0	3.2	$ 6,083
Funeral directors	2	2.3	6,421	0.4	0.9	c
Clerical						
Postal clerks	38	11.7	$ 7,963	28.0	4.2	$ 6,327
Skilled workers						
Carpenters	48	7.0	$ 4,601	1.0	0.2	$ 4,500
Unskilled workers						
Carpenters' helpers	10	1.5	$ 3,596	0.2	0.4	c
Construction laborers	134	19.0	4,431	3.0	4.8	$ 3,503

[a] The median earnings for the total labor force are lower than the median earnings for whites because the inclusion of black and latino workers' earnings effectively lowers the total.

[b] Includes dentists.

[c] Number of persons is too small to compute median earnings.

[d] Not listed.

Sources. Adapted from Department of Commerce, Bureau of the Census, *Detailed Characteristics: United States Summary, 1970 Census of Population* (Washington, D.C.: U.S. Government Printing Office, 1973), pp. 739-745; and Department of Commerce, Bureau of the Census, *Occupational Characteristics: United States Summary, 1970 Census of Population* (Washington, D.C.: U.S. Government Printing Office, 1973), Table 15, pp. 280-283.

PERSONS BY RACE, ETHNICITY, AND SEX AS A PERCENTAGE OF TOTAL

	LATINO						TOTAL LABOR FORCE					
	1,976 MEN			(1,906) WOMEN			(44,650) MEN			(26,574) WOMEN		
	Number (000) Omitted	Percent in Occupational Group, 1970	1969 Earnings	Number (000) Omitted	Percent in Occupational Group, 1970	1969 Earnings	Number (000) Omitted	Percent in Occupational Group, 1970	1969 Earnings[a]	Number (000) Omitted	Percent in Occupational Group, 1970	1969 Earnings[a]
	9.0	5.5	$17,379	1.0	1.0	$ 8,178	240	3.7	$25,000+	14	0.6	$ 9,989[b]
	17.0	14.7	11,841	0.3	0.1	c	1050	17.9	13,530	15	0.5	10,531
	2.0	0.2	13,634	0.1	0.02	c	203	3.8	19,985	8	0.3	10,717
	4.0	2.4	7,164	4.0	5.2	5,245	47	1.0	9,028	60	2.6	7,316
	6.0	0.5	9,650	3.0	0.03	4,804	178	5.2	13,643	33	3.1	9,045
	5.0	0.4	7,360	15.0	20.4	5,438	67	3.2	8,812	115	21.8	7,122
	5.0	0.5	$ 9,394	1.0	6.1	$ 6,104	226	4.9	d	d	5.2	d
	0.4	0.3	c	0.1	0.001	c	28	0.6	d	d	0.2	d
	7.0	0.5	$ 7,588	2.0	0.1	$ 5,223	128	5.2	$ 8,326	d	0.7	6,347
	33.0	8.3	$ 6,272	0.5	0.2	$ 3,787	402	7.8	$ 7,895	d	0.2	d
	4.0	1.8	$ 4,067	c	0.1	c	4	1.3	d	d	0.03	d
	46.0	22.1	5,125	1.0	4.6	4,058	108	16.6	6,270	d	3.0	d

tional discrimination is still very prevalent in American society; only now it is practiced more covertly.

Finally, if we look at the nonwhite employed by occupational group (Table 5.2), we see that even though there have been improvements in the nonwhite-to-white ratio, the most significant improvements are in the secondary occupations. Clerical workers increased their percentage by five times since 1948. One of every four nonwhites is a semiskilled worker. Using dual labor market categories, fully 40 percent of whites are placed in the primary labor market, whereas only 23 percent of nonwhites are. The proportions have remained fairly stable since the 1940s, with the exception of the 1960s, where large increases in primary employment were experienced by nonwhites. But, again, the broad occupational groups do not show that most of the increases were in the lower-status, lower-paying primary jobs. However, the fact that the proportion of nonwhites in primary jobs is increasing is viewed as a positive step in reducing occupational discrimination.

OCCUPA-
TIONAL MO-
BILITY

The movement of individuals, families, groups, strata, or entire societies from one position to another in a social system is social mobility. Social mobility measures the extent to which a social system is open or rigid. The most frequent context for measuring social mobility is occupation, although education, income, general prestige, and socio-economic status are sometimes used. Mobility can be vertical (upward or downward on an ordinal scale) or horizontal, and it can be measured over time, that is, intergenerationally, comparing differences between parent and offspring.[14]

Occupational mobility is considered by a great many sociologists to be *the* measure of social mobility. This view is given strong support by the Davis-Moore theory of stratification.[15] They emphasize that a person's contribution to society is measured by the socially valued services performed. In a different way, Marxists view occupation as closely tied to social mobility. Occupation is the foundation on which productivity of the society rests. It produces power through the occupational organization of workers, and status by means of an ideology or consciousness of kind.

A major study comparing the occupational mobility of blacks and whites was undertaken in a 1962 national sample of adult males, which showed the comparative effect of fathers' occupations on their sons' entry occupations. Comparison of intergenerational mobility rates between blacks and whites showed that blacks are lower than whites on the scale of occupational prestige regarding their first entry occupation. Black youths start from a lower occupational base (father's occupation), so they have this initial handicap to

success in higher-status occupations.[16]   Another study of census data takes
account of this handicap by setting up an expected frequency pattern of occupational mobility and the assumption that there would be equality of occupational mobility (no racism regarding hiring). Even with these adjustments
it still would require several generations for blacks to catch up to whites because of their low relative starting point.[17]

Blacks are more likely to enter the work force through manual occupations, such as service, farm, and laborer, and whites through white-collar and
skilled positions. Furthermore, the majority of blacks entering in lower-manual positions were not upwardly mobile, whereas the majority of whites rose
up the mobility ladder.[18] Increased education was less of an aid for upwardly mobile blacks than for upwardly mobile whites.[19] Also, downward mobility rates were higher from first to current job at all occupational levels for
blacks as compared to whites.[20] Still another national sample, this one of
noncollege employed youths 16 to 24 years of age, showed that although
blacks do move up the occupational ladder, whites move up proportionately
faster.[21] Among older males, "the occupational differences between whites
and blacks are greater in their current jobs than at the beginnings of their
careers."[22] For example, a study of material handlers (semiskilled) showed
that white handlers earned more than black handlers, holding constant education, age, marital status, job location, job experience, and characteristics of
the hiring establishment.[23]

UNEMPLOY- MENT AND THE EMPLOYED POOR

Differences in unemployment between whites and blacks over the past decade
have remained substantially unchanged at a ratio of 2 to 1. White unemployment has hovered at around 5 percent and black unemployment at about 10
percent.[24] An analysis of unemployment figures from 1954 to 1973 shows
that black unemployment rises proportionately higher than white when business conditions deteriorate and decreases more slowly when conditions improve.[25] The differential is greatest among clerical and sales workers.

Contrary to popular belief, the poor are not only the unemployed, or
even the part-time employed. They are the full-time employed as well. Six
percent of the employed are poor, as estimated by the Bureau of the Census
poverty level of $4275 for a four-person family (and as adjusted for single
persons and others). However, only 4 percent of the white working force is
poor, whereas 14 percent of the nonwhite force is. Therefore, proportionately
more nonwhite than white blue-collar workers are found in the poverty sector,
another indicator of racial discrimination. Table 5.5 delineates the employed

TABLE 5.5 THE EMPLOYED POOR, 1972, BY OCCUPATIONAL GROUPS AND RACE[a]

OCCUPATIONAL GROUP	WHITE TOTAL EMPLOYED	WHITE EMPLOYED POOR AS PERCENT OF EACH OCCUPATIONAL GROUP	WHITE PERCENT OF EMPLOYED POOR	NONWHITE TOTAL EMPLOYED	NONWHITE EMPLOYED POOR AS PERCENT OF EACH OCCUPATIONAL GROUP	NONWHITE PERCENT OF EMPLOYED POOR
Professional and technical	14.6	1.2	3.8	9.5	8.6	3.5
Managers and administrators	10.6	3.1	10.2	3.7	7.8	1.5
Sales	7.1	3.6	11.0	2.2	13.6	8.9
Clerical	17.8	—		14.4	—	
Total white-collar	50.0		25.0	29.8		13.9
Skilled craftsmen	13.8	3.4	16.1	8.7	12.9	7.9
Operatives	16.0	10.3	18.6	21.3	30.9	22.9
Nonfarm laborers	4.6	8.4	7.8	9.9	19.8	12.7
Total blue-collar	34.4		42.5	39.9		43.5
Private household workers	1.2	34.1	1.4	6.8	61.2	14.3
Other service workers	10.6	9.5	13.6	20.5	21.6	20.1
Total service workers	11.8		15.0	25.3		34.4
Farmers and farm managers	2.2	13.4	10.4	0.6	—	3.1
Farm laborers	1.6	27.9	7.1	2.4	48.5	5.1
Total farm	3.8		17.5	3.0		8.2
Total employed	100.0	4.0	100.0	100.0	14.0	100.0

[a]For families of four or more persons.

Sources. U.S. Department of Commerce, Bureau of the Census, Characteristics of the Low-Income Population, 1972, Current Population Reports, Series P-60, No. 91 (December 1973), pp. 95-96; U.S. Department of Labor, Office of Manpower Administration, Manpower Report of the President, 1974 (Washington, D.C.: U.S. Government Printing Office, April 1974), Table A-12, p. 269.

poor by occupational group and race. The most outstanding feature of this table is that nearly one of every two employed poor, both white and nonwhite, is a blue-collar worker (42.5 and 43.5 percent, respectively, a slight increase since 1969).[26] This indicates the existence of a class factor in addition to race.

The percentage of working poor of each occupational group is without exception greater for nonwhites. Three of every 10 (30.9 percent) employed black semiskilled workers are poor; 1 of every 10 (10.3 percent) employed white of the same group are poor. Other illuminating comparisons are at the professional and technical level, where nonwhites are more likely to be poor than whites in the ratio of 7 to 1, at the skilled craftsman level at 4 to 1, and among operatives at 3 to 1.

Using dual labor market categories, the percent of employed poor in the secondary market is 33 percent for whites and 70 percent for nonwhites. For the employed poor there is a definite racial dichotomy supporting the dual labor market theory.

It must be emphasized that the basis for measuring the poverty level varies depending on who is doing the defining. For example, the Bureau of Labor Statistics (BLS) estimates the level of a low-income family to be almost twice the amount of the Bureau of the Census ($7386 as compared to $4275, for 1972. As a consequence, using BLS standards, approximately one of every five employed persons in the United States falls below the poverty level (see Table 4.3). The relative proportions of nonwhite working poor to white working poor of Table 5.5 would *increase* if BLS statistics were applied, since a larger proportion of blacks than whites are found in the range of occupations with incomes falling between $3743 and $6960—the 1970 low-income family budgets for the Bureau of the Census and the BLS, respectively. This is indicated in Table 5.6 which, when compared to the same figures in Table 5.5, shows not only a much larger employed poor sector but also proportionately more nonwhites in it than the Bureau of the Census data show. This is estimated by comparing the "(A) minus (B)" columns of Table 5.6 to the "Employed Poor as Percent columns of Table 5.5.

Table 5.6 indicates some startling figures. For example, nearly one of every two nonwhite working families with heads in the professional and technical group (40.6 percent) had a total family income of less than $7000 in 1970. The rate of nonwhite working poor decreases in the managerial and sales occupations. But one must remember that these jobs, with much higher rates, are where nonwhite workers are found in disproportionately high numbers (see Tables 5.2 and 5.3).

Measuring social mobility on the basis of total family income (similar to the Bureau of the Census measure, see Table 5.6 footnote *b*), James Peterson sampled 370 black households in Chicago in 1970 and found a "great deal" of

TABLE 5.6 THE EMPLOYED POOR, OCCUPATIONAL CATEGORY AND GROUP, AND RACE, 1970

OCCUPATIONAL CATEGORY AND GROUP	(A) UNEMPLOYED 1970[a]	WHITE (B) EMPLOYED AND UNEMPLOYED (FAM- ILY INCOME LESS THAN $7000)	(A) MINUS (B) ESTIMATED BLS EMPLOYED POOR[b]	CENSUS BUREAU EMPLOYED POOR[c]
Total labor force	4.1	20.8	16.7	3.8
Professional and technical	2.0	10.8	8.8	2.0
Managers and administrators	1.3	10.1	8.8	2.3
Sales	3.5	16.2	12.7	3.1
Clerical	3.4	23.3	19.9	2.8
Total white-collar	2.6	15.1	13.5	2.6
Skilled workers	3.7	17.1	13.4	3.3
Semiskilled workers				
Operatives, except transport	6.7	26.5	18.7	5.4
Transport equipment operatives	9.3	24.3	28.0	9.3
Unskilled workers	6.6	37.3	19.7	5.9
Total blue-collar		26.3		
Service workers, except private household	4.9	36.2	31.3	8.4
Private household workers	3.4	76.8	73.4	35.6
Total service	4.2	56.5	42.3	22.0
Farmers and farm managers	—	49.9	—	16.7
Farm laborers and foremen	—	66.4	—	25.1
Total farm	2.2	58.2	56.0	20.9

		NONWHITE		
OCCUPATIONAL CATEGORY AND GROUP	(A) UNEMPLOYED 1970[a]	(B) EMPLOYED AND UNEMPLOYED (FAMILY INCOME LESS THAN $7000)	(A) MINUS (B) ESTIMATED BLS EMPLOYED POOR[b]	CENSUS BUREAU EMPLOYED POOR[c]
Total labor force	8.2	44.4	36.2	17.2
Professional and technical	2.2	42.8	40.6	5.5
Managers and administrators	1.7	20.9	19.2	6.8
Sales	9.1	35.3	26.2	10.8
Clerical	7.2	39.1	31.9	10.1
Total white-collar	5.0	34.5	29.5	8.3
Skilled workers	5.1	33.8	28.7	6.0
Semiskilled workers				
Operatives, except transport		43.7		
Transport equipment operatives	8.9	41.3	33.6	14.6
Unskilled workers	10.5	53.3	42.8	21.6
Total blue-collar	8.1	43.0	34.9	14.1

111

TABLE 5.6 THE EMPLOYED POOR, BY OCCUPATIONAL CATEGORY & GROUP, AND RACE, 1970 (CONTINUED)

	NONWHITE			
OCCUPATIONAL CATEGORY AND GROUP	(A) UNEMPLOYED 1970[a]	(B) EMPLOYED AND UNEMPLOYED (FAMILY INCOME LESS THAN $7000)	(A) MINUS (B) ESTIMATED BLS EMPLOYED POOR[b]	CENSUS BUREAU EMPLOYED POOR[c]
Service workers, except private household	7.6	55.9	48.3	21.4
Private household workers	5.4	85.9	80.5	57.3
Total service	6.5	70.9	64.4	39.4
Farmers and farm managers	–	72.6	–	–
Farm laborers and foremen	–	83.0	–	–
Total farm	5.7	77.8	72.1	52.5

[a]Computed from the following sources: U.S. Department of Commerce, Bureau of the Census, *The Social and Economic Status of the Black Population in the United States, 1970*, Current Population Report, Series P-23, No. 38, Table 50, p. 62; Bureau of the Census, *Detailed Characteristics: United States Summary: 1970 Census of Population*, PC(1)D-1, February 1973, Tables 227 and 228.

[b]U.S. Department of Commerce, Bureau of the Census, *Detailed Characteristics: United States Summary: 1970 Census of Population*, PC(1)-D1, February 1973, Table 255. Includes all income of all persons 14 years and older in a four-person family with heads in the experienced civilian labor force. This includes wages and salaries, public assistance income, social security incomes, and income from dividends, interest on savings, investments, royalties, and other income-producing investments.

[c]*Detailed characteristics*, calculated from Table 262, p. 998.

upward mobility and a "smaller but significant amount" of downward mobility.[27] However, these results are based on the Bureau's lower poverty-level figures of $3335 for those in poverty and $4275 for those in "near poverty." Using these cutting points, 6 out of 10 black women and 8 out of 10 black men in poverty moved out of poverty in the space of a few years. Therefore, Peterson concludes, escape from poverty is not difficult. The poverty class is not a stagnant group but, instead, is constantly changing.[28]

Because the BLS poverty level figure is nearly $7000 for a family of four, the large difference between that and the Census Bureau and Peterson's $4275 "near poverty" statistic would allow a large number of working people to still be included in the BLS poverty class; that is, they remain a part of the secondary labor force. Peterson's figures do not hold up. The racial differences are significant. Applying dual labor market categories to Table 5.6 figures, white primary labor force workers outnumber their nonwhite counterparts by more than two to one.

Arguing against the BLS poverty-level figures, Stanley Lebergott contends that the continued emphasis on consumption of goods as a measure of prestige guarantees that the standard of living will continue to rise. Therefore, the poverty level, based on the standard of living, will also rise, insuring that poverty will remain. Lebergott considers telephones, new automobiles, televisions, and the like as luxuries, as well as state laws against child labor and double-family occupancy in one domicile, and the elderly living away from their children.[29] If none of these "luxuries" existed, the Census Bureau's poverty level of $4275 could indeed be used with good justification.

Just how poor is poor can be gleaned from a quick look at the next higher BLS family bracket, the "intermediate," in which a budget of $10,664 provides, among other necessities:

A toaster that will last for thirty-three years, a refrigerator and a range that will each last for seventeen years, a vacuum cleaner that will last for fourteen years, and a television set that will last for ten years. The budget assumes that a family will buy a two-year-old car and keep it for four years, and will pay for a tune-up once a year, a brake realignment every three years, and a front-end alignment every four years. . . . The budget assumes that the husband will buy one year-round suit every four years . . . and one topcoat every eight and a half years. . . . It assumes that the husband will take his wife to the movies once every three months, and that one of them will go to the movies alone once a year. The average family's two children are each allowed one movie every four weeks. A total of two dollars and fifty-four cents per person per year is allowed for admission to all other events, from football and baseball games to plays or concerts. . . . The budget allows nothing whatever for savings.[30]

The existence of employed poor at the higher-prestige occupational levels should not be overlooked. One of every four employed poor whites (about 400,000 workers—this is using the more conservative Bureau of the Census statistics for poverty) is white-collar. The poor are not limited to the underemployed or the unemployed, nor to the lower-prestige jobs.

From the point of view of radical social theory this has important consequences. Karl Marx predicted that a vanguard of disillusioned intellectuals would lead the proletarian revolution.[31] Recent Marxist theorists hold that this vanguard will comprise the disaffected poor and dissatisfied affluent workers.[32] Others suggest that the unemployed professionals and managers (the primary sector) will provide the impetus for possible class action.[33] Whether in fact they will, *employed* poor white-collar workers should also be included in this list. As one socialist sociologist put it:

> *In short, it is far more realistic to look at the labor force as a continuum of working-class types, ranging from unemployed ethnics to even employed white-collar workers, than to look at it as a hopelessly split class, with better-off blue- and white-collar workers inevitable resting their aristocratic asses upon the backs of super-exploited or unemployed and unemployable Black and Latin workers.*[34]

SOME EFFECTS OF INEQUAL- ITY

From the statistics reviewed it seems that there has been little effect from the efforts of the various government agencies organized to insure the civil rights of minorities in employment. Definite gains have been experienced in some specific occupations targeted for enforcement, such as construction workers in federally funded projects, clerical workers in government organizations, and university teaching. But, overall, the effects are yet to be measurable across the occupational spectrum. Perhaps with the additional powers given the Equal Employment Opportunity Commission in 1972, further inroads will be made in state and local government hiring and promotion.

There is concern that the EEOC and the Office of Civil Rights of the Department of Health, Education and Welfare will overextend themselves in their zeal to apply the mandate of "affirmative action," and that their programs will result in a rigid quota system of employment. On the other hand, the need for change has never been more evident. On the basis of the rough estimates gained by examining the occupational structure, it can be concluded that the nonwhite underemployed in the United States runs somewhere between 30 and 40 percent of the work force. As one researcher finds, as late as 1960 blacks have had to practice "sponsored mobility" to be chosen by the elite on the basis of conformity in order to get ahead instead of engaging in "contest mobility," getting ahead by acting on one's own behalf (i.e., ambition).[35] One important indicator that this is beginning to change is the increasing number of blacks in political office at local and state levels across the country.

This also has direct effects on the kinds of occupations in which blacks are found. In the Southern states, until the dynamic events of the 1960s, blacks had to risk their lives as well as their jobs in order to exercise their right to vote, whereas most other ethnic groups took this right for granted. Thus, up until the 1960s, blacks in political occupations had to focus on the legal processes of *gaining* the franchise, of fighting in the courts, and not engaging in those occupations dealing with political mobilization and bargaining. They became legal warriers, not political ward leaders.[36]

CLASS, RACE, AND OCCUPATION: THE INTEREST GROUP APPROACH

The study of the relationship of social class to occupation can be analyzed theoretically from a functionalist or conflict point of view. Studies that use occupation as a measure of socio-economic status use a functional definition of class. Class is limited to economic or prestige strata. A major textbook in sociology defines class as "a stratum or aggregate of persons who share more or less the same occupational role of the household breadwinner(s) plus his/her inherited wealth."[37] A similar definition is used by Arthur Vidich and Joseph Bensman in their classic study, *Small Town in Mass Society.*

> *Particular groups of individuals who exhibit specified social and economic life styles . . . . Classes are identified in terms of productive activity, patterns of consumption, and other forms of social and economic behavior. The term does not necessarily imply a recognition of "belonging together" by members of the class.*[38]

Social classes are measured by the prestige standing of occupations. A relationship is found between social class and people's attitudes toward work and career expectations,[39] and leisure activity.[40] Also, it has been observed that the higher the social class, the higher the educational aspirations,[41] occupational attainment,[43] and intellectual achievement.[44]

One study by a dual-market economist relates class and race by means of a scale of occupational prestige.[45] Harrison attempts a test of the human capital theory for the elimination of poverty. This theory says that investment in human capital through education and vocational training by means of federal programs in manpower training, aid to education in ghetto areas, and the like, is the single best way to eliminate poverty. Harrison shows that whites in ghetto areas receive lower returns on their human capital than whites who are outside the ghetto, an indicator of class discrimination in addition to race discrimination. He then asks whether there are structural characteristics of the work force that are common to both black and white poor. He draws his sample from over 11,000 household interviews from the country's 12 largest SMSA's, completed in March 1966 and March 1967, by the Bureau of the Census. In addition, he includes data from the sample of 40,000 household interviews conducted by the Department of Labor in 1966. He examined the degree of upward mobility from the periphery (secondary market) to the core (primary market) of the economy. Three measures of "payoff" to investments of human capital were used: (1) weekly earnings, (2) average annual unemployment, and (3) occupational status.

Harrison found that first, ghetto nonwhites lag significantly behind ghetto whites on earnings and status and have a much higher unemployment rate. Second, there is no significant change upward or downward on these measures for nonwhites who move from the ghetto to other parts of the city or to the suburbs. Third, as education increases for ghetto nonwhites, their *occupational status* increases significantly, but wages do not increase and unemployment does not decrease significantly. Education does not bring most blacks and some whites out of the secondary labor market. Those who cannot escape secondary occupations tend to find their jobs boring and low paying and therefore *prefer* unstable employment. What the liberal economists call "subemployment" is really a "normal mode of employment in a backwater of that economy."[46]

In all of these studies class is treated as a stratum in society and not as a distinct entity with its own consciousness, cultural attributes, and so forth. It is viewed as a set of discrete groups (categories, interest groups, or status groups) or as a continuous hierarchical order (queuing or continuum, or pluralist). This is true of dual-market theorists as well. They lump together strata on the basis of occupation and occupational culture and, in some cases, income, to arrive at two or three major class divisions—an "interest group" approach to social class.

In one more recent example, Holger Stub summarizes the literature in this area and concludes that modern industrial societies, especially U.S. society, are comprised of status groups or communities in all but the highest and lowest groups. The middle class is not really a class in terms of its relation to the means of production (i.e., either dependent or independent) but more of a consortium of varying life-styles, status communities made up of middle-level professionals and administrators, a "middle mass" with highly stable careers, the organization men and women who seek out and obtain secure, low-risk occupations and who have a stake in maintaining them. There is no dominance over these occupational types; there is only interdependence between them and other communities and classes.[47]

THE MARXIST APPROACH

Traditional Marxists diverge from these definitions. Social classes are not only socio-economic strata, they are "polarized manifestations of the relations of social aggregates to the means of production."[48] They have a common ideology and political organization.[49] One class (the bourgeoisie, comprising landowners and petty bourgeoisie) owns the means of production; another class (the proletariat, made up of the general proletariat and a lumpenproletariat) provides labor, a primary instrument of production. Other Marxian theorists have modified the definition of the proletariat and the function it performs. The new "instruments of production" encompass "the rational organization of human and technical equipment that governs economic development," such as productivity, land management, the rationality of educational policies, the organization of communications, and authority systems in large organizations.[50] People from all levels of the occupational structure are needed for these tasks. These workers are consumption oriented in a society of abundance. They become highly integrated into the culture and are dependent on the ruling groups for proper organization and control.[51]

The only Marxist study to examine empirically the relation between race and class in the United States was conducted by John Leggett on a sample of Detroit blue-collar workers in 1960. He found a higher degree of class consciousness and a greater willingness to take class action among blacks than among whites. This relationship varies depending on a person's employment status and union status.[52]

CLASS CONSCIOUSNESS OR WILLINGNESS TO TAKE CLASS ACTION (IN PERCENT)

White employed	20	Black unemployed	56
White unemployed	32	Black unemployed, nonunion	27
Black employed	57	Black unemployed, union	80

Generally, race is the most important influence on class consciousness of blue-collar workers, over and above ethnicity. However, racial antagonisms

in America generally prevent the organizing of labor into a solidary organization crossing racial boundaries. Unemployment and unionization, however,
tend to increase class consciousness and interracial cooperation.[53]

THE INTEREST
GROUP
REBUTTAL

Interest group theorists say that where they differ from Marxists is in the emphasis on class as determined by persons' experiences associated with the relation to the means of production. From a national area-probability sample of
the adult population of the United States (N=923), Jackman and Jackman
conclude that these experiences "do not appear to be salient in the formation
of subjective class identification in the United States." Furthermore, blacks
were found to be insensitive to changes in their prestige resulting from statuses
they achieved. Instead, it was their ascribed status of race that was overwhelm-
ingly important to them and that they perceived as distinguishing them as a
separate group in their relationships to socio-economic prestige and income
(as opposed to the means of production).[54]

From this the authors conclude that a person's objective status (i.e., one's
occupation or race) is not enough to develop a subjective class identification.
One must share a common experience with others of the same status in order
to transform a group from a "class in itself" to a "class for itself.[55] A good
example on a microscale of this sharing of socio-economic experiences (derived
from family, life-styles, prestige) was demonstrated in a strike of the Professional and Staff Association, a union group of New York City's Museum of
Modern Art employees. The important issue was what underlay the money
issues—who constituted management and who constituted labor. Those people
whose socio-economic origins were similar to those of the museum's trustees
saw themselves as management. Those whose socio-economic origins were
from the middle class or lower class tended to see themselves as labor, regardless of amount of education and social mobility.[56]

In the same vein, two other sociologists emphasize that class and occupation are not necessarily related.

> *Even the occupational career of a particular practitioner will give him a*
> *different class perspective from that of his fellow practitioners. Class is*
> *something different from occupation if and when class emerges at all, and*
> *operates upon separate and often conflicting dynamics from that of oc-*
> *cupation.*
>   . . .
> *There is a different "reality" to which different occupations respond with*
> *different ways of perceiving that reality. But all of these multiple reali-*

ties and multiple perspectives are related to occupation, not to class. The problem in the analysis of class is to discover if there are any typicalities of classes of occupation, a problem of great complexity because of the vast number and variety of occupations in a complex society.[57]

The radical theory of labor market stratification is directly contradicted by these analyses. Social class determined on the basis of relation to the means of production—as measured by occupation, race, or labor organization—is not realizable. Therefore, to reverse the famous statement of Marx: it is not the existence of men (their relation to the means of production) that determines their consciousness (their occupational perspectives), but their consciousness that determines their existence. Alienation, the motive force behind class action, is consequently viewed as a *subjective* or social psychological phenomenon, where *individuals* describe, feel, and perceive themselves to be dissatisfied in their work or occupation. Marx, on the other hand, viewed alienation as an *objective*, structural phenomenon. The theorist describes what is alienating, but workers may not even realize that they are alienated (a situation Marx called false consciousness). In the structural conditions of capitalist society the workers are divested of their humanity. Beacuse the means of production are controlled by others. The worker becomes a commodity to be bought and sold on the market.[58]

The almost exclusive emphasis of American sociology is on the social psychological study of alienation and, as a consequence, the sociology of occupations has until quite recently practically ignored the Marxist approach.[59] Because of this, there is almost no research on the relationship between occupation, race, and class using this appraoch. As I have tried to show, the mere definition of social class will determine how this relationship is perceived.

SUMMARY
AND
CONCLUSIONS

Analysis of occupational stratification by race discloses that even though nonwhites have made significant occupational gains in relation to whites over the past two decades, they are found in the lower-paying, lower-status jobs within given occupations. Blacks are not geographically as mobile (from city to suburb), nor are they socially as mobile, because of educational and occupational blocks. Consequently, more nonwhites than whites are found among the employed poor, among the underemployed, and among the unemployed. When dual labor market theory is applied to the statistics, a clear racial difference is shown to exist. The human capital factors of education and vocational training seem to have little effect on occupational earnings and status.

However, interest group theorists suggest that the complex occupational mix in the United States prevents class organization on the basis of occupational category or group. These researchers treat worker alienation as an individual phenomenon. Worker satisfaction cuts across occupational boundaries, preventing class action. Neo-Marxists, on the other hand, believe that occupational status, as determined by one's relations to the means of production, is the important factor in the development of social classes. They also see race as a potent factor in developing a class consciousness that, paradoxically, also prevents interracial worker solidarity.

FOOTNOTES FOR CHAPTER 5—
OCCUPATIONAL CHARACTERISTICS BY RACE

[1] An urban area is defined as any area with a central city of 50,000 persons or more plus other incorporated fringe cities and other densely populated areas. In contrast, a standard metropolitan statistical area (SMSA) includes only "a county or groups of contiguous counties which contain at least one city of 50,000 inhabitants or more, or twin cities with a combined population of at least 50,000. In addition to the county, or counties, containing such a city or cities, contiguous counties are included in an SMSA if, according to certain criteria, they are socially and economically integrated with the central city." Thus, one SMSA (New London-Groton-Norwich, Conn.) has no urbanized area. U.S. Department of Commerce, Bureau of the Census, *General Social and Economic Characteristics: United States Summary* (Washington, D.C., U.S. Government Printing Office, 1972), Appendix A, p. 4.

[2] For a review of developments in this area see Bennett Harrison, *Urban Economic Development: Suburbanization, Minority Opportunity, and the Condition of the Central City* (Washington, D.C.: The Urban Institute, 1974).

[3] Special report of *The New York Times* (October 15, 1972), 58.

[4] Special report of *The New York Times,* 58.

[5] Special report of *The New York Times,* 58.

[6] Special report of *The New York Times,* 58.

[7] *General Social and Economic Characteristics.*

[8] J. F. Otero and Michael D. Boggs, "A New Awareness for Latino Workers," *New York Teacher* (June 16, 1974), 11-14.

[9] Department of Labor, Bureau of Labor Statistics, *Black Americans: A Decade of Occupational Change* (Washington, D.C.: U.S. Government Printing Office, 1972), pp. 2-3.

[10] See also, U.S. Department of Commerce, *The Social and Economic Status of the Black Population in the United States, 1972,* Current Population Reports, Series P. 23, No. 46 (July 1973), p. 49.

[11] Peter M. Blau and Otis Dudley Duncan, *The American Occupational Structure* (New York: John Wiley & Sons, 1967), pp. 239-241.

[12] See, for example, the summary statement of S. M. Miller and Ronnie S. Ratner, "The American Resignation: The New Assault on Equality," *Social Policy, 3* (May-June 1972), 5-15.

[13] These arguments are mentioned in a discussion in U.S. Department of Labor, Bureau of Manpower Administration, *Manpower Report of the President, 1973* (Washington, D.C.: U.S. Government Printing Office, 1973), p. 102.

[14] Summarized from Melvin M. Tumin, *Social Stratification: The Forms and Functions of Inequality* (Englewood Cliffs, N.J.: Prentice-Hall, 1967), pp. 87-88.

[15] Thomas E. Lasswell, *Class and Stratum* (New York: Houghton-Mifflin & Co., 1965), p. 102. James Peterson, *Escape From Poverty: Occupational and Economic Mobility Among Urban Blacks* (Chicago: Community and Family Study Center, University of Chicago, 1974), pp. 5-8, contends that occupational mobility must be considered a subdivision of social mobility, that total family income (see Table 5.6) is a more accurate measure of social mobility because: first, only males are included in occupational mobility studies, yet in the lower strata a disproportionate number of families are female-headed; and second, occupational mobility studies eliminate: (a) those whose power, wealth, and prestige (as the proper measures of social mobility) are not accounted for by their occupation alone, for example, those living from inherited wealth or welfare funds; and (b) working marital partner or children, who add to or subtract from factors determining social status.

[16] Otis Dudley Duncan, *Patterns of Occupational Mobility Among Negro Men* (Ann Arbor, Mich.: University of Michigan, Population Studies Center, 1967). Another researcher has shown that even if all blacks had been born into the higher white-collar group (i.e., professionals), only 10.4 percent would have remained in that group by the time they were in the labor force at ages 25 to 64, whereas the actual figure was 28.6 percent for nonblack workers. Samuel H. Preston, "Differential Fertility, Unwanted Fertility, and Racial Trends in Occupational Achievement," *American Sociological Review, 39* (August 1974), 502.

[17] Stanley Lieberson and Glenn V. Fuguitt, "Negro-White Occupational Dif-

ferences in the Absence of Discrimination," *American Journal of Sociology, 73* (September 1967), 188-200.

[18] Duncan, *Patterns of Occupational Mobility* . . . .

[19] Blau and Duncan, *The American Occupational Structure*, p. 210.

[20] Duncan, *Patterns of Occupational Mobility* . . . .

[21] Nathan Hare, "Recent Trends in the Occupational Mobility of Negroes, 1930-1960, An Intercohort Analysis," *Social Forces, 44* (December 1965), 166-173.

[22] Herbert S. Parnes et al., *The Pre-Retirement Years*, U.S. Department of Labor, Manpower Research Monograph No. 15 (Washington, D.C.: U.S. Government Printing Office, 1970), p. 118.

[23] David P. Taylor, "Discrimination and Occupational Wage Differences in the Market for Unskilled Labor," *Industrial and Labor Relations Review, 13* (April 1968), 389.

[24] *The Social and Economic Status of the Black Population . . . 1972*, p. 38.

[25] Curtis L. Gilroy, "Black and White Unemployment: The Dynamics of the Differential," *Monthly Labor Review, 97* (February 1974), 46.

[26] See Martin Oppenheimer, "The Sub-Proletariat: Dark Skins and Dirty Work," *The Insurgent Sociologist, 4* (Winter 1974), 17, for 1969 figures.

[27] Peterson, *Escape from Poverty*, pp. 48-52.

[28] Peterson, *Escape from Poverty*.

[29] Stanley Lebergott, "How to Increase Poverty," *Commentary, 60* (October 1975), 59-63.

[30] From a United Auto Workers study, as reported by Andrew Levison, "The Working-Class Majority," *The New Yorker* (September 2, 1974), 38.

[31] Karl Marx and Friedrich Engels, *The Communist Manifesto* (New York: International Publishers, 1948), p. 19.

[32] For example, Charles H. Anderson, *The Political Economy of Social Class* (Englewood Cliffs, N.J.: Prentice-Hall, 1974).

[33] For example, Ivar Berg, *Education and Jobs: The Great Training Robbery* (New York: Praeger Publishers, 1970), p. 191.

[34] Oppenheimer, "The Sub-Proletariat . . .," p. 18-19.

[35] James N. Porter, "Race, Socialization and Mobility in Educational and

Early Occupational Attainment," *American Sociological Review, 39* (June 1974), 303-316.

[36] Charles V. Hamilton, "Blacks and the Crisis in Political Participation," *The Public Interest,* No. 34 (Winter 1974), 191.

[37] Melvin L. DeFleur, William V. D'Antonio, and Lois B. DeFleur, *Sociology: Human Society,* 2 Ed., (Glenview, Ill.: Scott, Foresman & Co., 1973), p. 215.

[38] Arthur Vidich and Joseph Bensman, *Small Town in Mass Society* (Princeton, N.J.: Princeton University Press, 1958), p. 52.

[39] Jeffry Piker, *Entry Into the Labor Force: A Survey on the Experience of Negro and White Youths,* Institute of Labor and Industrial Relations, The University of Michigan and Wayne State University (December 1968), p. 149.

[40] Alfred C. Clarke, "Leisure and Occupational Prestige," *American Sociological Review, 21* (June 1956), 301-307.

[41] William H. Sewell, Archie O. Haller, and Murray A. Strauss, "Social Status and Educational and Occupational Aspiration," *American Sociological Review, 22* (February 1957), 73.

[42] Raymond Boudon, *Education, Opportunity, and Social Inequality: Changing Prospects in Western Society* (New York: John Wiley & Sons, Inc., 1974), pp. 131-133.

[43] Alan B. Wilson, "Residential Segregation of Social Classes and Aspirations of High School Boys," *American Sociological Review, 24* (1959), 836-845.

[44] Stephen Steinberg, *The Academic Melting Pot* (New York: McGraw-Hill Book Co., 1974).

[45] Bennett Harrison, "The Theory of the Dual Economy," in Harold L. Sheppard, Bennett Harrison, and W. J. Spring, *The Political Economy of Public Service Employment* (Lexington, Mass.: Lexington Books—D.C. Heath, 1972), pp. 41-63.

[46] Harrison, "The Theory of the Dual Economy."

[47] Holger R. Stub, "The Concept of Status Community," in Holger R. Stub (ed.), *Status Communities in Modern Society: Alternatives to Class Analysis* (Hinsdale, Ill.: The Dryden Press Inc., 1972), pp. 92-108.

[48] Jack L. Roach, Llewellyn Gross, and Orville Gursslin (eds.), *Social Strati-*

fication in the United States (Englewood Cliffs, N.J.: Prentice-Hall, 1969), p. 76.

[49] Karl Marx, *The Eighteenth Brumaire of Louis Bonaparte*, in Karl Marx and Frederich Engels, *Selected Works*, Vol. I (Moscow: Foreign Languages Publishing House, 1962), p. 334.

[50] Alain Touraine, *The Post-Industrial Society* (New York: Random House, 1971), p. 81.

[51] Touraine, *The Post-Industrial Society*, p. 74.

[52] John C. Leggett, *Class, Race and Labor: Working-Class Consciousness in Detroit* (New York: Oxford University Press, 1968), p. 82.

[53] Leggett, *Class, Race, and Labor*, pp. 117, 129.

[54] Mary R. Jackman and Robert W. Jackman, "An Interpretation of the Relation Between Objective and Subjective Social Status," *American Sociological Review, 38* (October 1973), 580.

[55] Jackman and Jackman, "An Interpretation of the Relation Between Objective and Subjective Social Status," pp. 570-571.

[56] Reported by Barbara Rose, "Strike Your MOMA?" in *New York Magazine* (November 19, 1973), 116-119. Class is even based on the fact of no occupational function (e.g., pensioners), or persons who have a common class origin, such as farm youth. See William R. Beer, "Chanzeux in Transition: Modernization in a Village of Anjou," Ph.D. thesis, The New School for Social Research, 1974, p. 152.

[57] Joseph Bensman and Robert Lillienfeld, *Craft and Consciousness: Occupational Technique and the Development of World Images* (New York: John Wiley & Sons, inc., 1973), pp. 338-339, 319.

[58] Karl Marx, *The Economic and Philosophic Manuscripts of 1844* (Moscow: Foreign Languages Publishing House, 1961), "Estranged Labor," pp. 67-83.

[59] George Ritzer, Richard Bell, Gale Miller, and Virginia McKeefery, "The Current Status of Occupational Sociology," Paper presented at the annual meetings of the Midwest Sociological Society, Omaha, Nebraska, 1974, pp. 28-29.

6 OCCUPATIONAL CHARACTERISTICS BY SEX

Throughout history men have played the dominant role in occupational life and have favored themselves with those occupations higher in prestige, power, and production of wealth. In antiquity women were considered as nothing more than chattel, as breeding machines to perpetuate the lines of the patriarchies of the tribe and the nation. An adulterous wife was often put to death, stoned, mutilated or, at the least, severely sanctioned by a public display of her guilt. In Greek and Moslem societies she was confined to the home and to the domestic chores therein. Men alone enjoyed the freedom of the outside world and the varied work of politics, the military, and the business that it afforded. In Greece, Rome, and India, women were not permitted to own or inherit property and had exceedingly limited civil rights.[1]

Very often during the last 200 years men have warned that the whole moral order of society would be threatened if woman's role were allowed to change rapidly; that feminine duties are the cornerstone of a stable society.[2] Perhaps this fear has a more practical meaning today, now that women are competing with men for higher status and higher-paying jobs. Men argue, for example, that women executives are not a good omen because they spend too much time away from their families, which destroys family stability. However, no one seems to be concerned about women travelling to foreign countries as domestic servants.[3]

Jane Prather has described the two major images of women held by men in American society.[4] The first sees women as sexual objects. Physical attractiveness is emphasized and intelligence and creativity are deemphasized. The result is that women are never taken seriously as persons but are seen more as playthings, as objects to have around to increase the male ego and status. Occupations that fit this image are that of airline hostess, model, and secretary.

The second image views women as servants. This view emphasizes the nurturant and caretaking role of women, stating that they are much better suited, biologically, to fulfill this role than men. The role implies that women are supported by working husbands. Therefore, for the work that women do, they will be paid less; they are not the "breadwinners" of the family. The "nurturant" occupations bear this out. They are mostly filled by women and are poorly paid—for example, social workers, nurses, and teachers.[5] Conversely, men are considered much more efficient in "instrumental occupations," that is, where rational, aggressive behavior is deemed necessary.

In this chapter I shall analyze the results of these images as reflected in occupational sex typing and the consequent occupational and income inequality between women and men. The analysis supports the hypothesis of a dual-labor market on the basis of sex discrimination.

OCCUPATIONAL
SEX TYPING

Sex typing in occupations occurs when one sex dominates an occupation in numbers and there is the expectation that this numerical dominance should be maintained.[6] In the United States, "half of all women workers are employed in only 21 occupations, whereas half of all male workers are more broadly distributed in over 65 occupations."[7] Valerie Oppenheimer has traced over time this overrepresentation (the ratio of observed to expected frequency) and has shown that it has decreased very slowly (see Table 6.1). By 1960, 81 percent of all women workers were in occupations where women were overrepresented. If these occupations had been 33 percent female, as they actually were in 1960, they would have accounted for only 38 percent of the female labor force.

Historically, women have been concentrated in occupations, so that they are numerically in the majority. For example, in 1960, three of every five women workers were in occupations where women were 70 percent or more of the workers. Preliminary 1970 census occupational data indicate that there is an increase in the concentration of women in several areas. Women as a proportion of all clerical workers rose from 68 percent in 1959 to 74 percent in 1970. As the total percent of women clerical workers, the increase was from 30 to 35 percent.[8] From a 1960 list of 500 specific occupations,

TABLE 6.1   WOMEN IN DISPROPORTIONATELY FEMALE OCCUPATIONS, 1900–1960

YEAR	FEMALES AS A PER-CENT OF TOTAL LABOR FORCE	PERCENT OF FEMALE LABOR FORCE		
		EXPECTED IN THESE OCCU-PATIONS[a]	OBSERVED IN THESE OCCU-PATIONS	RATIO OF OBSERVED TO EXPECTED
1900	18	21	74	3.5
1910	20	30	83	2.7
1920	20	33	86	2.6
1930	22	35	89	2.5
1940	24	36	89	2.5
1950	28	40	86	2.2
1960	33[b]	38	81	2.1

[a] This is the percentage of the female labor force that would have been observed in these occupations if their sex compositions had been the same as the sex composition for the work force as a whole.

[b] The 1960 occupational classification system is slightly changed and thus the figures are slightly offset by this change in classification.

Source. Valerie Kincade Oppenheimer, *The Female Labor Force in the United States: Demographic and Economic Factors Governing Its Growth and Changing Composition*, p. 69. Copyright © 1970 by the Institute of International Studies, University of California. Reprinted by permission of the publisher.

36 occupations accounted for almost two-thirds of all employed women. In 31 of these 36 occupations, women were in the majority. In 25 occupations they were 70 percent or more of the workers.[9] As Rosemary Park concludes:

> *Sex-typing of occupations tends to be a self-fulfilling prophecy. The more women in the occupation, the fewer men apply; and as a result women monopolize all openings, and it becomes a woman's occupation, which is apt to have discriminatory pay scales and to lack the honorific nature of most men's professions.*[10]

One quarter of all women workers are clustered around five occupations— secretary, retail salesperson, household worker, bookkeeper, and elementary school teacher.[11] This is evident in Table 6.2, which compares the percent of women to men by occupational group. The large number of women professional and technical workers is occasioned by overrepresentation in elementary and secondary school teaching and the large number of new occupations in the health services professions.

In the United States, women have always been underrepresented in the

TABLE 6.2 PERSONS IN THE EXPERIENCED LABOR FORCE, BY SEX, 1910-1970

MILLIONS OF WORKERS: OCCUPATIONAL CATEGORY AND GROUP	(29.8) (7.4) 1910[a]		(37.9) (10.7) 1930[a]		(42.2) (17.5) 1950[c]		(49.0) (29.7) 1970[c]		Median Earnings 1969	
	Male	Female	Male	Female	Male	Female	Male	Female	Male	Female
Professional and technical	3.1	9.2	4.0	13.6	6.4	10.2	14.0	14.5	$10,500	$4200
Managers and proprietors	27.8	5.1	24.2	4.7	22.8	7.0	14.2	4.5	10,300	4800
Clerical	9.9[b]	13.9[b]	12.8[b]	28.8[b]	7.2	26.3	7.1	34.5	6800	3600
Sales					5.6	8.2	5.6	7.1	6800	1200
Total white-collar	50.8	28.2	41.0	47.1	42.0	51.7	41.0	60.5		
Skilled workers	14.5	1.2	16.4	0.8	17.7	1.1	20.1	1.1	7900	4000
Semiskilled workers	11.2	27.9	14.4	23.7	20.9	19.1	19.6	14.5	6200	3100
Unskilled workers	18.2	1.4	16.1	1.5	8.1	0.5	7.3	0.5	5800	1900
Total blue-collar	43.9	30.5	46.9	26.0	46.7	20.7	47.0	16.1		
Private household service	2.0	24.9	2.7	21.6	0.2	10.1	0.1	3.6	400	400
Service other than private house	[d]	[d]	[d]	[d]	6.1	12.0	6.6	18.1	3700	1500
Farm laborers	14.0	16.4	9.5	5.4	4.8	5.6	5.3	1.8	800	300

[a] Persons 14 years and over.

[b] Combined clerical and sales workers.

[c] Persons 16 years and over.

[d] These occupations are included in blue-collar occupations for these census periods.

Source. Statistical Abstract of the United States, 1950 and Statistical Abstract of the United States, 1971 (Washington, D.C.: U.S. Government Printing Office); U.S. Department of Commerce, Bureau of the Census, Historical Statistics of the United States: Colonial Times to 1957 (Washington, D.C.: U.S. Government Printing Office, 1960), Series D72-122, p. 74.

higher-status occupations. In the work world women were considered physically incapable of handling many jobs traditionally considered male occupations, especially in managerial positions, in the "higher" professions of medicine, law, university teaching, the ministry, and in most crafts. Women were, and still are, considered the "weaker sex," physically, and are thus denied positions where heavy manual work is required in semiskilled and unskilled jobs. Even where machines now do the heavy work of moving, digging, and the like men still fill most of these positions (see Table 6.2). A woman's traditional status as homemaker and mother also has led many prospective employers to hesitate in hiring her because they do not expect her to remain in the labor force when marriage and children come along.[12] Thus, even though she might be equally or better qualified for the position, a man would be more likely to be hired.

Intergenerationally, men are more mobile than women. Even if the occupational structure of women and men were identical, sex discrimination would still alter the allocation of occupational destinations. Men would receive more of the higher-paying jobs.[13]

TABLE 6.3 WOMEN IN HIGHER PROFESSIONS BY SELECTED COUNTRIES, 1960s (IN PERCENT)

	MEDICINE	ENGINEERING	BARRISTERS
Soviet Union	76	37	38
France	22	3.7	19
Federal Republic of Germany	20	1	5
Austria	18	_[a]	7
Great Britain	25	0.06	4
Denmark	_[a]	_[a]	10
Sweden	13	_[a]	6.7
United States	6	0.07	3

[a] No data avaliable.

Source. Compiled from Evelyne Sullerot, *Woman, Society and Change* (New York: McGraw-Hill Book Co., 1971), Tables 5.6, 5.7, and 5.8, pp. 151-152.

Sex typing in the professions seems to be especially prominent in the United States. Compared to most European countries, the United States has fewer women in engineering, law and medicine (see Table 6.3). Although there are only three women working for every five men in the United States, there are almost twice as many women social workers as men. The ratio of women to men in elementary school teaching is 5 to 1 but, in the higher-status profession of college and university teaching, it is reversed in favor of men, 2 to 1. Women librarians outnumber men 5 to 1; male physicians outnumber women 10 to 1. The profession of clergyman is by tradition and rule (as well as by name) closed to women, but the lower-prestige occupation of nursing (listed as a profession in the census data) is almost exclusively made up of women.[14] Of the 12,000 women officers in the U.S. armed forces, almost three-quarters are nurses.[15]

And so it goes through all the occupational groups. As discussed in Chapter 5, even as a percentage of their own numbers in their occupational groups, women are in a poor position compared to men (see Table 5.4). With one exception (black female physicians), female physicians, engineers, lawyers, and university teachers are less a percentage of all women professionals than that of men for black, Latino, and white groups. For nonwhite women, then, there is a situation of double discrimination: first, as a member of an ethnic or racial minority and second, as a woman.

INCOME
INEQUALITY

The salaries of women are much lower than those of men. The median income of women age 14 and over in the United States in 1970 was $2328, only 36 percent of the median income of men, $6444.[16] Looking at specific occupations, annual earnings of women are much lower across the board (Table 5.4). For example, women accounting graduates averaged $793 per month in 1971, as compared to $845 for men. The differential is $30 a month for mathematics and statistics graduates and $14 a month for chemistry majors. It is not so much that less money is offered for the same job as it is that lower-status positions are offered for women hired into the same field.[17] As a result, the annual median earnings for women are considerably less. For full-time workers, in 1971 the median income of women was $5700, whereas for men it was $9630.[18] This is also reflected in the median earnings by occupational groups in Table 6.2. The median salary of professional women in 1969 was only $4200, compared to $10,500 for men. Similar large differences separate the sexes in all occupational groupings, with the exception of private household workers.

Thus, although there is improvement in the struggle for more jobs, there is a setback in job and income equality. "Women workers are measurably worse off today than they were in the 1950s."[19] In 1940, only 25 percent of the nation's women over 14 were in the labor force. By 1970, this had increased to 43 percent of all women over 16. However, whereas in 1955 the income of these women was 65 percent of their male counterparts, by 1970 this had *decreased* to 59 percent.[20]

SEX TYPING
AND SEX
ROLES

Sex typing has its effects on income differentials. In some male-dominated occupations there are hidden costs to being a female. For example, female executives often are barred from sharing in fringe benefits, insurance, stock option plans, and membership in exclusive men's clubs, where much business takes place.[21]

Because of role typing, even when occupational sex typing is overcome by a woman, she is governed by a much more rigid set of rules and obligations. Men are allowed the role of "mad genius," or "wild party man in town," but never a woman. The woman given to wild parties might easily become known as an "easy woman," and a woman careless or carefree in her dress or work would never reach the higher position to be considered a mad genius.[22] Likewise, women usually do not have as many and as long free blocks of time for their occupation as men do because they almost always retain responsibility for house and children, regardless of whether they are employed. Men will simply not respond to household crises—if they do, they become irritated or feign incompetence.[23]

In some cases, wives are considered part (an important part) of their husband's occupation. Their role is to be active in community activities, to hostess parties, and so forth. However, it is not possible to reverse the situation, to let the husband fill these peripheral yet important chores. The organization therefore gets more for its money by hiring male executives. It does not obtain the husband's services of a woman executive or administrator.[24]

The development of a separate role structure of work for women ran concurrent with the absorption of men into the work force as societies industrialized, urbanized, and bureaucratized. Women were given authority over children and homemaking tasks as men were required to spend more and more of their time away from home and in the factories and central place of commerce and industry. Most of women's jobs today are holdovers from these tasks: secretary, schoolteacher, nurse, waitress, housekeeper.

The work that most women do—homemaking—is not even considered an occupation by most people, although it does fit the definition given in this book. Almost half of the "nonworking" adult population, 34 million women, are housewives. Columnist Sylvia Porter, writing for the *New York Post*, asked executives of the Chase Manhattan Bank to compute the market value (1972 dollars) of the chores of the average metropolitan New York homemaker.[25] They concluded that the work of the homemaker can actually be classified under 12 conventional occupational titles, for a total of 99.6 hours of work per week at a cost of $257.53.

BREAKDOWN OF OCCUPATIONAL DUTIES OF THE AVERAGE HOUSE-
WIFE BY WEEKLY HOURS AND INCOME

OCCUPATION	NUMBER OF HOURS	RATE PER HOUR	TOTAL
Nursemaid	44.5	$ 2.00	$ 89.00
Housekeeper	17.5	3.25	56.88
Cook	13.1	3.25	42.58
Dishwasher	6.2	2.00	12.40
Laundress	5.9	2.50	14.75
Food buyer	3.3	3.50	11.55
Chauffeur	2.0	3.25	6.50
Gardener	2.3	3.00	6.90
Maintenance man	1.7	3.00	5.10
Seamstress	1.3	3.25	4.22
Dietician	1.2	4.50	5.40
Practical nurse	0.6	3.75	2.25
	99.6		$257.53

But because no statistical or definitional sources include it, it is virtually
impossible to categorize the housewife as an occupation in analyses of occupational data. As Helena Lopata notes in a book dedicated to this "new"
occupation:

> It has no organized social circle which judges performance and has the
> right to fire for incompetence, no specific pay scale, and no measurement
> against other performers of the same role or against circle members. It is
> vague, open to any woman who gets married, regardless of ability; it has
> no union and belongs to no organizational structure.[26]

What is needed is an occupational classification heretofore not considered.
Caroline Shaw Bell has suggested the title "consumer maintenance" and provides a job description:

> The chores of providing food, shelter, clothing, and personal care, no
> matter what type of household or family may be involved.[27]

The chores are a major function for hospitals, residential colleges, jails, rest
homes for the elderly, and the like. This social role clearly yields "social and
financial consequences" to the family unit. It is as homemakers, not as "housewives," that the role must be perceived. Men and single persons often fill this
role or share in its duties with the wife and mother, especially as more women

take on other occupational roles away from their families. The role would be viewed as an occupation, with all its implications for growth and change.

There are both Marxist and Freudian interpretations of the role of home-maker. The neo-Marxist approach is based on the assumption that sexual domi-nation is conditioned by economic factors of production, that the economic conditions of capitalism facilitate the repressive labor of females in household work. Additionally, women are necessary to reproduce and to socialize youth—the future work force. These activities, the basis for all other production in a society, only produce use value, a precapitalist function. Women must pro-duce exchange value but, contrary to some Marxist theorists, Carole Lopate argues that they will *not* achieve it by obtaining payment for housework.[28]

Demanding payment for housework only serves to take the emphasis away from the alienating nature of this work—its lack of meaning, its isolation in the home, its inability to obtain any sense of power through active participa-tion in work groups. In addition, it would be virtually impossible to institute a system of fair wage payments to housewives. Should all housewives receive a fixed minimum wage? This would certainly be too low for the more able to be a truly fair distribution. The logical source of disbursement of pay-ments would be the government. If the government were to take over this function, who will judge how much is to be paid and in what manner shall these 35 million persons be paid? Will some sort of caseworker be necessary to make the determinations, and on what basis? A weekly inspection of the home? Finally, bringing housework into the commodity market as just an-other commodity brings capitalism into the home, the last refuge of what meaningful activity is left to the family—love and care in the interstices be-tween drudgery.[29]

The neo-Freudian approach, developed most notably by Randall Collins, adapts aspects of Freud's theories in order to deal with the historical repres-sion of sexuality and aggression as developed in an "idealized moralism" specific to the twentieth-century West. The fundamental motive for male coercion of females is "the desire for sexual gratification rather than for labor per se."[30]

In the historical situation of private households in a market economy, just as with early forms of fortified households in a stratified society, men remain the household heads and control its property and monopolize all desirable oc-cupations as well. Marriage operates on a free market basis. Romantic love is used by woman as her major weapon in "capturing" a man. By making her-self both attractive and inaccessible, she develops her femininity to use as her bargaining tool for the male wealth and status acquired through the marriage contract. Her status is thereby enhanced. But, at the same time, romantic love maintains the cultural barriers between men and women. It confines women to a fantasy world apart from the reality of political and economic activities and aggressive sexual desires.[31] It results in both economic and sexual subjugation.

OCCUPATION-
AL CHOICE

Occupational choice is very closely tied to careers and to sex typing. Theories of occupational choice deal with "major kinds of events and phenomena which produce [career] patterns and determine their probability of occurrence."[32] Sex typing is one of the phenomena that results in a high proportion of women being placed in an occupation found in the secondary labor market. Persons in these occupations rarely have chosen their jobs. It is more likely that the occupation "chooses" them. They more or less fall into a job that has become available. There is very little from which to choose. It follows that if one stays in that job for a long enough time, one will acquire a set of values that fit the occupation in which one finds oneself. In occupations in the primary market, on the other hand, persons have more of an opportunity to choose from among a number of occupations and specialties. They receive a long grace period of several years of higher education, at which time they develop vocational and intellectual skills and attempt to pick an occupation that corresponds to their developed set of values.[33]

As previously noted, those in primary labor market occupations are also more likely to have careers, that is, elite positions characterized by graduated steps of increasing responsibility and with continual predictable rewards. Therefore, women are less likely than men to choose their occupation, and women's occupations, concentrated mainly in the secondary labor market, are less likely to have career patterns.

Increasing numbers of social scientists are pointing out that women have different values than men. The American male's role requires him to appear tough, objective, striving, achieving, competitive, and emotionally unexpressive. Also, the male's sex role affects his work role. Male psychotherapists often find it difficult to adapt to the "passivity" role of being warm and "bilaterally communicative" with their patients. Beginning male therapists more frequently want to take the active or instrumental role, as indicated by their selection of techniques such as hypnosis or reflection.[34]

The work role of women and men in scientific occupations is greatly affected by their sex roles. Jessie Bernard points out that the two major types of research approaches are sex typed.[35] The "agentic approach" is "identified with a masculine principle, the Protestant Ethic, a Faustian pursuit of knowledge...." It deals with mastery, repression, conquest. The scientist creates his own controlled reality, which he manipulates through simulation while remaining at a safe distance, uninvolved. It yields "hard" data. Methods used are quantitative indices, social indicators, and laboratory experiments. The "communal approach" disavows control because control contaminates results. It emphasizes fusion, expression, acceptance, and noncontractual cooperation (exchange). It yields "soft" data. Methods used are the case study, *Verstehen*, symbolic interaction techniques. It is "people-oriented." It is the *status* world of ascription, diffuseness, particularism, collectivity orientation, and affectivity, as compared to the agentic *cash-nexus* world of achievement, specificity, universalism, self-achievement, and emotional neutrality.

Women are preceived as being better fit for those scientific occupations that are defined as communal. As Table 6.2 clearly indicates, the "hard" science of engineering has few women. The physical sciences are comprised mostly of men. Women are found in greater numbers in the social sciences, although still at a much lower proportion than men.[36] The social sciences are called the "softer" sciences, where work is considered more suitable for women than work in the physical sciences.

From a national sample of scientists, Deborah David found that male scientists are higher by 14 percent than female scientists on an "intellectualism index," which measures the "freedom to select research areas," the "opportunity to work with ideas," and the "opportunity to be original and creative."[37] Men, more than women, want to be more original and creative and desire leadership roles. Women, more than men, stress the importance of being helpful to others and of wanting to work with people. The difference in values between sexes is greater than between occupations. David concludes that, in general, values determine occupation and they are sex-linked. Occupational sex typing discourages persons who are not preceived to have the appropriate value constellation from going into certain occupations—females from intellectually oriented occupations and males from people-oriented occupations.[38]

Sex typing of occupations by status orientation or cash-nexus orientation applies to a large range of occupations. Robinson, Athanasiou, and Head's examination of a range of *Dictionary of Occupational Titles* occupations revealed that people-oriented professions contain a larger percentage of women than data-oriented professions, with the exception of lawyers and the clergy being more people-oriented and dieticians and medical technicians being data-oriented.[39] There are other exceptions, and there are variations from country to country, which indicates that it depends very much on how one *defines* an occupation. For example, in the Soviet Union the profession of medicine is considered a nurturant occupation and so women are found in it in much greater numbers than other countries because of this designation.[40] A different reasoning suggests that women will go into occupations that allow regular schedules and the possibility of part-time work because of time demands of their families. However, this does not explain the disproportionate number of women in pediatrics, an occupation with unusual time demands and long hours.[41] Pediatrics is considered nurturant and therefore fit for women.

Therefore, the idea that women will gravitate toward certain occupations because they are mentally and physically more suited to them is not supported by these arguments. However, another theory states that there *are* certain biological differences between male and female that are "more basic and more diffuse" than sex typing. The complex endocrinological system of the human body makes for distinct and pervasive qualitative inner differences between the sexes in mentality, temperament, drive, and innovativeness.[42] Another argument suggests that cultural traits may be inherited, which means that there are genetic differences in ability and performance by sex or race. The arguments both for and against this view are too numerous to discuss here. With respect to occupations, the evidence has yet to be collected to show that biological factors are of themselves a significant determining element in social or occupational achievement.[43]

EMPLOYMENT INEQUALITY

Examination of the work force by sex and race (Tables 6.4 and 6.5) indicates that white women are found less in professional and technical and craft occupations and more in clerical occupations in proportion to men.

As Table 6.6 shows, size of the female white-collar category is extremely large for white women—65 percent of their numbers, and much smaller for blacks (36 percent) and Latinos (48 percent). However, estimating the primary labor market for women on the basis of dual labor market categories, the sizes are much smaller—less than half the white-collar category for each group: whites, 30 percent; blacks, 17 percent; and Latinos, 20 percent. Comparing men to women, one sees an almost complete reversal in proportions. The men's white-collar category is smaller than the women's. But the percentage of men found in primary occupations is larger than their percentage in white-collar occupations and twice the size of women in primary occupations. These are illuminating figures that support the contention of radical labor market theorists that the market is stratified by race, sex, and age.

In a trend analysis of the sexual division of labor in the United States from 1900 to 1960, Edward Gross found that over this period two of every three women workers would have to change occupations in order to attain full equality with male distribution in occupations.[44] This "index of sexual segration" has not changed over the years, despite major social changes such as war and depression, which have affected other aspects of the labor market significantly.

Male occupational groups tend to remain segregated and some even have become more segregative; all female occupational groups except skilled workers show a significant decrease in sexual segregation. The reduction in sexual seg-

TABLE 6.4 OCCUPATIONS OF EMPLOYED PERSONS BY SEX AND RACE, 1970

SEX AND OCCUPATION GROUP	WHITE	BLACK	LATINO
Men			
Number (thousands)	43,030	4,052	1,897
Percent	100.0	100.0	100.0
Professional, technical, and managerial workers	27.0	8.8	15.2
Sales workers	7.4	2.1	4.7
Clerical workers	7.6	8.1	7.6
Craftsmen and kindred workers	21.8	15.2	19.8
Operatives	18.7	29.6	25.2
Nonfarm laborers	5.7	15.8	10.1
Service workers (including private household workers)	7.3	16.0	11.3
Farmworkers	4.5	4.4	6.2
Women			
Number (thousands)	25,253	3,309	990
Percent	100.0	100.0	100.0
Professional, technical, and managerial workers	20.2	12.8	12.0
Sales workers	8.1	2.5	6.0
Clerical workers	36.9	20.7	30.0
Craftsmen and kindred workers	1.9	1.4	2.2
Operatives	14.1	16.5	24.1
Nonfarm laborers	0.9	1.5	1.3
Service workers (except private household workers)	15.4	25.5	18.5
Private household workers	2.0	17.9	4.0
Farmworkers	0.7	1.2	1.9

Source. U.S. Department of Labor, Bureau of Manpower Administration, *Manpower Report of the President, 1973* (Washington, D.C.: U.S. Government Printing Office, 1973), p. 99.

regation that is taking place, namely in female occupational groups, is created by men entering female occupations, especially the administrative positions in public elementary schools, nursing, and social work. However, when women move into a male occupation, the males tend to move out and leave the occupation sexually stratified.[45]

Another study of sexual segregation, based on the 1967 national Survey of Economic Opportunity, concluded that women are a reserve labor supply "crowded" into specific occupations.[46] Utilizing the human capital variables

TABLE 6.5 MINORITY GROUP EMPLOYMENT, BY SEX, 1969 (IN PERCENT)

OCCUPATIONAL CATEGORY AND GROUP	ORIENTAL (115)	(692)	AMERICAN INDIAN (52)	(28)	SPANISH SURNAMED AMERICANS (611)	(298)	BLACK (1736)	(975)
	MALE	FEMALE	MALE	FEMALE	MALE	FEMALE	MALE	FEMALE
Professional and technical	34.8	22.1	7.2	5.6	5.7	4.5	3.2	6.4
Managers and proprietors	7.3	1.9	7.2	2.5	3.0	1.0	1.7	0.9
Sales	5.8	6.5	5.4	13.8	4.1	6.8	2.8	5.0
Clerical	8.8	39.1	4.5	24.5	5.7	26.8	4.1	23.4
Total white-collar	56.7	69.7	24.2	46.4	18.4	39.0	11.8	35.6
Skilled workers	14.0	2.1	21.2	4.3	14.7	4.3	9.8	2.5
Semiskilled workers	11.9	11.2	29.5	27.5	32.7	28.4	37.9	24.9
Unskilled workers	7.8	6.9	19.7	10.8	23.9	16.9	25.5	12.6
Total blue-collar	33.8	20.1	70.4	42.6	71.4	49.7	73.2	40.1
Service workers	9.5	10.2	5.4	11.0	10.2	11.3	15.0	24.3
Total workers	100.0	100.0	100.0	100.0	100.0	100.0	100.0	100.0

Source. U.S. Department of Labor, Bureau of Labor Statistics, *Equal Employment Opportunity Report, 1969*, Vol. 1 (Washington, D.C.: U.S. Government Printing Office, 1969), p. 1. These figures represent about 35 percent of the total minority labor force. The survey of minority group workers was limited to employers of 100 or more employees. Government employees were exempted, and approximately one-quarter of the employers failed to respond. See pp. vii-x of the *Equal Employment Opportunity Report*, Vol. 1.

TABLE 6.6 PERCENT OF LABOR FORCE IN WHITE–COLLAR AND PRIMARY LABOR MARKET CATEGORIES, BY RACE AND SEX, 1970 (IN PERCENT)

	MEN			WOMEN		
	WHITE	BLACK	LATINO	WHITE	BLACK	LATINO
White-collar (professional, managerial, sales, clerical)	42	19	28	65	36	48
Primary labor market (professional, managerial, sales, craft workers, transport equipment operatives)	62	36	50	30	17	20

of education and on-the-job training, Stevenson constructed clusters of occupations with similar amounts of human capital. The occupations within these clusters, or "occlevels," are more closely related in regard to certain "objective" qualifications (of education and training) for work position than occupational groups are.[47]

The index of sexual segregation between occlevels was 36 percent for white females and 46 percent for black females, both considerably lower than Gross' figures (in the high 60s) for 1900 to 1960. However, within occlevels, the rates are higher, generally, in the 60th and 70th percentiles and are found as high as 93 percent. In addition, the greatest number of specific occupations in which there are no white males but only white and black females occurs at the lower occlevels, and the bulk of white-male-only occupations is found in the upper occlevels.[48]

Equality per human capital investment is never reached in any occlevel. Within each occlevel, white males consistently receive higher wages, generally followed by white women and than black women. Even where women had more education than men, in all occlevels they received lower wages.[49]

Within specific occlevels, taking the three most concentrated specific occupations, white males are the least concentrated, followed by white females and black females. Thus, "women are in fewer occupations than men, they are in different occupations than men, and they are more concentrated in a subset of occupations than are men." This is true within occlevels as well as across all occlevels.[50]

Women work in industries that are less profitable, less concentrated, and less capital-intensive than industries that employ men. These are the industries that are not able to pay high wages.[51] They are part of the secondary labor force.

The radical analysis carries this interpretation to the structural elements of society. Women are replacing those persons with weaker labor power—the young and the poor and uneducated older males. Postwar (Vietnam) inflation has risen more rapidly than wages and, as a result, the working class housewife has been forced into the labor market in order to help maintain the family. The group with the largest increase in numbers employed are the wives of working husbands. The working married woman must support the owners of capital by her labors in her various caring and support functions in the family *and* by her labors in the work force.[52]

There is no male-female breakdown on underemployment, but unemployment figures again indicate sex differences (see Table 6.7). With the single exception of transport equipment workers, of which there are very few women, the female unemployment rates are higher than that for males.

There has been considerable improvement in the job market for women over the past two decades. Since 1950 the proportion of women in the work

TABLE 6.7 UNEMPLOYED PERSONS BY OCCUPATION OF LAST JOB AND SEX, 1973

	TOTAL	MALE	FEMALE
Total	4.9	4.1	6.0
White-collar workers	2.9	1.8	4.0
Professional and technical	2.2	1.7	2.9
Managers and administrators	1.4	1.2	2.5
Sales	3.7	2.5	5.2
Clerical	4.2	3.0	4.5
Blue-collar workers	5.3	4.8	7.7
Skilled workers	3.7	3.6	5.9
Semiskilled operatives	6.1	4.9	7.9
Semiskilled transport equipment operatives	4.1	4.1	2.7
Unskilled workers	8.4	8.4	9.4
Service Workers	5.7	5.5	5.8
Farmers and farm laborers	2.5	2.3	3.5

Source. U.S. Department of Labor, Bureau of Labor Statistics, *Employment and Unemployment in 1973*, Special Labor Force Report 163 (Washington, D.C.: U.S. Government Printing Office, 1973), Table A.7, p. A-11.

force has increased by 13 percent (from 31 to 44 percent). However, most of the increase has come in secondary occupations, as I have traced them.[53] Chapter 17 will show that even though increasing education of women has prepared them for better jobs, all indications are that the limitations against women in the higher-status occupations (the primary market) will find a large number overtrained and underemployed unless they enter in large numbers into occupations that are traditionally the enclave of men.

MEN'S LIBERA-TION: SOCIAL POLICY FOR SEXUAL EQUALITY IN OCCUPATIONS

One of the suggested ways of opening up more of the primary market to women is the recommendation for a kind of reverse liberation, that is, of liberating men from the burden of their oppressive work. In his instrumental role of risktaker and family provider, the male is not supposed to be fearful or to show weakness, However, if men are freed from the restrictions of "agentic" occupations and are allowed to increase their choice of options by considering the traditional female occupations such as nursing, secretary, day care worker,

and the like, they will achieve a great deal of psychological and sexual liberation.[54]

Part of this expansion of choice may come as men find themselves more
and more in positions subordinate to women in the occupational setting and
consequently forced to take orders from them and be able to get along with
them. As equals they will also be able to engage in more "communal" behavior. Correspondingly, more women will have the opportunity to be aggressive in both business and personal relations as men get accustomed to more
equality in sex roles. Women will share in the more onerous responsibilities
such as overtime work and the pressure-cooker atmosphere of decision making
at the workplace. Husbands with wives as main breadwinners of the family
would be able to take on more of the expressive tasks of child care and be
able to be responsible for more of the housework, which is less achievement
oriented and less stressful.[55]

It is the combination of a carefully wrought women's *and* men's liberation
that can effectively open up the marketplace for jobs and allow a true sexual
equality in occupational choice.

SUMMARY AND CONCLUSIONS

Women are segregated into certain occupations in which they are numerically
in the majority. These occupations—secretary, public school teacher, social
worker, librarian, and the like—are the less prestigious within their respective
occupational groups. Like blacks, women as a minority group are geographically and socially less mobile. Their own occupation comes second to their
husband's.

Women are found disproportionately in secondary labor market occupations. Human capital investment for women does not pay off equally in terms
of salary or wages. Even though there has been improvement in the job market for women over the past 20 years, most of it has been in secondary market jobs. Sexual segregation in the labor market is still very strong.

FOOTNOTES FOR CHAPTER 6
OCCUPATIONAL CHARACTERISTICS BY SEX

[1] Evelyne Sullerot, *Woman, Society and Change* (New York: McGraw-Hill
Book Co., 1971), pp. 20-28.

[2] Sullerot, *Woman, Society and Change*, pp. 15-17.

[3] Sullerot, *Woman, Society and Change*, p. 40.

[4] Jane Prather, "Why Can't Women Be More Like Men?" *American*

Behavioral Scientist, 15 (November–December 1971), 173-175.

[5] Prather, "Why Can't Women Be More Like Men?" p. 175.

[6] Cynthia Fuchs Epstein, *Woman's Place* (Berkeley, Calif.: University of California Press, 1970), p. 152.

[7] Edward A. Robie, "Challenge to Management," in Eli Ginzberg and Alice M. Yohalem (eds.), *Corporate Lib: Women's Challenge to Management* (Baltimore: The Johns Hopkins University Press, 1973), p. 14.

[8] Valerie Kincade Oppenheimer, "Demographic Influence on Female Employment and the Status of Women," *American Journal of Sociology, 78* (January 1973), 949.

[9] Valerie Kincade Oppenheimer, "Rising Educational Attainment, Declining Fertility and the Inadequacies of the Female Labor Market," in Charles F. Westoff and Robert Parke, Jr. (eds.), *Demographic and Social Aspects of Population Growth*, Vol. I (Washington, D.C.: The Commission on Population Growth and the American Future, U.S. Government Printing Office, 1972), p. 312.

[10] Rosemary Park, "Like Their Fathers Instead," in Ginzberg and Yohalem (eds.), *Corporate Lib*, p. 49.

[11] U.S. Department of Labor, Women's Bureau, *1969 Handbook on Women Workers* (Washington, D.C.: U.S. Government Printing Office, 1969), p. 96.

[12] The figures do not support this assumption. See Edwin C. Lewis, *Developing Woman's Potential* (Ames, Iowa: Iowa State University Press, 1968), p. 295.

[13] Andrea Tyree and Judith Treas, "The Occupational and Marital Mobility of Women," *American Sociological Review, 39* (June 1974), 293-302. This analysis disagrees with the findings of an earlier study that concludes that there are no significant differences in intergenerational mobility between men and women. See Peter Y. DeJong, Milton J. Brawer, and Stanley S. Robin, "Patterns of Female Intergenerational Mobility: A Comparison with Male Patterns of Intergenerational Occupational Mobility," *American Sociological Review, 36* (December 1971), 1033-1042.

[14] Department of Commerce, Bureau of the Census, *Detailed Characteristics: U.S. Summary, 1970 Census of Population* (Washington, D.C.: U.S. Government Printing Office, 1973), pp. 718-724.

[15] Phyllis A. Wallace, "Sex Discrimination: Some Societal Constraints on

Upward Mobility for Women Executives," in Ginzberg and Yohalem (eds.), *Corporate Lib*, p. 71.

[16] *Detailed Characteristics*, p. 833.

[17] Caroline Bird, "Welcome, Class of '72, To the Female Job Ghetto," *New York Magazine* (May 1972), 30.

[18] E. J. Kahn, Jr., "Who, What, Where, How Much, How Many?" *The New Yorker* (October 15, 1973), 155.

[19] Bird, "Welcome, Class of '72...," 31.

[20] Kahn, "Who, What, Where...," 156.

[21] Wallace, "Sex Discrimination...," p. 77.

[22] William Goode, "Family Life of the Successful Woman," in Ginzberg and Yohalem (eds.), *Corporate Lib*, p. 105.

[23] Goode, "Family Life...," pp. 108-109.

[24] Juanita Kreps, "The Sources of Inequality," in Ginzberg and Yohalem (eds.), *Corporate Lib*, p. 89.

[25] *New York Post* (February 14, 1972).

[26] Helena Z. Lopata, *Occupation: Housewife* (New York: Oxford University Press, 1971), p. 139.

[27] Caroline Shaw Bell, "Implications for Women," *Social Policy, 3* (September–October 1972), 15.

[28] Carole Lopate, "Pay for Housework?" *Social Policy, 5* (September–October 1974), 27-32.

[29] Lopate, "Pay for Housework?"

[30] Randall Collins, *Conflict Sociology: Toward an Explanatory Science* (New York: Academic Press, 1975), pp. 227-232.

[31] Randall Collins, "A Conflict Theory of Sexual Stratification," *Social Problems, 19* (Summer 1971), 3-20. Also, Collins, *Conflict Sociology*, pp. 233-258.

[32] Edward Gross, *Work and Society* (New York: Thomas Y. Crowell Company, 1958), p. 196.

[33] The question of values influencing occupational choice and choices influencing values is taken up by Morris Rosenberg, *Occupations and Values* (Glencoe, Ill.: The Free Press, 1957).

[34] Sydney M. Jourard, *The Transparent Self* (New York: D. Van Nostrand Co., 1971), p. 48.

[35] Jessie Bernard, "My Four Revolutions: An autobiographical History of the ASA," *American Journal of Sociology, 78* (January 1973), 773-791.

[36] *Detailed Characteristics,* pp. 739-745.

[37] Deborah S. David, "Occupational Values and Sex: The Case of Scientists and Engineers," Paper presented at the Annual Meetings of the American Sociological Association, Montreal, Canada, August 27, 1974, pp. 10-12.

[38] David, "Occupational Values and Sex."

[39] John P. Robinson, Robert Athanasiou, and Kendra B. Head, *Measures of Occupational Attitudes and Occupational Characteristics* (Ann Arbor, Mich.: University of Michigan Survey Research Center, Institute for Social Research, 1969). p. 438.

[40] Epstein, *Woman's Place,* p. 159.

[41] Epstein, *Woman's Place,* p. 160.

[42] Florence Ruderman, "Sex Differences: Biological, Cultural, Societal Implications," in Cynthia Fuchs Epstein and William J. Goode (eds.), *The Other Half: Road to Women's Equality* (Englewood Cliffs, N.J.: Prentice-Hall, 1971), p. 49.

[43] The argument has focused on the issue of I.Q. in the literary magazines and journals recently. See, for example, Samuel Bowles and Herbert Gintis, "I.Q. in the U.S. Class Structure," *Social Policy, 3* (November–December 1972–January–February 1973), 65-96; Norman Podhoretz, "The New Inquisitors," Richard Hernnstein, "On Challenging an Orthodoxy," Ben J. Wattenberg and Richard M. Scammon, "Black Progress and Liberal Rhetoric," all in *Commentary, 55* (April 1973); George Purvin, "Intro to Hernnstein 101," Jerome Kagan, "What is Intelligence?" both in *Social Policy, 4* (May-June and July-August 1973), 76-87.

[44] Edward Gross, "Plus Ça Change...? The Sexual Structure of Occupations Over Time," *Social Problems, 16* (Fall 1968), 198-208.

[45] Gross, "Plus Ça Change...?" See also Harold L. Wilensky, "Women's Work: Economic Growth, Ideology, Structure," *Industrial Relations, 7* (May 1968), 241.

[46] Mary Huff Stevenson, "Determinants of Low Wages for Women Workers," unpublished Ph.D. dissertation, University of Michigan, 1974.

[47] The indicants of education and training are derived from ordinal scales used by the *Dictionary of Occupational Titles, 1966 Supplement.*

[48] Stevenson, "Determinants of Low Wages for Women Workers," pp. 110-115.

[49] Stevenson, "Determinants of Low Wages for Women Workers," pp. 93-95.

[50] Stevenson, "Determinants of Low Wages for Women Workers," pp. 116-118.

[51] Stevenson, "Determinants of Low Wages for Women Workers," p. 172.

[52] Ed Stover, "Inflation and the Female Labor Force," *Monthly Review, 26* (January 1975), 50-58.

[53] For further elucidation of the 1950 to 1970 rates of occupational discrimination by sex, see Robert Tsuchigane and Norton Dodge, *Economic Discrimination Against Women in the United States* (Lexington, Mass.: Lexington Books, 1974).

[54] Constantina Safilios-Rothschild, *Women and Social Policy* (Englewood Cliffs, N.J.: Prentice-Hall, 1974), pp. 86-88.

[55] Safilios-Rothschild, *Women and Social Policy,* pp. 78-86.

7 OCCUPATIONAL CHARACTERISTICS BY AGE

The relation of occupational structure to age can be examined from many aspects, including job employment rates, job entry requirements, degree of occupational mobility, relation of occupational aspirations to values, and effect of education, family background, and other variables on the original relationship of age to structure. Each of these is examined in this chapter.

EMPLOYMENT AND UNEMPLOYMENT

The adage that age has its limits certainly has its parallel in the work world. The younger that one is in the labor force or, conversely, the older that one is, the less are the opportunities for employment. Looking through the labor force statistics, it is obvious that this rule holds for just about all occupations, male or female, white or nonwhite.[1] Opportunities for employment in higher-status positions increase radically after age 18, the normal year for high school graduation. Likewise, the proportion of young people in service and laboring jobs decreases as they become older.[2]

Unemployment for full-time, out-of-school youth is much higher than the national average (see Table 7.1). One reason is that these people are more likely to be in lower-level occupations, which tend to have higher unemployment rates.

TABLE 7.1 UNEMPLOYMENT OF YOUTH NOT ENROLLED IN SCHOOL, BY OCCUPATION, AGE, AND SEX, OCTOBER 1972

OCCUPATIONAL CATEGORY AND GROUP	16–21 YEARS		22–24 YEARS		TOTAL 16–24 YEARS	
	MEN	WOMEN	MEN	WOMEN	MEN	WOMEN
Professional and technical	2.4	2.2	6.5	8.0	3.9	4.2
Managers and administrators	1.3	0.2	3.4	2.3	2.1	0.9
Sales workers	1.8	6.6	6.5	4.6	3.5	5.9
Clerical workers	5.8	23.5	9.1	39.5	7.0	29.0
Total white-collar	11.4	32.5	25.5	54.4	16.6	40.0
Craftsmen	10.7	1.4	13.7	—	11.8	0.9
Operatives	25.8	12.2	22.1	18.4	24.4	14.3
Laborers	18.5	1.6	22.1	0.4	19.8	1.2
Total blue-collar	55.0	15.1	57.8	18.8	56.0	16.4
Private household workers	—	1.2	—	0.4	—	0.9
Service, except private household	11.6	17.9	7.2	20.7	10.0	18.9
Total service workers	11.6	19.1	7.2	21.1	10.0	19.8
Farm workers	2.7	1.4	2.7	1.1	2.7	1.3
No previous work experience	19.4	31.9	6.8	4.6	4.7	22.5
Totals	100.0	100.0	100.0	100.0	100.0	100.0

Source. U.S. Department of Labor, Bureau of Labor Statistics, *Employment of School-Age Youth, October, 1972,* Special Labor Force Report No. 158, 1973, p. A-17, Table I.

The rates vary by sex. Males are more likely to be unemployed in blue-collar positions and females in white-collar clerical and service occupations. With one exception (male service workers), unemployment rates *increase* as these youths get older, an indication of the effects of the lack of continuing education at the college level.

The unemployment rate by age, length of unemployment, and number of spells of unemployment (Table 7.2) also gives a view of the special problems of young people in the job market. Young people are not unemployed for as long periods of time as older people but, generally, they are out of work more frequently and tend to float from one job to another. Table 7.2 clearly shows the effects of discrimination by race, age, and sex. Middle-aged, white males

TABLE 7.2 EXTENT OF UNEMPLOYMENT BY AGE, SEX, AND RACE IN 1971

AGE AND RACE	PERCENT OF TOTAL WORKING OR LOOKING FOR WORK WHO WHERE UNEMPLOYED AT SOME TIME DURING 1971		PERCENT UNEMPLOYED THREE MONTHS OR LONGER		PERCENT WITH TWO OR MORE SPELLS OF UNEMPLOYMENT	
	MALE	FEMALE	MALE	FEMALE	MALE	FEMALE
White						
16-17	25.8	22.9	46.7	36.3	41.0	31.8
18-19	30.6	31.4	48.2	41.8	41.3	32.8
20-24	30.7	23.9	49.5	43.4	35.7	28.3
25-34	16.8	16.4	49.7	45.4	32.7	23.2
35-44	12.1	14.1	48.2	50.2	31.4	27.8
45-54	10.5	10.3	52.7	55.0	35.0	29.6
55-64	11.0	9.8	55.9	58.3	35.4	26.1
65-	7.8	6.0	69.4	67.6	43.9	35.1
Nonwhite						
16-19	41.0	45.8	52.5	43.6	38.8	29.3
20-24	38.4	35.8	57.5	49.2	36.6	34.1
25-44	18.7	23.0	58.8	55.3	40.5	34.1
45-54	15.1	11.6	54.4	60.9	36.7	29.9
55-64	13.1	12.6	61.1	a	50.7	a
65-	7.6	4.4	a	a	a	a

[a] Percent not shown where base is less than 75,000.

Source. Adapted from U.S. Department of Labor, Bureau of Labor Statistics, *Work Experience of the Population in March 1972,* Special Labor Force Report No. 162, 1974, Table C-1, p. A-49.

in the primary occupations (see also Table 6.6) are the most fully employed. Young, nonwhite females experience the highest rates of unemployment. One out of almost every two female black teenagers was unemployed at some time during 1971. It is likely that two out of every three of these teenagers was underemployed during that same year.

A poignant story relating to this predicament is told by Nat Hentoff:

The Secretary of Labor has told of stopping a teenager in Harlem this past spring and asking him if he was looking for a job. The boy's answer was, "Why?" That answer, I submit, was a healthy reaction. I would think it meant: I've stopped letting myself be conned. I have eyes. I see what jobs are available to the adults in the ghetto. I know the lousy schooling I've had. Where am I supposed to look? And to put it where it is, why should I think things will change? Nobody out there gives a damn about me.[3]

On the whole, in the early 1970s 3 of every 10 persons 18 and 19 years of age had experienced some unemployment, as well as one of every four persons 20 to 24 years old. For students the overall rate of unemployment is around 12 percent, or one of every eight persons. A constant factor that keeps cropping up in analyses of these data is the large number of job changes among young people. They are seen by employers as a cheap source of temporary employment in secondary jobs. When the job market becomes tight, minimum age requirements tend to rise, thus causing rapid and extreme fluctuations in youth's work force participation rates.[4] Therefore, even though the size of the teenage work force is expected to increase at a *decreasing* rate during the remainder of the 1970s (as compared to the increase at an *increasing* rate during the 1960s),[5] this should not reduce teenage unemployment. Employers will merely look to other sources of cheap labor—especially the working poor and the older unemployed. Or, they will see to it that the age level of children permitted to work is reduced.

There has already been a slight but steady reversal of the strict child labor laws enacted during the early 1900s to ameliorate the harsh child labor conditions experienced during the American industrial revolution. For the first time since these laws were enacted, the limits on age are being removed selectively. For example, in Utah since 1973 children 10 years and older are permitted to be employed in jobs such as shoe-shining, delivery of handbills, and caddying. Employment certificate requirements are waived in many instances for these very young workers. Colorado now allows persons under 16 to work 6 hours a day after school, up from 4 hours, and Illinois allows a minimum age of 10 for farmwork, which is one of the most strenuous types of manual labor. Lowering the legal age of majority to 18 years has reduced the minimum age for obtaining certain occupational licenses and for employment in certain places dependent on them.[6] However, there are no conditions of child labor that can compare to those of the past.

EMPLOYMENT AND EDUCATION

While all age categories of the labor force will have increased the amount of education received, younger workers will have increased their advantage over older workers with regard to college studies. This means that the more difficult problem of retraining and placing older workers will be added to the problem of employing and retraining workers.[7] However, even with a college education, young workers will face employment problems in the higher-prestige occupations. According to relatively conservative reports,[8] there will be an oversupply of college graduates in the 1980s, which may average about 140,000 persons per year. This will mean competition for jobs with nongraduates and, unless there is a general rise in hiring and promotion requirements, the unemployment rates for upper-level, white-collar occupations will skyrocket. So, even though the number of professional and technical jobs will continue to grow faster than jobs in other occupational groups, there will be an oversupply in that group. The vast majority of the 60 million job openings expected to become available between 1972 and 1985 will be open to persons with less than 4 years of college education.[9] These will be mostly "tertiary sector" jobs in the secondary labor market.

The U.S. Department of Education has developed a new program of career education that, pending government legislation, it plans to institute in the nation's elementary and secondary schools. This program separates school curriculums into 15 "job clusters."[10] All known jobs can be placed into one or another of these clusters:

Construction.
Manufacturing.
Transportation.
Agri-business and natural resources.
Marine science.
Environment.
Business and office.
Marketing and distribution.
Communication and media.
Hospitality and recreation.
Personal services
Public service.
Health
Consumer and homemaking education.
Fine arts and humanities.

Table 7.3 represents the major occupational areas in the marketing and distribution cluster.

TABLE 7.3 CLUSTER FOR MARKETING AND DISTRIBUTION OCCUPA-
TIONS

Elementary Education	Pre-Vocational and Exploratory	Skill Development and Related Knowledge		Options After Grade 12
Grades 1-2-3-4-5-6	Grades 7-8-9	Grades 10-11-12		
What Are The Occupations?	Marketing System	Retail Trade	General Merchandise Group Dealership and Franchises Specialty Stores Rental Operations	Job Placement
		Wholesale Trade	Merchant Wholesaling Manufacturing Merchandise Brokerage Farm Products Assembly Petroleum Plants and Terminals	
Who Works In These Occupations?		Service Trades	Lodging Personal Services Business Services Auto and Miscellaneous Repair and Services Travel, Recreation and Entertainment	
		International Trade	Automatic Merchandising Mail Order Direct Selling	
		Non-Store Retailing	Foreign Operations Exporting	Apprenticeship and Adult Education
		Industrial Selling	Production and Engineering Business Operations	
What Is The Life Style Of People?	Sales and Services	Trade Selling	Retail Resale Wholesale Resale Home and Institutional Resale	
		Consumer Selling	Apparel, Accessories and Personal Care Hardware, Materials Equipment Housing, Property and Household Products Food Products and Services Automotive, Transportation and Petroleum Products Intangibles	
		Industrial Purchasing	Purchasing Procedures Vendor Relations	
Who Do People Work With?	Buying	Buying for Resale	Buying Offices Chain Operations Independent Operations	
		Procurement	Bid Advertisement Direct Negotiation	Post-Secondary Occupational Skill Training
		Advertising	Media Organizations	
	Sales Promotion	Display	Display Houses Windows and Interiors	
Where Are These Jobs?		Public Relations	Customer and Community Services Trade Relations Publicity	
		Product Transport	Carriers Traffic Shipping and Delivery	
	Physical Distribution	Storage	Warehousing Inventory Control	
		Materials Handling	Receiving and Marketing Assembling and Packing	Advanced Education (4-Year College Or More)
How Do Workers Accomplish Their Jobs?		Finance	Banking Institutions Exchanges	
	Marketing Services	Credit	Consumer Credit Commercial Credit	
		Insurance	Personal Insurance Business and Property Insurance	
		Research	Marketing Information Product Analysis and Development	

Source. The Occupational Outlook Quarterly, 17 (Winter 1973), 19.

Learning about these clusters begins during the child's first 6 years of schooling. All children receive the same education, including a brief review of each of the job clusters. In grades 7 to 9, persons select the clusters that are of most interest and, in conjunction with their basic courses in English, mathematics, and social studies, they examine the chosen clusters in more depth. In the tenth grade each student selects one cluster and is trained in an entry-level skill in one occupation, such as typist, social work aide, or construction helper. Depending on the student's interest in pursuing work in a particular cluster, he or she will be counseled and placed for the eleventh and twelfth grades, either in intensive job preparation, study for postsecondary occupational programs, or study for college.

Supposedly, if an individual loses a job in one occupation through technological change or changing job requirements, that person should be able to be retrained relatively quickly for work in another occupation in the cluster. If training has been broad enough, the individual should be flexible enough to manage the quick transition.

OTHER FACTORS

In the 1930s and 1940s there was considerable job discrimination against both older and married women. But this has now changed, since the job market for women has improved from the 1950s to the present. The cause of this is given by Valerie Oppenheimer as the dominance of women in several occupations that are now expanding as part of the tertiary sector of the economy—nurses, teachers, librarians, telephone operators, stenographers, secretaries, typists, and the like. Also, at the same time, just when the demand for female workers began to rise sharply, the supply of young women decreased rapidly—both married and unmarried—between 1940 and 1960. This was due to the secular decline in American fertility in the 1930s. In addition, the higher fertility of women following World War II (the "baby boom" period) reduced the number of women available for work, the marriage age continued its long decline from the 1940s to the 1950s, and there was a rise in the proportion of women enrolled in school.[11]

A question that immediately comes to mind is whether the baby boom will increase the labor supply of young women and put older women out of work from 1970 to 2000. Oppenheimer feels not, because of the increased demand for women in the tertiary sector occupations, the increased amount of schooling of women, and the fact that fertility has leveled off and likely will remain fairly stationary. This is likely to lead to a "more extensive integration of women into the economy at all points in the family life cycle."

What seems to be happening is that factors such as occupational commitment are becoming more important and family status less important in determining women's labor force status.[12]

ENTRY INTO
THE LABOR
FORCE

Entry into the labor force is a process of gaining "intermediate positions," that is, of taking part-time jobs while in school, of completing work-training programs either on the job or in vocational schools, and of being unemployed. Once young people have begun job training or have obtained their first job, they have begun a series of incremental movement into the work world.[13]

Job entry is not a random process. A person is involved either actively or passively in choosing an occupation. "Choice" can refer to concerns with individual motivation, which leads to years of planning and training, or to broad societal forces, which restrain the individual into certain patterns or categories. In its broader meaning, it includes both. As I have already indicated, generally, the lower the prestige and skill level of the occupation, the less the people in it control their work situation, the less each has the ability to develop a career, and the more the work of each is shaped by external forces. Since so few entry jobs are at the upper levels of the occupational hierarchy, the "entry job" concept is not very useful as a career concept. However, it is useful as a tool in analysis of occupational choice.

Occupational choice is a process in which an individual makes decisions (or does not) and is influenced by the environment or attempts to change these influences where possible, the result of which is to close off certain avenues of possible occupational activity and to open others. Factors involved in the process are the individual's choice of high school curriculum, college major, whether and when to marry, the state of the job market at the person's time of entry, race or ethnic background, place of residence (rural or urban), the person's knowledge of occupations at the time of entry, and family background. Occupational choice is based on a combination of accident (external events beyond one's control), impulse (internal unconscious motives), and rationally planned and organized efforts by the individual. It is a *developmental process* in which the individual becomes more and more aware of his or her personal likes and dislikes, abilities, and values.[14]

Young people going into secondary market jobs are mostly those with a high school diploma or less. Their educational training has prepared them for the less skilled manual and clerical jobs in the labor market. Their jobs of entry are mostly accidental and impulse motivated. Numerous studies have found that the grapevine (i.e., friends and relatives) is the most important source of available jobs for both black and white lower-manual jobs.[15]   A national sample of out-of-school youths in 1963 indicated this to be true for blacks (54 percent) and important but less true for whites (32 percent).[16] A sample of 1963 high school graduates of three Detroit high schools disclosed that the graduates generally had very little knowledge of job wages, working conditions, chances for advancement, and the like, not only at the time of first jobs but also later, when making voluntary job changes. They drifted into their jobs because no others were available at the time.[17]

The entry jobs of youth reflect the discrimination by race and sex in the occupational structure. In a sample from 21 Detroit public senior high schools of 1963 graduates and dropouts, the percentage of entry jobs in office work was much higher for women than for men (66 percent versus 13 percent) and the same for semiskilled and unskilled jobs (54 percent versus 7 percent). Entry service jobs were much higher for nonwhites than whites (22 percent versus 8 percent), and entry skilled jobs was low for both whites and nonwhites, although much higher for the former (8 percent) than for the latter (2 percent).[18] Blacks relied more on informal sources for jobs, which tended to restrict them to local job markets, whereas whites could depend more on formal agencies and had a wider market for their skills from which to choose.[19]

For the poor and the nonwhite, "career agents" (i.e., persons or organizations important to an individual in his passage from one status to another),[20] are significant to entry jobs. Not only are parents and friends important sources of job information, but the federal government also can be effective through its various training programs.

As more information is collected on persons' entry jobs into the work force, there is mounting evidence that family background plays an important part in the level at which one enters. The attainment of educational credentials, the meal ticket to jobs, are found to rely heavily on family background, even more so than on ability and merit. However, the effects of family background and education tend to decrease as one's "career" progresses, a point discussed further in Chapter 17.

OCCUPATIONAL MOBILITY

If family background is so important, what happens to the sons of fathers when they go out into the occupational world? Do they follow in their fathers' footsteps or not? Table 7.4 gives a quick overview of intergenerational mobility patterns for males in the United States in 1962. Notice that 7 of every 10 sons of fathers who were white-collar workers ended up as white-collar workers themselves. Six of every 10 blue-collar sons become blue-collar workers. It is only among farmers' sons that the pattern of intergenerational occupational inheritance does not hold, because of the large decrease of farm jobs forcing these sons mostly into blue-collar occupations. These patterns are magnified for nonwhite workers.[22]

TABLE 7.4 OCCUPATIONS OF MEN WORKING IN 1962 (25 TO 64 YEARS OLD) AND OF THEIR FATHERS

FATHER'S OCCU-PATION WHEN SON WAS 16	SON'S OCCUPATION IN MARCH 1962			
	TOTAL	WHITE-COLLAR	BLUE-COLLAR	FARM
White-collar	100.0	71.0	27.6	1.5
Blue-collar	100.0	36.9	61.5	1.6
Farm	100.0	23.2	55.2	21.6
Total	100.0	40.9	51.4	7.7

Source. Frank Ackerman et al., "The Extent of Income Inequality in the United States," in Richard Edwards, Michael Reich, and Thomas E. Weisskopf (eds.), *The Capitalist System: A Radical Analysis of American Society,* p. 217. Copyright © 1972 by Prentice-Hall, Inc. Reprinted by permission of the publisher. Figures are calculated from data in Peter M. Blau and Otis Dudley Duncan, *The American Occupational Structure* (New York: John Wiley & Sons, 1967), Table J2.1.

When the analysis is refined from occupational categories to occupational groups, many divergencies occur. There is much more movement between groups but mostly within categories (Table 7.5). For example, there is a great deal of intergenerational movement from managerial to professional occupations, and vice versa. However, there are problems in interpreting these percentages. The sons of self-employed (free) professional fathers are twice as likely to enter salaried professions as they are to follow their fathers' footsteps into the free professions. But this is partly because salaried professionals outnumber free professionals 7 to 1. In fact, the sons of fathers in the free professions fill a much larger proportion of the positions in the free professions than they do in the salaried professions. This is depicted in Table 7.6, which compares the observed mobility to expected mobility. In a perfectly mobile society, that is, one in which occupational chances are completely randomized, observed and expected mobility are equal and have the value of 1.0. This is based on the ratio of the total labor force in the occupational group (bottom row of Table 7.5) to the observed percent from a given origin in one occupational group.[23] For example, Table 7.5 indicates that sons of free professionals should replace their fathers by a ratio of 1.4 to 1. Instead, they replace them 11.7 to 1, or approximately 12 times as many sons as expected (row 1, column 1 of Table 7.6).

The ratios in table 7.6 show that upward mobility (to the left of the diagonal) is more prevalent than downward mobility (to the right of the diagonal). Also, of those sons who are either upwardly or downwardly mobile, most move only one group from their fathers. Thus, one must be cautious in interpreting the amount of upward mobility as being a strong indicator of a loose occupa-

TABLE 7.5 MOBILITY FROM FATHER'S OCCUPATION TO 1962 OCCUPATION, FOR MALES 25 TO 64 YEARS OLD: OUTFLOW PERCENTAGES

FATHER'S OCCUPATION	RESPONDENT'S OCCUPATION IN MARCH 1962																	
	1	2	3	4	5	6	7	8	9	10	11	12	13	14	15	16	17	Total[a]
1 Professionals, self-employed	16.7	31.9	9.9	9.5	4.4	4.0	1.4	2.0	1.8	2.2	2.6	1.6	1.8	0.4	2.2	2.0	0.8	100.0
2 Professionals, salaried	3.3	31.9	12.9	5.9	4.8	7.6	1.7	3.8	4.4	1.0	6.9	5.2	3.4	1.0	0.6	0.8	0.2	100.0
3 Managers	3.5	22.6	19.4	6.2	7.9	7.6	1.1	5.4	5.3	3.1	4.0	2.5	1.5	1.1	0.8	0.5	0.1	100.0
4 Salesmen, other	4.1	17.6	21.1	13.0	9.3	5.3	3.5	2.8	5.4	1.9	2.6	3.7	1.7	0.0	0.8	1.0	0.3	100.0
5 Proprietors	3.7	13.7	18.4	5.8	16.0	6.2	3.3	3.5	5.2	3.9	5.1	3.6	2.8	0.5	1.2	1.1	0.4	100.0
6 Clerical	2.2	23.5	11.2	5.9	5.1	8.8	1.3	6.6	7.1	1.8	3.8	4.6	5.6	1.0	1.8	1.3	0.0	100.0
7 Salesmen, retail	0.7	13.7	14.1	8.8	11.5	6.4	2.7	5.8	3.4	3.1	8.8	5.1	4.6	0.1	3.1	2.2	0.0	100.0
8 Craftsmen, manufacturing	1.0	14.9	8.5	2.4	6.2	6.1	1.7	15.3	6.4	4.4	10.9	6.2	4.6	1.7	2.4	0.4	0.1	100.0
9 Craftsmen, other	0.9	11.1	9.2	3.9	6.5	7.6	1.5	7.8	12.2	4.4	8.2	9.2	4.6	1.2	2.8	0.9	0.3	100.0
10 Craftsmen, construction	0.9	6.7	7.1	2.6	8.3	7.9	0.8	10.4	8.2	13.9	7.5	6.2	5.2	1.1	4.3	0.8	0.6	100.0
11 Operatives, manufacturing	1.0	8.6	5.3	2.7	5.6	6.0	1.4	12.2	7.3	3.2	16.9	6.9	5.1	4.0	3.5	0.8	0.6	100.0
12 Operatives, other	0.6	11.5	5.1	2.5	6.6	6.3	1.4	7.1	9.3	4.9	10.4	12.5	5.9	2.1	4.2	0.9	1.1	100.0
13 Operatives, service	0.8	8.8	7.4	3.5	6.0	9.0	1.9	8.0	6.4	5.4	11.7	8.1	10.5	2.7	3.3	1.0	0.2	100.0
14 Laborers, manufacturing	0.0	6.0	5.3	0.7	3.3	4.4	0.7	10.7	6.0	2.8	18.1	9.4	9.4	7.1	5.8	1.7	0.9	100.0
15 Laborers, other	0.4	4.9	3.5	2.5	3.5	8.7	1.7	7.7	8.2	5.7	12.7	10.6	8.1	3.4	9.9	0.9	1.1	100.0
16 Farmers	0.6	4.2	4.1	1.2	6.0	4.3	1.1	5.6	6.9	5.8	10.2	8.6	4.8	2.4	5.4	16.4	3.9	100.0
17 Farm laborers	0.2	1.9	2.9	0.6	4.0	3.5	1.2	6.4	6.6	5.8	13.1	10.8	7.5	3.2	9.2	5.7	9.4	100.0
Total[b]	1.4	10.2	7.9	3.1	7.0	6.1	1.5	7.2	6.1	4.9	9.9	7.6	5.5	2.1	4.3	5.2	1.7	100.0

[a] Rows as shown do not total 100.0, since men not in experienced civilian labor force are not shown separately.
[b] Includes men not reporting father's occupation.

Source. Peter M. Blau and Otis Dudley Duncan, *The American Occupational Structure*, Table 2.2, p. 28. Copyright © 1967 by John Wiley & Sons, Inc. Reprinted by permission of the publisher.

TABLE 7.6 MOBILITY FROM FATHER'S OCCUPATION TO OCCUPATION IN 1962, FOR MALES 25 TO 64 YEARS OLD: RATIOS OF OBSERVED FREQUENCIES TO FREQUENCIES EXPECTED ON THE ASSUMPTION OF INDEPENDENCE

FATHER'S OCCUPATION	RESPONDENT'S OCCUPATION IN MARCH 1962																
	1	2	3	4	5	6	7	8	9	10	11	12	13	14	15	16	17
1 Professionals, self-employed	11.7	3.1	1.2	3.0	0.6	0.7	0.9	0.3	0.3	0.5	0.3	0.2	0.3	0.2	0.5	0.4	0.5
2 Professionals, salaried	2.3	3.1	1.6	1.9	0.7	1.2	1.1	0.5	0.6	0.2	0.7	0.7	0.6	0.5	0.1	0.2	0.1
3 Managers	2.5	2.2	2.5	2.0	1.1	1.2	0.7	0.8	0.7	0.6	0.4	0.3	0.3	0.5	0.2	0.1	0.1
4 Salesmen, other	2.9	1.7	2.7	4.1	1.3	0.9	2.2	0.4	0.8	0.4	0.3	0.5	0.3	0.0	0.2	0.2	0.2
5 Proprietors	2.6	1.3	2.3	1.9	2.3	1.0[a]	2.1	0.5	0.7	0.8	0.5	0.5	0.5	0.2	0.3	0.2	0.2
6 Clerical	1.6	2.3	1.4	1.9	0.7	1.4	0.8	0.9	1.0[a]	0.4	0.4	0.6	1.0[a]	0.5	0.4	0.2	0.0
7 Salesmen, retail	0.5	1.3	1.8	2.8	1.6	1.0	1.7	0.8	0.5	0.6	0.9	0.7	0.8	0.1	0.7	0.4	0.0
8 Craftsmen, manufacturing	0.7	1.5	1.1	0.8	0.9	1.0	1.1	2.1	0.9	0.9	1.1	0.8	0.8	0.8	0.6	0.1	0.1
9 Craftsmen, other	0.6	1.1	1.2	1.2	0.9	1.2	1.3	0.5	1.7	0.9	1.1	1.2	0.8	0.6	0.6	0.2	0.2
10 Craftsmen, construction	0.6	0.7	0.9	0.8	1.2	1.3	0.5	1.4	1.1	2.8	0.8	0.8	0.9	0.5	1.0	0.2	0.4
11 Operatives, manufacturing	0.7	0.8	0.7	0.9	0.8	1.0[a]	0.9	1.7	1.0[a]	0.6	1.8	0.9	0.9	1.9	0.8	0.2	0.4
12 Operatives, other	0.4	1.1	0.6	0.8	0.9	1.0	0.9	1.0	1.3	1.0	1.0[a]	1.7	1.1	1.0	1.0	0.2	0.7
13 Operatives, service	0.5	0.9	0.9	1.1	0.9	1.5	1.2	1.1	0.9	1.1	1.2	1.1	1.9	1.3	0.8	0.2	0.1
14 Laborers, manufacturing	0.0	0.6	0.7	0.2	0.5	0.7	0.5	1.5	0.8	0.6	1.8	1.2	1.7	3.3	1.4	0.3	0.5
15 Laborers, other	0.3	0.5	0.4	0.8	0.5	1.4	1.1	1.1	1.1	1.2	1.3	1.4	1.5	1.6	2.3	0.3	0.7
16 Farmers	0.4	0.4	0.5	0.4	0.9	0.7	0.7	0.8	0.9	1.2	1.0[a]	1.1	0.9	1.1	1.3	3.2	2.3
17 Farm laborers	0.1	0.2	0.4	0.2	0.6	0.6	0.8	0.9	0.9	1.2	1.3	1.4	1.4	1.5	2.1	1.1	5.5

[a] Rounds to unity from above (other indices shown as 1.0 round to unity from below).

Source. Peter M. Blau and Otis Dudley Duncan, *The American Occupational Structure*, Table 2.5, p. 32. Copyright © 1967 by John Wiley & Sons, Inc. Reprinted by permission of the publisher.

tional structure. Many moves that are tabulated as upward vertical mobility
on the tables are really horizontal shifts in the secondary labor market. As
shown in Chapter 4, moving from police officer (service) to carpet installer
(craftsman) or counter clerk (clerical) is not a case of upward vertical mobility.

The gradual change from manual to nonmanual occupations and from
lower-status to higher-status occupations continues to take place in the United
States. However, this trend is quite limited for young people and will likely
become even more limited as the occupations at the lower end of the prestige
hierarchy (service workers, laborers, and farmers) tend to decline.[24]

The criticism has been raised, however, that there really is a much more
open occupational mobility structure than the statistics present, that in fact
there is a good deal of upward mobility *within* occupational groups that goes
unrecorded and that increased specialization opens up many new positions for
those aspiring to be upwardly mobile.[25] However, the evidence is mounting,
especially in studies of professions, that this is not as true as it may have been
earlier in the century. Even within a specific occupation, sons of fathers from
occupations higher in status than engineering are found in higher-status positions within the engineering profession. Similarly, sons of fathers in low-status
occupations are found disproportionately in low-status positions in engineering.[25]

A major question facing youth today is, "Are people affected negatively
by accepting low-level jobs as their first full-time job?" In an analysis of occupational mobility data from seven United States SMSAs covering 1957 to
1967, Jonathan Kelley concludes that occupational work patterns have a very
limited history. Once a "career" is launched, one's future depends mainly on
present occupation and very little on past occupation or income. Also, family
background has only a marginal bearing, operating through the factors of education and occupation. "In short, as a man's career progresses, past failures are
forgiven and past success forgotten."[27]

However, young people are finding it more and more difficult to break
out of secondary labor market jobs. Local and regional studies in the United
States indicate that it is especially difficult for low-income workers to improve
in their occupational status from their first full-time occupation.[28]

ASPIRATIONS
AND VALUES

There are two views of occupational choice and career potential for youth: a
radical view that a person's first job is important in determining future work
positions, and a conservative view that a person's socio-economic status depends
largely on his or her present efforts. Neither is conclusive in the scientific
proof of its hypothesis. Are young workers' aspirations ultimately fulfilled?
Do they become locked into their first jobs or their first labor market place-

ment? What are their aspirations and their expectations? Both sides tend to agree on one point, that there is a major contradiction between occupational aspiration and the existing job market in the United States today. Not only upper-middle class youth but, more and more, youth from working class and lower-middle class families are hopeful of obtaining upper-middle class income and status from their jobs plus a high degree of meaningfulness and creativity from their work. This is caused by the rising expectations of the increasing number of people with at least some college education, if not the bachelor's degree itself, the aspirations of women generated by the feminist movement, and the various affirmative action programs of government.[29]

This is the first time that occupational aspirations have preceded instead of followed changes in the type of production. The industrial revolution was followed by changes from blue-collar to white-collar work. And the kinds of values that existed supported this movement—achievement through hard work, accountability to oneself (and through oneself to his God), and deferred gratification. In other words, the Protestant Ethic.[30]

Now, when aspirations are not met, young workers tend more frequently to drop out of the labor market and take on a new set of values that reject work as demeaning and trivial. They take jobs where and when they can get them in order to "get by," to support their life-style of simple leisure activities. Whereas unemployment was once seen as irrational and destructuve, it is now seen as a rational response to an irrational work system.[31] Others argue that young people have never lost the values of the Protestant Ethic—of independence, freedom, and risk—and that their commitment to work is as high as ever but that they expect more creative and interesting work.[32] Another study points out that what adolescents aspire to is not necessarily what they expect and that expectations more closely parallel the existing occupational structure.[33]

Following this line of thought is the culture-of-poverty idea that the values and aspirations of lower-class youth are different, that they do not value success as much, that they aspire less to the goals that would aid in their success, and that they realize that they have less opportunity to achieve success if they want it. These values reduce an individual's striving to attain a better position. For example, when asked about how they would choose jobs, lower-class persons chose less frequently the occupations that involved economic risk (e.g., professions) and more frequently those with immediate economic security (skilled manual occupations).[34] As I have already pointed out, there is considerably more long-term economic security in professions than in craft occupations—fewer spells of unemployment, higher salaries, and so forth. Lower-class youth have as high, and even higher, aspirations than middle-class youth when starting occupational levels of fathers are held constant.[35]

The poor are keenly aware of the differences between conventional norms and values and their own. They must and do accept " a number of modifications and qualifications to mainstream values." The acceptance of female-centered families is necessary, although it is not the wished-for ideal.[36] Thus, the lower-class accepts an alternative set of values (expectations) while still holding on to the values of the larger society (aspirations). However, their commitment to these general values is not as strong. They are considered more valid but less attainable.[37]

Young, poor people experience the same discrimination as their parents, and the probabilities are that they will end up in the same position as their parents. They are subject to the same inequities, such as poor schooling, dead-end jobs, and lower-paying jobs. On one work-training project youths were complaining because they were shoveling manure. "What demon tricked them into believing that this experience was not increasing their employability?"[38] New jobs at various occupational levels, if and when they are created, will likely *not* be available to the underemployed, a large number of whom are young, untrained workers, unless there is a major revolution in thinking, about training for needed skills in a greatly expanded work-training program.

SUMMARY AND CONCLUSIONS

Young people have lower rates of employment than their elders. Much of this difference is caused by their enrollment in school and their lack of job training and experience. However, both out-of-school youth with little education and college graduates face serious employment problems. The former are competing on a job market that is shrinking faster than their own numbers are being reduced, and the latter are competing on a job market that is expanding slower than their own numbers are expanding.

Although there is considerable upward occupational mobility of sons as compared to their fathers, there are increasing limits to a young person's ability to move from a secondary labor force job to a primary labor force career. This has not had much of an effect on the general occupational aspirations of youth, which remain high. However, occupational expectations are reduced to adjust to the hard realities of the work world. Aspirations remain high, and youth react by perceiving work as alienating.

FOOTNOTES FOR CHAPTER 7
OCCUPATIONAL CHARACTERISTICS BY AGE

[1] Department of Commerce, Bureau of the Census, *Occupational Characteristics: United States Summary: 1970 Census of Population* (Washington, D.C.: U.S. Government Printing Office, 1973), Tables 40 and 41, pp. 609-637.

[2] *Occupational Characteristics....*

[3] Nat Hentoff, "Whose Existential Crisis?" in Eliot E. Cohen and Louise Kapp (eds.), *Manpower Policies for Youth* (New York: Columbia University Press, 1966), p. 17.

[4] William G. Bowen and T. A. Finegan, "Labor Force Participation and Unemployment," in Arthur M. Ross (eds.), *Employment Policy and the Labor Market* (Berkeley, Calif.: University of California Press, 1965), pp. 115-161.

[5] Department of Labor, Bureau of Labor Statistics, *The U.S. Labor Force: Projections to 1990*, Special Labor Force Report No. 156, pp. 4-5.

[6] For a detailed summary, see David A. Levy, "State and Labor Legislation Enacted in 1973," *Monthly Labor Review* 97 (January 1974), 28.

[7] U.S Department of Labor, Bureau of Labor Statistics, *Education of Workers: Projections to 1990*, Special Labor Force Report No. 160, 1974, p. 27.

[8] News release of the U.S. Department of Labor, Office of Information, December 11, 1973.

[9] U.S. Department of Labor, Bureau of Labor Statistics, *Occupational Outlook Handbook*, 1974-1975 Edition (Washington, D.C.: U.S. Government Printing Office, 1974).

[10] A brief summary of this program can be found in *The Occupational Outlook Quarterly, 17* (Winter 1973).

[11] Valerie Kincade Oppenheimer, "Demographic Influence on Female Employment and the Status of Women," *American Journal of Sociology, 78* (January 1973), 951-952, 956-957.

[12] Oppenheimer, "Demographic Influence on Female Employment....," pp. 958-960.

[13] The discussion in this section owes much to the research of Jeffry Piker, *Entry into the Labor Force: A Survey of the Literature on the Experience of Negro and White Youths* (Ann Arbor, Mich.: Institute of Labor and Industrial Relations, The University of Michigan—Wayne State University, 1968).

[14] This definition is summarized from Piker, *Entry into the Labor Force*, pp. 66-67; Peter M. Blau et al., "Occupational Choice: A Conceptual Framework," *Industrial and Labor Relations Review* (July 1956), 531; Eli Ginzberg et al., *Occupational Choice: An Approach to a General*

Theory (New York: Columbia University Press, 1951); Eli Ginzberg, "Toward a Theory of Occupational Choice: A Restatement," *Vocational Guidance Quarterly, 20* (March 1972), 169-176. For a review of the literature, see Robert Hoppock, *Occupational Information*, 2nd Ed. (New York:: McGraw-Hill Book Co., 1963), Chapter 7.

[15] Paul Jacobs, *Unemployment as a Way of Life* (Berkeley, Calif.: University of California, Institute of Industrial Relations, 1966).

[16] Vera C. Perrella, Forrest A. Bogan, and Thomas E. Swanstrom, "Out-of-School Youth, February, 1963," *Monthly Labor Review, 87* (November-December 1964), 1260-1268, 1416-1424.

[17] Larry Singell, "Some Private and Social Aspects of Juvenile Labor Mobility," Bowling Green State University, Department of Economics, as quoted in Piker, *Entry into the Labor Force*, pp. 95, 128.

[18] Fred Cook and Frank Lanham, "Opportunities and Requirements for Initial Employment of School Leavers with Emphasis on Office and Retail Jobs," (Detroit: Wayne State University, College of Education, 1966), as quoted in Piker, *Entry into the Labor Force*, p. 19.

[19] Alice H. Kidder, "Interracial Comparisons of Labor Market Behavior," Unpublished Ph.D. thesis, Massachusetts Institute of Technology, August 1967.

[20] Erving Goffman, *Asylums* (Garden City, N.Y.: Doubleday Anchor Books, 1961), pp. 135-169.

[21] Although there is more crossing of nonmanual to manual occupations, mostly by persons who take part-time jobs in manual occupations until they receive employment again in their nonmanual occupations. Seymour M. Lipset and Reinhard Bendix, "Social Mobility and Occupational Career Patterns," *American Journal of Sociology, 57* (January 1952), 366-374.

[22] Piker, *Entry into the Labor Force*, p. 32.

[23] Peter M. Blau and Otis Dudley Duncan, *The American Occupational Structure* (New York: John Wiley & Sons, 1967), p. 35.

[24] Robert M. Hauser and David L. Featherman, "Trends in the Occupational Mobility of U.S. Men, 1962-1970," *American Sociological Review, 38* (June 1973), 307, 309.

[25] Wilbert E. Moore, "Changes in Occupational Structures," in Neil J. Smelser and Seymour M. Lipset (eds.), *Social Structure and Mobility in Economic Development* (Chicago: Aldine Publishing Company, 1966), p. 212.

[26] Robert Perrucci, "The Significance of Intraoccupational Mobility: Some Methodological and Theoretical Notes, Together with a Case Study of Engineers," *American Sociological Review, 26* (December 1961), 874-883. A high degree of direct occupational inheritance into father's specific occupation exists for eight professions. See Ronald M. Pavalko, *Sociology of Occupations and Professions* (Itasca, Ill.:   F. E. Peacock Publishers, Inc., 1971), p. 72.

[27] Jonathan Kelley, "Causal Chain Models for the Socioeconomic Career," *American Sociological Review, 38* (August 1973), 481-492.

[28] Ruth Fabricant Lowell, *The Dual Labor Market in New York City* (The City of New York Human Resources Administration, Office of Policy Research, December 1973), pp. VI-4-VI-6.

[29] Brigitte Berger, " 'People Work'—the Youth Culture and the Labor Market," *The Public Interest,* No. 35 (Spring 1974), 55-66.

[30] Berger, " 'People Work'...."

[31] Larry E. Reavic, "The Myth of Unemployment," *National Review,* April 12, 1974, p. 427.

[32] *Work in America,* Report of a Special Task Force to the Secretary of Health, Education, and Welfare (Cambridge, Mass.:   the MIT Press, 1973), p. 48.

[33] W. P. Kuvesky and R. C. Bealer, "A Clarification of the Concept 'Occupational Choice,' " *Rural Sociology, 31* (September 1966), 265-276.

[34] Herbert H. Hyman, "The Value Systems of Different Classes: A Social Psychological Contribution to the Analysis of Stratification," in Seymour M. Lipset and Reinhard Bendix (eds.), *Class, Status and Power* (Glencoe, Ill.:   The Free Press, 1953), pp. 426-441.

[35] Lola M. Irelan (ed.), *Low-Income Life Styles,* U. S. Department of Health Education, and Welfare (Washington, D. C.:   U.S. Government Printing Office, 1966).

[36] Charles H. Anderson, *Toward a New Sociology,* Rev. Ed. (Homewood, Ill.:   The Dorsey Press, 1974), p. 168.

[37] Anderson, *Toward a New Sociology,* p. 169. See also: Aaron Antonovsky and Melvin J. Lerner, "Occupational Aspirations of Lower Class Negro and White Youth," *Social Problems, 7* (Fall 1959), 132-138; H. Roy Kaplan and Curt Tausky, "Work and the Welfare Cadillac: The Function of and Commitment to Work Among the Hard-Core Unemployed," *Social*

Problems, 19 (Spring 1972), 469-483; Leonard Goodwin, *Do the Poor Want to Work?* (Washington, D. C.: The Brookings Institution, 1972); Alan S. Berger and William Simon, "Black Families and the Moynihan Report: A Research Evaluation," *Social Problems, 22* (December 1974), 145-161.

[38] S. M. Miller, "The Exiles: Dropouts in the Affluent Society," in Louise Cohen and Eli E. Kapp (eds.), *Manpower Policies for Youth.* (New York: Columbia University Press, 1966), p. 28.

PART 2

OCCUPATIONAL DYNAMICS

Most work today is done in large organizations. The division of labor has created job specialization, and this has been followed by the increasing organization and bureaucratization of work. The role of occupations in dealing with this phenomenon is treated in several ways in Part 2. First, in Chapter 8, the nature of bureaucratic organizations is examined and the reaction of occupational groups to bureaucratization is analyzed. The kinds of reactions are manifested in whether and how the body of knowledge of an occupation is developed. Professionalized occupations (Chapters 9 and 10), because they contain mostly primary labor market workers, are quite active in maintaining or developing their professional knowledge and autonomy.

Autonomy is the freedom of an occupation's members to determine the knowledge to be used in their occupation and how that knowledge is to be applied. It is reduced when an occupation's work roles and body of knowledge are rationalized. Technology and alienation, two factors that significantly affect autonomy, are recurring themes in Chapters 9 to 15. In addition to a review of the descriptive analyses of occupations, each of these chapters discusses worker alienation. Chapters 10 and 11 point to the low amount of alienation experienced by professionals, administrators, and managers. However, indications are that this pattern is beginning to change for some occupations within these groups.

Because they have less control over their body of knowledge than professionals, semiprofessionals (Chapter 12) have less autonomy and are more alienated from their work. In general, autonomy is further reduced and alienation increased in clerical and sales occupations (Chapter 13), in many working-class occupations (Chapter 14), and in most lower-class occupations (Chapter 15). However, as pointed out in these chapters, there are some exceptions, such as transport equipment operatives and highly skilled craft workers, who do not fit the pattern. As depicted in Chapter 14, these workers may even develop a false consciousness, that is, be distracted into accumulating consumer goods as the measure of prestige, what Marx referred to as commodity fetishism. Dual labor market theory is applied to show how the primary and secondary labor market categories are measures of autonomy in terms of worker control over the work process. This helps to refine the definition of working class and lower class by autonomy instead of by occupational skill, prestige, or life-style alone.

8 OCCUPATIONS AND ORGANIZATIONS

The goal of an occupation's members is to develop and maintain work autonomy. Those occupations in which the body of working knowledge is less rationalized (i.e., less organized and accessible) tend to be more powerful and more autonomous. They are primary labor force occupations. Their members must protect themselves from infringements by other occupations and by clients and must counter the attempts to dominate them by the bureaucratic structure in the organizations in which they work.

This chapter introduces three concepts needed to analyze the dialectic between the rationalizing of occupations and occupational autonomy: rationalization, bureaucratization, and professionalization. Unions and professional associations, organizational structures that grow up around these three forces, are examined, as are the effects of administrative authority and technology on these structures. Some of the larger social effects of occupational development are also discussed.

RATIONALIZATION

Rationalization is the development in organizations of standardization, formalization, codification, systematization, accessibility, and availability of knowledge.[1] It is an extensive process, ranging from the highly rationalized knowledge of bureaucratic organizations to the nonrationalized knowledge of religion and mysticism (see Chart 8.1).[2] *Traditional knowledge* is charismatic knowledge, the "vision" of a political leader or religious prophet.

CHART 8.1 CONTINUUM OF RATIONALIZATION OF THE KNOWLEDGE BASE OF ORGANIZATIONS

Innovation by extension (extending uncertainty)			Innovation by rationalization (reducing uncertainty)
Traditional or charismatic knowledge	Professional knowledge	Experts	Technical or bureaucratic knowledge
Inspirational strategy[a]	Judgmental strategy[a]		Computational strategy[a]

[a] From James D. Thompson, *Organizations in Action* (New York: McGraw-Hill, 1967), p. 134.
Source. Adapted from Wolf V. Heydebrand and James J. Noell, "Task Structure and Innovation in Professional Organizations," in Wolf V. Heydebrand (ed.), *Comparative Organizations: The Results of Empirical Research* (Englewood Cliffs, N.J.: Prentice-Hall, 1973), pp. 314-315.

There are no rules, no technical complexity. *Professional knowledge* is characterized by moderate technical complexity. For example, technical and administrative rules are internalized by means of formal education and job socialization. These are represented by the premodern professions of law, medicine, and university teaching. *Technical knowledge* is characterized by a fully organized set of externalized technical and administrative rules for the coordination of people and materials by bureaucratic means. Task complexity is routinized and ultimately automated.[3]

Innovation takes place at all levels. *Innovation by extension* deals with the creation of new knowledge. *Innovation by rationalization* has to do with the maintenance of already developed knowledge by further systematization and routinization of complex tasks. Bureaucrats and managers naturally favor innovation by rationalization because it increases their power to control production at higher organizational levels and decreases their dependence on professional experts. Professionals tend to favor some combination of innovation by extension and innovation by rationalization. The latter is acceptable only if it can be controlled by the profession, because the more the body of knowledge, services, and goals of the profession become certain (specifiable), the more likely professional autonomy is reduced.[4] All occupations attempt to maintain as much autonomy as possible.

Heydebrand and Noell take the Weberian point of view that the tendency of modern society is toward increasing rationalization. The number of generalist professions has decreased significantly. Today most information and knowledge can be rationalized into specialist occupations in large organizations and sold as commodities to be manipulated on the market.[5] We seem to be advancing toward the "iron cage" of bureaucracy that Max Weber warned us about years ago. This is a trap that leads to increased conformity and the likelihood of totalitarian government.

Others have viewed increasing rationalization with a great deal more optimism. Karl Mannheim saw the "functional rationality" of the planned society as a regulated unity helping humanity to attain a more perfect society.[6] The "free-floating" intellectuals were the group that was to lead the way to this society.[7] Daniel Bell represents this position today:

> *The methodological promise of the second half of the twentieth century is the management of organized complexity . . . , the identification and implementation of strategies for rational choice in games against nature and games between persons, and the development of a new intellectual technology.*[8]

This new intellectual technology substitutes algorithms (problem-solving rules) for intuitive judgments. The *codification of theory* becomes the basis for innovation in science, technology, and economic policy. The professional occupations are the groups that will carry out these managerial tasks.[9]

The opposite view that society is evolving toward a less rationalized, "organic" form is put forth by Azumi and Hage, the authors of a recent book on organization theory.[10] Another writer, Richard Simpson, argues that bureaucracies are growing but are becoming *less* rational, and that "rational values are in retreat." By coopting the new activist movements of the 1960s, bureaucracies absorb their ideas. As a result, there is a gradual institutionalization of values toward a better quality of life and less toward productivity for profit, for a more person-based and less role-based society. This comes largely from the services-sector occupations—research, social- and services-delivery planning, TV, broadcasting, advertising, and various governmental agencies.[11]

The position is taken in this book that organizations and occupations fluctuate in their degree of rationalization over periods of time as new knowledge is developed by them. The degree of rationalization can, to some extent, be

balanced by the degree of innovation introduced. Both these forces are governed by the amount of bureaucratization and professionalization present in the
organization or occupation.

BUREAUCRAT- IZATION AND PROFESSION- ALIZATION

Occupations both adapt to and change organizations because most occupations
cannot exist without some sort of formal organization, and all organizations
with a division of labor are divided by occupational skills, techniques, and
functions. There is no way in which to separate one from the other. However,
they can be analytically viewed as distinct societal forces by utilizing ideal-type
concepts. These concepts, in their perfect or ideal state, exist only in the mind
of the observer, but they are used to obtain approximations to that ideal. The
approximations are then compared to one another.[12] The two major ideal types
are bureaucracy and professionalization.

Bureaucracy represents the extremes of rationality and control. In fact, it is
defined ideally as a system of organization, administration, and control, consist-
ing of a division of labor and a hierarchical system of responsibility of lower officials to higher officials, with each office holding more authority than those below it. Operations of the organization are governed by a consistent system of
abstract rules and procedures developed in order to efficiently carry out the
organization's goals. Individuals conduct their roles formally and impersonally
in order to minimize emotional involvements, which could possibly lead to favoritism and inequitable treatment.[13] The fully developed bureaucracy "maximizes
organizational efficiency." This is the function of bureaucracy, the most important form of social organization in modern society. In contrast, professionalization represents, ideally, the lack of rationality and control, accomplished by the
occupation's successful control over its own body of knowledge by means of a
mandate awarded to it by the state. The work autonomy of the individual is
thereby fully protected. Autonomy permits one to be free to engage in those
activities circumscribed only by that mandate, allowing more room for creativity
and innovation.[14]

Sociologists have examined organizational structure on the basis of the degree
of its bureaucratization. The formal characteristics of bureaucracy, each of which
is an ideal type, are viewed as measurements for placing an organization on a continuum of bureaucracy.[15] Following the guidelines of Miller and Form,[16] we
can chart some examples of modern organizational structures on this continuum
(see Chart 8.2). Thus, the most bureaucratic organizations will exhibit the greatest division of labor, the most elaborate system of abstract rules, the most extensive degree of specialization of work tasks, and the greatest degree of rationality.

CHART 8.2 CONTINUUM OF BUREAUCRATIZATION OF ORGANIZATIONS

	Increasing Bureaucratization →				Decreasing Bureaucratization →		
Military organizations	Large governmental organizations	Large corporation	Large union	Large university	Small college	Voluntary organization	Solo practitioner
Catholic church			Large public school system	Large hospital	Public school	Large professional firm	Small professional firm
					Political party	Small business	Suite
					Small church		Social circle

However, a decrease in bureaucracy does not necessarily mean an increase in professionalization. Organizations on both ends of the continuum of bureaucratization have professional representation. (There does, however, seem to be some correlation of size to bureaucratization, a point which will be discussed shortly.) People in some occupations experience more bureaucracy because the majority of them work in complex organizations, for example, public relations men and women, marketing research directors. Similarly, some organizations are more professionalized because a large number of their personnel are professionals of one type: law firms, medical groups, and public accounting firms.

In several respects bureaucracy and professionalization display similarities.[17] The decisions of both are governed by universalistic standards; that is, they are based on the objective criteria of a body of knowledge that is independent of the case of the client under consideration. This allows for the specificity of expertness in which the person is qualified to deal with the client's problems in a strictly limited area. For example, the physician tells the patient what to eat but not which friends to choose. Likewise, the corporate executive will tell workers which products to manufacture but not what to eat for lunch. But neither tell them which religion to practice or which school to attend, this more diffuse authority being assigned to parents. In addition, in their relations with clients both are governed by norms of affective neutrality, which condemn emotional involvement. Detachment insulates the "producer" from the client so that the former may exercise reasoned judgment. Thus, it is in the area of control of knowledge in a rationally organized manner on the basis of expertise that the two are most alike.[18]

The source of authority is one of the most important differentiating factors between bureaucracy and professionalization. The social control of professionals comes mainly from outside the organization; it is the colleagual authority developed by professional associations. Decisions are reviewed by the *occupational* colleague group, and discipline emanates from them. In a bureaucracy the management of the *organization* reviews and disciplines. The major systems of social control of the source of authority in both organizations and occupations can be analyzed on the basis of the degree to which bureaucratic and professional factors are present in them.

ORGANIZA-
TIONAL
CONSTRAINTS

Depending on the functions they perform in an occupation, people will find alternative kinds of organizational structures available—professional, corporate, and union. These structures can vary considerably by size, complexity, and degree of formalization. Almost all occupations are limited in their organiza-

tional structure by two major constraints.[19]   The first constraint is the nature
of the technology—how does it set up one's work? Automobile assembly
line workers are highly organized formally in order to meet the demands imposed by the unvarying speed of delivery of the materials to be processed.
However, in fully automated auto plants, there is less formalization because
workers are freed from the routine of a set standard of delivery on which
they must perform their work tasks. Instead, periodic checks are made to
examine the quality of machine-produced items. Smaller groups operate on
a more informal schedule and maintain a higher rate of production.[20]

The second limit to organization is the power-command constraints, that
is, the limit imposed by the bureaucratic chain of command in the organization, especially in the forms of management direction. Administrative decision making can lead to changes in the occupational groups within the organization. If, in a large corporation, it is decided that production, sales, and
distribution scheduling must be computerized, then some groups will be removed, others decreased, and still others increased in order to adapt to the
changes. Bookkeepers will be let go, whereas computer programmers will be
brought in.

Individual members of an occupation practicing on their own as "solo
practitioners" or in small professional groups will have more power to choose
how to maintain and develop their practice. However, the client can at times
greatly influence the work of the professional. Solo lawyers and physicians
are mostly chore boys for their clients. They have less freedom to choose a
specialty than those who work in large organizations, less access to a wide
range of clients and equipment, less contact with colleagues, and less ability
to counter the client's whims and opinions. The "free" practitioner becomes
a captive to clients.[21]

PROFESSIONAL ASSOCIATIONS AND UNIONS

In order to counter excessive administrative control, people in occupations
have banded together either in professional associations or in unions. Professional associations are groups of professionals organized to initiate and
promote general objectives of the entire occupation or of segments that the
organizing persons represent. The functions of unions are directly opposed
to professionalized occupations. Such efforts on the part of union leaders
as attempting to reduce the autonomy of management by negotiating terms
of remuneration and worker security, by developing a collective force through
the threat of strike, and by fostering a class consciousness are antithetical to
a professionalized environment.

Professions are generally highly organized internally through their associations, establishing fees, conditions of work, and rules for recruitment and training. Autonomy is guaranteed when, after it has shown its power to organize internally and externally, the profession attains a monopoly over its area of expertise in the form of a mandate from the state. "Indeed, the ideology and extensive occupational organization of some professions is such that it is beneath them—a loss of status—to bargain or negotiate with clients or management."[22] The normative conflict of collective bargaining practiced by unionized occupations is avoided by the established professions. Authority relations are considered an internal matter, governed by colleague control through a written code of ethics. All practitioners are considered as equals. Unionization would not normally confer higher social status.

In examining the various occupational groups in the U.S. occupational structure, it is interesting to note that unionism is not only weak among the highest organized occupations, but also among the least organized. Among unskilled laborers and farm workers, for example, there has traditionally been very little unionization. This is attributed to the low level of awareness of the importance of organized occupational activity to improve working conditions. There has been, however, a large increase in unionism of these occupations over the last decade. This is also true of several professions. For example, small but rapidly increasing numbers of dentists, physicians, and university teachers are unionizing. As more professions are faced with the loss of autonomy resulting from their placement in large bureaucratic structures, they turn to the only other source of power available to them: the collective power of unionism. Unionism does not have as one of its explicit goals the reduction of bureacracy, but it does establish lines of authority and, consequently, it clarifies areas of professional and managerial autonomy.

Unionized professionals, including even those of the highest ranks, have become part of the "new class" of service occupations, which is being heralded as the major hope for reforms in American institutions. But the impact of these union movements will be minimal unless the present large number of organizing craft unions (an organization of workers of a single occupation) merge into industrial-type unions [composed of all workers in one or more factories or all members of an occupational group (i.e., all professionals, all skilled workers, all clerical workers)].[23] In this event, unions would likely take the place of professional associations as a mode of collective advance of social mobility. Craft unions are already competing with professional associations in low-level occupations and the stratified service bureaucracies such as nursing, engineering, public school teaching, social work, and counseling.[24]

To summarize, the power of the organization can range from the high occupational solidarity of professional groups to the total administrative control of corporate groups. Etzioni has distinguished the two as *professional authority* and *administrative authority*, respectively.[25] They can be visualized on a continuum as follows:

Professional authority   Administrative authority
|——|

Organizational types:

Professional   Union   Corporate

   Administrative authority is found in traditional industrial labor—labeled as jobs or positions in a general skill class instead of as occupations. These position are constructed, changed, and dissolved by management on the basis of what will increase productivity and profits. "They have no social or economic foundation for their persistence beyond the plants, agencies or firms in which they exist."[26]

   Professional authority, on the other hand, withholds from management the authority to "create and direct the substance, performance and even the goals of work itself. ... It [is] a source of control which may well rival that of management." A profession is an occupation so well organized that its members can depend on receiving a concrete particular identity, a lifelong career, and the opportunity to continue to practice the same skills regardless of the organization in which they work.[27] Jobs extend *across* organizations; they are independent of any particular organization. In professional departments it is the professionals who control the work itself, even though management controls the terms and conditions of work. In union organizations the situation is exactly reversed: management controls the production process and the worker bargains on issues of pay and working conditions.[28]

   In her analysis of labor market shelters, Marcia Freedman illustrates the dynamics of these two forms of authority. Structure, in the form of labor market segmentation, enters the labor market when the continuity of employment becomes the norm. There is less freedom to vary one's occupation on the market. "The division of labor becomes a source of restraint rather than a source of freedom in the market.... It encompasses a range of activities, hierarchically spelled out in different job titles, and resulting in organizational rather than occupational attachment."[29]

   However, for those who manage to set up market shelters and gain control of the state regulating apparatus, there is some freedom in terms of job autonomy. They have "obtained public power to serve the interests of their members." This power takes the form of professional association campaigns, new unions of professionals, and support of protectionist legislation by unions.[30]

PROFESSIONAL
BUREAUCRACY

More and more professionals are working in bureaucratic organizations. The resulting conflict between the structure and values of the professional and bureaucratic modes creates serious built-in strains in several areas.[31] As an example, one of the most common situations is that of a group of scientists in a research and development department in a large corporation. As employees in a bureaucratic organization, they will find that the nature of the goal sought by this organization will differ from their own. The corporation's goal is profit. The scientists' goal is to develop basic research. And, although basic research can and does turn up profitable new ideas and products, the scientists cannot guarantee results in any regularized schedule. As a consequence, the emphasis of management is to push applied research at the expense of basic research, a task not pleasing to "pure" scientists. A second area of strain develops when the professionals become more engaged in administrative tasks and less in scientific work. Most professionals hope to avoid administrative tasks in order to devote their time fully to their research. A third problem arises with the kind of incentives sought by the professionals. They want to be recognized by colleagues in the profession (a "cosmopolitan" identity) more than they do by persons within the organization (a "local" identity). This is difficult to do if they are busily engaged in administrative work or applied research for the firm. A fourth possible strain develops in the area of decision making. The dilemma for scientists is that if they join the administration, they will not have the time to maintain their work and reputation in their specialties. Management faces the same problems of how to balance the organization's goals with the professionals' goals and yet maintain the autonomy and thus creativity of the professionals.

There appears to be an inverse relationship between the degree of bureaucratization and the professionals' attitudes. Bureaucratic procedures tend to inhibit professional development, and professional values are not compatible with bureaucracy. However, the workable compromise that results from this conflict of forces is called "professional bureaucracy." It is found in corporate organizational structures as well as in professional organizations. In professional organizations it operates most efficiently through a system of work procedures and rules of behavior external to the organization in which the professional works. These procedures and rules are "devised by professional associations and the government and supported by a professional milieu and public opinion which is generally favorable to the enforcement of these regulations."[32] The canons of the bar association, the code of ethics of the various professional associations, and the work procedures set up such as the "generally accepted auditing standards" for CPAs are all examples that govern the work behavior of professionals and that promote personal autonomy in the form of freedom from close internal supervision.

The balance between professional and bureaucratic elements is a temporary one and constantly fluctuates with the growth and development of the organization and with occupations directly impinging on the organization. For example, certain companies find it advantageous to emphasize professional autonomy over managerial control. At Arthur D. Little, a large management consulting firm, top management considers its role to be that of facilitating the work of the professional staff by providing staff services that relieves the professional of bureaucratic details in record-keeping, hiring, and the like. Thus, employees are more often being "administered" by their subordinates.[33] On the other hand, persons in the traditionally "freer" professional organizations, because of their increasing size and specialization, may not be any more autonomous than colleagues in industrial organizations. One researcher found that legal departments in large organizations were not more bureaucratized than private law firms of comparable size.[34]

Careful analysis of the modern organization has shown that the bureaucratization process has been blunted considerably by the entrance of large numbers of professionals and other experts at the various staff levels in large-scale organizations. Even though this creates a more complex division of labor, it also generates more innovation. Furthermore, if there is a tall hierarchy (i.e., many levels of authority), then there is a strong tendency for the organization to be more highly effective when professionals are present in considerable numbers because they provide a "continuous source of error detection and correction"[35] when added to the normal complement of managers. In addition, even though complexity (levels of hierarchy) increases in the larger organization of which the professional is a part, there is decreased complexity within the professional departments because a system of equals (collegial authority) is predominant.[36] The differences between professional and bureaucratic organizational goals are summarized in Chart 8.3.

Most empirical studies of professionals in bureaucratic organizations have shown how bureaucracy is antithetical to professional norms and goals. In her analysis of military psychiatrists, Arlene Daniels[37] indicates how independent initiative and professional judgment is severely limited by the military organization. Instead of acting as therapists, these psychiatrists limit themselves to making recommendations on whether a person should or should not be discharged because of mental illness. They are transformed from counseling agents to control agents for the organization. They become captives of the wishes of the military commanders for whom they work. Consequently, "for a successful bureaucratic adaptation, [these] professionals need to develop a primary commitment to the larger aims or general rationale of the organization they serve."[38]

The autonomy of the jail school teacher is compared to the public school teacher by Phyllis Stewart and Muriel Cantor.[39] They find that the jail school teacher has more autonomy than the public school teacher in what to teach,

CHART 8.3 COMPARISON OF PROFESSIONAL AND BUREAUCRATIC STRUCTURES

PROFESSIONAL	BUREAUCRATIC
A set of complete skills together with a complete set of internalized standards. Tasks and responsibilities are broadly defined and adjusted and redefined in interactions with organizational members.[a,c]	Partial skills with external controls. Tasks and responsibilities are rigidly defined in narrowly defined functional roles.[a,c]
Necessity for longer period of training allows for strong internalized controls to be established regarding work-related values and norms established by professional association.[a]	Shorter training period does not usually permit strong establishment of values and norms.[a]
Necessity for training institutes because practitioners cannot afford time and expense necessary.[a]	Values and norms are established by the organization and acquired on the job.[a]
Generalized and flexible work.[a]	Specialized and inflexible work.[a]
More creative and change oriented.	Methodical, disciplined, prudent, and stability oriented.
Reliance on horizontal consultation (colleague control).[b] Personal autonomy.[b]	Reliance on vertical supervision (hierarchical control).[b] Organizational control.[b]
Organic—the content of communication is information and advice. There is commitment to tasks, and importance and prestige is attached to affiliations and expertise in the larger environment (cosmopolitan orientation).[c]	Mechanistic—the content of communication is instructions and decision issued by superiors. There is loyalty and obedience to superiors as a high value, and importance and prestige is attached to identification with the organization itself (local orientation).[c]

[a] W. Richard Scott, "Professionals in Bureaucracies—Areas of Conflict," in Howard M. Vollmer and Donald L. Mills (eds.), *Professionalization* (Englewood Cliffs, N.J.: Prentice-Hall, 1966), pp. 267-268.

[b] J. Victor Baldridge, *Power and Conflict in the University* (New York: John Wiley & Sons, 1971), p. 158.

[c] Tom Burns and G. M. Stalker, *The Management of Innovation* (London: Tavistock Publications, 1961). The mechanistic and organic structures are condensed in Gerald Zaltman, Robert Duncan, and Jonny Holbek, *Innovations and Organizations* (New York: John Wiley & Sons, 1973), p. 131.

how to teach it, and whom to teach. This is because the public school teacher must adhere to the unstated goal of keeping classroom discipline, whereas for the jail school teacher this is no problem. If an inmate misbehaves, that person will be removed permanently from the classroom, thus eliminating all opportunity for the break in prison routine that the classroom offers.[40] In prisons the teacher does not have to be concerned with antagonistic boards of education, dissatisfied parents, or unruly students. The teacher has more freedom in choosing curriculum and teaching methods.

However, other studies indicate that professional and bureaucratic processes are interdependent in many large organizations. Peter Blau found in large government personnel agencies that professionals were given the feeling of personal autonomy because there were substitutes for direct supervision such as detailed statistical records of performance.[41] Studies of large law firms[42] and large public accounting firms[43] disclosed other substitutes for direct supervision—ethical codes and norms constructed for the firms by occupational associations.

Eugene Litwak has suggested that it is not so much the degree of professionalization of the occupation as it is the degree of uniformity of the organization's or occupation's tasks that determines the kind of organizational structure. Organizations that successfully combine both uniform and nonuniform events are *professional bureaucracies.* Examples are hospitals, research organizations, and graduate schools.[44] Examining the supervisory relationships among physicians in an outpatient clinic in a large teaching hospital, Mary Goss describes how these events are controlled.[45]

It has even been suggested that as professional work is being located more often in bureaucratic settings, new methods of cooperation and accomodation between professionals and bureaucrats indicate "increased compatibility" instead of just "interdependency."[46] As salaried employees, professionals are less concerned with financial problems and tend to see their rewards in colleague recognition of their work. Likewise, in group practice there is greater peer and public evaluation of the professional's work. Computer storage and retrieval of information gives other professionals access to the decisions of colleagues. Likewise, more professionals will end up dealing with the client, thereby offering a more complete set of services.[47]

But, as with all other forms of human organization, professional bureaucracy has both good and bad features. More openness in the large organization means less privacy in the traditional professional-patient relationship. Engel and Hall point out that greater technical interdependency threatens the power of professionals as people begin to realize that no longer can a single profession have all the knowledge necessary for client treatment, that other professionals must be relied on. In the process of increased division of labor among professionals, the problem of the dehumanization of the client becomes paramount.[48]

Finally, as professional knowledge becomes more highly rationalized, professionals are transformed into experts. Their autonomy is threatened as their knowledge becomes subject to control by administrators.[49] Michel Crozier makes this point in his analysis of a French clerical agency and an industrial monopoly.[50] As the expert's work becomes more easily organized, it can be translated into rules and procedures and taken over by less highly trained people.

This analysis of professional bureaucracy suggests that professional organizations are becoming more bureaucratic and that bureaucratic organizations are becoming more professionalized.[51] But one must keep in mind that even though some professional departments in corporations are less bureaucratic than some professional organizations, and vice versa, "there is...a general tendency for the autonomous professional organization to be less bureaucratic than the heteronomous organization or the professional department. This suggests that the nature of the occupational groups in an organization affects the organizational structure."[52]

OCCUPATIONS AS SOCIAL CONTROL UNITS

The goal of an occupation's conscious efforts to improve is to provide autonomy for its members. Historically, the most successful way of accomplishing this has been to professionalize the occupation. Usually, the first step is to develop the occupation's body of abstract knowledge. Then it impresses on the public or government the importance of this knowledge to society (whether in fact it is important) in order to obtain a mandate for exclusive use and application of this knowledge. Professionalism, instilling beliefs in the practitioner and the public that only this occupation could organize and use this knowledge properly, is an important process in obtaining control and monopoly of the ideas and technology of a field that often was organized and maintained by another occupation.

Very few researchers have analyzed occupations as social control units. William Goode, in his studies of librarians, saw not only individuals in organizations competing with one another in their efforts to achieve in the class system, but also occupations engaged in the same competition. They may, he states, "move up or down in power, prestige, or income."[53]

Both systems may be viewed as zero-sum games. The income which one individual receives cannot be claimed by another. If an occupation rises in income level or in prestige ranking, necessarily the other will lose.... An expanding economy may yield more real income for nearly all occupations; but at any given time there is only so much income to be distributed, each occupation has a higher or lower average income than others, and those which have risen have done so at the expense of others.[54]

Thus, if librarians wish to professionalize (and thereby receive the power, prestige, and income that goes with autonomy), they must be willing to develop and control areas of knowledge, some of which may impinge on the expertise of other professions. They also must develop scientific principles to serve as guidelines for their work. For example, they could apply communications theory to routing and sorting of knowledge entering the library in all forms. They would accept the task of judgmental decision making in areas of values (e.g., book selection for public or for specialist reading).[55] They could, in a word, create a structure of lay uncertainty that would provide them with the power and the potentiality for autonomy in an area of expertise.

After conducting an historical study of the elite of the medical profession in France, two researchers concluded that alternately, or sometimes simultaneously, a profession attempts to rationalize its practice by making it more technical and by codifying it, and to make its practice secret by monopolizing its knowledge (i.e., keeping it from the outside world by means of ideological generalizations).[56] A very good example of keeping the practice secret is an analysis completed by a British researcher, Michael Burrage, comparing American occupations to British occupations.[57] Burrage contends that British occupations are largely *occupationally based.* That is, there is little occupational rationalization, but there is early occupational socialization and "normatively coordinated behavior." One is expected to serve one's entire career within a single class of occupational positions that correspond closely to the class structure of British society. Likewise, the boundaries of the unions and associations correspond with the formal class divisions of the occupations. On the other hand, most American occupations are *bureaucratically based.* They have weaker group sanctions on individual behavior and make less of an effort to produce early occupational socialization. Because of the rationalizing process, there is less emphasis on inherited, traditional occupational relationships within an organization and more emphasis on individual innovation and making it on one's own.[58]

In the British and French health service professions emphasis is given to the esoteric nature of the knowledge base. This results in a quite different historical development of professional autonomy. As a result, rigorous administrative rationalization was not developed because of the guildlike arrangement between doctor and patient. Specialists were limited in their abilities to develop a close personal relationship with patients by this arrangement.[59] In England general practitioners performed their own surgery and were oriented to the patient at home. Compare this to the American practice of development of the formal scientific aspect of medical training, with the resulting high rationalization of the work process. Likewise, with British manual occupations, both unions and management see workers as divided naturally into occupational groups. A craft- or trade-structured union movement has been retained. Workers recognize themselves as having collective interests as well as individual interests. U.S. unions see workers as a "vast undifferentiated mass of individuals—who happen to be employed in a particular industry but have no permanent occupational identity." Characteristically, in Britain the workers organized as an occupational group and *then* created an administrative structure; in the United States it was usually the reverse—unionists went out to organize workers. It is therefore not surprising that in Britain labor unions have recruited 38.7 percent of the labor force and that in the United States labor unions have recruited only 28.5 percent of the labor force, as of 1965.[60]

Thus, the British workers are generally better prepared to face struggles with management. However, the emphasis on keeping a tight in-group structure and, for the professions, a protected body of knowledge, does have serious drawbacks. The unwillingness to rationalize the mystery of the professional expertise, for example, forestalls most attempts at innovation. Practitioners do not feel any change is necessary or desirable. In this sense, the low amount of rationalizing is to a considerable extent detrimental to change in an occupation. As Kenneth Boulding sees it, "Where the rigidities of a professional subculture do not allow the image [knowledge] of its practitioners to change rapidly enough, new images will arise, outside the profession or established subculture, and create professions and subcultures of their own."[61] The unwillingness or inability of the occupation to innovate will result in the loss of power, wealth, and prestige that occurs with the rationalizing process.

In the U.S. situation, innovation and creativity are much more in evidence because the process of rationalizing the esoteric knowledge in their occupations forces professionals to develop a new mystique in place of the old. Occupations that are rapidly rationalized by newly introduced techniques or administrative practices become weakened or in many instances cease to exist if they have not developed mystique or if they do not have the administrative strength to control it.[62] New occupations will have successfully competed for the areas of uncertainty that are up for grabs.

For example, let's take the case of the development of electronic data processing (EDP) and its effect on the business professions. One of the first professions to utilize EDP in industry was management consulting. These people were very effective in setting up mathematical, econometric, and other models for the production of goods in manufacturing plants. But it was the CPAs who, with their knowledge of "internal control systems," both financial and human, began to plan with the aid of EDP for "total information systems" for their clients. They now compete successfully with management consultants in important areas such as executive placement, arranging for mergers and acquisitions, advising of foreign governments, and purchase or sale of securities. More important, they now give a total package plan by integrating the management consulting work with the annual audit of the client. This is a function that others are prevented by law from doing, since CPAs alone are permitted to audit a publicly traded corporation (a corporation that sells its stock on a major stock exchange).[63]

Thus, even though they are partly unaware, all professions that advise large-scale organizations are involved in a struggle for the status and prestige that results from it. The sociologist, Paul Lazarsfeld, commented on this phenomenon to public accountants:

> The computer is invading all divisions of business and this raises the issue of who should control the computer. A power fight could develop between accountants and other groups, for the division which controls the computer also controls the investments of the company. The stakes are high in this conflict or collaboration issue, for the status and prestige of the various professions will be dependent upon the outcome.[64]

This prediction is limited to corporation accountants. But we can "modernize" it by giving it an occupational focus:

> The computer has invaded all types of economic organizations. This raises the issue of which profession can best utilize the computer to provide a total information service for the administrative groups of society. A power fight has developed between accountants and other professions. The stakes are high in this conflict or collaboration issue, for the status and prestige of the various professions involved will be dependent upon the outcome.

The battle has been engaged. The CPAs have expanded their services to all forms of economic organization, including banks, public utilities, transportation companies, churches, universities, and federal, state, and local governmental agencies. Many other professions are either directly or peripherally involved: management consulting, law, banking, actuary and, to a limited degree, administrative science and sociology.

THE ROLE OF TECHNOLOGY

Technology plays a very importnat role in occupational control. Discussing this on an organizational level, Terrebury states that uncertainty, as exemplified by developments in technology, is the dominant characteristic of organizational environments with "turbulent fields," and in large-scale organizations this is becoming more predominant.[65] At the occupational level, Richard Peterson emphasizes that if only the two forces of bureaucracy and professionalization were at work in society, then a "rigidly bureaucratically bounded occupational structure would develop," one reminiscent of the craft guilds of the Middle Ages.[66] The various stages that the occupation of ceramic engineering went through were, he shows, also greatly influenced by technology. First, for centuries, ceramics were made by craftsmen potters. Second, earlier twentieth-century technology, in the form of electric power, allowed for development of ceramic insulators that in turn lead to the rise of the occupation of ceramic engineering. The third period developed with the introduction of plastic insulators that made ceramic engineering obsolete; and the fourth period saw the resurgence of ceramic engineering in the production of new uses for ceramics in atomic energy plants and space vehicles.

Because of technological and organizational changes a host of new occupations have arisen. As Hughes has emphasized, in medicine the physician has gradually handed over many activities to nurses, and nurses to aides.[67] The entire paraprofessional structure in public school teaching and in the health services occupations has led to the creation of scores of new occupations and occupational titles. English architects are being forced into new areas by rapid technological change, especially in areas of building design. Others are trying to branch out by casting themselves as leaders of multiprofessional teams,[68] much in the way that CPAs have organized in the United States. In the academic occupations, as each new discipline developed, philosophy has been reduced somewhat in its scope of expertise. Philosophers have counteracted by developing subspecialties in areas that parallel these new fields, for example, the philosophy of science, political philosophy, social philosophy, and the philosophies of art, history, and math.[69]

We all know of occupations made obsolete by technology. The invention of the automobile led to the demise of occupations providing for horse-and-buggy travel: horseshoers, saddle-makers, and other skilled crafts in leather making. New occupations were opened, from petroleum engineering and geology to gas station attendant and auto mechanic. However, just as the British overinvested in railroads in the nineteenth century, the United States has done so with automobiles in the twentieth century and consequently has drastically affected highways, jobs, and the shape of cities. Political pork barreling discouraged alternative modes of transportation, built a favorable tax structure and, in the process, wasted a tremendous store of energy resources and fostered environmental destruction. The great occupational movement to fuel the automotive industry is now coming to an end. There will be some attrition as emphasis is placed on new or increased forms of urban mass transportation and, hopefully, in the human services occupations.

However, even if there is this turnover in occupations, old ones dying and new ones growing, the probabilities are high that is is the same class of people who were found in the declining occupations who will replace themselves in the newer, developing occupations. The analyses in Chapters 4 to 7 and Chapter 17 substantiate this fact.

SOCIAL EFFECTS

Changes in social attitudes have also been important in the development of occupational prestige and power. Sometimes these attitudes are affected by technological developments and sometimes not. In the United States there have been waves of antiprofessionalism during its history that have affected the course of development of entire occupational categories. In the revolutionary era the professions were suspected of being un-American and undemocratic. Several states opened the practice of law to anyone, with no formal preparation. And again, in the Jacksonian era of the mid-1800s, the American civil service system was reformed by eliminating educational and experiential background as requisites for a position. This, of course, had a disastrous effect on the professions, and another long period of deprofessionalization set in.[70]

The scientist's and the academic's scholarly detachment is a deviation least tolerated by laymen in periods of crisis. For example, the attack on the Supreme Court followed its decisions on civil rights. The attack on professors came during the era of McCarthyism. Hughes remarks that "social unrest often shows itself precisely in such questioning of the prerogatives of the leading professions."[71]

We have just begun to move into another era where professions are under attack by an increasing number of persons in U.S. society. Clients are now organizing and demanding their share of their rights—the right to have the services they *want*. This "client revolt," as some call it,[72] is taking many forms (local cooperatives, national voluntary associations such as Nader's Raiders, the Sierra Club, etc.). It is making itself felt in the organized action of these groups, and indirectly in court decisions in favor of the client. More and more, professions and large-scale organizations are being held accountable for their actions by the lay public. Client advocacy is becoming an established phenomenon in our society today.

SUMMARY AND CONCLUSIONS

The general tendency in modern industrial society is for organizations and occupations to increase in rationalization of the work process. However, in occupations, and especially in professionalized occupations, there are continual attempts to develop new knowledge or control existing knowledge. This innovation and control of areas of uncertainty acts as a counterbalance to the bureaucratization of organizations for occupations. Bureaucratization creates administrative control, whereas professionalization creates occupational control.

Persons who work in large organizations face particularly difficult problems in maintaining occupational autonomy. In organizations with a preponderance of professionals, the larger organizations tend to provide more independence from client influence than the smaller organizations. Increasing organizational size and complexity generally lead to professional bureaucracy, a constantly changing balance between the two forms of order.

The development and control of a structure of uncertainty provides occupational autonomy. However, occupations are constantly rationalizing other parts of their work tasks. This simultaneous innovation and rationalization is a necessary dialectic process because the lack of rationalization of an occupation's knowledge results in occupational stagnation. One of the major functions of rationalization is to transfer power and control from the occupation to the organization, thus stimulating a need for innovation by the occupation.

This process is interposed by the segmentation of the labor market. Secondary occupations develop high organizational attachment, and low occupational attachment and primary occupations develop just the opposite kinds of attachments.

Within the work organization, conflict occurs between those practicing occupationally based knowledge and those practicing bureaucratically based knowledge. Overemphasis on keeping practice of an occupation esoteric by monopolizing knowledge usually means that a more highly developed normative system exists. As a result there is little bureaucratization but tremendous internal control over members, to the extent that it can become authoritarian for both the occupation's members working in an organization and for the management of the organization. Overemphasis on innovation, on the other hand, can lead to rapid changes unacceptable to members of the occupation.

FOOTNOTES FOR CHAPTER 8
OCCUPATIONS AND ORGANIZATIONS

[1] Wolf V. Heydebrand and James J. Noell, "Task Structure and Innovation in Professional Organizations," in Wolf V. Heydebrand (ed.), *Comparative Organizations: The Results of Empirical Research* (Englewood Cliffs, N.J.: Prentice-Hall, 1973), p. 295.

[2] This broader definition of rationality transcends the issue of legal-rational authority versus bureaucratic authority as presented by Parsons, Udy, and others. Instead of concentrating on the norms of organization, the focus is on the conflict by opposing interests over the control of specialized knowledge and resulting control over the definition of tasks in the organization and over the control of its goods and services. Thus, traditional

and charismatic knowledge can be viewed as more inspirational, as more uncertain and less accessible to the public than bureaucratic and technical knowledge, which is more computational. Professional knowledge in modern organization tends to accommodate the two in a "judgmental strategy." Heydebrand and Noell, "Task Structure and Innovation...," pp. 295-296, 311-315.

[3] Heydebrand and Noell, "Task Structure and Innovation...," pp. 294-298.

[4] Heydebrand and Noell, "Task Structure and Innovation...," pp. 300-302.

[5] Heydebrand and Noell, "Task Structure and Innovation...," p. 321.

[6] Karl Mannheim, *Man and Society in an Age of Reconstruction*, Rev. Ed. (New York: Harcourt, Brace & World, 1940).

[7] Karl Mannheim, *Ideology and Utopia* (New York: Harcourt, Brace & World, 1936).

[8] Daniel Bell, *The Coming of Post-Industrial Society* (New York: Basic Books, 1973), p. 28.

[9] Bell, *The Coming of Post-Industrial Society*, pp. 29, 35. For a discussion of the contradictions in Bell's argument, see Chapter 3 above.

[10] Koya Azumi and Jerald Hage, *Organizational Systems* (Lexington, Mass.: D. C. Heath, 1972), p. 216. The "organic" and "mechanistic" models of organization, comparable to the traditional and technical forms of knowledge (see Chart 8.1), are defined by Tom Burns and G. M. Stalker, *The Management of Innovation* (London: Tavistock Publications, 1961). The mechanistic is "appropriate to stable conditions," whereas the organic is "appropriate to changing conditions, which give rise to constantly fresh problems and unforseen requirements for action which cannot be broken down or distributed automatically arising from the functional roles defined within a hierarchic structure."

[11] Richard L. Simpson, "Beyond Rational Bureaucracy: Changing Values and Social Integration in Post-Industrial Society," *Social Forces*, 51 (September 1972), 1-6.

[12] The ideal type is fully described by Max Weber in his "'Objectivity' in Social Science and Social Policy: Part II," in his *The Methodology of the Social Sciences*, ed. and trans. by Edward A. Shils and Henry A. Finch (New York: The Free Press, 1949).

[13] This definition of bureaucracy follows that of Max Weber. See Hans Gerth and C. Wright Mills (eds. and trans.), *From Max Weber: Essays*

in Sociology (New York: Oxford University Press, 1958), pp. 196-198.

[14] The importance of the mandate has been stressed by Everett C. Hughes, *Men and Their Work* (New York: The Free Press, 1958).

[15] Richard H. Hall, *Organizations* (Englewood Cliffs, N. J.: Prentice-Hall, 1972), p. 67.

[16] Delbert C. Miller and William H. Form, *Industrial Sociology*, 2nd Ed. (New York: Harper & Row, 1964), p. 11.

[17] These are listed in Peter M. Blau and W. Richard Scott, *Formal Organizations* (San Francisco: Chandler Publishing Co., 1962), pp. 244-247.

[18] Charles Perrow, *Complex Organizations: A Critical Essay* (Glenview, Ill.: Scott, Foresman & Co., 1972), p. 55, notes that Max Weber emphasizes the point that expertise is the basis of bureaucratic control, just as it is for professionalization. See also Richard H. Hall, "Professionalization and Bureaucratization," *American Sociological Review, 33* (February 1968), 102-103; George Ritzer, "Professionalization, Bureaucratization and Rationalization: The Views of Max Weber," *Social Forces, 53* (June 1975), 627-634.

[19] Elliott A. Krause, *The Sociology of Occupations* (Boston: Little, Brown & Co., 1971), p. 242.

[20] The classic example is given by Robert Blauner, *Alienation and Freedom: The Factory Worker and His Industry* (Chicago: The University of Chicago Press, 1964).

[21] Everett C. Hughes, "The Professions in Society," *The Canadian Journal of Economics and Political Science, 26* (February 1960), 61.

[22] Lee Taylor, *Occupational Sociology* (New York: Oxford University Press, 1968), p. 145.

[23] Elliott Krause distinguishes between "organization by setting," where the goals of the workers are the goals of the management, and "organization by occupation," where workers are unionized across factories. See his *The Sociology of Occupations,* p. 79.

[24] Marie Haug and Marvin B. Sussman, "Professionalization and Unionism," *American Behavioral Scientist, 14* (March-April 1971), 538-540.

[25] Amitai Etzioni (ed.), *The Semi-Professions and Their Organization* (New York: The Free Press, 1969), pp. x-xii.

[26] Eliot Freidson, "Professionalization and the Organization of Middle-Class

Labour in Postindustrial Society," in Paul Halmos (ed.), *Professionalization and Social Change*, The Sociological Review Monograph No. 20 (Staffordshire, England: University of Keele, December 1973), p. 54.

[27] Freidson, "Professionalization and the Organization of Middle-Class Labour . . . ," p. 54. Freidson calls them the "administrative principle" and the "occupational principle." See his "Professions and the Occupational Principle."

[28] Freidson, "Professions and the Occupational Principle," p. 24.

[29] Marcia Freedman, *Labor Markets: Segments and Shelters* (Montclair, N. J.: Allanheld, Osmun, 1976), Chapter 2.

[30] Freedman, *Labor Markets*, Chapter 9.

[31] These strains are listed by William Kornhauser, with the assistance of Warren O. Hagstrom, *Scientists in Industry: Conflict and Accommodation* (Berkeley, Calif.: University of California Press, 1962), pp. 11-12.

[32] Erwin O. Smigel, *The Wall Street Lawyer* (New York: The Free Press, 1964), p. 278.

[33] George E. Berkley, *The Administrative Revolution* (Englewood Cliffs, N. J.: Prentice-Hall, 1971), p. 34.

[34] Hall, *Organizations*, p. 191.

[35] Hall, *Organizations*, p. 279.

[36] Hall, *Organizations*, pp. 121-122. Smallness does not avoid the problem of hierarchy. If anything it intensifies it, since the average differential between positions at different levels is greater in small organizations because of their fewer levels going from bottom to top positions. Size appears to have little effect on hierarchy if chains of equal length (i.e., number of levels) are compared. Arnold S. Tannenbaum, et al., *Hierarchy in Organizations* (San Francisco: Jossey-Bass, 1974), p. 95.

[37] Arlene K. Daniels, "The Captive Professional: Bureaucratic Limitations in the Practice of Military Psychology," *Journal of Health and Social Behavior*, 10 (December 1969), 225-265.

[38] Daniels, "The Captive Professional . . . ," p. 264.

[39] Phyllis L. Stewart and Muriel G. Cantor (eds.), *Varieties of Work Experience* (Cambridge, Mass.: Schenkman Publishing Co., 1974), pp. 193-194. The jail school teacher study appears in this volume. See Lewis A Mennerick, "The County Jail School Teacher: Social Roles and External Constraints," pp. 142-158.

[40] Stewart and Cantor, *Varieties of Work Experience.*

[41] Peter M. Blau, *The Dynamics of Bureaucracy,* Rev. Ed. (Chicago: University of Chicago Press, 1963), Chapter 3.

[42] Erwin O. Smigel, *The Wall Street Lawyer* (New York: The Free Press, 1964), pp. 275-286.

[43] Paul D. Montagna, "Professionalization and Bureaucratization in Large Professional Organizations," *American Journal of Sociology, 74* (September 1968), 138-145.

[44] Eugene Litwak, "Models of Bureaucracy Which Permit Conflict," *American Journal of Sociology, 62* (September 1961), 182. Elizabeth Morrissey and David F. Gillespie, Technology and the Conflict of Professionals in Bureaucratic Organizations," *The Sociological Quarterly, 16* (Summer 1975), 319-332.

[45] Mary E. W. Goss, "Influence and Authority Among Physicians in an Outpatient Clinic," *American Sociological Review, 26* (February 1961), 39-50.

[46] Gloria V. Engel and Richard H. Hall, "The Growing Industrialization of the Professions," in Eliot Freidson (ed.), *The Professions and Their Prospects,* pp. 75-88.

[47] Engel and Hall, "The Growing Industrialization of the Professions."

[48] Engel and Hall, "The Growing Industrialization of the Professions."

[49] Heydebrand and Noell, "Task Structure and Innovation in Professional Organizations," pp. 314-315.

[50] Michel Crozier, *The Bureaucratic Phenomenon* (Chicago: University of Chicago Press, 1964).

[51] Hughes has stated a similar proposition: "As the professions become more organized, business organizations become more professionalized." Everett C. Hughes, "Professions," *Daedalus, 92* (Fall 1963), 665. See also George Strauss, "Professionalism and Occupational Associations," *Industrial Relations, 2* (May 1963), 9.

[52] Hall, "Bureaucratization and Professionalization," p. 103.

[53] William J. Goode, "The Librarian: From Occupation to Profession?" *The Library Quarterly, 31* (October 1961), 306.

[54] Goode, "The Librarian: From Occupation to Profession?" p. 306. Recently, Goode has noted that over a long period of time the zero-sum

concept does not always apply. Society and other professions may benefit without loss from another occupation's advancement in quality performance. William J. Goode, *Explorations in Social Theory* (New York: Oxford University Press, 1973), p. 349.

[55] Goode, "The Librarian: From Occupation to Profession?" pp. 311-315.

[56] H. Jamous and B. Peloille, "Professions or Self Perpetuating Systems: Changes in the French University Hospital System," in J. A. Jackson (ed.), *Professions and Professionalization* (London: Cambridge University Press, 1970), pp. 117-118.

[57] Michael Burrage, "Democracy and the Mystery of the Crafts: Observations on Work Relationships in America and Britain," *Daedalus, 101* (Fall 1972), 141-162.

[58] Burrage, "Democracy and the Mystery of the Crafts."

[59] Burrage, "Democracy and the Mystery of the Crafts."

[60] Burrage, "Democracy and the Mystery of the Crafts."

[61] Kenneth E. Boulding, *The Image: Knowledge in Life and Society* (Ann Arbor, Mich.: University of Michigan Press, 1956), p. 141.

[62] Carolyn F. Etheridge, "Lawyers Versus Indigents: Conflict of Interest in Professional-Client Relations in the Legal Profession," in Eliot Freidson (ed.), *The Professions and Their Prospects* (Beverly Hills, Calif.: Sage Publications, 1973), p. 263, shows that as the courts bureaucratize by substituting rules and procedures for the lawyer's mystique the professional control of the lawyer decreases. The balance between bureaucratic and professional principles of work is destroyed.

[63] Paul D. Montagna, "The Public Accounting Profession: Organization, Ideology, and Social Power," *American Behavioral Scientist, 14* (March-April 1971), 475-491.

[64] Paul F. Lazarsfeld, *Profile of the Profession, 1975, From the Viewpoint of a Sociologist* (New York: American Institute of Certified Public Accountants, 1964), p. 12.

[65] Shirley Terrebury, "The Evolution of Organizational Environments," *Administrative Science Quarterly, 12* (March 1968), 590-613.

[66] Richard A. Peterson, *The Industrial Order and Social Policy* (Englewood Cliffs, N. J.: Prentice-Hall, 1973), p. 61.

[67] Everett C. Hughes, "The Study of Occupations," in Robert K. Merton,

Leonard Broom, and Leonard S. Cottrell, Jr., (eds.), *Sociology Today: Problems and Prospects* (New York: Basic Books, 1959), p. 454.

[68] Philip Elliot, *The Sociology of the Professions* (New York: Herder and Herder, 1972), p. 125.

[69] Joseph Bensman and Robert Lilienfeld, *Craft and Consciousness: Occupational Technique and the Development of World Images* (New York: John Wiley & Sons, 1973), pp. 101-103.

[70] Burrage, "Democracy and the Mystery of the Crafts;" Krause, *The Sociology of Occupations*, pp. 26-33.

[71] Hughes, "The Study of Occupations," p. 449.

[72] Marie R. Haug and Marvin B. Sussman, "Professional Autonomy and the Revolt of the Client," *Social Problems, 17* (Fall 1969), 153-160.

9 THE PROFESSIONS: APPROACHES TO THEIR STUDY

The professions have long been prominent in the comments of social theorists, but it is only recently that a sociology of professions has emerged as a distinct subfield in the discipline. Three major approaches to the area have emerged. The first was led by Everett C. Hughes at the University of Chicago. Known as the Chicago School or the symbolic interactionist approach, its theorists emphasize the generative nature of social interaction. Occupations are viewed as role performances that must be constantly reexamined because of the changing nature of the situational environment of social interaction. The conflict orientation predominates. Internal conflicts, self-interests, and competition come under the scrutiny of the participant observer's eye.[1]

The second major approach, the Ivy League School or structuralist approach of occupational sociology (also frequently referred to as the functionalist school), followed the development of the Chicago School in time by about two decades. The advent of this competing school dates from the publication of Talcott Parsons' *The Structure of Social Action* in 1937.[2] Highly abstract and theoretical, this approach is much different from the descriptive ethnographies of the Chicago School. Professions are viewed as essentially stable institutions that reflect community values and goals. As such, they are considered most important to the occupational and social structure of society. The professions are emphasized as functioning units that perform certain needed tasks for society. The focus is on social structure, and occupations are important social institutions that provide underlying support for the society. Professions have certain unique characteristics or attributes that are a measure of professionalization. In contrast, the interactionist approach views a profession as a social control system that is supported by its own ideology and mystique. The emphasis is on social processes and change.

The third approach, the social class approach, is based on the Marxist definition of class as a nationally organized group with its own ideology and willingness to act. Theorists of this approach predict that the contradictions of capitalism will lead certain occupations to class formation and class action to transform the capitalist mode of production.

Because professions have been examined more than any other occupational groups, discussion of these approaches is aided by a large number of studies. From 1946 to 1959, studies of professionals comprised a majority of all articles on occupations found in major journals.[3] There are several reasons for this popularity. First, professionals are similar in socio-economic background to those who study them and thus are easier to associate with, especially in interview and fieldwork situations. Second, professionals are also likely to be more empathetic to the research goals of the sociologist—they share the same desire to discover and test. Third, the work of professional people is more glamorous and carries more prestige and consequently may affect the researcher's judgment as to whom to study.[4] Fourth, because the work of professionals is functionally important to society, some sociologists consider it necessary to know as much as possible about each of the professions. Fifth, more people are now in the professions (from 4 percent in 1900 to 14 percent in 1970). In addition, large numbers of professionals are employed in large corporate and union organizations, which creates new role conflicts that demand explanation and solutions. Finally, the attempt of other occupations to model themselves after the professions in order to attain wealth and status places the professions in a position where workers in many other occupations want a set of do-it-yourself instructions on how to professionalize. The structuralist approach of listing attributes seems to be particularly suited to meet this request, although it is not its manifest purpose.

THE STRUCTURALIST APPROACH

Most structuralists have approached the study of professions by either explicitly or implicitly constructing a continuum of the degree of professionalization of occupations. The characteristics commonly attributed to a profession are: a body of knowledge and a developed intellectual technique with a formulated systematic theory or set of theories. This knowledge is transmitted by a formalized educational process and testing procedure set up by members of the profession. A code of ethics governs relations with colleagues, clients, and the public. This formally establishes the set of values of the profession, in which a service orientation is emphasized. There is the idea of a career, a "calling" in the service of the public which, through authority in its sphere of knowledge, monopoly in all matters related to its service, and objectivity in its theory and technique, will advance social progress. On the basis of this the public will grant the profession its mandate, the formal recognition of status by means of state and federal licensing. The more of these attributes an occupation has and the more developed each of these attributes is, the more professionalized the occupation is.[5]   On this basis, occupations are charted on a continuum of professionalization (see Chart 9.1).

CHART 9.1 CONTINUUM OF PROFESSIONALIZATION OF OCCUPATIONS

DECREASING PROFESSIONALIZATION		INCREASING PROFESSIONALIZATION	
←		→	
Librarian	Social worker	Dentist	Physician
Stockbroker	Nurse	Chemist	Lawyer
Insurance adjuster	Chiropracter	CPA	Judge
Real estate sales-person	Vocational counselor		

Ritzer extends this continuum by stating that "*all* occupations can be placed on a continuum [of six attributes] ranging from the nonprofessions on one end to the established professions on the other."

1. General, systematic knowledge.
2. Authority over clients.
3. Community rather than self-interest, which is related to an emphasis on symbolic rather than monetary rewards.
4. Self-control through occupational associations, training in occupational schools, and existence of a sponsor rather than outside control.
5. Recognition by the public as a professional.
6. A distinctive occupational culture.[6]

Each of these "characteristics" in turn can be measured on a subcontinuum:[7]

1. Body of   Insights and
    abstract theory   practical knowhow

2. | Client unable to judge / or satisfy own needs | Customer judges own needs / and evaluates the ability of services or commodity to satisfy those needs |

	Client unable to judge	Customer judges own needs
2.	or satisfy own needs	and evaluates the ability of services or commodity to satisfy those needs
3.	The individual emphasizes	Individuals emphasize
	helping others (code of ethics, protecting client)	helping themselves
4.	Authority to control knowledge	No licensing—
	(licensing by community) provides autonomy	no autonomy
5.	Recognition on the basis of	No attainment—no
	attainment of previous four characteristics	recognition as a profession
6.	Training schools and formal and	No professional
	informal groups produce values, norms, and symbols	culture

It is Ritzer's hope that these definitions will ultimately be operationalized to measure quantitatively the degree of professionalization of an occupation. He suggests that the degree of general systematic knowledge will be most important in this measurement.[8] From the knowledge base a strong public relations effort by the occupation will be able to build public confidence that will support a mandate to grant authority over clients in all matters relating to that body of knowledge.[9]

Careers and Socialization

Structuralists view careers as predictable courses through organizations. They are organized "life-plans" that coordinate actions of the individual with reference to a definite goal; they are "functionally rational."[10] A major study headed by Robert Merton[11] of medical school students views these students as *tabula rasa,* as blank minds ready to be shaped by the norms and values of the major socializing institutions of medicine. Social norms *allow* persons to choose their occupations.[12] Once chosen, students adopt professional role models (of teachers or famous practitioners) that they set up as ideals with which to compare their own performance. The more professional the occupation, the more likely will entering students have a role model and the more likely will they not change careers.[13]

Occupational socialization is defined as the process by which people selectively acquire the culture of an occupation, that is, its values, attitudes, knowledge, and skills. "*Socialization* refers to ways in which *individuals* are shaped by their culture."[14]   Culture is a distinct and separable feature of the group. The individual develops the norms of this culture and applies them consistently.   This results in a basically harmonious social system of a profession in equilibrium, not conflict.   "There is a behavior norm covering every standard interpersonal situation likely to recur in professional life," which is not encountered in nonprofessional occupations.[15]

Professions as Communities

Structuralists view professions as relatively stable communities.   Its members have a sense of common identity, members have a permanent status, there is a common set of values and language, and the professional community has power over its members through recruitment and training.   Even bureaucratic organizations that employ professionals do not usually break the continuity of the professional community.[16]

Although structuralists do emphasize order and structure, it does not mean they ignore change.   Conflict within and encroachment among professions is discussed.   Moore notes that physicians have paid little attention to the mouth, so dentists have moved in; dentists have paid little attention to the feet, so podiatry has grown; podiatrists have ignored the eyes, so optometry has increased.   Jurisdictional disputes are common because of the new knowledge continually being developed.   It is rarely possible for a profession to keep control over a new specialty, particularly if that specialty challenges the currently accepted orthodoxy.   Some examples of challenges come from chiropracty, osteopathy, medical psychiatry, and clinical psychology.[17]   Goode emphasizes the encroachment on other professions being practiced by psychology, sociology, and medicine.[18]

Some Problems of the Structuralist Approach

Examining this "attributes" or "traits" model of professionalization presents many problems to the user.   Can one assume that occupations are unidimensional; that is, can they be placed on a single continuum on the basis of the attributes of a profession?   There are some high-prestige occupations that do not aspire to develop many of the characteristics of professionalization.   The occupation of mathematician, for example, does not emphasize several of the attributes of a profession, such as the service motive and a code of ethics.   So, where does it fit on the continuum?   How does one assign weights to each of the characteristics?   For example, what weight do we give to a code of ethics as compared to the body of knowledge?

The validity of each of the attributes has been questioned repeatedly by critics of this model.[19]   One points to the problem of overemphasis on the role of scientific knowledge resulting from the reliance on the medical profession as the model for a knowledge base.   For example, the law profession's body of knowledge is not scientific. It comprises a body of social norms and the procedures for their application.[20] It is not an internally consistent "system of abstract propositions that describe in general terms the classes of phenomena comprising the profession's focus of interest."[21] Under this definition, law is not a profession and neither is sociology. As Phillips points out, even if sociological data could be collected with little respondent bias, as it rarely is, sociologists have not been able to explain their data adequately. In empirical research they have explained only about 10 percent of the variance in dependent variables as caused by independent variables—not a reliable figure.[22] Yet both law and sociology are considered professions by the public.

The question of professional ethics remains a serious problem in the measurement of professionalization. Do ethical codes protect the client or are they really only a mask for greater professional control of the market for the client's services? For example, restrictions on advertising are found in the codes of many of the established professions. These restrictions presuppose that prospective clients know the weaknesses and strengths of the various professional practitioners or groups and can successfully pick the best qualified persons to serve them—a situation that is rarely, if ever, attained. Another labor market constraint is the regulation against "raiding"—offering employees of other professional firms jobs through the client or otherwise. Similar restraints exist for bidding for customer services.[23] Is not being able to bid for these services always in the best interests of the client?

Others have argued that a code of ethics is more than just an ideology serving the occupation; that it "informs the public that the profession has met and is meeting its responsibilities, it is also part of an implicit contract between a profession and members of society."[24] However, evidence from an increasing number of studies indicate that in cases where a new profession emerges, ethical codes serve the profession more than they serve the client.[25] It is part of a "defensive strategy" to present credentials in order to obtain licensing from the state. In the most advanced, accepted, and powerful professions the profession itself has control over recruitment, education, and certification. Daniels demonstrates that this control invites abuses within the system; that professionals are not sufficiently guided by their own ethics—that, for example, the importance of research is so overriding in the best medical schools that the study of clinical medicine suffers.[26]

The ideal-typical model of solo practice in a fee-for-service structure actually reduces the quality of services to the client instead of increasing it (through the development of autonomy over services). The solo professional's work cannot be reviewed easily. There is contact only with the client, who must review and judge the professional's work. But, in the professions, the only persons capable of judging one's work are other professionals and not the client. There is some suggestive evidence that there is better quality performance among professionals in group practice where there is controlled surveillance and supervision by peers and other related professional practitioners and also by clients. Daniels concludes that the existence of professional autonomy does not seem to support the contention that professional autonomy contributes to high standards of service. In fact, in real-life situations the more powerful the profession (in terms of autonomy), the more charges seem to be leveled against it for lack of client protection.[27]

The measurement of professional autonomy must also take into account the degree of bureaucratization of the organization in which most professionals work. For example, in practicing specialized medicine, autonomy is threatened by dependence on a large hospital bureaucracy. Colleague control can reduce a professional's autonomy regarding decisions made in reference to the client more than client control can. Also, specialists depend on the complex machines and administrative organization of work teams to carry out their tasks. The very circumstances that create autonomy (i.e., a special service that no others can do as well) also end up precluding autonomous practice. Thus it is that in many cases a given level of professionalization can be maintained only if an equilibrium can be maintained between it and a certain level of bureaucratization.[28]

Another problem is the lack of comprehensiveness of the list of attributes. One attribute that is rarely included in the list, effective interpersonal relations, is very important in some professions. This is especially true in university teaching, in which personal traits such as congeniality, cooperativeness, and general likeability are extremely important. In a content analysis of a sample of 110 letters of recommendation for faculty candidates to departments of chemistry and English, Lionel Lewis found these personal factors to be the capital concern of the employing professionals.[29]

Still another problematic area is concerned with the large jump from nonprofessional to professional occupations. There just does not seem to be a gradual climb into full professional status. Some writers have noted that if an occupation does not have an adequate body of knowledge, all else seems to founder. William Goode has shown[30] that librarians have no firm knowledge base and thus they are not recognized by the public as a profession, where complex intellectual activities are taking place when the public is not there. The public, or the officials who grant licensing, must *believe* that a valuable service is being performed before it will grant any measure of autonomy or freedom from lay supervision and control. It believes presently that libraries, but not librarians, are important to society. Libraries are like supermarkets. Everything is self-service. Thus, concludes Goode, what really distinguishes professions from nonprofessions is autonomy in their area of expertise.[31] This is accomplished gradually by means of a professional ideology, which helps to gain legitimate control over work, and not by various traits or attributes.[32]

To summarize the structural model of professions, professions are service occupations that: "(1) apply a systematic body of knowledge to problems which (2) are highly relevant to central values of society."[33] This creates special problems of social control, because lay persons cannot judge professional performance. The two most common forms of social control, bureaucratic supervision and customer judgment, are useless in this situation. The emphasis is instead on the professional's self-control, as developed in a long socialization process into the ethics of the profession and supplemented by colleague pressures. In return for the selflessness of the professional, society grants privileges such as high income and prestige and protects the professional's autonomy from lay interference and control. This is accomplished by norms that restrict certain forms of competition, laws against quacks (nonlicensed practitioners), and the like.[34]

Structuralists have also indicated that the development of professions is affected by attitudes and beliefs. Following the work of Hall,[35] Ritzer has suggested that the six characteristics of a profession have both structural and attitudinal (individual) components. *Professionalization* represents a measurement of the six structural characteristics of an occupation, whereas *professionalism* represents a measurement of six individual characteristics within an occupation.[36] The latter are the same as the six subcontinua measuring professionalization, except that they refer to individuals' attitudes regarding the profession. A particularly good example of professionalism is the phenomenon of professional socialization, where students are taught the skills, norms, and values needed for them to view themselves and to be viewed by others as professionals. Professionalism measures how an individual feels about an occupation. These attitudes really do not have much effect on professionalization unless the occupation "continually fail[s] to adequately socialize its new members."[37]

Thus, professionalization is affected very little by attitudes and beliefs. More important, professionalism is limited to how persons in their own occupation perceive themselves. There is no reference to how others perceive the occupation—a key explanatory factor of Chicago School theorists.

THE INTERAC-
TIONIST AP-
PROACH

Interactionists view a profession as a set of role relationships between expert and client. The expert provides an esoteric skill in a service given to a client. The client in return gives trust and payment of an equitable fee. The key factors, as set forth by Everett Hughes in numerous essays, are: (1) autonomy of the professional in the work setting (i.e., autonomy, or freedom from control over one's work), and (2) trust of the client that the professional is working in the best interests of the client. "A profession [as a type of occupation] is a social role defined by the nature of the relationship between the professional and his client."[38] Professing to know certain skills better than clients and professing to use them for their clients' benefit *and* having clients believe this is the basis for the claim for the exclusive right to practice in a given area. The motto is not *caveat emptor* (let the buyer beware), but *credat emptor* (let the buyer believe in us). This gives the professional the authority over this area of knowledge—the most important characteristic of a profession.[39]

Often, the professional's exclusive work takes the form of bearing the burden of the client's guilty knowledge. For example, the lawyer, policeman, physician, reporter, scientist, diplomat, private secretary—all keep knowledge that a lay person would be required to reveal. "Most occupations rest upon some bargain about receiving, guarding, and giving out communications. The license to keep this bargain is the essence of many occupations."[40] Often again, exclusive work is "dirty work," either mental or physical. The physician must deal with disease; he is responsible for bringing people back to health (health is cleanliness). Ranking in the medical occupations is by degree of cleanliness: physician, nurse, practical nurse, nurse's aide, hospital attendant.[41] The process of making an occupation professional often includes the attempt to transfer dirty work to some other workers in the field.[42]

Because clients are not familiar with the knowledge of the professional, they are not in a position to judge for themselves the quality of the services received. They are protected from their own incompetence by giving the right to perform the service over to the professional. In return, professionals are protected from their own incompetence (mistakes) and from allegations that they make them by the fiction that all licensed practitioners can be judged only by their peers.[43]

Professions and Power

To maintain the autonomy of a profession in order to protect it from outside control, its body of knowledge must remain secret, a mystique must be built up around its practices. This is more common among the applied professions, which "pursue knowledge to improve practice" than among those that pursue knowledge merely to increase knowledge—the academic professions.[44] The ability to make good judgments in uncertain situations is the mark of a true professional. A study of orthopedic surgery residents disclosed that the emphasis in training and practice in this specialty is on the great deal of uncertainty stemming from four areas of work, all of which require good judgment on the part of practitioners. Decisions are not scientifically based, that is, on a simple deductive conclusion arrived at logically after considering certain obvious alternatives. Instead, decisions are reached on the basis of what works best in the face of ambiguous circumstances. These include:

1. *The body of knowledge:* Regular meetings are held to point out how solutions to essentially the same problem are reached on the basis of choosing vastly different alternatives—the "gray areas" of the knowledge. For example, the Journal Club is a group that meets monthly, at which time residents present an exhaustive review of the literature involving certain selected cases.
2. *Unique characteristics of the physician:* Decisions may vary depending on what works best in the hands of the individual practitioner.
3. *Unique characteristics of the patient:* Any social, psychological, or physical characteristics that are different.
4. *Situational constraints:* These are constraints such as administrative policies, relationships with other staff members (e.g., sharing responsibility for patient with anesthesiologist), work pace, and work load. These external constraints are considered the dirty work of the occupation by these physicians.[45]

To insure autonomy, professionals will often attempt to strengthen the mystique of the profession by introducing new and complex ideas and practices. This is especially true of professions threatened by computerization and by the rationalization of the body of knowledge. CPAs have entered some areas of management consulting and actuarial work as they find more of their traditional auditing work computerized and simplified.[46] Similar patterns of rationalization among supervisors in a French industrial plant have occurred without any follow-up of new knowledge by the supervisors. The loss of professional autonomy in this instance was significant.[47] This phenomenon will be examined in greater detail later in this chapter and in Chapter 10.

Careers and Socialization

Careers are defined by Hughes as an "immense area of problems, embracing a great many of the problems of formation of social personality and adjustment of individuals to their social surroundings." In contrast to the structuralist definition and the one given in this book, a career is a broad concept, involving a person's entire life processes in which the individual chooses from among alternative activities while moving in time and age within the institutional system in which the occupation exists.[48] A person's career is his "ultimate enterprise, his laying of his bets on his one and only life."[49]

Another term, *status passage,* is used to link the concept of careers to occupational socialization. Status passages are sets of mutually accepted behavior patterns that facilitate easy acceptance of norms and beliefs about aging and career development of individuals.[50] In contrast to structuralists, interactionists perceive occupational culture as arising from role performance and role relationships and not from organizational-regulatory mechanisms of social control. As Becker and others show in their study of midwestern medical students,[51] individuals experience new situations that are constantly changing. Individual perspectives can become long-term group perspectives if enough persons accept them. However, unlike norms, these perspectives are not "imperative." Medical students will follow a particular "mood" and will maximize generalized values. For example, they will absorb new knowledge according to how their peer group (either fraternity or married) perceives the kind of knowledge necessary for their role as physician. These cultural perspectives are stable, but they are changeable if new role performances or new problematic situations are introduced that require a new perspective to be formulated. Culture is not a distinct and separable feature of the group.[52]

In an examination of symphony orchestra musicians and major league hockey players, Robert Faulkner demonstrates that careers are sequences of status passage by which persons come to grips with the objective reality of their position in their work organization and occupation.[53] Age is a critical variable in completing this analysis. Faulkner shows how employee turnover into and out of the "major league" (the elite organizations within occupations) differentiates occupations. In hockey only one of every three major league players (in the 14 National Hockey League teams) had been in the League 6 years or more, whereas three of every four major symphony orchestra musicians had (Boston, Chicago, Cleveland and Philadelphia symphonies, and the New York Philharmonic Orchestra).

The average length of stay in the major league for musicians is 18 years, for hockey players 5 years. The promotion of hockey players from the minor leagues is much more rapid. Sixty percent of all those promoted to major league hockey had been promoted before they were 24 years old. Only 1 in 10 stay to become regulars. Only 1 in 3 stay 6 years or more. They move up young, there is high attrition, and they stay for only a short time. In contrast, musicians stay at the top longer and have a much lower rate of attrition from the major to minor orchestras. However, in both occupations, the launching of a successful career in the majors takes place over a very short span of time—in the early twenties for hockey players and by the early thirties for musicians.

This means that there are heavy demands placed on the worker to be recognized by management and to demonstrate talent quickly. Along with the knowledge that one's chances will deteriorate rapidly as time passes, this puts an enormous strain on persons as they grow older without promotion.[54] The same pattern is experienced by some academic professions. For example, in physics and chemistry, high performance is expected early in one's career—well before age 40. In history it is just the opposite. One is not expected to reach one's peak of productivity (i.e., publication) until after age 40.[55]

The typical status passage of individuals in hockey and symphony orchestra music is one of high expectations up through the twenties (the period is about twice as long for musicians as it is for hockey players—10 years versus 5), followed by a period of indecision and then, in their thirties, the construction of new mobility outlooks and motivations. Regarding the latter, the workers define their situations as one of "relative success." They do not make it to the top, so they rationalize their position by emphasizing the roots they have laid down in the community with family and friends and the price one must pay for being in the big league (constant traveling, uncertainty over the future for hockey players, etc.). These function as a "cooling out" process for those who fail to make it. This allows one to admire those who do make it without being bitter about not making it oneself. Also, the occasional older person who does make it holds out hopes for all older workers that someday they, too, might make it.

In moving from one job to another, professionals may move downward in mobility organizationally but in the process may experience personal upward or horizontal mobility. For example, a third violinist in a major league orchestra can move upward in personal mobility by accepting a first violin position in a "minor league" orchestra, although it is downward mobility, organizationally.[56] The author also discovered that when relatively large numbers of people are taken into the elite groups on a trial basis, as they are in music and hockey, there will be greater dissatisfaction regarding their social mobility. Because more people have been allowed at least a temporary spot in the major leagues, the expectation is developed that everyone be given this chance. The expectation is not met and dissatisfaction is the result.[57]

Careers, then, are "a basic activity through which knowledge of an occupation is detected and displayed." The reality of the occupational world is seen. It is "occupational adulthood," the coming of occupational age. Contingencies of status passage (e.g., promotion and demotion processes) are linked to persons' beliefs and the social organization of success and failure. In addition to a symbolic interactionist examination of "changes in the mobility motivations, purposes, and expectations of the individual,"[58] Faulkner views status passage in terms of hierarchical settings in organizations and their mobility routes. This combination helps to uncover the interrelationships between the organizational contexts of occupational mobility patterns and the career concerns of individuals.

Faulkner has attempted to do for interactionists what Ritzer has attempted to do for structuralists: to relate the individual to the social structure. Faulkner charts the occupational behavior of individuals by using the concept of status passage. Ritzer has used the concept of professionalism to incorporate individual phenomena into the analysis. Interactionists, however, give this latter term of professionalism a much different emphasis.

Professions, Professionalization, and Professionalism

Interactionists define professionalization as a process comprising three basic activities:

1. The founding, proliferation, or transformation of an institution in which a new profession and other interested occupations struggle over their respective roles in the new areas of work.
2. The development and strengthening of a training school, first outside and then inside the university.
3. The standardization of schooling, which acts as a basis for licensing to work in the occupation.[59]

A profession is not a structure, nor is it a state of mind. It is a social object. It is not the rules, but the activity that gives the profession its social reality. People agree to its existence and its legitimacy and then act accordingly.[60]

Professionalism, on the other hand, *is* a state of mind.[61] Professionalization is what actually exists; professionalism is what is legitimated by society or its representatives, regardless of what exists. It is an ideology, a system of shared beliefs and values that legitimate the collective claims of the profession and of those outside the profession.[62] Professionalism is an advocacy, not a behavioral fact. As such, it serves as a political force to protect and enhance the position of the profession in society. As one view states: "Professionalism is ...a label used by occupations to win power and prestige."[63]

Professionalism is what is thought about a profession. But because what is thought about it in large part defines what it is and what it gets in terms of power and prestige, professionalism greatly affects an occupation's ability to professionalize (to become licensed, set up a training school, control new areas of knowledge, etc.). Professionalism is the internal pressure to organize and set up a code of ethics. Professionalization is the measure of depth and adherence to the code. Professionalism is what practitioners *say* about their honesty. Professionalization is *a measure* of how honest they are.

Professionalization is also a process. As the result of professionalism, it "represents the efforts of some members of a vocation to control and to monopolize their work. They will seek to wrest power from those groups that traditionally have controlled the vocation."[64] The objective is to attain collective mobility of members of an occupation. Those who are unwilling or unable to be mobile are turned out of the occupation. Those in control do not give up the fight to maintain the social movement. Thus, professionalization is often a militant process.[65]

The professional ideology is important to all aspects of the maintenance and development of an occupation. The range and diffusion of the public stereotype will determine to a considerable degree the number and variety of persons an occupation can recruit.[66] A profession's belief in its autonomy will determine what actions it will take as a group in order to professionalize. Autonomy, the key variable in measuring professionalization, is itself an important ideology.[67]

A good example of professionalism exists in the medical profession. Physicians have obtained direct control over the development and maintenance of the body of knowledge and the specialized expertise resulting from it. There is a high degree of autonomy. In a comprehensive analysis of the American medical profession, Eliot Freidson concludes that physicians receive autonomy when state officials *believe* that their profession has attained certain attributes, whether in fact they have. They then confer on it a mandate and license to control its work.[68]

Control of knowledge also can lead to attempts to mystify knowledge in order to keep it away from the public and other professions. Freidson describes how medicine began to compete strongly with religion and law in the nineteenth and twentieth centuries. With areas such as hysteria, neurosis, and depression being defined as illnesses instead of sin or crime, medicine has narrowed the limits if not weakened "the jurisdictions of the traditional control institutions of religion and law."[69]

However, social control over different areas of knowledge can fluctuate historically. In 1914, federal legislation made heroin use a crime and thus took away drug addiction treatment from the medical profession. But the growth of methadone maintenance in response to the tremendous increase in heroin addiction in the 1960s allowed the medical profession to regain much of the control over addiction. The profession contends that addiction is a metabolic disease and as such belongs in the realm of medicine.[70]

Like control of knowledge, control over training in imparting that knowledge is an important aspect of professionalism. The amount and duration of training is secondary in importance to control of the training process. "Power and persuasive rhetoric are of greater importance than the objective character of knowledge, training and work."[71]

Also, there is no reliable information to indicate that the service orientation is a strong and widespread attribute among professionals. "It too, like training, can be deliberately created so as to attempt to persuade politically important figures of the virtues of the occupation."[72]

Professions as Coalitions

Whereas structuralists view professions as well-integrated communities, interactionists view them as subgroups or segments that are in conflict with one another. A segment in a profession is a coalition that is in opposition to other coalitions. A large part of its activity is a power struggle for the profession of institutional arrangements or some kind of place within them. Professions are "loose amalgamations of segments pursuing different objectives in different manners."[73] Even though they are organized under a common name and work for a common cause, they are less a community than they are "extensive coalitions, which ... frequently run the risk of fragmentation and even

dissolution." Professions are constantly changing. They are "temporary rest-
ing places within a historical stream of events."[74]

Interactionists emphasize the centrality of power as an explanatory variable in examining professions. As such, a historical and comparative analysis
of occupations is emphasized. Professions are classified into three major
"streams" of professionalization:[75] (1) those of medieval origin (law, ministry,
medicine); (2) those that developed later from lower-order occupations to professional occupations (accounting, psychiatry, architecture); and (3) the recent
emergence of scientific occupations to professions (chemistry, physics, engineering). Conflict often occurs between occupations in these three categories.

THE SOCIAL CLASS AP-PROACH

In reviewing the analyses of professions as social classes, the Marxian definition
of social class will be used as the basis for measurement. A social class is a
group of people with basically the same economic life chances, organized
society-wide, and who have their own ideology, cultural configuration, and
propensity to act. As discussed in Chapter 2, conventional American definitions
include only the first of these characteristics. Occupational prestige, as measured by the NORC scale and Duncan Socio-Economic Index, is taken to be
the measure of social class, since social class becomes synonymous with social
status. In the major analyses of U.S. class structure by Warner, Hollingshead,
the Lynds, and Centers, the economic base of stratification is measured by
occupation.[76] Duncan's objective measure of social status, obtained by measuring the income and education of those in a given occupation, is highly correlated to the findings of the NORC study. These occupational ratings are
easily translated into social class categories of upper class, middle class, working class, and the like by the reseacher (the "objective" technique of stratification). Or, less commonly, the social class categories obtained by techniques
used in the earlier community studies (i.e., the subjective and reputational
techniques, as defined in Chapter 2—see "Occupational Prestige") are assigned
occupations on the basis of occupational prestige scales or even the U.S.
Bureau of the Census occupational classification system.

Most recent studies of the U.S. class structure continue in this tradition,
which means that income and education are accorded primary importance.
One of the best known analyses is by Peter Blau and Otis Dudley Duncan.[77]
A large number of these status group studies support the human capital theory
that ability plus education lead directly to class (i.e., occupational) mobility.
However, Blau and Duncan do point to variations by race. As I document in
Chapter 11, a few U.S. sociologists (e.g., C. Wright Mills and G. William Dom-
hoff) have attempted to uncover the weaknesses of this approach by examining

what they consider to be the basis for a national upper class by utilizing the Marxist definition of social class. However, it is not until the limited and selective effects of education are documented by recent empirical studies (see Chapter 17) that the dominance of the "status group" emphasis has begun to decline and the "social class" emphasis has gained momentum.

The large majority of adherents of both emphases do not view the professions *per se* as a social class. They are not considered to be united in belief and action. The emphasis in the professions is on separation, autonomy, and the individual career.[78] Talcott Parsons argued that professions are not groups that put forth a new social ideology. They function like businessmen, primarily in their self-interests.[79] Or, as Robert Merton has declared, professionals do not have to feel altruistic but only must act altruistic because the professional community has institutionalized altruistic behavior.[80]

The most fully developed argument that occupations, and especially professions, are not the basis for social classes is given by Joseph Bensman and Robert Lilienfeld. They say that occupational perspectives do not necessarily lead to class perspectives. Occupations at similar status levels may have entirely different rates of growth, expansion, and decline and thereby differentially color the perspective of the worker.[81] Workers do not develop a similar consciousness from similar experiences because they perceive the same experiences (social relations) in different ways. A prime example is the ability of an artist, psychoanalyst, or intellectual to serve either the elite or the masses. There is no consciousness of a common fate to pull workers together because the conditions of true exploitation do not exist. Nor does the ideology, usually developed by the intellectuals, help them to unite.[82]

Social class is a phenomenon of collective action. A bureaucracy, on the other hand, attempts to have its members identify their ideas and interests with the organization instead of engaging in collective action.[83] As partial bureaucracies, the professions are not organized as a social class. Nor do most writers think they will be. Their view is that not only the interests of bureaucracy but also self-interests prevent this organization. The most that can be hoped for is sets of conflicting interest groups.

However, others see the possible successful combining of certain segments of professional workers with other occupational workers into a functioning class structure. The ideas of two of these theorists have already been discussed in Chapter 3. Gartner and Riesmann see a vanguard class of service workers who are developing a consciousness of their common fate as secondary workers and as consumers. They are the minorities, women, and young people in the human services occupations, including lower-level occupations and some professions. They conclude that the very strength of neocapitalism will produce the seeds of its change when the service worker as consumer becomes alienated from work and dissatisfied with consumption.[84]

The core of the "new working class," as it is called by many, is for Touraine the public health experts, consulting engineers, accountants, educators, and skilled workers.[85] Harrington suggests that the professional-managerial-clerical groups plus the blue-collar group, if joined together by a belief in the socialization of corporations into publicly owned and directed collectives, could become a new working class majority to forge a political economy of humanistic organization.[86] Anderson finds a new working class consciousness developing amongst white-collar people who work in production-related scientific and technical jobs and whose moderate earnings are not derived from "surplus created by others' labor."[87]

Radical Marxists believe that professionals are coopted into the elite group and are therefore not part of the new class. Braverman sees a constantly growing working class, now comprising 7 of every 10 workers in the country (not including professional and technical and managerial occupational groups). This class is defined as those persons who sell their services to capital in return for their subsistence.[88] Flacks says that the social class movement will not be led by occupational organizations and groups but by the family, especially through the women's liberation struggle, which is attempting to transform at the level of values the role of the mother and the functions of the family.[89]

The more moderate and more radical interpretations do not hold out much hope for societal change through professionalization. The professions represent nothing more than another form of labor market segmentation, a balkanization of occupations, which promotes level consciousness instead of class consciousness. Those who fall somewhere in between are optimistic that a strong collective movement among professions will develop as the contradictions in the capitalist economy reach their extreme forms. Some suggest that the continued combined high unemployment and high inflation in the United States will initiate this movement.

One example is the situation of chemists. Between 1961 and 1970, the consumer price index for chemists of middle-range income rose 29 percent, whereas their income increased by 47 percent. However, chemists under 25 earned less than $7000 yearly (four-person family income) and had a 25 percent unemployment rate.[90] Thus, certain professionals (older white males) may be developing as part of the national upper class (see Chapter 11), but others within the same profession are becoming part of a new working class movement. In the case of the established professions, practically all members have well-paid, secure positions.

Therefore, the professions are split along the dimensions of a dual-labor market instead of as an autonomous class or stratum. This will also be true of other occupational groups, as I point out in succeeding chapters. If it materializes, the "new working class" will be comprised of the disaffected workers from across the occupational spectrum. Professions, then, are much the same as any other occupational group, with the exception that more of them are generally in higher power positions than nonprofessional occupations.

SUMMARY AND CONCLUSIONS

There are three basic approaches used to study the professions: interactionist, structuralist, and social class. They are also known as the Chicago School, the Ivy League School, and the Marxist approaches, respectively. The interactionist approach follows symbolic interactionist theory quite closely, whereas the structuralist is based on functionalism. The social class approach relies mostly on conflict theory. The primary basis for explaining occupational stratification for each approach is social power (interactionist), social status (structuralist), and social class (social class). As noted in Chapter 2, these three bases are the major elements for grading people socially.

Structuralists generally view the professions as containing attributes not present in other occupations or present only to a minor degree. In its emphasis on structure and stability, this approach has ignored the ideological component of professional occupations, that is professionalism. Interactionists have shown clearly how professionals often are able to use professionalism, that is, to obtain legitimation of their work without necessarily possessing the attributes required for such legitimation. Because of this, there quite often is conflict within and between professions.

Adherents to the social class approach perceive in this conflict the ultimate disenchantment of some professionals and intellectuals, who will then become part of the growing new working class. In the remaining chapters, this book demonstrates that along with the professions, other occupational groups contain workers who for reasons of poverty or alienation are prime candidates for this class.

FOOTNOTES FOR CHAPTER 9
THE PROFESSIONS: APPROACHES TO THEIR STUDY

[1] The major writings of Hughes are collected in his *The Sociological Eye*, 2 Vols. (Chicago: Aldine-Atherton, 1971).

[2] Talcott Parsons, *The Structure of Social Action* (New York: McGraw-Hill Book Company, 1937).

[3] Erwin O. Smigel et al., "Occupational Sociology: A Reexamination," *Sociology and Social Research*, 47 (July 1963), 474.

[4] These are listed by Smigel, et al., "Occupational Sociology ...," p. 474.

[5] Among the more notable sources listing these attributes or traits of a profession are: Abraham Flexner, "Is Social Work a Profession?" in *Studies in Social Work*, No. 4 (New York: The New York School of Philanthropy, 1915); Alexander Carr-Saunders and P. A. Wilson, *The Professions* (London: Oxford University Press, 1933), pp. 284-287; Ernest Greenwood, "Attributes of a Profession," *Social Work*, 2 (July 1957), 44-55; Richard H. Hall, "Bureaucratization and Professionalization," *American Sociological Review*, 33 (February 1968), 93; Wilbert E. Moore, in collaboration with Gerald W. Rosenblum, *The Professions: Rules and Roles* (New York: Russell Sage Foundation, 1970), Chapter 1; George Ritzer, *Man and His Work: Conflict and Change* (New York: Appleton-Century-Crofts, 1972), p. 331; William J. Goode, *Explorations in Social Theory* (New York: Oxford University Press, 1973), Chapter 14.

[6] Ritzer, *Man and His Work*, pp. 49, 54.

[7] Ritzer, *Man and His Work*, pp. 54-63. Moore, *The Professions*, also depicts professions as being measurable on subcontinua.

[8] George Ritzer, "Professionalisn and the Individual," in Eliot Freidson (ed.), *The Professions and Their Prospects* (Beverly Hills, Calif.: Sage Publications, 1973), p. 67.

[9] Ritzer, *Man and His Work*, p. 61.

[10] Karl Mannheim, *Man and Society in an Age of Reconstruction*, Rev. Ed. (New York: Harcourt, Brace & World, 1940), p. 56.

[11] Robert K. Merton, George Reader, and Patricia L. Kendall (eds.), *The Student Physician* (Cambridge, Mass.: Harvard University Press, 1957).

[12] Natalie Rogoff, "The Decision to Study Medicine," in Merton, Reader, and Kendall (eds.), *The Student Physician*, p. 109.

[13] Wagner Thielens, Jr., "Some Comparisons of Entrants to Medical and Law School," in Merton, Reader, and Kendall (eds.), *The Student Physician*, pp. 131-152.

[14] Merton, Reader, and Kendall (eds.), *The Student Physician*, pp. 287-290.

[15] Sigmund Nosow and William H. Form (eds.), *Man, Work, & Society* (New York: Basic Books, 1962), p. 215.

[16] William J. Goode, "Community within a Community: The Professions," *American Sociological Review*, 22 (April 1957), 194, 197.

[17] Moore, *The Professions*, pp. 178-179.

[18] William J. Goode, "Encroachment, Charlatanism, and the Emerging Profession: Psychology, Sociology, and Medicine," *American Sociological Review, 25* (December 1960), 902.

[19] For a summary of several criticisms see Julius A. Roth, "Professionalism: The Sociologist's Decoy," *Sociology of Work and Occupations, 1* (February 1974), 6-23.

[20] Dietrich Reuschemeyer, "Doctors and Lawyers: A Comment on the Theory of the Professions," *Canadian Review of Sociology and Anthropology, 1* (February 1964), 21.

[21] Greenwood, "Attributes of a Profession," p. 46.

[22] Derek L. Phillips, "Sociologists and Their Knowledge: Some Critical Remarks on a Profession," *American Behavioral Scientist, 14* (March-April 1971), 563-582.

[23] Joseph A. Pichler, "An Economic Analysis of Accounting Power," in Robert R. Sterling (ed.), *Institutional Issues in Public Accounting* (Lawrence, Ka.: Scholars Book Co., 1974), pp. 61-64.

[24] Dean S. Dorn and Gary L. Long, "Brief Remarks on the Association's Code of Ethics," *The American Sociologist, 9* (February 1974), 34.

[25] Arlene Kaplan Daniels, "How Free Should Professions Be?" in Freidson (ed.), *The Professions and Their Prospects*, pp. 45-46.

[26] Daniels, "How Free Should Professions Be?" pp. 49-51.

[27] Daniels, "How Free Should Professions Be?" pp. 54-56.

[28] Richard H. Hall, "Professionalization and Bureaucratization," *American Sociological Review, 33* (February 1968), 104.

[29] Lionel S. Lewis, "The University and the Professional Model," *American Behavioral Scientist, 14* (March-April 1971), 541-562.

[30] William J. Goode, "The Librarian: From Occupation to Profession?" *The Library Quarterly, 31* (October 1961), 306-318.

[31] Goode, "The Librarian: From Occupation to Profession?"

[32] Eliot Freidson, *Profession of Medicine* (New York: Dodd, Mead & Co., 1970), pp. 79-82.

[33] Reuschemeyer, "Doctors and Lawyers...," p. 17.

[34] Reuschemeyer, "Doctors and Lawyers...," p. 18.

[35] Hall, "Professionalization and Bureaucratization."

[36] George Ritzer, Gale Miller, Richard Bell, and Virginia McKeefery, "The Current Status of Occupational Sociology," Paper presented at the annual meetings of the Midwest Sociological Society, Omaha, Nebraska, 1974, pp. 20-22.

[37] Ritzer, "Professionalism and the Individual," p. 71.

[38] Everett C. Hughes, *Twenty Thousand Nurses Tell Their Story* (Philadelphia: J. B. Lippincott, 1958), p. 236.

[39] Everett C. Hughes, "Education for a Profession," *The Library Quarterly*, *31* (October 1961), 336; Everett C. Hughes, "Professions," *Daedalus, 92* (Fall 1963), 657.

[40] Everett C. Hughes, "The Study of Occupations," in Robert K. Merton, Leonard Broom, and Leonard S. Cottrell, Jr. (eds.), *Sociology Today* (New York: Basic Books, 1959), p. 449.

[41] Hughes, *The Sociological Eye*, Vol. 2, p. 307.

[42] Hughes, *The Sociological Eye*, Vol. 2, p. 314.

[43] Everett C. Hughes, *Men and Their Work* (New York: The Free Press, 1958), pp. 46-55.

[44] Hughes, "The Professions," p. 660.

[45] Gary Burkett and Kathleen Knafl, "Judgment and Decision-Making in a Medical Specialty," *Sociology of Work and Occupations, 1* (February 1974), 82-109.

[46] Paul D. Montagna, *Certified Public Accounting: A Sociological View of a Profession in Change* (Lawrence, Ka.: Scholars Book Co., 1974), Chapter 8.

[47] Michel Crozier, *The Bureaucratic Phenomenon* (Chicago: University of Chicago Press, 1964), pp. 100-107.

[48] Hughes, "The Study of Occupations," pp. 457-458.

[49] Hughes, *The Sociological Eye*, Vol. 2, p. 406.

[50] Barney Glaser and Anselm Strauss, *Status Passage* (Chicago: Atherton, 1971).

[51] Howard S. Becker et al., *Boys in White: Student Culture in Medical School* (Chicago: University of Chicago Press, 1961).

[52] Becker et al., *Boys in White*, pp. 431-432. For a concise summary of several of these points see Philip Elliott, *The Sociology of the Professions* (New York: Herder and Herder, 1972), pp. 82-89.

[53] Robert R. Faulkner, "Coming of Age in Organizations: A Comparative Study of Career Contingencies and Adult Socialization," *Sociology of Work and Occupations, 1* (May 1974), 131-174.

[54] Faulkner, "Coming of Age in Organizations."

[55] Theodore Caplow and Reece J. McGee, *The Academic Marketplace* (New York: Basic Books, 1958).

[56] The aborted World Football League would have allowed much more upward personal (through downward organizational) mobility for professional football players. The lack of an organized minor league prevents such a possibility presently. Once a person is out of college he has no opportunity to remain in national professional football unless he remains in the major league.

[57] Faulkner, "Coming of Age in Organizations," pp. 151-152.

[58] Faulkner, "Coming of Age in Organizations," p. 134.

[59] Anselm Strauss, *Professions, Work and Careers* (San Francisco: The Sociology Press, 1971), pp. 69-70.

[60] Ralph L. Blankenship, "Professions, Colleagues, and Organizations," in Ralph L. Blankenship (ed.), *Colleagues in Organization* (New York: John Wiley & Sons, in press). For structuralists, a profession is definitely a social fact, that is, it is a separate material entity with structure and institutions. See George Ritzer, *Sociology: A Multiple Paradigm Science* (Boston: Allyn and Bacon, 1975), p. 73. Two writers have affirmed the social factist position, theoretically, in recent books. Arnold S. Tannenbaum et al., *Hierarchy in Organizations* (San Francisco: Jossey-Bass, Inc., 1974), p. 205, concludes that "social structure rather than interpersonal relations is the more substantial basis for understanding outcomes such as the distribution of reactions and adjustments within a system." Peter M. Blau, *The Organization of Academic Work* (New York: John Wiley & Sons, 1973), reaches this conclusion in the preface to his book. He notes that his previous position that social structure was socio-psychological is now reversed, that social theory requires a conceptual framework of macro-sociological properties—of the characteristics of organizations, societies, and other collectivities—and necessarily excludes interpersonal factors because the theory would not be "consistent," that is, interpersonal factors would be too complex and cumbersome, impossible to test.

[61] F. J. C. Seymour, "What Is Professionalism," in Howard M. Vollmer and Donald L. Mills (eds.), *Professionalization* (Englewood Cliffs, N. J.: Prentice-Hall, 1966), p. 129.

[62] The definition of ideology is from Burkhart Holzner, *Reality Construction in Society*, Rev. Ed. (Cambridge, Mass.: Schenckman Publishing Co., 1972), Chapter 10.

[63] Marie R. Haug and Marvin B. Sussman, "Professionalism and the Public," *Sociological Inquiry, 39* (Winter 1968), 57. Ritzer has expanded his analysis by stating that the characteristics of the professions are either derived from the power of the professions or do not actually exist in given professions, but that people have been convinced that these characteristics do exist. George Ritzer, "The Emerging Power Approach to the Study of the Professions," paper presented at the Annual Meetings of the American Sociological Association, August 24-30, 1975.

[64] Ronald G. Corwin, *Militant Professionalism: A Study of Organizational Conflict in High Schools* (New York: Appleton-Century-Crofts, 1970), p. 8.

[65] Corwin, *Militant Professionalism,* p. 44.

[66] Howard S. Becker and Anselm L. Strauss, "Careers, Personality, and Adult Socialization," *American Journal of Sociology, 62* (November 1956), 255.

[67] Phyllis L. Stewart and Muriel G. Cantor, *Varieties of Work Experience* (New York: John Wiley & Sons, 1974), pp. 356, 359. Roth, "Professionalism: The Sociologist's Decoy," says that attributes merely serve to enhance and protect the standing of an occupation.

[68] Eliot Freidson, *Profession of Medicine* (New York: Dodd, Mead, 1970), pp. 186-187. In a structuralist analysis, William Goode, *Explorations in Social Theory*, pp. 345-373, also agrees that autonomy is important but then locates the key factor, the "substance of the problem," in the personal relations with the client. The more "the client *must* allow the professional to know intimate and possibly damaging secrets about his life if the task is to be performed adequately," the more professional the occupation. This ends up in the confusing situation where aeronautical engineering is more intimate than social work and veterinary more intimate than nursing or chiropracty. He concludes that close personal relations between client and practitioner prevent any strong professional ideology from developing to overtake the public.

[69] Freidson, *Profession of Medicine,* p. 249.

[70] Ron Miller, "Towards a Sociology of Methadone Maintenance," in Charles Winick (ed.), *Sociological Aspects of Drug Dependence* (Cleveland: CRC Press, 1974), pp. 169-198.

[71] Freidson, *Profession of Medicine,* pp. 78-79.

[72] Freidson, *Profession of Medicine,* pp. 81-82.

[73] Rue Bucher and Anselm Strauss, "Professions in Process," *American Journal of Sociology, 66* (January 1961), 326.

[74] Strauss, *Professions, Work, and Careers,* p. 77.

[75] Strauss, *Professions, Work, and Careers,* p. 77.

[76] See W. Lloyd Warner and Paul S. Lunt, *The Social Life of a Modern Community* (New Haven: Yale University Press, 1941), p. 81; August B. Hollingshead, *Elmtown's Youth and Elmtown Revisited* (New York: John Wiley & Sons, 1975), p. 55, first published in 1949; Robert S. Lynd and Helen Merrell Lynd, *Middletown* (New York: Harcourt, Brace & Co., 1929), p. 21; Richard Centers, *The Psychology of Social Classes* (Princeton: Princeton University Press, 1949), Chapter 6.

[77] *The American Occupational Structure* (New York: John Wiley & Sons, 1967).

[78] Elliott, *The Sociology of the Professions,* p. 61.

[79] Talcott Parsons, "The Professions and Social Structure," *Social Forces, 17* (May 1939), 457-467.

[80] Robert K. Merton, *Some Thoughts on the Professions in American Society,* Brown University Papers No. 37 (July 8, 1960), p. 13. See also Joseph Ben-David's review of the functionalist position in his "Professions in the Class System of Present-Day Societies," *Current Sociology, 12* (1964), p. 248.

[81] Joseph Bensman and Robert Lilienfeld, *Craft and Consciousness: Occupational Technique and the Development of World Images* (New York: John Wiley & Sons, 1973), p. 2.

[82] Bensman and Lilienfeld, *Craft and Consciousness,* pp. 171-172.

[83] Reinhard Bendix, *Work and Authority in Industry* (New York: John Wiley & Sons, 1956), p. x.

[84] Alan Gartner and Frank Riessman, *The Service Society and the Consumer Vanguard* (New York: Harper & Row, 1974), pp. 26-27.

[85] Alain Touraine, The *Post Industrial Society* (New York: Random House, 1971).

[86] Michael Harrington, "Why We Need Socialism in America," *Dissent, 17* (May-June 1970), p. 276.

[87] Charles H. Anderson, *The Political Economy of Social Class* (Englewood Cliffs, N. J.: Prentice-Hall, 1974), pp. 125-126.

[88] Harry Braverman, *Labor and Monopoly Capital: The Degradation of Work in the Twentieth Century,* Special issue of *Monthly Review, 26* (July-August 1974), 111.

[89] Richard Flacks, "Strategies for Radical Social Change," *Social Policy, 1* (March-April 1971), 7-14.

[90] Martin Oppenheimer, "The Proletarianization of the Professional," in Paul Halmos (ed.), *Professionalisation and Social Change,* The Sociological Review Monograph No. 20 (Staffordshire, England: University of Keele, December 1973), pp. 216-217.

10 THE PROFESSIONS: LABOR MARKET STRATIFICATION

Although the professions are among the most dominant occupations in their share of wealth, prestige, and power in the occupational system, there are significant differences *within* the professions regarding these factors. Labor market stratification by sex and race explains a large part of these differences. These differences within professions are also reflected in the amount of alienation experienced by professionals. In addition, the amount of alienation will fluctuate with changes in the size of the organization in which professionals work—with increased size and complexity there is more conflict between professional and administrative authority. Social changes in professional occupations are conditioned by both labor market discrimination and the conflict of authority. Each of these areas is examined for its impact on professional change.

SEX STRATIFICATION

There is no question that the professions are sex typed. Approximately two-thirds of all persons in the semiprofessions are women, whereas only one-tenth of all persons in the professions are women.[1] Despite the expanding job opportunities for women in the early 1970s, they still are not entering the traditionally male professions to any great extent, nor do they appear to be preparing for them. Of the total persons awarded bachelor's degrees as of June 1972, only 7 percent of the

women majored in science and mathematics, compared to 24 percent of the
men. On the other hand, almost 50 percent of the women majored in education (semiprofession), but only 11 percent of the men chose this major.[2]

Sex Typing within Professions

Just as there are male and female professions, there are male and female
specialties within professions. Women lawyers are concentrated in family law,
trusts and estates, and domestic relations. Women physicians are found mostly in pediatrics, psychiatry, and public health medicine. Public health allows
for the compatability of the sex and professional roles: regular work hours,
manageable work load, no need to build a practice, and the immediate income
that comes from it. There is liberation from the entrepreneurial role and
there is association with males who also dislike that role.[3] The nurturant role,
the "woman-as-servant" image, is fulfilled in these specialties.

Women who strive to attain a high occupational position find themselves
in a "double bind." In order to attain such a position a woman must emulate
masculine characteristics considered essential for the job. Upon doing so, she
is labeled "unfeminine" or "aggressive"; by traditional male values she is less
desirable as a wife or a companion. If, on the other hand, she does not
adopt the masculine characteristics, she is considered inadequate for the job.[4]

ACADEMIC WOMEN. College and university teaching has long been a
male-dominated profession. Women presently comprise about 20 percent of
the American academic faculty. They are located mostly in the smaller colleges and universities and in the lower ranks at these institutions. Even at the
training level discrimination is evident and has been on the increase. In 1920,
women comprised 47 percent of undergraduates in the United States and 15
percent of the Ph.D.s. By 1970 they made up only 40 percent of undergraduates and 10 percent of Ph.D.s.[5] Between 1958 and 1963 women Ph.D.s in
academia earned about $700 a year less than men Ph.D.s.[6] By 1968 the gap
had increased to $1200.[7] Women also are less likely to be given tenure or
to be promoted, especially in the sciences. They are found in lesser proportions
to their numbers in the sciences and in greater proportion to their numbers in
the humanities and education. All this, even though women have published
as much as men and are as active, generally, on committees and in other related
professional work.[8]

In a study of women political scientists in prestige departments in western
U.S. colleges it was found that women are placed outside the academic prestige system. Only 5 percent of these departments are staffed by women,
mostly in lower-level positions. In those departments, of all the teaching
Ph.D. candidates, only 2 percent are women[9] —not much of a model for aspiring women Ph.D. candidates. The key point for career advancement is at the
point of entry into graduate school: admissions. There is a great deal of

discrimination against women candidates at this point. In addition, there is a significant self-selection factor where women take themselves out of the race by not applying. They have high anticipatory fears caused by their realization of discrimination.[10]

A national study of academic women in sociology disclosed similar circumstances. Women sociologists made up only 5 percent of the full professors at graduate departments of sociology in the United States in 1972.[11] There are more women in lower positions in sociology than in the other fields; therefore, their median salary is that much lower than males as compared to other fields. In 1968 the salary differential between males and females in sociology was $1700, compared to $1200 for all fields.[12]

Women students in sociology are constantly reminded that a woman has to be "better than men" in order to be accepted for graduate school.[13] Once in graduate school, they find very few career models. Their chances of having a female teacher are only about 1 in 10.[14] Promotions for married women are even fewer. The feeling of the (mostly male) appointments committee is generally that married women will not have the necessary long hours to devote to a career. Therefore, they are not good risks. One woman candidate reported about her interview that:

Not one question at lunch was directly related to my work. They wanted to know what kind of arrangement I had with my husband, who baby-sat when, and what we did when the children were sick.[15]

And, in a reverse of the "women-as-a-sexual-object" image, Caplow and McGee give the following example:

We had one young woman come down here from one of the Big Ten. She had the M.A. and was working on her doctoral dissertation and we would have very much liked to have gotten her, but when she saw the Dean, he turned her down. He didn't like the way she was turned out, thought she was too stylishly dressed. We had thought she looked very lovely.[16]

The idea that married women are not as productive is just a myth. In fact, they are as much or more productive than men, even with their added family responsibilities.[17] Many did not even interrupt their careers. More than 7 out of every 10 women who received Ph.D.s from 1957 to 1958 had not interrupted their careers up through 1964.[18] Considering the marriage statistics of this group, some of these most certainly were married and others had children. When comparing positions attained at higher academic ranks in colleges and universities, it was found that not only are men Ph.D. sociologists favored over women Ph.D. sociologists, but also that those in the latter group who were unmarried were chosen more frequently for the higher ranks than the married.[19]

WOMEN IN SCIENCE AND ENGINEERING. A recent analysis of American scientists and engineers revealed that males in these professions score higher in creativity and lower in people orientation than females. Women tend to maintain the values impressed on them at an early age, an indication that one's values do not necessarily determine one's career choice.[20] However, this seems to be true only of those women who are determined to stick it out in these male-dominated professions. Most women are eliminated from competition long before they even would consider these occupations as a possible choice of career. Their personality characteristics seem to lead them away from these professions. For most women, then, values do determine their choice of occupation.

Alice Rossi points out that the major characteristics of outstanding scientists are just those that are basic to the socialization of boys and not of girls: (1) high intellectual ability; (2) persistence in work to produce personal satisfaction; (3) extreme independence; and (4) low interest in social activities. Boys are encouraged to stand on their own, to aim for a high goal. Girls are prompted to be cooperative and responsive to people and to minister to their needs. Thus, women who do manage to become scientists are more frequently found teaching science than doing science.[21] In a major study of occupational choice in the 1950s, Rosenberg concluded that the occupational value of orientation toward people is the most important one differentiating career choices of men from women. Women tend to work with people and men with things.[22] All the studies of scientists and engineers in this section indicate that this is true even with professions.

David sees a further insidious socialization of women to their subordinate role as members of the professions of science and engineering.[23] Men tend to set up an "intellectual double standard" in which women are considered inferior in the important characteristics of the field, even though in some cases they may be superior. Women's creativity is ignored because it is simply not seen as part of the female role. Also, their people-oriented role is perceived as useless at best and possibly harmful. The author suggests that an important reason for this male hostility is that experience has shown that once women begin to enter an occupation in large numbers, the prestige of that occupation drops. Men feel they are only trying to protect the social status of "their" occupation.[24]

DUAL-CAREER FAMILIES. Having a profession means several things. It means wholehearted dedication to one's career: a willingness to move at any time your employer asks or to stay put when that is necessary; the requirement of a proper address in a certain section of town or suburb; and only one member of the family is permitted to work in the same organization (rules against nepotism). All these factors support the assumption that only one member of a family can have a career and that the interests of all the other members will be subordinated to it.[25]

In an in-depth study of 20 couples in which the wife had a Ph.D. and an independent career, Holmstrom found that in a majority of cases the husband's job was seen as more important than the wife's when deciding where to live. Only in a few cases was the situation reversed. Usually, the wife had to take the risk—the couple would move before the wife had located a position or even before she had job hunted.[26]

The budgeting of time becomes extremely important in dual-professional career families because most professional occupations demand long work hours and a rigid schedule that requires that both professionals be at work at the same time. Thus, duties of child care cannot be shared. The isolation of the nuclear family (no relatives present) also requires that a parent or some substitute be with the children when both parents are working—which is usually all day.[27]

With regard to family roles, Poloma and Garland note that there are no significant changes in the dual-career family. The woman careerist still plays the subordinate, nurturant role. Only when the wife's income (not education or occupational achievement) exceeds the husband's are the power relations shifted in favor of the wife in the American family. The husband's dominant role is clearly threatened. No wives in the sample wanted to earn more than their husbands, even though some, in fact, did.[28]

The wife's taking on a professional role does not mean a dramatic change for the family. In no cases did research detect a genuine equality of role tasks. The wives were expected to keep their domestic roles of housecleaner, child care, and cooking, and the husbands would assist when necessary. "Wives are constrained by their own idea of ideal feminine roles." The consequences are: first, they must channel their energies into two roles—home and profession; and second, they cannot give enough time and energy to plan and work at their careers, thus making professional success more difficult.[29]

The continuing increase in the number of hours worked by professional people further complicates the difficulties encountered by women in these dual-career families. Finally, the fact that upward mobility in professional careers occurs early in the career further reduces the limited chances of married professional women. It is at this time that the husband will be most likely to move, that the family may move to the suburbs (where fewer jobs are available), and that children will be born. All these contribute to the obstruction of women's career development.

CONCLUSIONS. The argument that discriminatory practices alone cause certain professions to become sex typed is a very weak one. A considerable amount of self-imposed exclusion occurs, even to the point of self-delusion. A study of women professionals in civil service and industry showed that these women are socialized to the point that they measure their career progress in terms of those women who have not made it instead of comparing themselves to their male peers.[30] In all probability, these very women are also discriminated against. They have had to be superior professionals just to compete with the "average" male professional. It is very likely they should be in even higher positions than they are.[31] But women generally consider their own sex inferior even when the facts do not support the belief, especially when it involves intellectual and professional competence. This is true not only of male occupations but of female occupations, too, including popular occupations such as elementary school teaching and dietetics.[32]

Although there is little or no public support for sex-typing occupations, there is still a value system that operates to keep women out of the higher positions and occupations. Women perceive, correctly for the most part, that the opportunity structure in our society is biased against them. They are encouraged by males to train in traditionally female occupations, and they are denied access to male-dominated training schools in the higher professions.[33]

The value system of highly educated and highly trained women does not allow them to internalize occupational values to the extent that men do. Values and attitudes toward the sexual division of labor, especially regarding the organization of the family system, have to change before there can be any significant change in the female professional labor force.

Although married professional women still have primary responsibility for children, their role responsibilities in the home are decreasing. At the same time, their husbands are spending even more time in occupational pursuits. This unbalanced set of role allocations can only bring added problems to the family. Many feel that solutions such as maternity leave, child care centers, antidiscriminatory legislation, and the like are mere palliatives that do not confront the issues.[34] They hope that the educational system will provide the basic structure and forum for the redefinition of sex roles, especially those in the family. Perhaps here women themselves will be able to take an active role in changing the underlying value system.

Sex Stratification between Professions

Because most occupations that large numbers of women work in are "women's occupations," other occupations that work in close synchronization with them are carefully ranked higher in prestige, power, and income. Physicians have authority over nurses, administrators over public school teachers, and academic professionals over librarians.

The structure of authority is nowhere clearer than in the relationship between physicians and nurses in a hospital. Anselm Strauss details this relationship in the psychiatric wing of a Chicago general hospital.[35]

The psychiatrists are quick to manifest their authority over the nurses when the situation demands it. However, in daily practice, the nurse is given much freedom of decision regarding the patient, depending on the particular method of practice of the attending physician. The somaticist is more medically oriented (primarily using drugs and electrotherapy shock treatments) and tends to utilize the psychiatric nurses in more traditional medical fashions—simple nursing care and patient management. The ex-resident relies more on psychotherapy, including the use of the ward as a therapeutic device. In this "ward strategy" he must rely on the nursing staff to give the patient a proper milieu for therapy. Some ex-residents do give more weight to their own psychotherapy treatments; others give almost equal weight to the involvement of other patients and the staff. The latter will rely on nurses to "place" the patient in the right section of the right ward—whatever they consider to be the best therapeutic setting. But the nurse is always perceived to be in a subordinate position.

The complexity of the hospital bureaucracy requires several hierarchical levels of physicians and nurses. The M.D. unit administrator of a ward is overseen by the M.D. unit coordinator. The unit coordinator in turn receives general policy decisions from the hospital's central administration. The psychiatric unit's staff nurses receive orders from the physicians, and their work schedules are organized by nursing supervisors, who in turn are administered by the assistant head of services. Staff nurses, in turn, have authority over nurses aides, nursing assistants, and practical nurses.

The two hierarchies (physicians and nurses) are separate, but there is no question as to where final authority lies. The usual point of contact is the interaction between the unit administrator and the staff nurse. However, for emergency cases and other unusual situations, higher-level personnel become involved. At this point lines of communication become involved and often confused regarding who is responsible for which decisions with respect to patient care. For example, a physician may persuade a unit resident to urge the staff nurses to "work on" an unruly patient and to attempt to block a potential transfer. Sometimes such an agreement may mushroom into a problem where nurses become unwilling to "give up" on the patient. Finally, the nurses' actions are overruled, although usually with reluctance, by a unit coordinator or an even higher administrator.

THE SITUATION
OF BLACKS

Bureau of Census statistics for 1973 indicate that 7 percent of the black labor force were professional and technical workers compared to 14 percent for whites (see Tables 5.2 and 5.3). But if one looks at the proportion of blacks in the higher professions as compared to whites (see Table 5.4), a different picture emerges. Blacks are found in disproportionate numbers in the least professionalized professions or, as they are referred to in this book, the semiprofessions (e.g., social workers and elementary school teachers). One writer suggests that because blacks have established a beachhead in the semiprofessions, they should aspire to this level instead of attempting to enter the professions which, for the most part, are still unachievable by blacks due to past and, in some cases, present discriminatory practices. The generational mobility pattern for black professionals has been from manual labor to clerical positions, then to the semiprofessions. The final step to the professions should take place with the next generation of black workers.[36]

A brief examination of recent data analyzing minority recruitment in sociology is another indicator of just how limited the number of blacks is in the professions today. In 1967 there were only 121 black Ph.D.s in sociology, only 6.5 percent of all sociology doctorates.[37] Since there are more than 200 graduate departments of sociology in the United States, black graduate students in sociology would have very little opportunity to receive encouragement from professionals of their own minority group. There has been almost no improvement of black representation in sociology since the 1960s. In 1974, the percent of black faculty members in graduate sociology departments was 4.9 percent of all faculty. Those at the full professor level were only 2.6 percent of the total full professor faculty.[38] Also, new black Ph.D.s in sociology in 1970 averaged about 3 percent of all Ph.D.s granted during that year. This percentage has not changed up through 1974.[39]

The Special Case of Black Professional Women

From an analysis of census statistics, Bock has concluded that black women have an "unnatural superiority" in the American labor market. Seven percent of black female workers were in the professions in 1960, whereas only 3 percent of black male workers were.[40] This phenomenon occurs because black women are less feared sexually and are less threatening occupationally.[41] Therefore, they are better prepared through enculturation to adapt to the white-dominated world. Parents see that there are more opportunities for black females than for black males, and they see higher education as a better investment for the female. Therefore, daughters are given preference in education and, as a result, are better prepared for migration to urban areas. These women went into public school teaching jobs especially, whereas males were better prepared for factory employment and manual labor. As a result, the median income of black professional women is higher than that of white professional women and poses a threat to the black male's masculine role of chief breadwinner.[42]

The black male is severely limited in the number and types of jobs open to him. He has a better chance of obtaining work in professions open to women than in entering professions open to whites.[43] Black females, then, have more of a chance to break out of the secondary labor market than any other minority group workers. But, even for them, it is a difficult process and is the exception, not the rule. However, Bock's theory of the "farmer's daughter effect" does not apply to persons already within an occupation. Interviews with young black men and women psychologists disclosed that more women felt restrictions on their careers than men.[44]

Black Physicians

The black physician has had to struggle under very difficult circumstances in order to become a licensed physician. As of 1970, the U.S. census lists only 5200 black physicians, 1000 of them women. Michel Richard describes how in earlier times they were turned away from white medical schools, hospital affiliations, membership in professional associations, and white patient referral networks.[45] Because 90 percent of their patients are black, black physicians do not receive as high incomes as white physicians. Consequently, they do not have the money to support training in a medical specialty, which ultimately would increase their income. They even had great difficulties in starting a practice during the depression of the 1930s. There were many instances in which new M.D.s accepted work in other occupations until they could build up a clientele. One physician recalls how he worked as an elevator starter at Macy's after receiving his degree. Another told of his job as a railroad dining car waiter.[46]

Richard points out that this rigid pattern of discrimination is now beginning to change. More black physicians, especially the younger ones, are now members of the American Medical Association, the major professional association of American doctors. Also, most are now hospital affiliated, even if mostly in black hospitals, and an increasing number have a reciprocal arrangement of patient referrals with white colleagues.

Richard notes that this coopting of black physicians into the white power structure was interpreted by E. Franklin Frazier and Frantz Fanon as another form of internal colonialism. They are part of an intellectual elite of a minority group, and they could lead this group out of its lowly position. However, because they are relatively privileged, they have taken on some of the worst features of their oppressors.[47]

Even though some resistance to change has developed, Richard describes how black physicians as a whole were found to be more change oriented and liberal than their white colleagues. They desired more group practice and more government participation in the health services professions.[48] Futhermore, even though black physicians were found to be more upwardly mobile than white physicians (and, accordingly, they would be more conservative according to social mobility theory), they were more liberal than their white colleagues. Also, the more status discrepancy[49] experienced by black physicians, the more liberal they were found to be. This relationship remains unchanged regardless of the degree of social mobility of the physician.[50] This appears to disprove the radical theories of Frazier and Fanon, who suggested that the willingness to follow the orders of the majority group goes with high status, even when their own minority suffers.

There are studies that contradict these findings, however. Back and Simpson discovered that black students training for the professions differ in their attitudes toward open competition from whites. Those from higher-income families tend to want more protection from open competition, and those from lower-income families want less protection.[51]

In a similar study David Howard interviewed black dentists, lawyers, physicians, and public school teachers.[52] He found that they were ambivalent about open competition with whites; they were "considerably less than enthusiastic." The author interprets this to mean that black professionals have their own monopolies on services in ghetto areas. They want to keep the status quo in order to maintain their relatively high incomes and standard of living; they do not want to lose them to white competition. Their dilemma is that, on the one hand, they are obligated to show commitment to the democratic ideal of open competition but, on the other, they have special interests in their minority group that inhibit open relations and favorable attitudes toward competition with whites. But their democratic commitment prevents them from expressing this hostility toward open competition—thus, the ambivalence.[53]

In a much broader analysis, Will D. Tate reviews the rise of the new conservative middle-class black professional during the 1960s. Its source of growth was the large expansion of center-city funding projects (e.g., model cities) and the implementation of civil rights laws in governmental agencies. This large group has more to lose in wealth and prestige than the "traditional" (pre-1960) black professional and, as a result, is less willing to accept social and institutional changes.[54]

In summarizing this research on black professionals, one dilemma is apparent. Although younger black professionals appear to be becoming more change oriented and liberal, at the same time there is the enticement offered by a closed market for their services. Although through their professionalizing they now constitute an important potential elite of leadership, they are in danger of succumbing to the internal colonialism described by Frazier and Fanon.

WORK
ALIENATION

The enormous literature on alienation expresses the significance that people attach to it. It is, however, a very broad concept and, as is the case with all such terms, has many meanings. An excellent summary of the history and development of the concept is given by Israel.[55] Alienation can refer either to individuals or to social structures. Most American sociologists have used it at the individual or psychological level, listing five basic states: powerlessness, meaninglessness, normlessness, isolation, and self-estrangement. At this level we deal with the *process* of estranging; alienation is a subjective phenomenon.[56]

On the social structural level or sociological level, alienation is viewed as a *state* of estrangement. It is an objective phenomenon in that a researcher can study observable behavior of individuals. In this sense the study of alienation is also psychological. However, the observations of individuals are seen to be independent of the persons being observed. That means that the interpretation of the researcher may not agree with his or her subjective state. The assumption here is the Marxist one: the individuals may be unable to realize that they are alienated.[57]

The sociological level emphasizes the impossibility of individuals attaining their goals because they are blocked by society. Discussion usually involves how to *change* society to meet these goals. Theories developed are primarily conflict theories. At the psychological level, emphasis is put on social demand that cannot be met by individuals because they are deviating from society's norms and rules. The consensus needed to maintain equilibrium is not reached because of a lack of individual *social adjustment.*[58]

Work commitment and work alienation are opposite sides of the same coin of involvement. Involvement can be defined as the absorbing, emotional occupying of one's self, either positively (commitment) or negatively (alienation).

Nearly all research indicates that the more professionalized the occupation, the less alienated and more committed are those in it.[59] The more personal autonomy people have in work, the more involved they are in their occupation. However, this relationship tends to vary by type of organizational structure.[60] The more rigid organizations, those that experience a greater degree of centralization, codification, and enforcement of rules, have the more alienated professionals. This is true for professionals working in health and welfare agencies,[61] for priests and their assistants,[62] and for engineers in the aerospace industry.[63]

The relationship made between occupation and involvement in work can also be made for occupation and involvement in leisure; that is, the more professionalized the occupation, the more involved the person is in leisure activities. From a Marxist point of view, people who are not alienated from themselves and their work are more productive and human and thus are able to be positively involved in their work. This position, of course, necessarily assumes that organizational structure at work (and in leisure) will affect the relationship in leisure just as it does work. If people are made dull and weary by their work, it will also affect their ability to become creatively involved in leisure.

In addition, those whose needs are frustrated at work may vary in the type of leisure involvement attained. In a 1957 national sample of the adult

U.S. population, Veroff and Feld found that persons who experienced frustrated achievement motivation in work (inability to feel a sense of accomplishment or self-expression) do not seem to be able to compensate with achievement in leisure. On the other hand, those who have a frustrated affiliation motivation (inability to be with or see people with whom one works) seem to easily compensate with affiliation gratification in leisure.[64]

The conceptual difficulties increase when some persons (especially those in professional occupations) say that their work is their leisure. Not only do professional people spend more time at their work than any other occupational group,[65] they also tend to choose work over leisure, given a theoretical extra 2 hours in a day.[66] Professional people also tend to mix work with leisure. The weekend away is often combined with a convention or with visits to clients, the evening cocktail party to meet prospective clients, and the golf game to close a contract.

Is leisure "rest for work's sake," a need peculiar to the capitalist state, or does it have intrinsic value as an end in itself? Marx viewed the ideal state as one in which leisure took the place of work as the measure of an individual's wealth. On the basis of his analysis of capitalism, he concluded that work deprives the worker of any satisfying activity. Work is external to the worker, imposed by the social conditions of capitalism. It is not the worker's work but work given over to the owner for the creation of private property. Humanity is self-estranged, alienated in capitalist society.[67] In modern terms, people do not have a "central life interest" in their work, with the exception of the more prestigious occupations.[68]

PROFESSIONAL CHANGE

There are many factors impinging on the process of professionalization, helping to create change. Ronald Corwin has analyzed the struggle for control of administration and teaching in American high schools.[69] He states that professionals engage in conflicts more frequently than nonprofessionals. They are more innovative. They create new ideas and produce new objects or events that collide with accepted practice and create conflict. Professionalization is often a militant process that creates a reaction of increasing bureaucratization. Attempting to professionalize a highly bureaucratized, publicly supported occupation such as public school teaching is likely to provoke militancy.[70]

There are some exceptions to this rule. Increased professionalization in the more bureaucratized *and* professionalized schools results in less conflict than in those schools in which professionalization is developing and on the increase. Bureaucratization helps to contain conflict in the least professionalized schools and, conversely, highly professionalized persons tend to police themselves and do not need to resort to more militant stands.[71]

Corwin concludes that organization is a response to the forces of bureaucracy and professionalization. The more highly organized the system, the more bureaucratic it is. "Organization evolves in reaction to conflict; the greater the external and internal threat to the organization, the more highly organized the system will become. Bureaucratization is the product of this race between organization and control."[72] Chart 10.1 displays the two extremes of this conceptualization.

CHART 10.1 DEGREE OF ORGANIZATION OF OCCUPATIONS

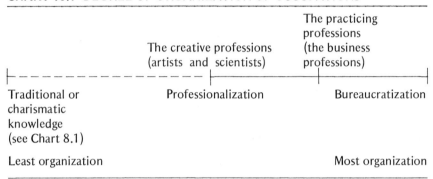

In and of itself, bureaucracy most likely is not a threat to professionalization and is not a major cause of deprofessionalization.[73] Instead, there is something about the process of professionalization itself that leads to deprofessionalization, that is, the rationalizing of the body of knowledge, of which bureaucratization presents the extreme case and professionalization the intermediate case.[74]

In a different but related discussion, Albert Mok describes the two major role models in the professions: the producers of knowledge and the users of knowledge. The former create new knowledge and the latter are the appliers of knowledge.[75] Looking at Chart 10.1, we can place the creative professions to the left on the continuum of organization of occupations and the applied professions to the center. Looking back to Chart 8.1, the continuum of rationalization, one can see that Corwin's conceptualization of organization covers the right half of that continuum. Mok's creative professionals practice innovation by extension, whereas the applied professionals practice innovation by rationalization.

Mok summarizes his observations, stating that the tendency of the emerging postindustrial society is for the professionals to choose the role model of the user of knowledge. Scientists, more and more engaged in large-scale projects, have become more dependent on governmental aid and thus tend to gear their studies to governmental problems and to finding practical solutions to these problems instead of "transforming" knowledge. In addition, the public puts pressure on the professional to *use* science for its benefit and not to stay aloof in the ivory towers of basic knowledge studies.[76]

There are two major results of this condition. First, the professional becomes highly dependent on the government or the public. Autonomy is threatened as a system of client patronage builds up. Any organization of professionals as a social movement is required by the funding institutions to be ameliorative instead of radical in intent.[77] The political and economic elite become the ultimate client. Freidson contends that all professions are found in this category:

> *A profession attains and maintains its position by virtue of the protection and patronage of some elite segment of society which has been persuaded that there is some special value in its work.*[78]

The second result is that although postindustrial society depends on innovation by extension, it is creating the very conditions for its destruction by structurally not promoting that innovation.[79] The rationalization of society has increased and, conversely, professional autonomy has decreased as goals, tasks, products, and services become more certain (specifiable) and are specified by others, as the knowledge base becomes more rationalized (i.e., standardized and routinized and thus more generally available and accessible to clients, audiences, and markets), and as professional control over resources is restricted or shifted to other power groups (e.g., owners, managers, boards of trustees).[80] As the knowledge occupations decrease, occupational authority decreases.

Most studies show that the greater the professionalization, the greater the receptivity to change.[81] However, among professionalizing occupations, there is a notable rejection of change, at least among the members of these occupations who emphasize professionalism. Those more committed to an ideology are more likely to feel threatened by rapid change.[82]

In terms of who they serve—the middle class and especially the elite—the professions have always been known to be defenders of the status quo. The defenders of the disadvantaged and the poor are in the small minority. The Perry Masons and Marcus Welbys are part of the professionalism of the majority, the corporate lawyers and the Park Avenue psychiatrists who serve those who can afford their higher fees. Social workers and psychiatrists working in the areas of drug abuse have been able to "decriminalize" certain behavior by developing a legitimate treatment plan for their middle-class patients in place of the usual sanctions against criminality. They will plead difficult work pressures or family conflicts to explain a client's behavior and will obtain judgment in favor of the treatment plan. The court will often define the middle-class person's breaking of a societal norm as noncriminal, but the same action by a lower-class person will be seen as criminal. The helping professions are, then, a halfway house toward decriminalization, especially for the middle and upper classes.[83]

The case of physicians is even more apparent. In some ghetto areas of the New York City SMSA there are fewer than 10 doctors per 100,000 people, while the average for the SMSA as a whole is over 200 doctors per 100,000 people. In Great Neck, a rich suburban community in the New York City SMSA, there are about 750 doctors for each 100,000 people.[84]

There are also structural constraints on an occupation's willingness to change. Wilensky discusses how highly stable careers in the middle ranks of the professions and administrative occupations attract people who value security instead of high risk and independence. This is caused by the structural attributes of certain types of organizations and occupations that are growing in number in advanced industrial societies:

1. Organizations with tall hierarchies; careers with many stages affording a quick and steady climb.
2. Organizations with a high ratio of managers to managed. These have careers with administrative posts at the end.
3. Organizations with a history and prospect of continued growth, for example, an organization or occupational group that produces a wide variety of products and services (e.g., a diversified conglomerate that serves to cushion against fluctuating demand) or an indispensable service in continual demand (e.g., education).
4. Long, prescribed training in a professional school or executive training program.
5. Multiple units, geographically scattered.[85]

Labor market analysts also have pointed out that many occupations are locked into their present positions by their sex, age, and minority group stratification. Because they are so heavily discriminated against, "female occupations" are at a distinct competitive disadvantage. Practices of licensing and sex typing keep nurses, airline hostesses and secretaries out of the running for the jobs of physician, airline pilot, or executive. These sheltered male occupations are rarely breached.

To conclude, there are at least two ways in which occupations react to external impingements. The first is a method to prevent change, that is, to severely limit access to its body of knowledge, to build a mystique around its functions. Uncertainty is thereby maintained; problems remain unanalyzable, and the profession becomes oriented to the status quo. A corollary to the first is for the profession to limit strictly the number of risks it is willing to take. By controlling the production, development, and application of its body of knowledge, it can control its risks.

A second way of reacting is to attempt to change by increasing the exceptions to routine production. This means developing new knowledge or taking over knowledge from another area by maintaining a high degree of unanalyzability in the profession. Taking some of our previous examples from Chapter 9, public accounting moves into management consulting and architecture moves into administrative services.[86]

Taking more risks by attempting to professionalize new areas of knowledge is becoming more difficult in our highly organized, highly rationalized society. With increasing specialization, the professions become fractionated into small groups of experts. The development of "basic" science or innovative art is seriously compromised in the university as methods of application and productivity norms become emphasized. The development of expertise has similar consequences for the applied professions.[87] As each specialty becomes more developed, as the knowledge base becomes more rationalized, the power that goes with control of that knowledge is reduced. Psychologists are worried when many of their principles are codified for lay training of teachers and parents in counseling. CPAs are concerned when their annual audit is partly computerized and is called the "annual nuisance." As Crozier emphasizes:

> The expert's success is constantly self-defeating. The rationalization process gives him power, but the end results of rationalization curtail this power. As soon as a field is well covered, as soon as the first intuitions and innovations can be translated into rules and programs, the expert's power disappears.[88]

Finally, we should be aware that the various factors affecting group and role autonomy of professions—bureaucracy, the political system, technology—make it impossible to draw a simple linear progression of professionalization.[89] Any of these factors may aid professionalization as well as hinder it. The continuum models used in this and other chapters are only graphic illustrations of a very complex schema of interrelated societal organizations and forces, a constantly changing multidimensional kaleidoscope.

SUMMARY AND CONCLUSIONS

The professional labor market is stratified by age, sex, and race. Especially noticeable is the degree of sex typing within professions, as studies in the academic and health-service professions point out. Less advertised but as commonly practiced is the sex stratification between professions. Males tend to become physicians and physical scientists; women tend to become nurses and social scientists. Race stratification in the professions is also quite apparent. Therefore, once conflict occurs within or between professions for control over a body of knowledge, the professions or segments within that are dominated by white males are most successful.

Chapters 9 and 10 have demonstrated that, as a whole, professions provide autonomy and reduce alienation. They provide ideologies to protect that autonomy, and they innovate to counteract the loss of power.

However, despite their striking growth during the last 50 years, the professions do not operate as a strong political or social force in U.S. society. In fact, unionization, as a collective mode of social mobility, is strongly competing with professional associations, especially in the lower-level public service occupations. Although one sociologist sees the personal service professions as enabling humanity to devote more attention to serving its personal needs, to healing its soul, and to developing shared participation,[90] others see professional judgment as a threat to democratic principles because it allows only the expert to make decisions—an elitist view of social order.

As professionals are found more and more in large organizations, they face the power and authority of management. Whether professionals are able to gain more power in the near future will depend on the extent to which management can determine the character of the task, who will perform it, the way it is to be performed and evaluated, and the way it will be related to other occupations. If management does control these processes, then administrative authority will predominate. If the division of labor is developed and controlled by the occupations into which work is organized, that is, by licensing and control of knowledge, then occupational authority will predominate.[91] However, there are many indications that adjustments can be and are being reached between the two.

Conflicts exist within and between the professions both in terms of labor market stratification and in terms of the bureaucratization of the organizations in which professionals work.

FOOTNOTES FOR CHAPTER 10
THE PROFESSIONS: LABOR MARKET STRATIFICATION

[1] Athena Theodore, "The Professional Woman: Trends and Prospects," in Athena Theodore (ed.), *The Professional Woman* (Cambridge, Mass.: Schenkman Publishing Co., 1971), p. 4. The definition of profession used here is limited to the "higher" or "traditional" professions such as law, medicine, university teaching, and the clergy, and the new "full" professions that are given high status by the public and that are fully professionalized in terms of attributes (e.g., scientists, CPAs, and architects). The semiprofessions (e.g., social work, nursing, engineering, and public school teaching) are discussed in Chapter 12.

[2] U.S. Department of Labor, Bureau of Labor Statistics, *Educational Attainment of Workers, March 1973*, Report No. 161, p. 60.

[3] John Kosa and Robert E. Coker, Jr., "The Female Physician in Public Health: Conflict and Reconciliation of the Sex and Professional Roles," *Sociology and Social Research, 49* (April 1965), 294-305.

[4] Jane Prather, "Why Can't Women Be More Like Men?" *American Behavioral Scientist, 15* (November-December 1971), 172, 180.

[5] Patricia Albjerg Graham, "Women in Academe," *Science, 169,* No. 3952 (1970), 1284-1290.

[6] Rita James Simon, Shirley Merritt Clark, and Kathleen Galway, "The Woman Ph.D.: A Recent Profile," *Social Problems, 15* (Fall 1967), 227.

[7] Michael A. LaSorte, "Sex Differences in Salary Among Academic Sociology Teachers," *American Sociologist, 6* (November 1971), 305.

[8] Simon, Clark, and Galway, "The Woman Ph.D."

[9] Joyce M. Mitchell and Rachel R. Starr, "A Regional Approach for Analyzing the Recruitment of Academic Women," *American Behavioral Scientist, 15* (November-December 1971), 191.

[10] Mitchell and Starr, "A Regional Approach for... Academic Women," pp. 195-198.

[11] Helen MacGill Hughes (ed.), *The Status of Women in Sociology 1968-1972* (Washington, D. C.: American Sociological Association, 1973), p. 31.

[12] LaSorte, "Sex Differences in Salary," p. 305.

[13] Helen MacGill Hughes (ed.), *The Status of Women in Sociology 1968-1972,* p. 20.

[14] Alice Rossi, "Status of Women in Graduate Department of Sociology, 1968-69," *American Sociologist, 5* (February 1970), 6.

[15] Helen MacGill Hughes (ed.), *The Status of Women in Sociology 1968-1972,* p. 34.

[16] Theodore Caplow and Reece J. McGee, *The Academic Marketplace* (New York: Basic Books, 1958), p. 107.

[17] Simon, Clark, and Galway, "The Woman Ph.D.," p. 231.

[18] Graham, "Women in Academe."

[19] Sylvia F. Fava, "Marital Status and the Status of Women in Professional Sociology." Paper presented at the Annual Meetings of the Society for the Study of Social Problems, New Orleans, La., August 26, 1972.

[20] Deborah David, "Male Values and Female Professionals: Women in Science and Engineering." Paper presented at the Workshop in the Employment of Women, National Research Council, National Academy of Science, September 24, 1974. A previous study came to essentially the same conclusion. See Robert Perrucci and Joel E. Gerstl, *The Engineers and the Social System* (New York: John Wiley & Sons, 1969), pp. 208-210.

[21] Alice S. Rossi, "Women in Science: Why So Few?" *Science, 148*, No. 3674 (1965), 1196-1202.

[22] Morris Rosenberg, *Occupations and Values* (New York: The Free Press, 1957).

[23] David, "Male Values and Female Professionals."

[24] David, "Male Values and Female Professionals." The "deprofessionalization" of an occupation caused by an inflow of women is discussed by Howard M. Vollmer and Donald L. Mills (eds.), *Professionalization* (Englewood Cliffs, N.J.: Prentice-Hall, 1966), p. 340.

[25] Linda Lytle Holmstrom, *The Two-Career Family* (Cambridge, Mass.: Schenkman Publishing Co., 1972), p. 29.

[26] Holmstrom, *The Two-Career Family*, p. 37.

[27] Linda Lytle Holmstrom, "Career Patterns of Married Couples," in Theodore (ed.), *The Professional Woman*, pp. 516-524.

[28] Margaret M. Poloma and T. Neal Garland, "The Myth of the Egalitarian Family: Familial Roles and the Professionally Employed Wife," in Theodore (ed.), *The Professional Woman*, pp. 741-761.

[29] Poloma and Garland, "The Myth of the Egalitarian Family." In an analysis of female Ph.D. mathematicians married to male Ph.D. mathematicians, Helson found that the males held the more important positions at the prestigious universities. Most of the women did not teach graduate students, and one-third of the women Ph.D.s held no job at all, fear of nepotism being suspected as the major reason. Ravena Helson, "Women Mathematicians and the Creative Personality," in Bernice Eiduson and Linda Beckman (eds.), *Science as a Career Choice* (New York: Russell Sage Foundation, 1973), pp. 563-574.

[30] Irene Tinker, "Nonacademic Professional Political Scientists," *American Behavioral Scientist, 15* (November-December 1971), 206-212.

[31] Tinker, "Nonacademic Professional Political Scientists."

[32] Philip Goldberg, "Are Women Prejudiced Against Women?" *TRANSaction, 5,* No. 5 (1968), 28-30.

[33] Theodore, "The Professional Woman," p. 31.

[34] Theodore, "The Professional Woman," p. 34.

[35] Anselm Strauss et al., *Psychiatric Ideologies and Institutions* (New York: The Free Press, 1964).

[36] E. Wilbur Bock, "Farmer's Daughter Effect: The Case of the Negro Female Professionals," *Phylon, 30* (Spring 1969), 26.

[37] James E. Conyers, "Negro Doctorates in Sociology: A Social Portrait," *Phylon, 29* (Fall 1968), 213.

[38] Joan R. Harris, "Women and Minorities in Sociology," *ASA Footnotes, 3* (January 1975), 4-5.

[39] Harris, "Women and Minorities in Sociology." See also *ASA Footnotes, 3* (April 1975), 4.

[40] Bock, "Farmer's Daughter Effect."

[41] Jessie Bernard, *Marriage and Family Among Negroes* (Englewood Cliffs, N.J.: Prentice-Hall, 1966), pp. 68-70.

[42] Bock, "Farmer's Daughter Effect."

[43] Bock, "Farmer's Daughter Effect," p. 22.

[44] Lauren Wispé et al., "The Negro Psychologist in America," *American Psychologist, 24* (1969), 148.

[45] Michel P. Richard, "The Negro Physician: Babbitt or Revolutionary?" *Journal of Health and Social Behavior, 10* (December 1969), 265-274.

[46] Richard, "The Negro Physician."

[47] Richard, "The Negro Physician."

[48] Richard, "The Negro Physician."

[49] Status discrepancy or status inconsistency states that discrepancy in a person's status is a source of radicalism. Status inconsistency of black physicians is a classic case: as blacks, they are at the bottom of the

caste ladder but, as physicians, they are at the top of the status ladder of the professions.

[50] Michel P. Richard, "The Ideology of Negro Physicians: A Test of Mobility and Status Crystallization Theory," *Social Problems, 17* (Summer 1969), 20-29.

[51] Kurt W. Back and Ida Harper Simpson, "The Dilemma of the Negro Professional," *Journal of Social Issues, 20* (April 1964), 60-70.

[52] David H. Howard, "An Exploratory Study of Attitudes of Negro Professionals Toward Competition with Whites," *Social Forces, 45* (September 1966), 20-26.

[53] Howard, "An Exploratory Study of Attitudes of Negro Professionals."

[54] Will D. Tate, *The New Black Urban Elites* (forthcoming).

[55] Joachim Israel, *Alienation: From Marx to Modern Sociology* (Boston: Allyn & Bacon, 1971).

[56] Israel, *Alienation*, p. 6.

[57] Israel, *Alienation*, pp. 6-7.

[58] Israel, *Alienation*, p. 12.

[59] Robert J. Havighurst, "Youth in Exploration and Man Emergent," in Henry Borow (ed.), *Man in a World of Work* (Boston: Houghton Mifflin, 1964), p. 228.

[60] Wilensky has set up three types of work orientation: work alienation, work indifference, and work attachment. He shows that a person's work milieu and the type and size of the organization one works in are the significant determinants of degree of work involvement. Harold L. Wilensky, "The Problem of Work Alienation," in Frank Baker, Peter J. M. McEwan, and Alan Sheldon (eds.), *Industrial Organization and Health: Volume I: Selected Readings* (London: Tavistock Publications, 1960), p. 557. Wilensky's three types are comparable to a typology by Amitai Etzioni, *A Comparative Analysis of Complex Organizations* (New York: The Free Press, 1961), pp. 8-11.

[61] Michael Aiken and Jerald Hage, "Organizational Alienation: A Comparative Analysis," *American Sociological Review, 31* (August 1966), 497-507.

[62] R. Richard Ritti, Thomas P. Ference, and Fred H. Goldner, "Professions and Their Plausability: Priests, Work, and Belief Systems," *Sociology of Work and Occupations, 1* (February 1974), 24-51.

[63] George A. Miller, "Professionals in Bureaucracy: Alienation Among Industrial Scientists and Engineers," *American Sociological Review, 32* (October 1967), 755-768.

[64] Joseph Veroff and Sheila Feld, *Marriage and Work in America* (New York: Van Nostrand Reinhold Co., 1970), pp. 286-293.

[65] Harold L. Wilensky, "The Uneven Distribution of Leisure: The Impact of Economic Growth on 'Free Time,'" *Social Problems, 9* (Summer 1961), 32-56.

[66] Alfred C. Clarke, "Leisure and Occupational Prestige," *American Sociological Review, 21* (June 1956), 301-307.

[67] Karl Marx, *Economic and Philosophic Manuscripts of 1844* (Moscow: Foreign Languages Publishing House, 1961), pp. 67-83. People may be alienated from their work and yet still be satisfied with their jobs in terms of the modern definition of work satisfaction. For example, certain professionals may be specifically satisfied with their improved material conditions of living as provided by their occupation, but suffer a "psychological deprivation" if their work is an activity undertaken for ulterior ends and is not in itself a satisfying activity. C. Wright Mills, *The Marxists* (New York: Dell Publishing Co., 1962), p. 86.

[68] The concept of the central life interest is examined in detail in Chapters 11 and 12.

[69] Ronald G. Corwin, *Militant Professionalism: A Study of Organizational Conflict in High Schools* (New York: Appleton-Century-Crofts, 1970).

[70] Corwin, *Militant Professionalism*, pp. 175, 291-293.

[71] Corwin, *Militant Professionalism*, pp. 296-297.

[72] Corwin, *Militant Professionalism*, p. 12.

[73] Nina Toren, "Deprofessionalization and Its Sources: A Preliminary Examination," *Sociology of Work and Occupations, 2* (November 1975), 328.

[74] Weber used the examples of the English and American law professions, the former being a good example of the lawyers' fight against the "rational codification of law." Hans Gerth and C. Wright Mills (eds. and trans.), *From Max Weber: Essays in Sociology* (New York: Oxford University Press, 1947), p. 217. Toren, "Deprofessionalization and Its Sources," distinguishes between professions that emphasize their knowledge base (scientific professions) and those that emphasize the service ideal (human welfare professions). However, the rationalization process overarches both types, as explained in footnote 86 below.

[75] Albert L. Mok, "Professional Innovation in Post-Industrial Society," in Freidson (ed.), *The Professions and Their Prospects*, pp. 107-109.

[76] Mok, "Professional Innovation in Post-Industrial Society," p. 111.

[77] John D. McCarthy and Mayer N. Zald, "The Trend of Social Movements in America: Professionalization and Resource Mobilization," (Morristown, N.J.: General Learning Press Module, 1973), p. 26.

[78] Eliot Freidson, *Profession of Medicine* (New York: Dodd, Mead, 1970), p. 72.

[79] Mok, "Professional Innovation in Post-Industrial Society," p. 114.

[80] Wolf V. Heydebrand and James J. Noell, "Task Structure and Innovation in Professional Organizations," in Wolf V. Heydebrand (ed.), *Comparative Organizations: The Results of Research* (Englewood Cliffs, N.J.: Prentice-Hall, 1973), p. 300.

[81] Jerald Hage and Michael Aiken, *Social Change in Complex Organizations* (New York: Random House, 1970), pp. 33-38.

[82] Irwin Epstein, "Professionalization, Professionalism and Social-Worker Radicalism," *Journal of Health and Social Behavior, 11* (March 1970), 67-77.

[83] Mary D. Howard and John R. Howard, "Toward a Theory of Decriminalization," in Sawyer F. Sylvester, Jr. and Edward Sagarin (eds.), *Politics and Crime* (New York: Praeger, 1974), pp. 148-157.

[84] Mark Kelman, "The Social Costs of Inequality," *Dissent, 20* (Summer 1973), 295.

[85] Harold L. Wilensky, "Work, Careers, and Social Integration," *International Social Science Journal, 12* (1960), 543-560.

[86] Thomas S. Kuhn's analysis of paradigms helps to explain these two processes of occupational change. See his *The Structure of Scientific Revolutions*, Rev. Ed. (Chicago: The University of Chicago Press, 1970). Although Kuhn limited his examples to the sciences, I believe they can be expanded to nonscientific disciplines as well. A paradigm refers to an occupation's conceptual, methodological, and theoretical commitments, what it feels should be done and how it is to be accomplished. Once "an existing paradigm has ceased to function adequately in the exploration of an aspect of nature," once an anomaly has been created, a new paradigm will develop and compete with the old. Once the group developing the new paradigm is well organized and achieves power, it has to produce mechanisms for maintenance of that power at the occupational

level. This is the task of what Kuhn refers to as "normal science."
Normal science clarifies and extends the paradigm's precision and scope;
it reduces uncertainty and provides mystique. These are "mopping up"
operations, which engage the large majority of scientists throughout their
careers. Once the power base of the accepted paradigm is threatened, its
defenders may attempt to expand its knowledge base by coopting the
intruding paradigm. This may or may not end in a transformed paradigm.
In other words, paradigms do not necessarily stagnate once they are established. Kuhn makes the important observation that normal science,
the research done under a paradigm already accepted, itself induces paradigm change.

The knowledge base of paradigms within an occupation provides that
occupation with a power base to prevent other occupations from encroachment on its domain. In this regard, the struggle for new knowledge means
a struggle of competing paradigms between as well as within occupations.
In most cases it is not merely a struggle between theories within the same
paradigm, for example, between Marxist and functionalist theories, both
of which operate in the structuralist paradigm in sociology. Instead, it
deals with major conceptual differences, such as the holistic versus atom-
istic approaches in sociology, or the public accountant as reactor versus
the public accountant as initiator of interpretations of economically
valued social events. For discussion of the sociological paradigms, see
George Ritzer, *Sociology: A Multiple Paradigm Science* (Boston: Allyn
& Bacon, 1975); George K. Zollschan and Walter Hirsch (eds.), *Explorations in Social Change* (New York: Houghton Mifflin, 1964); Percy Cohen,
Modern Social Theory (New York: Basic Books, 1968).

[87] Kuhn, *The Structure of Scientific Revolutions*, pp. 64, 84, notes that as a
paradigm is developed, it calls for the construction of elaborate equipment, an esoteric vocabulary and skills, and a refinement of concepts
away from their common-sense origins. This "professionalizing" process,
Kuhn says, leads to "an immense restriction of the scientist's vision" and
to a resistance to paradigm change. A paradigm change requires changes
in some of the profession's most elementary theoretical generalizations.

[88] Michel Crozier, *The Bureaucratic Phenomenon* (Chicago: The University
of Chicago Press, 1964), p. 165.

[89] Phyllis L. Stewart and Muriel G. Cantor, *Varieties of Work Experience*
(New York: John Wiley & Sons, 1974), p. 359.

[90] Paul Halmos, "Sociology and the Personal Service Professions," in Eliot
Freidson (ed.), *The Professions and Their Prospects* (Beverly Hills, Calif.:
Sage Publications, 1973), p. 294.

[91] Eliot Freidson, "Professionalization and the Organization of Middle-Class Labour in Postindustrial Society," in Paul Halmos (ed.), *Professionalization and Social Change*, The Sociological Review Monograph No. 20 (Staffordshire, England: University of Keele, September 1973), p. 56.

11 EXECUTIVES, MANAGERS, SUPERVISORS, AND PROPRIETORS

The modern, large-scale organization requires several levels and types of management to maintain its flow of operations. Several occupational titles are used to designate these levels, which at the same time provide a person's status in management. The most common titles are: administrator, manager, executive, supervisor, official superintendent, and director. The Bureau of the Census summarizes all managerial occupations under the occupational group "Managers and Administrators." In 1972, 8 million persons (9.8 percent of the labor force) were in this group.[1]

Often, different names are given to a single managerial position within a firm or to persons doing the same work in different organizations. For example, those in the highest positions in a corporate organization are called top management, or executives, or administrators. Superintendents are usually the top management of nonprofit organizations such as training institutions (e.g., West Point Academy) or prisons. Likewise, officials are considered the administrators or managers of nonbusiness organizations.[2] Proprietors are the owners of the businesses, and they are most always managers of their organizations. The problem is that more than one name is used for a single position. For example, the president of a corporation can be considered top management, an executive, an administrator, or the top official. There are also several

levels in "middle management" that include both line and staff positions.
Supervisory positions are often included here.

The three major levels of management that are most commonly found
in the literature will be used in this chapter. In the order of their authority,
from higher to lower, they are: executives, managers, and supervisors. Managers are separated into line and staff occupations. Proprietors will constitute
a separate category; they are special cases because of their usually small
organizational size. Where the data exist, each of these occupations will
be examined with regard to role relations of its occupants with those in
similiar occupations at other levels, race and sex discrimination power relations, and work alienation.

EXECUTIVES

Executives are the highest officers of the organization, the elite of leadership.
They set the major overall policies and organizational objectives, coordinate
the functions performed to meet these objectives, train and maintain a group
of junior executives, and delegate responsibility to the various managers.[3] In
the most widely known treatment of the work of the executive, Chester Barnard lists three major functions of the executive.

1. To provide channels of communication.
2. To secure essential services from individuals by coordinating their
   activities in a cooperative relationship with the organization.
3. To formulate and define the purposes, objectives, and ends of the
   organization.[4]

These functions combine into an organic whole, into a working system of
organization that involves two opposing forces: individualism and community.
Individualism initiates with the executives who create moral codes for the
workers. In its extreme form individualism is a dogmatism that prevents the
cooperation necessary to control social conflict. Community, in its extreme
form, provokes overcoordination, regimentation, and subordination of personal
initiative. Executives, Barnard concludes, maintain an equilibrium between
the two by guiding and directing the process of administration. They are
especially well suited for this important task of leadership because they have
a "will to effort." They have a strong private code of morals that serves as
the basis of their responsibility.[5]

Technology and the Social Organization of Work

Barnard's view has been vigorously contradicted by a number of studies
that portray the executive as a member of a closed elite group who make
major organizational decisions in their own interests.[6] In a historical analysis of the steel industry from 1890 to the present, emphasizing 1890 to 1920,

Katherine Stone shows that the development of hierarchy in the labor force was not the result of increased complexity of jobs, but the result of management's attempt to stop or cover up the increasing simplicity and homogeneity of jobs.[7]

At the turn of the century, employers instituted a program of output incentives. Individual workers were paid premiums for higher productivity. This pitted workers against each other in competition for higher wages. At the same time, employers rationalized the work process by dividing labor into highly specialized operations, in which certain physical skills but fewer mental skills were needed. Mental skills were transferred to foremen, and the skilled jobs were placed on job ladders in which many levels of slightly higher skills were needed to rise from one rung of the ladder to the next. This, too, kept the workers' minds on getting ahead and competing with others instead of organizing to participate in planning production, as they did in guilds and early capitalist enterprises when they had control of all aspects of their work, including how a product was to be constructed or treated.

If, as employers were fond of saying in those days, a worker could be trained for most skilled jobs in 7 weeks, then certainly, Stone contends, the training necessary for most jobs did not require a ladder that took several years to reach such a position. "This redivision of labor was not a necessary outgrowth of the new technology, but rather was an adaptation of employers to meet their own needs, as capitalists, to maintain discipline and control."[8]

Unionization of the steelworkers in the 1930s did not reverse the control of employers over employees. Seniority systems were set up and finally agreed to by management, but the job ladders remained long. Workers still are trained for the jobs long before they are able to move into them, showing that the promotion hierarchy is just as artificial today as 75 years ago. Also, seniority prevents minority group members from staying on the job during hard times. This creates conflict among workers and diverts them from organizing collectively. Unions attempt only to increase wages and fringe benefits and are not at all concerned with changing the nature of work. Stone emphasizes that unions failed to change the rules regarding the *content* of the company training courses. They only demanded to partake in the establishment and operation of training programs.[9]

Hierarchy at the point of production was crucial in the struggle for occupational control of the working class. Administrative authority is the dominant force in industry. Executives, not workers, define the structure and dynamics of labor market institutions. Technological innovations only refine the realm of possibilities.

The division of labor and the centralized organization of factory work deprive workers of control of their work. Management organizes production on the basis of these two factors, not to increase productivity (i.e., providing

more outputs with the same inputs) but to increase control.[10] This social
organization of production by management shapes technology and not vice
versa. The loom shop was seen as a real threat by independent weavers in the
sixteenth century. But the loom shop was ultimately set up because the management of factories wanted it. In the early 1900s steel company manage-
ments introduced machines to replace *skilled* workers, not the semiskilled or
unskilled workers. Skilled workers were the power group among employees
at that time. Thus, organization of production is determined by the exercise
of power and not by the degree of technological innovation.[11]

Aronowitz brings attention to what he considers an important segment of
the working class, the white-collar occupations of technically trained workers,
especially those in automated industries who are directly involved in production. These are the lab technicians and the directors of operations and maintenance who work within limits set by higher management. They are the new
"front-line" production workers, whose jobs are highly rationalized. They
have limited authority in the hierarchy of labor, but have no control over their
own labor or that of the organization. They have been highly trained, but
their expectations are not met. Their responsibility and power are limited.
They become bored. This is the "proletarianization of the professions," the
transformation of technical labor from independence to dependence.[12]

Social Background

In the last 20 years the percent of executives with a college education has
nearly doubled, from 43 percent to about 80 percent.[13] Most executives
have followed in their fathers' footsteps—62 percent of fathers were in business occupations. Nearly half of all executives studied engineering and science,
but only one-third of them rose to their present positions through these fields.
One of every seven executives attended law school, but only about 1 in 12
has used it at work.[14]

Business Executives

Because executives make major decisions affecting the lives of a great
many people, they have been studied intensively by social scientists in hopes
of finding what kinds of personality characteristics are necessary for good
executive leadership. An early study of business executives by William Henry
covers most of the characteristics noted by successive analyses. He concludes
that successful business executives show:

- High achievement drive, which stresses accomplishment rather than the
  glory received from it.
- A personal feeling of work well done and not the social reputation
  that results.

- Authority as helpful and necessary, and not destructive and prohibitive.
- Able to organize unstructured situations.
- Decisive—able to decide among alternatives without being unnerved by the process.
- Strong self-identity.
- Active and aggressive.
- Interested in the practical, the immediate, and the direct, that is, reality oriented.
- Personalizes relations with superiors and impersonalizes relations with subordinates.[15]

Overall, these are the attitudes and values accepted and admired by middle-class Americans. Some of the negative aspects or costs of this personality type are fear of the uncertain, the inability to be introspective, and the fear of failure.[16]

After interviewing 50 top-level executives and 50 first-line supervisors (i.e., foremen), two researchers found that executives perceived themselves pretty much as Henry described them.[17] They also perceived supervisors as having few or none of these characteristics. Supervisors generally agreed with these perceptions, realizing that their handicaps were a lack of education and training, a different sociocultural background, and different occupational opportunities. Executives named the drawbacks to their work as the adverse effects of a pressure environment on personal health, their lack of leisure time for themselves and with their families, and the loneliness resulting from the isolation of the position. Supervisors listed the same drawbacks the executives did. They used this as a rationale for not wanting to become executives.[18]

Chris Argyris points out that the relationship between the executive and the supervisor is always a dependent one, no matter how "democratic" the executive tries to be.[19] In their day-to-day administration effective executives will get subordinates to compete for rewards and privileges. They will keep subordinates apart by working with them separately and by defining their important goals for them. Argyris contends that this superior-subordinate relationship and competition will not change as long as industrial organizations are structured the way they are.[20]

Federal Executives

Federal executives are high-level appointees of politicians who direct and manage governmental agencies and programs. They are drawn primarily from families in which the father holds a professional or executive position. The father's occupation is an important influence on the career pattern of the federal executive, but after 15 years this influence is largely dissipated.[21]

After accounting for the effects of father's occupation, college education was found to be most important in attaining a federal executive position. Eighty-one percent were college graduates. Even though they have a distribution of occupational origins similar to that of men, women tend to be concentrated at the lowest-level positions in the traditional women's jobs: social security, child welfare, public assistance, and vocational rehabilitation.[22]

Federal executives are placed in a position where role conflict and strain are almost inevitable. They must be both "public servant" and "federal executive." They must react with sensitivity to government officials and the public and show them deference. At the same time, they are expected to be decision makers, to be action oriented, to shape and execute policy and not to respond in a passive and reactive manner. They must act cooperatively and interdependently and at the same time firmly and independently. These executives are people who like to innovate and create; they have ideals and visions of what they want to carry out. Yet they must be able to operate in the constricted environment of politicians who require that certain political courses be followed one year and others the next. They must not push issues to a crisis stage.[23]

Federal executives lack privacy in official and home life, work with a less homogeneous group of executives than their corporate counterparts, and often deal with problems that have a much less clearly defined purpose.[24] Naturally, they are well paid for their work, not as well as corporate executives, but well enough to qualify for the life-style of the upper middle class.

The Elected Public Official
In the case of elected public officials, certain strains are caused by their adjusting to a new position or to a new occupation. These strains are patterned along the structure of roles or norms that comprise the system. William Mitchell discusses these strains.

- Insecurity regarding tenure as a result of not knowing whether a job will follow the next election.
- There is the conflict between public roles. For example, the role of administrator versus the role of the advocate of public issues.
- Private versus public roles. The role of the public official as community oriented and altruistic versus the role of businessman to maximize profits.
- Time and pressure demands. Frustration over making important decisions with so little time and the press of petty demands of constituents.
- Status insecurity caused by lowered status resulting from vilification by the public.

Most of these role strains and conflicts are found only among elected officials.

The Union Leader

Labor union leaders are executives who must wear several hats. They act as innovators for their members in bargaining with management and are conservative and authoritarian in protecting what they perceive as highly vulnerable positions. In the bargaining role labor leaders must act decisively and quickly in order to secure a position of security for their unions and especially for themselves.[26] At the same time, they are overly concerned with their ambivalent social status and image. They want to be accepted by "respectable society." Warren Van Tine concludes that with this "embourgeoisement" of its leaders during the past 80 years, "whatever radical potential had existed in the labor movement was defused."[27]

This increasing conservatism has led to a centralization of union functions and decision making. As a union grows larger, union conventions are held less frequently, and channels of upward influence are blocked by leaders who wish to remain in power. A union executive board that is somewhat representative of the membership is formed, but the centralization of power is such that the union president can, in most cases, control the executive board.[28] Union leaders have taken over the duties of collective bargaining and grievance procedures from shop stewards. They tend to become entrenched in their jobs for fear of losing them. Because of their limited education, they have fewer job possibilities outside the union and may even have to go "back to the bench."[29] However, the position has become more of a career in the twentieth century than it was in the nineteenth century.[30]

Since they deal with upper-class and upper middle-class industry leaders, union leaders become accustomed to this style of life and do not care to return to their former style. Obtaining a strategic oligarchic position allows them to attain their ambitions of power and security. They become highly authoritarian, even though they are supposed to operate in a democratic manner.[31] Often in such situations a union executive will be able to develop and exploit an aura of charisma. The modern large trade union thus becomes a bureaucratic hierarchy with a legion of devoted followers tied to their leader by a belief in the leader's extraordinary powers, or more often, by the belief that this is the path to prosperity.[32] This has been the history of a large part of the American labor movement over the past 50 years.

S. M. Lipset provides a case study of the exception to this rule—the democratic union. The International Typographers Union functioned for several decades as a workable union democracy because there was a large nucleus of aspiring union officials; the union was not so large that one could not know at least some of the rank-and-file workers; there was no division between the elite and the uneducated, untrained masses. The membership was, as a whole, reasonably well educated, and a large number of internal groups were in constant interaction with union leaders.[33]

C. Wright Mills's portrait of the labor leader summarizes this discussion well.

The labor union is an army; the labor leader is a generalissimo. The union is a democratic town meeting; the leader is a parliamentary debator. The union is a political machine; the leader is a political boss. The union is a business enterprise, supplying a labor force; the labor leader is an entrepreneur, a contractor of labor. The labor union is a regulator of the workingman's Industrial animosity; the labor leader is a salaried technician of animosity, gearing men at work into an institution and then easing that institution through the slumps and wars and booms of American society.

. . .

[As entrepreneurs, union leaders must] . . . regulate the conditions of employments within an occupation, or an industrial market for labor. . . . The labor leader organizes and sells wage workers to the highest bidder on the best terms available. He is a jobber of labor power. He accepts the general conditions of labor under capitalism and then, as a contracting agent operating within that system, he higgles and bargains over wages, hours, and working conditions for the members of his union. The labor leader is the worker's entrepreneur in a way sometimes similar to the way the corporation manager is the stockholder's entrepreneur.[34]

Labor executives must at one time be innovative and at another conservative, at one time bureaucratic and at another charismatic. Often, these roles are in conflict, producing severe role strain for these leaders. As is the case with all leadership positions, for labor union executives there are some problems where the decisions made are totally unacceptable to one or more of the opposing groups that they administer.

Minority Union Leaders

There are very few blacks serving as heads of labor unions. Most blacks in positions of leadership are at the level of union locals. In one of the few sociological analyses of black union officials, Kornhauser notes that there are two possible reasons to select a black for higher union office. One is that there is a strong political movement of the black membership of the union for a black union official. Another is that white leaders face conflict in the union between whites and blacks and so move for election of a black union leader. The black union leader is, in effect, a token black used to win the support of black members. In this situation minority union leaders often face a dilemma. They owe allegiance to the white leadership that likely got them elected, but they also see themselves as "ambassadors" of the minority groups.[35]

Women in high elected and appointive union positions are very rare in the 177 unions in the United States. In 1972, in elective positions only two were presidents of unions (Veterinarians and Stewards and Stewardesses), and only 13 are in secretary-treasurer positions.[36] In terms of their proportion of union membership (around 13 percent), their representation in leadership is extremely low.

There are many obstacles to women attaining positions as labor union officials of any rank. First, when a union promotes a woman to its national staff, it usually puts her in a "woman's job." For example, she is placed in an education, political action, or health services department and not on the "service staff," which does the negotiating and bargaining for an entire plant or industry. She has much difficulty in operating at an equal policy-making level in the union. Second, the family woman has home responsibilities that she finds difficult to avoid. The husband wants his wife at home to cook and clean. The union woman also finds job-related travel difficult because she cannot easily socialize with men after hours in bars and restaurants. Only 5 percent of all union officials are women.[37]

Other Executive Positions

Conflicts in work roles are prevalent in all executive occupations. Bankers in smaller communities derive power merely on the basis of office—they have control over much of the area's liquid capital. Therefore, they usually participate in community decisions of any importance. They are in a position to manipulate people easily; yet they are very vulnerable to public opinion and must maintain a conservative image of cautiousness and reliability, or it will hurt their business.[38]

Other examples of role strain are cited in studies of prison officials,[39] controllers,[40] and executives in small companies.[41]

ARE EXECUTIVES A NATIONAL UPPER CLASS?

Because of their importance in making decisions that affect other people's lives and because they own or control a large portion of this country's wealth, a continuing argument has been carried on whether top executives constitute a national upper class. The pluralist position (see Chapter 2) is that there are a large number of competing interest groups, rich and nonrich, that tend to veto each other. No group is cohesive enough to put through its own ideas without significant influence from other groups. The upper class does not act cohesively as an organization with a single ideology and the desire to act in common for the good of the group. Arnold Rose states the pluralist position well when he says that top executives "scarcely understand it [the power structure] much less control it." He proposes a "multi-influence" hypothesis, that there are several economic and political elites, each operating largely independently of the others.[42]

In a series of studies, G. William Domhoff has traced the social relationships of the wealthy in the United States. He finds a large number of wealthy families from all over the country in a set of interlocking social circles. They perceive each other as equals, attend prep schools and colleges together, intermarry with a high degree of frequency, interlock in corporate directorships, and are members of the same exclusive clubs and policy groups.[43] The clubs and policy groups are particularly important, because they strengthen the social cohesiveness of the top executives of industry, government, the military, banking, and education. Eighty-five percent of the 800 largest nongovernment organizations in the country have at least one top executive in the 11 top social clubs and four top policy groups. These groups are "a major means by which the ideas and norms of the ruling class in general are related to the business sector." Thus, Domhoff concludes, the upper class does act cohesively as an organized group with an ideology, and it does attempt to act in its own interests.[44] It is a social class.

This radical attack on the pluralist position in gaining many adherents as research continues to disclose a very large number of interconnections among members of this group. More information on ideology and decision making leading to consensus will further substantiate this theory and place the pluralists on the defensive.[45] The latter view, however, has been and still is the dominant view in sociology and among the general public.

MANAGERS

Managers are lower than executives in the hierarchy of authority in organizations and higher than supervisors. Managers plan, organize, integrate, and measure the general policy decisions of executives.[46] They utilize supervisors, sometimes several levels of them, to monitor these objectives in the day-to-day activities of the rank-and-file workers.

A major division of labor in the organization occurs at the managerial level, that between the line management and staff management.[47] Line managers are directly responsible to the executives for the implementation of policy. They are the ones put on the carpet if quotas are not met. The staff manager, or "career professional," is technically not a manager but an advisor who usually reports directly to top management (executives), just as the line manager does.

The manager must balance and adjust the communications and conflicts between the formal and informal parts or the "front" and the "back" of the organization. The front of the organization is its physical plant, its product or services, and other items used specifically to portray its image. The back region is the place where, as part of the persons' performances, impressions given or received are "knowingly contradicted as a matter of course." These are the actions and communications (documents, memos, informal conversations) that contradict the official line.[48]

Disregard of either the front or back regions can lead to disastrous consequences for managers. Front and back regions are relative to a given performance. "The same performance before different audiences or different performances before the same audience can radically alter the use of front and back in a given situation." Managers may give the impression that they are on the side of employees when, in fact, they are not.[49] The successful manager is guarded in talk, controlled in aggressions, master of the mobile face, and an expert engineer of events and associates.[50]

Organizations tend to develop in one direction or another as mechanistic or organic (see Chapter 8). In mechanistic organizations (managers relate to one another in prescribed ways and the flow of influence and information is standardized) the manager's good relations with superiors will enhance relationships with subordinates. In organic organizations (managers relate to one another on the basis of conflict and politics) the manager's good relations with one party tend to be followed by poor relations with the other. For example, the foreman gets along well with workers but not with management. Or managers get along well with executives but not with foremen.[51]

Line Managers

Very often organizations are assigned new goals that conflict with the old ones, creating conflict in role expectations among organization members who hold opposing views. In prison facilities when there is a change from a treatment-oriented to a custodial-oriented warden, supervisory personnel have a difficult time adapting to the change. New formalized rules and their rigorous enforcement produce a sometimes violent reaction on the part of prisoners.[52] Conversely, a changeover to a treatment-oriented manager could have serious negative consequences also. Although there are improvements in the inmate-guard relations, there remains a great deal of antagonism among staff members with different orientations and a general dislike of the centralization of policy making.[53]

Another example of role conflict among managers is given by Gladys Kammerer in a study of city managers. The conflict between city managers and publicly elected mayors is very serious because many of the bargaining and administrative tasks of the managers are taken over by the mayors. It is significant that in less than 50 percent of the cities studied was there a mayor in the city along with the manager.[54] There is no clear role differentiation between the two positions.

The research administrator in a large organization is in a special situation of role conflict and ambiguity. The job requires taking charge of the purchasing, payrolls, maintenance of the building or section of the building, arrangements for travel, and so forth of the scientific research staff of the organization. Research scientists know more about their work than the administrator. Yet the administrator is placed higher in the formal authority structure than the scientist, even though the latter considers the administrator's position to be a lower one in the organization.[55]

Also, there are divergent perceptions by the two parties regarding the necessity for various administrative procedures. For example, scientists usually do not see the need for requisition forms, whereas administrators do. They may see them as a waste of time and feel that administrators are purposely antagonizing them with "bureaucratese." In addition, research administrators have few chances for upward mobility. They are usually not Ph.D.s, a qualification necessary to attain the position of research director (an executive position). Their major reference groups are business associations, whereas the scientists' reference groups are professional associations.[56]

Research administrators work in a *bureaucratic* setting. That is, they work in an organizational setting where the source of authority is administrative and the organizational structure is corporate. The work setting of scientists is one of *professional bureaucracy.* They are subordinated to the authority structure of the organization, but the source of authority for their body of knowledge is from outside the organization—from their professional associations.

Research administrators are caught between the needs of the scientist and the demands placed on them by the research director or company executives. They have a different field of training from scientists, but are placed on a higher level of authority. Salary is somewhat lower than what could be earned elsewhere because it must conform somewhat to the scientists' lower salaries. Finally, these administrators cannot reach the top level of research administration unless they attain the Ph.D., which is usually not the case.[57]

In a study of industrial engineers in one large and several small corporations, Ritti found that these employees were somewhat dissatisfied with their work because of the centralization of decision making at the top levels of administration and because of the nature of the technology, and not because of any conflict between an "administrative" orientation of the engineers. Engineers are administratively oriented in that they define advancement as achieving a higher position in management, and not as gaining prestige from an outside association.[58] They are not typical of the research orientation of many of the other scientists in industry. Their work setting is not *professional bureaucratic,* but more *bureaucratic.* In fact, engineering is not considered to be a true profession by one person who has studied it extensively.[59]

Organizational Experts

Experts are technically not managers. They operate as advisors to executives and managers. They use their knowledge to develop plans and programs to present to management. Managers, on the other hand, are in the direct line of authority in the organization. They are responsible to top management for the results of policies and programs set by themselves and top management.

To some, experts are considered part of the executive group.[60] Others see them functioning only partly as executives in that their advice is used in making policy decisions. However, they do not coordinate the work of other managers, including experts. This is done by the executive alone.[61] It is easiest to consider the expert as part of middle management.

Personnel managers are experts in industrial relations. They oversee contract negotiations, wage and salary administration, employment, employee safety, job descriptions, job evaluations, grievance handling, employee training, employee benefit programs, and the like. Often the personnel manager is head of the industrial relations department and may even be included among the organization's several vice-presidents.[62] This person is the consultant to whom employees go if they have problems or gripes.

Because of their unusual tasks of handling employee personal and social problems and benefits, hiring, training, and the like, personnel managers frequently have developed a dual loyalty to both the organization (i.e., loyalty to employees through counseling) and the occupation (they believe in the need for professionalization of personnel administration). As a result, they are viewed by some as people with no backbone, "who always find some way to accommodate the wishes of the strongest forces acting on [them]."[63]

The public relations manager is a case of another managerial occupation attempting to professionalize. In a survey of public relations managers in large industrial corporations, Kenneth Henry found that, like engineers, public relations managers see their employers (top management) as their most important reference group (the group that provides one's primary social identity).[64] Their work setting is *bureaucratic.*

There is a large number of experts working in labor unions. Wilensky categorizes three types: the "facts and figures man," who furnishes technical intelligence (economists, lawyers, statisticians); the "contact man," who has skills in manipulating the ideas and feelings of people in the community (lobbyists, public relations people, press relations persons); and the "internal communications man," who has skills in manipulating the ideas and feelings of union members (editors, education and recreation directors).[65]

These union intellectuals have little real power in the union. They depend on the union leader for their jobs and thus become conservative in their policy suggestions; they tend to become the mouthpiece for the leader in policy matters.[66] These staff experts are *expected* to act as advocates. They must relate to the organization as well as their occupation; they must become, in part, organization men.[67] The role orientations of most union experts diverge greatly from the model of the *professional bureaucrat.* They operate under a crisis atmosphere and in an atmosphere of antiintellectualism.[68]

Although most organizational experts are painted as soft-spoken, conservative advisors to management, without real power and unable to professionalize, some experts do attain a great deal of power in organizations. They are the rationalizers, the spoilers of the old ways, the systems analysts and information specialists—often buried in the accounting system. As Mills points out, they become the key persons in the power center of the corporation. These managers are not the experts in technology but the "executors of property."[69] Some of these people are hired from the outside as consultants but are around, year after year, auditing the assets and inventories, estimating land valuations and leasing arrangements, hiring executives, advising on acquisition or sale of property, equipment, bonds, stocks, and other investments, and generally making themselves invaluable. These are the professional experts in the large CPA firms, law firms, and management consulting firms.[70] But, mostly, they are the personnel in the CPA firms.

SUPERVISORS
Foremen

Much has been written about foremen—the first-line supervisors—describing their unique position in industry as those persons who are the go-between for management and the worker. In 1948, Robert Leiter wrote that to be effective the foreman must relate successfully to both management and worker, which had become a very difficult task. Whereas foremen used to have much more authority (they hired and fired, trained, settled grievances, planned production, and often set wages—each was the owner's direct representative in the plant), with job segmentation and the centralization of administration and control, they lost much of this authority and prestige to specialist managers and staff.[71]

This was pretty much the sentiment of reviewers of the industrial scene at that time. Foremen were no longer viewed as "the men in the middle" or as an integral part of the "line." They were more often regarded by workers as "well-meaning," or as troublemakers to be straightened out by talking to top management.[72] Mills noted that the work of the foreman had become systematized, centralized, and then rationalized and redistributed among the new positions of personnel specialist, safety expert, and time study engineer. This "diminishes the foreman's authority and weakens the respect and discipline of subordinates."[73]

However, only 5 years later (1956), three researchers were able to say:

The foreman, the forgotten man of a few years ago, has become almost the most talked about in the industrial world. Any employer who does

not declare that his foreman is a member of management's team, and that
he occupies a peculiar place of honor as management's "front-line" repre-
sentative, is behind the times.[74]

These researchers do note that on the assembly line foremen do not determine
the number of units to be produced, the rate of production, or the amount
or type of work to be done by individual workers. Also, they have only the
authority to make very minor changes in use of tools or the work process of
individuals, except in less rationalized industries, where they have much more
authority. They are usually responsible for setting up the job, setting scheduling, moving materials, and other duties.[75]

However, the many problems of human relations at work and their ultimate effect on production have not been solved by engineers. It is here that
the foreman is still very important to the production process. Foremen generally felt that the assembly-line method did create many more problems of
personal adjustment and morale. Conformity to the rigorous schedule and
work on highly simplified tasks made the job boring. It was the responsibility
of foremen to maintain the dignity of the individual. They were involved in
many varied personal relations. Their job was not boring at all. As the researchers note in their conclusion, the effective foreman will "act as the inter-
mediary between the purposes of management and the attitudes and activities
of his men.... He interprets company policy to his men ... [and] also trans-
mits the needs, complaints, and attitudes of his men to management and de-
fends and interprets the workers' viewpoint." This is no dull job shorn of
responsibility and prestige.[76]

It took only another 5 years (1961) for the mood to again change entirely.
William Foote Whyte wrote at the time that the work of foremen as intermediaries has a serious built-in dilemma. If they try to keep close to the
workers, the foremen are accused by management of being too close to them;
consequently, they are not trusted by management. If they conform to management's expectations, workers will feel they have been sold out. Some foremen have tried to play both ends against the middle by agreeing with management when with them and going along with the workers when with them. This
is usually not successful and often meets with anger on the part of both management and the workers.[77]

In addition, many companies were now recruiting college graduates for
foreman positions, whereas years ago people used to move up from skilled
blue-collar positions to fill these supervising jobs. This overeducated boss is
seen as an outsider, taking away a position that they feel rightly belongs to
one of their own members.[78]

The reality, then, is that the human relations problems are quite often not
being ameliorated by the foremen. Without the authority they once possessed,

they have no power to act as effective intermediaries. They are viewed at best as a necessary evil and at worst as an interloper in the generally smooth running plant operations.

A comprehensive sociological analysis completed at the same time as the Walker, Guest, and Turner research indicates that the mood of optimism of the 1950s was not substantiated with enough evidence; that, in fact, the foremen's authority was minimal and they experienced a great deal of job dissatisfaction.[79] Halpern found that unionization of the plant was the determining factor in foreman effectiveness. Examination of over 1000 foremen in 56 large industrial firms showed that regardless of how the foreman felt about his degree of participation in management, those in nonunionized plants experienced a greater sense of participation than unionized plant foremen. Foremen in unionized plants experienced much greater job dissatisfaction, with the exception of those who identified highly with management—these exceptions they felt that they were accorded enough status and recognition by management.[80]

In union-management relationships the authority of foremen is reduced because in large organizations a grievance in one department can become the basis for justifying a grievance anywhere in an entire industry or organization. As a result, they must refer nearly all decisions to management specialists. In many cases these specialists do not even bother to inform the foremen of latest developments in collective bargaining or grievance results. Often they receive the specialists' decisions from the shop steward (the union representative of the workers) or management. Foremen in nonunionized plants are more likely to feel that success depends on external forces such as luck and business conditions. This is especially true of those who identify with the rank and file.[81]

In sum, there is a narrowing of opportunity for achievement and self-expression and more of a sense of deprivation in the job of foreman. However, this can vary, depending on unionization and how foremen perceive their role in the administration of the organization.[82]

Union Stewards

Union stewards represent the union in the shop. They mediate between the rank-and-file worker and the union leaders. Just as the power and authority of the foreman waned when management was centralized, the power of the union steward declined when unions placed decision making of many matters at the international union level. Stewards have tried to overcome this reduction in authority by playing an important role in informal communications channels in the factory.[83] Regardless of their success in their work roles, stewards are extremely limited in their vertical mobility. They have virtually nowhere to go because they lack the formal education required of higher-level positions.[84]

Shop stewards remain marginal people. They receive too much abuse from the rank and file and too little authority from the union leadership. The workers blame them for poor union decisions and unpopular contract agreements, even though the stewards have had almost no input into the negotiations.[85]

The union steward faces problems of divided loyalty and job restrictions, the same as those of the foreman.

PROPRIETORS

It is the dream of millions of Americans to work for themselves. In fact, about 5.3 million nonfarm workers (7 percent of the work force) were self-employed as of 1971.[86] The proportion of self-employed among the total nonfarm work force has been declining since World War II. This is mostly because of competition from large department stores and food chains, which force the small owner-operated general store out of business by operating on a lower profit margin and by offering attractive fringe benefits not available to the self-employed. The self-employed fall into three major groups.

- Professional persons such as lawyers, doctors, dentists, veterinarians, and optometrists. More than half the workers in each of these occupations are self-employed. Other occupations in this category include accountants, architects, writers, artists, and entertainers.
- Persons in relatively low-paying enterprises that require few specialized skills and little monetary investment. Examples are street peddlers and hucksters, private household cleaners, and baby-sitters.
- People who own their own business. This is the largest group of self-employed and includes those who own factories, barbershops, gasoline stations, and repair shops.

There are certain advantages to being your own boss. Generally, the self-employed have a much lower rate of unemployment (in 1971 it was 1.3 percent as compared to 6.2 percent for all nonfarm salaried workers). Also, the self-employed make more money (in 1970, the average wage was $11,292, as compared to $10,031 for salaried workers). However, the self-employed work longer hours (an average of 51.5 hours per week compared to 42.4 for salaried), have a great deal more financial insecurity because of weather, uncertainties, seasonal fluctuations, and location, and have a much higher rate of failure. Only one of every two private firms lasts more than 18 months, and only one of every five lasts 10 years.

The self-employed manage to exist if they have picked a good location (this seems to occur mostly through chance instead of planning), if they have enough capital to sustain them through the crucial first 2 years, and if they have some experience or training in management techniques.[87]

Most minority-owned businesses are proprietorships. Only 1 percent of them employed 50 or more workers in 1969, and only 2.4 percent collected more than $1 million in gross earnings.[88] Most of these businesses are located in minority ghetto areas of the major cities in the country.

A recently popularized liberal view is that most ghetto businesses are neither absentee-owned nor staffed by nonghetto, mostly white residents. However, a 1968 study of sample ghetto areas of Chicago, Washington, D.C., and Boston disclosed that:

- Blacks own 32 percent of the business establishments in the sample, yet these establishments draw only 22 percent of all customers, draw only 9 percent of employees, pay only 12 percent of all wages, and represent only 14 percent of total personal income.
- As a comparison, chain businesses owned by whites but managed by blacks comprise only 7 percent of the businesses, yet their overall economic impact is one-third as great as that of total black-owned businesses.
- Most of the employees of white-owned ghetto firms (83 percent) live outside the ghetto area.
- White-owned firms employ over 80 percent of the persons employed in ghetto businesses.
- More than 8 out of 10 white-controlled businesses are owned or managed by persons living outside the ghetto.
- The majority of locally owned businesses in the ghetto are owned by blacks. Only 69 percent of these black-owned businesses made a profit. On the average, they earned less than $7000 in 1967, and the highest income earned in this group was under $15,000. In contrast, 16 percent of the absentee owners made less than $7000 and 23 percent earned over $25,000.[89]

Thus, the high rate of failures among small businesses is especially characteristic of black-owned companies in ghetto areas. Additionally, the majority of jobs and the major part of income from ghetto businesses flows outside the ghetto. Absentee control is an important factor governing the rate of flow.

The two reasons usually given for the lack of black business development are: (1) unfair competition, and (2) lack of capital because of prejudice on the part of bankers.[90] The explanation for reason 1 is that European Jews came from occupations that were mostly commercial, so they had a background of training and experience.[91] Also, as they moved up from the working class into the middle class, they tended to move to the suburbs but to keep their businesses in the city. Blacks moved into the emptying Jewish ghettos, and thus the situation of absentee landlords was established.

The second reason is supported by the evidence that although blacks did not have a more difficult time than whites in obtaining consumer, mortgage, and commercial loans, there were some barriers. The white businessman is free to set up business anywhere he wants, but blacks are limited to the ghetto. Tracing the growth of black businesses in Philadelphia from the 1700s onward, the researcher found that the number and sizes of these businesses grew and then shrank as racism became open in the 1820s through the end of the century, keeping blacks out of any melting pot. As a result, blacks are no further advanced in business today than they were in 1820.[92]

PROFESSIONAL-IZATION AND IDEOLOGY

Most of the occupations discussed in this chapter are business occupations. The question is often raised (mostly by businessmen) whether business is a profession. Those in business, especially those in large corporations, have been agreeing that business should and is becoming more responsible to the community while it maintains its individual interests.[93]

Bernard Barber analyzes the professionalization of business by utilizing four criteria: (1) a high degree of generalized and systematic knowledge; (2) orientation primarily to community interest instead of to self-interest; (3) a high degree of self-control of behavior by means of a written code of ethics; and (4) a system of rewards (money and honors) seen as symbols of work achievement, as ends in themselves and not as means to the ends of self-interest. He finds that businessmen score high on criterion 1, having developed new scientific principles of administration and attaining college educations. But there is only moderate improvement of the always minimal service to the community, and there is no significant development of a code of ethics or rewards as ends in themselves.[94]

Business has made "some progress," according to Barber, but it is not an established profession. Unless the "structure of the social and cultural situation in which they have to act" (i.e., the basic values of social and economic life) is changed in business, professionalization will remain an ideology instead of a fact for businessmen.[95]

The public statements and personal opinions of business executives help to shed further light on whether business is professionalizing. In a content analysis of a sample of speeches of big business leaders from 1934 to 1970, Maynard Seider found five major ideologies.

1. *Classical.* Free enterprise, profit motive, and a self-regulating market.
2. *Social responsibility.* Emphasizes the role of business in fighting social problems.
3. *Trustee.* Balances the rival claims of stockholders, workers, the public, and government.

4. *Professionalization.* Emphasizes the unique skills necessary for the operation of large organizations.
5. *Nationalism.* The belief that the country is important to work for and to protect.[96]

Although classicalism ranks highest, no single major theme emergies. Classicalism is used in 52 percent of the speeches, nationalism in 31 percent, social responsibility in 19 percent, trustee in 9 percent, and professionalization in 6 percent. The latter three types comprise Barber's criteria for the professionalization of business. This would amount to only 35 percent of the speeches, assuming that they all occurred in separate speeches. Even the ideology of professionalizing (i.e., professionalism) is not strong among the public utterances of America's business elite. These findings also bring into question Francis X. Sutton's hypothesis that there is an ideologically unified big business elite.[98]

Seider hypothesizes that ideology develops in response to structural factors impinging on the large-scale capitalist organizations instead of in response to individual factors caused by role strain. Pressure to develop ideology varies according to the type of firm and industry. It also varies according to the businessman's social class and the type of business community in which he finds himself. Eleven industries are examined to discover their ideological types. Defense industries and industries concerned with foreign markets and investments (aerospace, steel, banking, automobile) are highly nationalistic. Retail and service industries (retail businesses, petroleum sales, automobile) are closest to the consumer and are social responsibility oriented. Private utilities fear government takeover and are classically oriented.[99]

When questioned about whether workers should have a larger role in the management of the plant where they work, a sample of executives of the nation's leading economic, political, labor and voluntary organizations responded favorably as follows.[100]

Minority organization leaders	83%
Liberal organization leaders	82%
Labor union leaders	65%
Mass media executives and professionals	48%
Conservative organization heads	39%
Career civil servants	33%
Democratic politicians	33%
Republican politicians and officials	16%
Business owners and executives	12%

Even though labor union leaders scored quite high on this question, they did not register highly on others. Only 17 percent agreed that big corporations should not be privately owned. Ninety percent of them subscribed to the Horatio Alger myth that the young working-class person of today can get ahead in our present system.[101]

Political leaders were ideologically split. Republicans tended to support the ideology of business, and Democrats fell midway between the conservative position of business leaders and the liberal position of labor leaders.[102]

Proprietors, including most small business owners, as part of the rapidly disappearing old white-collar group, are considered to be right-wing oriented in their political views.[103] This theory is supported in a Weberian analysis of social class in the United States by Norbert Wiley. Class interests are pursued in three different markets: the *labor market* of employees versus employers; the *money market* of debtors versus creditors; and the *commodity market* of buyers (or tenants) versus sellers (or landlords). Some occupations experience inconsistent class (or market) attributes. For example, small business owners are employers, creditors, and sellers—consistent attributes—but in most cases they are also debtors and buyers from more powerful sellers—inconsistent attributes when matched to the employer.[104]

As noted previously in this chapter, the great majority of minority-owned businesses are small businesses. It would be interesting to know whether these business owners (also employer, debtor, buyer) follow Wiley's hypothesis that all "people with inconsistent class attributes are especially prone to support right-wing groups," especially since Wiley notes that blacks are a unique case in the American experience. He admits that the labor market is the most serious economic problem of blacks, but he also believes it is the commodities market that contains the most powerful symbols of social status. The black situation emphasizes the need for commodities, which blacks cannot afford or are prevented from buying or renting.[105] If black business owners cannot buy on the commodity market, does their status as employer make any difference? That is, the importance of the commodity market may far outweigh their status inconsistency—they will be an integral part of the black lower-class radical movement. Or are they coopted to become a part of Franklin Frazier's black bourgeoisie? There are questions that need further research before any definite conclusions can be drawn.

WORK ALIEN- ATION

It is generally assumed that most people in leadership positions are satisfied with their work. A general hypothesis, yet to be tested on a significant number of persons at this level, is that the more professional the occupation, the more committed to their work the persons in it are. According to this hypothesis, people in leadership occupations are alienated from their work because their occupations are not professionalized.

A few empirical studies exist that lend support to this theory. The Report of the Special Task Force to the Secretary of Health, Education, and Welfare concluded that alienation at work is taking place at upper-level occupations as well as lower-level occupations. The report mentions a survey conducted by the American Management Association that one of every three managers in the United States indicates some willingness to join a union as work becomes more factorylike.[106] The majority of middle managers and specialists in seven Midwestern business firms have their central life interest outside of work. They view their work and career as a means to success in other-than-work institutional settings. However, these people are attached in important ways to the formal and technical features of their work organizations, if not in behaviors that can be carried out in either the work or nonwork setting.[107]

It was found that managers and specialists who are committed to their work have upwardly anchored careers; that is, they value top-level positions highly and strive for them throughout their occupational lives. Those not committed to their work are downwardly anchored; they value most highly occupational progress already experienced. Career anchorage points are better indicators of a person's central life interest than education or age. In general, the specialists were found to be more work oriented than the managers. Therefore, they had a central life interest in their work. This is attributed to the fact that they are professionals.[108]

Research by George Miller further clarifies this difference.[109] He noted that both scientists (professional experts) and engineers (as part of line management) experience alienation, but for different reasons. In a company where the policy is to encourage basic research and deemphasize supervision, scientists are less alienated than engineers. In this situation, engineers feel slighted by top management. They feel a lack of power and participation in the organization. Scientists, on the other hand, feel alienated when they lack autonomy to pursue work that interests them but does not necessarily interest the organization.[110] Therefore, it depends on the orientation of both the worker and the organization, either administrative or occupational, as to whether workers will feel alienated from their work.

Does this mean that executives and professional experts are not as alienated as middle managers and supervisors, and that managers and supervisors are less alienated than ghetto proprietors? Probably, but the evidence is lacking for the most part. The question of work alienation is covered more fully in the next three chapters, where more data are available for comparison, after which the position of occupations discussed in this chapter will be reassessed.

SUMMARY AND CONCLUSIONS

Occupations that require leadership or supervisory capabilities are occupations with considerable role conflict. From the first-line supervisory positions up to the organizational leaders, there is conflict between public and private roles, between loyalty to those in upper-level versus lower-level positions, and between innovation and order.

Most of these occupations are part of the primary sector of the labor force. As such, they are stratified by sex, race, and socioeconomic status. In addition to the statistics presented in Part 1, case studies in this chapter have emphasized sex discrimination in federal executive and union leader positions and race discrimination in union leader and proprietorship positions.

The trend in lower- and middle-management occupations is toward decreasing job autonomy. Foremen have lost the power to decide who is to be hired and the quality and rate of production. But there still exists a strong belief, even by union leaders, that if individuals work hard and diligently, they will get ahead. The Horatio Alger myth of success through hard work holds on even in the face of contrary evidence.

Another argument, presented by radical economists, demonstrates that workers are faced with increased levels of hierarchy imposed by a management desirous of maintaining power. Workers are given the illusion that they are advancing in a career pattern in this largely unnecessary hierarchy of authority. Management can thus use technological innovation where it fits into its plans.

"Getting ahead" is still quite possible, as Tables 7.5 and 7.6 on social mobility indicate. But the upward mobility has little meaning to the worker lodged in a meaningless hierarchy.

FOOTNOTES FOR CHAPTER 11
EXECUTIVES, MANAGERS, SUPERVISORS, AND PROPRIE-TORS

[1] U.S. Department of Labor, Bureau of Manpower Administration, *Manpower Report of the President, 1974* (Washington, D.C.: U.S. Government Printing Office, 1974), p. 355.

[2] Richard H. Hall, *Occupations and the Social Structure*, 2nd Ed. (Englewood Cliffs, N.J.: Prentice-Hall, 1975), p. 137.

[3] The Editors of *Fortune, The Executive Life* (Garden City, N.Y.: Doubleday Anchor Books, 1956), pp. 17-18.

[4] Chester I. Barnard, *The Functions of the Executive* (Cambridge, Mass.: Harvard University Press, 1938), pp. 217-231.

[5] Barnard, *The Functions of the Executive*, p. 282.

[6] These include: C. Wright Mills, *The Power Elite* (New York: Oxford

University Press, 1957); Francis X. Sutton et al., *The American Business Creed* (Cambridge, Mass.: Harvard University Press, 1956); David Finn, *The Corporate Oligarch* (New York: Simon & Schuster, 1969); G. William Domhoff, *The Higher Circles* (New York: Vintage Books, 1971); G. William Domhoff (ed.), *New Directions in Power Structure Research*, a special issue of *The Insurgent Sociologist, 5*, No. 3 (Spring 1975).

[7] Katherine Stone, "The Origins of Job Structures in the Steel Industry," *The Review of Radical Political Economics, 6* (Summer 1974), 113-173.

[8] Stone, "The Origins of Job Structures in the Steel Industry," p. 142.

[9] Stone, "The Origins of Job Structures in the Steel Industry."

[10] Stephen A. Marglin, "What Do Bosses Do? The Origins and Functions of Hierarchy in Capitalist Production," *The Review of Radical Political Economics, 6* (Summer 1974), 60-112.

[11] Marglin, "What Do Bosses Do?"

[12] Stanley Aronowitz, *False Promises: The Shaping of American Working Class Consciousness* (New York: McGraw-Hill, 1973), pp. 305-306.

[13] Figures are compared from *The Executive Life*, p. 33, and Derek C. Bok and John T. Dunlap, *Labor and the American Community* (New York: Simon & Schuster, 1970), p. 181.

[14] *The Executive Life*, p. 37.

[15] William E. Henry, "The Business Executive: The Psychodynamics of a Social Role," *American Journal of Sociology, 54* (January 1949), 286-291.

[16] Henry, "The Business Executive."

[17] Charles H. Coates and Roland J. Pellegrin, "Executives and Supervisors: Contrasting Self-Conceptions and Conceptions of Each Other," *Administrative Science Quarterly, 22* (April 1957), 217-220.

[18] Coates and Pellegrin, "Executives and Supervisors."

[19] Chris Argyris, *Executive Leadership* (New York: Harper and Row, 1953), pp. 40-41. In this instance Argyris is referring to upper-level supervisors, or middle management, since executives rarely interrelate with foremen.

[20] Argyris, *Executive Leadership*, pp. 42-46.

[21] W. Lloyd Warner et al., *The American Federal Executive* (New Haven: Yale University Press, 1963), pp. 29, 150, 176.

[22] Warner, et al., *The American Federal Executive*, pp. 108, 176-187.

[23] Warner, et al., *The American Federal Executive*, pp. 243-250.

[24] Marver H. Bernstein, *The Job of the Federal Executive* (Washington, D.C.: The Brookings Institution, 1958), pp. 32-37.

[25] William C. Mitchell, "Occupational Role Strains: The American Elective Public Official," *Administrative Science Quarterly, 3* (September 1958), 210-228.

[26] Lois MacDonald, *Leadership Dynamics and the Trade-Union Leader* (New York: New York University Press, 1959), p. 137.

[27] Warren R. Van Tine, The *Making of the Labor Bureaucrat: Union Leadership in the United States, 1870-1920* (Amherst, Mass.: University of Massachusetts Press, 1973), p. 181.

[28] Philip M. Marcus, "Union Conventions and Executive Boards: A Formal Analysis of Organizational Structure," *American Sociological Review, 31* (February 1966), 61-70.

[29] MacDonald, *Leadership Dynamics...*, pp. 70-72, 125. Only 17 percent of the top executives of unions had college educations in 1970. Bok and Dunlap, *Labor and the American Community*, p. 181.

[30] Van Tine, *The Making of the Labor Bureaucrat.*

[31] MacDonald, *Leadership Dynamics...*, p. 76.

[32] Harold L. Wilensky, *Intellectuals in Labor Unions: Organizational Pressures on Professional Roles* (New York: The Free Press, 1956), p. 276.

[33] Seymour M. Lipset, "Democracy in Private Government: A Case Study of the International Typographical Union," *British Journal of Sociology, 3* (March 1952), 55.

[34] C. Wright Mills, *The New Men of Power: America's Labor Leaders* (New York: Harcourt, Brace, 1948), pp. 3-4, 6.

[35] William Kornhauser, "The Negro Union Official: A Study of Sponsorship and Control," *American Journal of Sociology, 57* (March 1952), 443-452.

[36] Virginia A. Bergquist, "Women's Participation in Labor Organizations," *Monthly Labor Review, 97* (October 1974), 3, 8.

[37] Patricia Cayo Sexton, "Workers (Female) Arise!" *Dissent, 21* (Summer 1974), 388.

[38] Emory Kimbrough, Jr., "The Role of the Banker in a Small City," *Social Forces, 36* (May 1958), 316-322.

[39] Elmer H. Johnson, "The Professional in Correction: Status and Prospects," *Social Forces, 40* (December 1961), 168-176.

[40] Dale A. Henning and Roger L. Moseley, "Authority Role of a Functional Manager: The Controller," *Administrative Science Quarterly, 15* (December 1970), 482-489.

[41] Donald B. Trow, "Executive Succession in Small Companies," *Administrative Science Quarterly, 6* (September 1961), 228-239.

[42] Arnold M. Rose, *The Power Structure: Political Process in American Society* (New York: Oxford University Press, 1967), pp. 490-493.

[43] G. William Domhoff, "Social Clubs, Policy-Planning Groups, and Corporations: A Network Study of Ruling-Class Cohesiveness," in Domhoff (ed.), *New Directions in Power Structure Research*, pp. 179-181. Also, Domhoff, *The Higher Circles.*

[44] Domhoff, "Social Clubs, Policy-Planning Groups, and Corporations." These executives do not include labor leaders or members of minority groups. The most prestigious Jewish social club, for example, has almost no members who are interlocking executives in banking or elsewhere, contradicting the common view that "Jewish interests" control financial markets.

[45] In a comprehensive analysis of Marxist theories of the state, three writers contend that because their emphasis has been on "social and political groupings rather than classes defined by their relationship to the means of production," Domhoff and the rest of the "instrumentalist" perspective have failed to transcend the pluralist framework. That is, the state is not merely an "instrument" in the hands of the ruling class. There are many autonomous functions. Instead, it is the structures of society and its social mechanisms that guarantee the state's influence and ultimate control of productive policies of capitalists. David A. Gold, Clarence Y. H. Lo, and Erik Olin Wright, "Recent Developments in Marxist Theories of the Capitalist State," Parts I and II, *Monthly Review, 27* (October and November 1975), 29-43, 36-51.

[46] Peter F. Drucker, *Management* (New York: Harper and Row, 1973), pp. 393-394; *The Executive Life*, p. 19.

[47] See Chapter 8 for a discussion of the differences between line and staff management.

[48] Aaron V. Cicourel, "The Front and Back of Organizational Leadership: A Case Study," *Pacific Sociological Review, 1* (Fall 1958), 55.

[49] Cicourel, "The Front and Back of Organizational Leadership," p. 55.

[50] Melville Dalton, *Men Who Manage* (New York: John Wiley & Sons, Inc., 1959), pp. 252-253.

[51] Peter B. Smith et al., "Relationships between Managers and Their Work Associates," *Administrative Science Quarterly, 14* (September 1969), 338-345.

[52] Oscar Grusky, "Role Conflict in Organization: A Study of Prison Camp Officials," *Administrative Science Quarterly, 3* (March 1959), 452, 472.

[53] Grusky, "Role Conflict in Organization," pp. 468-469. A similar study of a gypsum plant was done by Alvin W. Gouldner, *Patterns of Industrial Bureaucracy* (New York: The Free Press, 1954).

[54] Gladys M. Kammerer, "Role Diversity of City Managers," *Administrative Science Quarterly, 8* (March 1964), 421-442.

[55] Norman Kaplan, "The Role of the Research Administrator," *Administrative Science Quarterly, 4* (June 1959), 34.

[56] Kaplan, "The Role of the Research Administrator," p. 39.

[57] Kaplan, "The Role of the Research Administrator," p. 39.

[58] R. Richard Ritti, *The Engineer in the Industrial Corporation* (New York: Columbia University Press, 1971).

[59] Robert Perrucci, "Engineering: Professional Servant of Power," in Eliot Freidson (ed.), *The Professions and Their Prospects* (Beverly Hills, Calif.: Sage Publications, 1973), pp. 119-134.

[60] Drucker, *Management*, p. 394.

[61] *The Executive Life*, p. 23.

[62] William Foote Whyte, *Men at Work* (Homewood, Ill.: Richard D. Irwin, 1961), pp. 500-510.

[63] George Ritzer and Harrison M. Trice, *An Occupation in Conflict: A Study of the Personnel Manager* (Ithaca, N.Y.: New York State School of Industrial and Labor Relations, Cornell University, 1969), pp. 41-45, 82.

[64] Kenneth Henry, *The Large Corporation Public Relations Manager: Emerg-*

ing Professional in a Bureaucracy? (New Haven: College and University Press, 1972).

[65] Harold L. Wilensky, *Intellectuals in Labor Unions: Organizational Pressures on Professional Roles* (New York: The Free Press, 1956).

[66] Mills, *The New Men of Power*, pp. 282-283.

[67] Kermit Eky, "The Expert in the Labor Movement," *American Journal of Sociology,* 57 (July 1951), 32.

[68] Wilensky, *Intellectuals in Labor Unions,* p. 276.

[69] C. Wright Mills, *White Collar* (New York: Oxford University Press, 1951), pp. 106-107.

[70] For a review of the advisory functions of these firms see: Daniel Guttman and Barry Willner, *The Shadow Government* (New York: Pantheon Press, 1976); Paul D. Montagna, *Certified Public Accounting: A Sociological View of a Profession in Change* (Houston, Texas: Scholars Book Co., 1974); Erwin O. Smigel, *The Wall Street Lawyer* (New York: The Free Press, 1964); Richard M. Lynch, "Professional Standards for Management Consulting in the United States," unpublished Ph.D. thesis, Graduate School of Business Administration, Harvard University, 1959.

[71] Robert Leiter, *The Foreman in Industrial Relations* (New York: Columbia University Press, 1948), pp. 32-36.

[72] Donald E. Wray, "Marginal Men of Industry: The Foreman," *American Journal of Sociology,* 54 (January 1949), 298-301.

[73] Mills, *White Collar,* p. 88.

[74] Charles R. Walker, Robert H. Guest, and Arthur N. Turner, *The Foreman on the Assembly Line* (Cambridge, Mass.: Harvard University Press, 1956), p. 1.

[75] Walker, Guest, and Turner, *The Foreman on the Assembly Line,* p. 10.

[76] Walker, Guest, and Turner, *The Foreman on the Assembly Line,* pp. 32, 124. The quote is on p. 137.

[77] Whyte, *Men at Work,* p. 380. An interesting parallel exists in the case of department chairpersons of colleges and universities in their relations with administration and faculty. For a discussion that focuses on this interrelation see Rue Bucher, "Social Process and Power in a Medical School," in Mayer Zald (ed.), *Power in Organizations* (Nashville, Tenn.: Vanderbilt University Press, 1970), pp. 3-48.

[78] Whyte, *Men at Work*, pp. 382-384.

[79] Richard S. Halpern, "Employee Unionization and Foremen's Attitudes, *Administrative Science Quarterly, 6* (June 1961), 75.

[80] Halpern, "Employee Unionization and Foremen's Attitudes," pp. 80-84.

[81] Halpern, "Employee Unionization and Foremen's Attitudes," pp. 75, 85-86.

[82] Halpern, "Employee Unionization and Foremen's Attitudes," p. 87.

[83] Arthur B. Shostak, *Blue-Collar Life* (New York: Random House, 1969), pp. 95-96.

[84] Michael J. F. Poole, "Towards a Sociology of Shop Stewards," *The Sociological Review, 22* (February 1974), 57-82.

[85] Leonard R. Sayles and George Strauss, *The Local Union: Its Place in the Industrial Plant* (New York: Harper & Bros., 1953), pp. 234-235.

[86] Gloria Stevenson, "Working for Yourself ... What's It Like?" *Occupational Outlook Quarterly, 17* (Spring 1973). The information in this and the following paragraph relies on this article.

[87] Kurt B. Mayer and Sidney Goldstein, *The First Two Years: Problems of Small Firm Growth and Survival,* Small Business Research Series No. 2 (Washington, D.C.: U.S. Government Printing Office, 1963).

[88] U.S. Bureau of the Census, *Minority-Owned Businesses, 1969* (Washington, D.C.: U.S. Government Printing Office, 1971).

[89] Albert J. Reiss, Jr. and Howard Aldrich, "Absentee Ownership and Management in the Black Ghetto: Social and Economic Consequences," *Social Problems, 18* (Winter 1971), 319-338.

[90] Eugene P. Foley, "The Negro Businessman: In Search of a Tradition," *Daedalus, 95* (Winter 1966), 107-121.

[91] This view of the occupational origins of Jews is described as being grounded in the material conditions of their existence in European middle-class occupations. Stephen Steinberg, *The Academic Melting Pot* (New York: McGraw-Hill Publishing Co., 1974).

[92] Foley, "The Negro Businessman."

[93] Bernard Barber, "Is American Business Becoming Professionalized?" in Edward A. Tiryakian (ed.), *Sociological Theory, Values, and Sociocultural Change: Essays in Honor of Pitirim A. Sorokin* (New York: The

Free Press, 1963), pp. 121-146. A recent statement is given by Peter F. Drucker, a strong advocate of business ethics, in his book, *Management*, (p. 810): Whereas the division of labor and specialization were the keys to accomplishing individual success in past centuries, that is, "private vices make public benefits," organization is the key to accomplishing social purposes today, or "personal strengths make social benefits." This is the new moral principle on which the legitimacy of managerial authority must be based.

[94] Barber, "Is American Business Becoming Professionalized?" George Strauss is a bit more optimistic. See his "Professionalism and Occupational Associations," *Industrial Relations, 2* (May 1963), 12-13. Daniel Bell is more pessimistic in his *The Coming of Post-Industrial Society* (New York: Basic Books, 1973), p. 374.

[95] Barber, "Is American Business Becoming Professionalized?" p. 142.

[96] Maynard S. Seider, "American Big Business Ideology: A Content Analysis of Executive Speeches," *American Sociological Review, 39* (December 1974), 802-815.

[97] An excellent example of classicalism, utilizing the concept of uncertainty to establish its importance, is presented in Milton H. Spencer and Louis Siegelman, *Managerial Economics* (Homewood, Ill.: Richard D. Irwin, Inc., 1959), pp. 23-24: "When managers have less reason to fear the possibility of loss due to a wrong decision because such loss will be largely protected [by insurance], the incentive for greater efficiency and improved planning is substantially weakened. Uncertainty has created a venturesome spirit as the essence of American capitalism and free enterprise, and it seems neither possible nor desirable that this be sacrificed for an organized scheme of profit protection."

[98] Francis X. Sutton, et al., *The American Business Creed* (Cambridge, Mass.: Harvard University Press, 1956).

[99] Seider, "American Big Business Ideology."

[100] Allen H. Barton, "Consensus and Conflict Among American Leaders," *Public Opinion Quarterly, 38* (Winter 1974-1975), p. 514.

[101] Barton, Consensus and Conflict Among American Leaders," pp. 516-517.

[102] Barton, "Consensus and Conflict Among American Leaders," p. 526.

[103] For example, Martin Trow, "Small Businessmen, Political Tolerance, and Support for McCarthy," *American Journal of Sociology, 64* (November 1958), 270-281.

[104] Norbert Wiley, "America's Unique Class Politics: The Interplay of the Labor, Credit, and Commodity Markets," *American Sociological Review, 32* (August 1967), 531, 536.

[105] Wiley, "America's Unique Class Politics," pp. 536, 539.

[106] *Work in America* (Cambridge, Mass.: The MIT Press, 1973), pp. 40-42.

[107] Daniel R. Goldman, "Managerial Mobility Motivations and Central Life Interests," *American Sociological Review, 38* (February 1973), 119-125.

[108] Goldman, "Managerial Mobility Motivations," p. 123.

[109] George A. Miller, "Professionals in Bureaucracy: Alienation Among Industrial Scientists and Engineers," *American Sociological Review, 32* (October 1967), 755-767.

[110] Miller, "Professionals in Bureaucracy."

12 SEMIPROFESSIONALS AND PROTECTIVE SERVICE WORKERS

Semiprofessions are occupations that do not measure highly on some or all of the attributes of a profession but are attempting to professionalize. The work roles of the people in a semiprofession have a direct and dependent relationship to a profession. The semiprofession applies knowledge derived from a profession instead of creating knowledge.[1] Therefore, the semiprofession cannot gain exclusive control over its function. It is partly governed by those who create or control the knowledge, for example, physicians over nurses or the state over social workers.

Semiprofessions are the servants of professions. Etzioni comments on the unusual relationship between the full-scale employment of semiprofessionals and the employment of women in the United States. If the majority of semiprofessions were male dominated, many of the relations between professionals and semiprofessionals might not be possible, for example, nurses and doctors, schoolteachers and superintendents, social workers and supervisors.[2] This corresponds to Veblen's view that most men's jobs are of an "exploit" nature and most women's jobs are "drudgery."[3]

Compared to professionals, semiprofessionals are held accountable for their performance by superiors and by the organization. They usually work in a more bureaucratic setting—there is a more formally structured hierarchy and system of rules. As one goes higher in this hierarchy, the jobs become mostly administrative. People are thus rewarded more highly for their administrative tasks than for their primary work tasks. This reduces emphasis on autonomy. For professionals it is performance of their main tasks and not organizational position that brings the highest rewards. For semiprofessionals it is just the opposite.[4]

However, tensions that appear to be a result of the conflict between professional authority and administrative authority are really partly the result of the sex composition of the labor force. In the case of the semiprofessions, especially nursing, social work, and teaching, not all of the differences between them and the full professions can be attributed to differences in the degree of professional authority. These semiprofessions are female-dominated occupations. Since women are less conscious of organizational status and have fewer years of higher education, they are, in general, culturally more amenable to administrative control than men.[5] It is difficult to determine how much of the difference in professional authority between professionals and semiprofessionals is because the semiprofessions are female occupations and how much is because the organizational setting is large scale. It is likely that both factors influence each other.[6]

Most of the people in the semiprofessions are women. Consequently, the organizations in which semiprofessionals work have high worker turnover rates. This results in considerable savings for employers, who can continually hire new employees at beginning salaries.[7] These occupations constitute a small but important segment of the secondary labor market.

Simpson and Simpson argue that the role of women in modern industrial society tends to aid their entrance into the semiprofessions. Women have a stronger allegiance to their family roles and thus do not have time to develop the strong colleague relations needed for professions. The semiprofessions attract people who want to work with people, who want to be well liked, and who do not want to dominate. They have people-oriented values. They are compliant, less leader oriented, and submit easily to bureaucratic administration. These are values more characteristic of women than of men.[8]

To cite a few examples, both nurses and nonnurses see nursing as an occupation that calls for hard work, sacrifice, and drudgery. Both see the nurse as basically unoriginal and subservient to supervisors and physicians.[9] Males occupy most of the administrative positions in the traditionally female semiprofessions because stigmas are not attached to administrative roles, only to careers in the work of the occupation itself, where sex is culturally prescribed as relevant.[10] The number of male head librarians is almost equal to the number of female head librarians, although the occupation is 82 percent female. Males are more likely than females to be head librarians of larger colleges and universities by a 2 to 1 margin, and women preside over men in small colleges by the same 2 to 1 margin.[11]

Finally, the role conflict of the professional woman appears to be mediated by her orientation toward her work, either service or academic. If she is service oriented (e.g., social work) she sees her work as merely an extension of her family role (to offer help, to nurture, etc.). Therefore, she does not experience a conflict because she does not see her home and work roles as incompatible. On the other hand, an "intellectual" social worker, looking for different satisfactions than those received at home (i.e., in ideas involved in her work), may experience role conflict.[12]

In order to obtain a more complete view of the semiprofessions, several will be examined at close range: nursing, social work, public school teaching, public relations, chiropracty, and pharmacy.

NURSING

The role of nursing was taken from the Victorian notion of women as "ministering angels" to their families and to humanity in general. The very fact that most of the nurses recruited in England during the early 1900s were from the servant class probably defined the status and function of the nurse. Her role was impoverished or "regressive" as a result of early twentieth-century emphasis on the scientific sterile environment, so that nurses were kept busy with cleanliness tasks and had little time for the important affective role of humanitarianism, of supplying emotional gratification or "narcissistic supplies" to patients.[13]

The "organistic-scientific" approach of medicine does not recognize the healing qualities of tender, loving care in most instances. In addition, because of their insecure professional position, nurses are often forced to display an excessive professional attitude, which harms the relationship with patients and does not allow them to display affective behavior. The sequestering of nursing students in nursing schools only adds to this dilemma.[14]

Most nurses work in hospitals, which are locations where professions, the guardians of knowledge, are integrated with the hospital organization, which harnesses this knowledge and relates it to practical situations.[15] In health care the scientific method reigns supreme, and physicians control the scientific body of knowledge that is applied. The role of the nurse is to overcome the problems that science either cannot deal with or that it creates as a result of its application. The nurse prevents physicians' errors from reaching the patient, the patient's family, or outside authorities. The nurse is a silent but unequal partner in guarding these mistakes. Exposure of physicians' mistakes is never made, but those of the nurse are made public and are heavily censured.[16]

If physicians make an error, psychiatric nurses will not confront them with it. Instead, they will work through the ward chief or some other person in authority. This strategy of deference is necessary so that nurses do not upset the normative balance of the doctor-nurse relationship. The nurses' strategy is what Goffman calls "deference behavior," which tends to protect their position and to confirm their conception of themselves.[17] Nurses go along with the whole rationale, even if it means blocking or distorting information. They act as "sponges" or "buffers." In one study it was found that when an obstetrician failed to show up to deliver a baby, the nurses would deliver it themselves and claim that the doctor delivered it.[18]

This inequality amounts to what Katz considers to be a caste system. Nurses are second-class citizens in the hospital. They can be totally ignored on medical issues, even though they might be right. They are often treated as nonpersons. Individual nurses may be treated fondly and their expertise appreciated, but in no instance are they recognized as equals. This parallels the treatment of blacks in the South, who were often cared for and liked individually but had to "keep their place."[19]

Role Conflict

As an occupation that is attempting to professionalize, nursing experiences a great deal of role conflict. Ronald Corwin analyzes this conflict by examining nurses' professional and bureaucratic role organization. He lists four types: (1) high professional and high bureaucratic, (2) high bureaucratic and low professional, (3) low bureaucratic and high professional, and (4) low bureaucratic and low professional.[20] These can be diagrammed in a property space as follows.

		Professional Role Organization	
		HIGH	LOW
Bureaucratic	HIGH	(1)	(2)
Role			
Organization	LOW	(3)	(4)

In relating nurses' and student nurses' role discrepancy (i.e., the difference between what they thought their role *should be* and what *actually* existed)[21] to their role organization, Corwin found that "degree" student nurses, those taking a general liberal arts education, are low bureaucratic-high professional. "Diploma" student nurses, those with a hospital education only, are high bureaucratic-low professional. After graduation, degree nurses tend to become type 1; high professional-high bureaucratic, and diploma nurses tend to become type 4; low professional-low bureaucratic. The role discrepancy is faced by the degree nurses. They represent the part of nursing that is attempting to professionalize.[22]

Bureaucracy in Nursing[23]

Nursing is located within a hierarchy of authority. At the top of this
hierarchy are the physicians, followed by nurses, then nurses aides and practical nurses. The growth of the occupation was phenomenal in the early part
of the twentieth century—from 11,000 nurses in 1900 to 300,000 nurses in
1930. However, since nursing schools were affiliated with hospitals, there
was almost no emphasis on professionalizing. The hospital administration saw
nursing as a low-level service occupation. Concurrently, women's colleges
were successfully competing with nursing for the most able women. This
resulted in nursing's development of university-based schools to attempt to
professionalize. But nursing graduate school education for nursing teachers
was attached to schools of education and not to schools of arts and sciences,
which severely limited their prestige.

The administrative hierarchy within hospital nursing is:

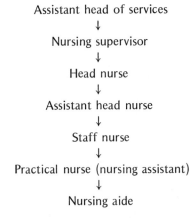

Assistant head of services
↓
Nursing supervisor
↓
Head nurse
↓
Assistant head nurse
↓
Staff nurse
↓
Practical nurse (nursing assistant)
↓
Nursing aide

Nurses also specialize in different work areas such as public health nursing,
hospital nursing, and psychiatric nursing. Although the profession generally
does not want to specialize beyond this level because it wants to maintain
the image that nurses can be used in any bedside situation, nurses do specialize further according to medical or administrative subdivisions: obstetrics,
geriatrics, general surgery, radical surgery, intensive care, and so forth.

Because of its attempts to professionalize, nursing has become the luxury
of the rich. By controlling the relationships between nurses and other health
occupations through their code of ethics, by developing their body of knowledge by means of renaming old practices into new expert approaches of "total
patient," "psychodynamics," and "interpersonal relations," and by influencing
the direction of nursing education, nurses have limited themselves to certain
"choice" clients. Degree nurses hold almost exclusive control of the private

nursing market, while the untrained aides and partly trained practical nurses work in the state and municipal hospitals.

Degree nurses in hospitals encounter the role conflict engendered by their strong value system of the bedside nursing ideal, crystallized around the themes of service, motherliness, and efficient housekeeping, as opposed to glamour, fashion, and success. These are given the names "traditionalizer" and "professionalizer" by Habenstein and Christ.[24] The professionalizer role usually wins out, with the result that nurses rarely see patients at the bedside anymore even though they are much more technically and professionally informed than the aide. Thus, while nurses are preventing the profession from being "diluted" by untrained outsiders, they are not in direct contact with the client.

Some of this isolation is forced on them from above. Nurses have found than an increasing amount of their time must be spent in accounting for the tasks assigned to them by doctors. Tasks must be broken down into detailed assignments for nurses' aides and other attendants, and then records must be kept of all these activities to see that they are properly carried out.[25] The number of forms required to record a patient's temperature has tripled, and the number of persons indirectly involved in recording, filing, and checking the recording and filing has also tripled. The actual carrying out of the bedside nursing tasks is accomplished more and more by the nurse's aide.

Occupation and Personality

Nurses have "feminine" work characteristics. They tend to be conformist and accepting of traditional female role attributes such as nurturance, dependency, and lack of aggressiveness.[26] They are dependable, methodical, conscientious, and deferent.[27] As Everett Hughes describes them:

> In the drama of treatment of the ill and the injured, the nurse is in the center of the action in every scene. Never the prima donna, she is the stalwart character who must always be ready to pick up a missed cue. She keeps the action moving.[28]

Social work, considered by many as another semiprofession with feminine work characteristics, differs radically from nursing. Social workers are independent, spontaneous, assertive, and highly liberal in their social attitudes. This suggests that personality "chooses" occupation in these semiprofessions.[29] Persons select nursing as an occupation because it is comfortable for the way they think and feel. However, other studies indicate that chance factors are very important in the choice of nursing as a career.[30]

In line with the emphasis on personality, it is interesting to note that among the health services occupations, both nursing and social work gained public recognition outside the field of medical knowledge. Physicians have never given nurses separate professional status as they have to radiologists, pathologists, or anesthesiologists. The nurse anesthetist was displaced by the physician anesthetist.[31] Likewise, the psychiatrist eliminates whatever full professional aspirations social workers may have in the present medical hierarchy. The power of the medical profession is evident. Personality type does not seem to have much effect on the success (or lack of it) of semiprofessionals in establishing a place in medicine.

The Male Nurse[32]

The male nurse is a marginal man—his status is poorly crystallized. He faces the contradiction that even though he is working in an occupation with a high degree of security and reasonable prestige, he feels inadequate because he cannot feel successful in a woman's occupation unless he achieves a position of high authority in it. Even then there is a feeling of abnormality, because in American society a male successful in competition with women is not in a prestigious position.

Male nurses feel much more strongly than female nurses that nursing should be professionalized. Much to the physician's consternation, they attempt to reduce the social distance between themselves and the doctors by questioning their expertise more frequently.

Not being able to play the male role at work (i.e., performing tasks that require large amounts of power, skill, or physical strength instead of displaying characteristics of the nurturant role) is perceived by the male nurse as a severe limitation. One tends to use one's occupation as a sign of virility in our society, and this is not permitted the male nurse.

Work Alienation

Work is a central life interest for a large majority of nurses.[33] Almost four out of every five nurses have a commitment to work-centered goals; for factory workers, the relationship is just the opposite—three of every four are committed to activities and goals outside the workplace.[34]

Among nurses, approximately three-fifths found personal satisfaction and meaningful informal group relations at work. The other two-fifths, or 40 percent, found them off the job.[35] These latter persons play the "utilizer" role orientation. They are doing the work of nursing "just as a job." They are "calculatively" involved in their work. They are the low bureaucratic-low professional group—type 4 of Corwin's model.

The nurse's most important formal organizational attachments are at work. Nine of every 10 answered that this was true for them personally.[36]

Nurses as Functionally Indispensable

The argument has been raised that nursing is an indispensable occupation in society today, that nurses are functionally powerful because if they suddenly were to disappear, the result would be chaos in the hospitals. Patients would die from lack of daily treatment, and physicians would be helpless to diagnose cases properly and to carry out most of their own "indispensable" functions.[37]

This is the same argument given by sanitation workers, police officers, and many other occupations. They all can paralyze the system immediately. They become *central* to the proper functioning of complex society. But only a few occupations—the higher professions—are not *replaceable*. In medicine only the physicians are functionally powerful; that is, they have centrality *and* are virtually irreplaceable, except in the very long run. They are in the key places in the division of labor, and this is reflected in their political power, prestige, and material rewards.[38]

SOCIAL WORK

Social work is a semiprofession that covers a wide range of services on several levels. Each level is analyzed by Nina Toren in order to dramatize the major problems or dilemmas in social work as an occupation attempting to professionalize.[39] One problem of social work centers around its ideological world view. One segment of the occupation emphasizes the social reform approach of improving social conditions through public welfare agencies. Social problems are considered the result of certain social structures, particularly capitalism. The other, more conservative "Freudian" segment emphasizes the casework approach of private counseling of individuals, families, and correctional institution inmates.[40]

Casework is seen to be more professional than public welfare agency work. Even so, many caseworkers find it difficult to perceive themselves as professionals. A large majority considered themselves "investigators" on the basis of how they felt they were perceived.[41] Also, the social worker in general has a low degree of assigned prestige. "The public does not differentiate between the public assistance worker (a technician or clerk of sorts) and the 'professional' worker with a master's degree in social welfare; both are identified as tenders of the welfare state."[42]

Another problem of social work centers around the question of mediation (see Chapter 9). The social worker does not decide who the clients will be or what their rights are. This is the "social welfare" approach to social work. The "therapy" approach tries to get around this by going into private practice.[43] Therapists believe that social work must become more professional by defining its own goals. Presently they are "captive" professionals of their hiring organizations. This system of bureaucratic authority "denies the [social worker's] claim that the task is too esoteric, sacred, or private to be evaluated by anyone but the practitioner."[44]

A third problem faced by social work is at the individual level of social role. The social worker customarily deals with routine tasks of eligibility determination of the client and the determination and administration of financial assistance. However, the social worker has recently become more interested in bringing about changes in people's behavior. The dilemma here is: how can a social worker who determines the client's financial needs offer therapeutic service also? The client's financial needs may be judged by the social worker according to whether the client was willing to accept services— a definitely unethical practice.[45]

Bureaucracy in Social Work

Social work agencies are what Scott calls "heteronomous professional organizations," groups in which persons other than the professional members set most of the administrative or professional goals and norms.[46] Heteronomous organizations also exist in secondary school teaching and nursing. Many semiprofessions fit this pattern of organization. Using Corwin's typology (see section above on Nursing—Role Conflict), another researcher, Andrew Billingsley, found that both supervisors and caseworkers are bureaucratically oriented to the agency and professionally oriented to the clients and the community. These are type 1 role organizations (high professional-high bureaucratic), or what Billingsley calls the professional role orientation.[47]

The important factors in social work seem to be that there are no restrictions on licensing to practice and no developed theoretical body of knowledge. This lack of professionalization is caused by a circular process from which the occupation cannot disengage itself: because the majority of social workers are women, they are accorded less job autonomy; and because there is less autonomy (and thus more bureaucracy and less prestige), it is difficult to recruit men into social work. Furthermore, the bureaucratic emphasis on rigid categorization of clients and routinization of relationships makes dealing on a personal basis with clients with severe problems very difficult.[48]

In their daily work interactions, social workers face a dilemma. They are pressed on one side by bureaucratic procedures (e.g., the close control by the social work supervisor has no parallel in the professions) and by the client on the other. Rigid hierarchical structure inhibits innovation in both public and voluntary agencies. If the social workers attempt to act as an advocate for the client, the supervisor will reprimand them. Also, the caseworker method of the one-to-one relationship with the client is still regarded as one of the most important methods for behavior change. This makes the social worker more dependent on the good will and cooperation of the client, which does not help the professionalization of social work. In addition, the fact that most social workers are employees of public organizations tends to lessen client confidence that the social worker is working solely for the client's benefit.[49]

Innovation and Risk in Social Work Agencies

As mentioned in Chapter 10, the greater the professionalization, the greater the receptivity to change. Because social work is a semiprofession, its members are not anxious to take risks by innovating by extension, that is, by creating new knowledge or new administrative methods. Dawn Day's study of adoption agency placements shows how a semiprofessional organization attempts to reduce its chances of making a mistake by limiting its placements to those that are sure bets, thus insuring a high success rate of adoptive parents.

The factor of organizational size complicates this situation. The larger social work agencies cater only to adoptive applicants because the division of labor separates foster care work from adoptive applicants so that the social worker has little or no contact with the children of prospective adopters.[50] It is known that the large social work agencies are less bureaucratized because of substitute methods of modern administration, such as detailed statistical records of performance, which check on the work of subordinates and attain information on operations without direct supervision.[51] However, Day's study shows that size and degree of professionalization do have a limiting effect on the amount of innovativeness of members, that bureaucratization is a serious problem in large social work agencies.

PUBLIC SCHOOL
TEACHING

Teaching is the single largest occupation in the professional and semiprofessional group. Fifty percent of all professional women are teachers. The teacher is an employee, a salaried worker subject to the authority of school administrators, the school board, and parents. Although teachers obtain job tenure and have a degree of control over the classroom, they are unable to determine what is taught. They do not have a systematic body of knowledge on pedagogical techniques, nor do they have a long training and socialization process.[52]

There are nearly 20,000 separate school districts in the United States, but less than 4 percent of them enroll half the pupils. A mere 2 percent of all school districts employ more than 40 percent of the nation's teachers.[53] Yet, even with this concentration, unions have not been very successful in gaining more power over the content of teaching. Union negotiations have been concerned with removing teachers from clerical and related chores, for example, milk distribution, supervision of playgrounds, cafeterias, and buses, book distribution, and scoring of standard tests. Salary schedule, teacher benefits, and teacher-pupil ratios are bargainable but, in most cases, assignment of teachers to schools and classes, curriculum, methodology, and textbook selection, pupil discipline, and selection of a principal or superintendent are considered administrative policy decisions and not "professional" decisions.[54]

Public school teachers, then, are not highly professionalized. School principals have a great deal of power in the daily life of the teacher. Yet, their ability to assess teacher performance has decreased as the specialization and expertise of both increase. Each is incapable of accurately judging the work of the other because neither is any longer familiar with the specialized tasks of the other. This problem is compounded by the sheltered, nonvisible environment of teaching.[55]

The belief that boys need to identify with a father figure was largely responsible for the heavy recruitment of males into secondary teaching.[56] Males in high school teaching increased from 40 percent in 1950 to a majority in 1960. However, the sex role is stronger in this profession than in all other occupations because the public wishes to define teaching as a feminine role. Consequently, most males do conform to this role definition. They are not seen as authority figures by their students, and maintaining discipline becomes more of a problem for male teachers than for female teachers. The entire situation tends to make males more politically conservative which, in turn, creates more problems of discipline. Placing a male in a feminine teaching role and keeping him there for many years at a low income and without much hope of advancement or change in role makes for a situation of personal rigidity and overemphasis on the hierarchy of authority between student and teacher. He has less tolerance for change and more need for respect.[57]

Vertical and Horizontal Mobility

Social mobility in public school teaching is mostly horizontal. The only vertical positions open to teachers are the limited number of principal and superintendent positions. Consequently, teachers tend to move horizontally through the system. They look for the school in which the problems of work are least aggravated and most susceptible to solution. In a study of Chicago public school teachers, Becker found that most teachers give up attempts at vertical mobility for the security of horizontal mobility.[58] A teacher will move from one school to the next and one district to the next in order to find a spot that is comfortable and safe. Most teachers do not request a move to a slum school, for example. Others will look for students with lifestyles similar to their own.

But there are always unanticipated consequences in teaching. "Ecological invasion" may produce changes once one's career is settled. Old ethnic groups move away and new ones move in. Or a change in principal will bring in someone with totally different ideas about the allocation of privileges and influence. These are the risks one takes in place of the uncertainties that go with vertical mobility, that is, a prolonged apprenticeship in school administration and possible assignment to a low-prestige school.[59]

Professionalism and Change

In some cases professionalism can act as an inhibitor to needed social change. In examining the total population of black teachers in black public schools in Washington, D.C., Catherine Silver found that the problems of school functioning, specifically, lowered student achievement, was not caused by "culture clash," that is, misunderstanding between the middle-class teachers and the lower-class students. Peer relations (discussion of professional matters among teachers) was the crucial variable affecting educational achievement in ghetto schools because it was here that threats to professional status were greatest. To compensate for the professionally difficult circumstances of lack of discipline in the classroom, the defensive teacher subculture redefined the situation by assuming that students were doing well academically, regardless of whether they were or not.[60]

Changes in school characteristics such as racial balance and better working conditions were not conducive to higher professional achievement, and thus indirectly did not benefit students educationally. Among school faculty, peer relations were important. The racial segregation problem therefore masks a potentially equally serious problem of teachers experiencing satisfaction and gratification only at the expense of their students. The professional attributes (the body of knowledge with a special technique, etc.) are used by these teachers as a device to insure against a sense of failure. They wrap themselves in a cloak of professionalism and disregard the student. Silver concludes that the race of the teacher is less important than the social composition of the schools (the socio-economic status of the student body and its influence on the faculty) in the total effect on educational achievement.[61]

PUBLIC RELA-
TIONS MAN-
AGER

In a survey of public relations managers in large industrial corporations, public relations counsel (solo practitioners in public relations), and newspaper business page editors, Kenneth Henry measured the degree to which status claims of each of these three groups were recognized among themselves (perceived prestige) and by others (assigned prestige—see footnote 21 above).[62] The independent counsel considered public relations a profession much less frequently (43 percent) than public relations managers (48 percent) or editors (51 percent) did. Managers felt that they were treated as being less professional than counsel. As an employee, then, the public relations manager experiences the pressure of bureaucratic organization when compared to the solo practitioner. Moreover, managers saw their employers (top management) as their most important reference group, that is, the group that provides one's primary social identity.

The editors ranked their top management (the publisher) as their most important reference group in only one of every three cases. The public relations counsel fall somewhere in between. About half rank client management as their most important reference group.[63]

Managers rarely rank the values of their peers highly (only 12 percent), but journalists show just the opposite inclination to rank them highly (71 percent). Again, counsel falls somewhere in between these two extremes. Almost no editors saw managers as important reference groups, whereas public relations managers and counsel valued editors highly. This is true because public relations people depend on editors to place publicity in the newspapers. Editors were more highly satisfied with their work than either managers or counsel. They also felt their work to be more steady and more respected, even though generally less well paid.[64]

Henry concludes that the corporation seems to impede the emergence of a professional identity among public relations managers to the status of established profession, at least to the level of news editor. A lack of personal autonomy and authority with their client (the reading public) prevent professionalization among these managers.[65]

CHIROPRACTY

The chiropracter's role is considered a marginal one by most occupational researchers. The role of chiropracty was until recently not accepted in several states. This often results in inconsistently applied sanctions. At one time chiropracters will be prosecuted for practicing illegally, and at other times they will be left alone by the legal authorities.[66] To some, then, they are professionals with all attendant rights and perquisites, but to others they are quacks and should be banished from practice.

There are two basic methods of chiropracty, the "orthodox," which emphasizes manipulation of the vertebrae as the principal way to cure illness, and the "contemporary" which, in addition to manipulation of the vertebrae, considers diathermy, exercise, diet regulation, and counseling to be equally important. This has led to a split in the occupation, including two separate occupational associations.[67]

Frequently, patients are not convinced that chiropracty is legitimate, that it actually can help. As a result, chiropracters must spend more time convincing the patient of their methods—they become more friendly and less impersonal. Patients who see chiropracters do not have organic defects (i.e., they have illnesses normally not able to be cured by physicians). This type of patient is more hypochondric or psychoneurotic. Suggestion plays more of a part in the relationship between chiropracters and their clients; they are more "patient oriented." They legitimize the sick role of these people. They perform this important service, one that the M.D. cannot or will not perform.[68]

As with nursing, physicians are loathe to give any power to chiropracters in the way of knowledge. Nearly all physicians are totally against chiropracty as a legitimate form of knowledge.[69] However, as more people turn to other forms of medicine for alleviation and cure, occupations such as chiropracty and acupuncture will grow in popularity and acceptance. This process may be helped considerably as the entire field of medicine becomes more mediated by governmental intervention. For example, chiropracty recently received a boost toward legitimacy when many states gave it health insurance coverage.

It is significant that the chiropracter is permitted to offer services of a broader range than any profession except physicians. For example, a dentist cannot treat stomach ulcers, a psychologist cannot prescribe medication for a heart condition, and an optometrist cannot treat epilepsy. However, a chiropracter can offer treatment for any of these and for many more illnesses. Chiropracters have attained this privilege solely through political action—special interest lobbying, especially through client pressure on politicians whenever legislation is pending.[70]

Chiropracters are now licensed to practice in all 50 states and, as of 1975, their services are covered by medicare and medicaid. Yet they have the least educational training of any of the major health professions. Two years of college and 4 years of professional school are required, compared to the physician's 4 years of college, 4 years of medical school, and 4 years of residency.[71] Furthermore, once chiropracters graduate, they generally have no contact with their colleagues; they do not have a hospital association as do M.D.s.

Although chiropracty does not have all the attributes of a profession and is less professionalized in those that it does have, it may attain full public recognition of its knowledge base soon and thus will obtain the wherewithall to professionalize fully.

PHARMACY

Retail pharmacists are limited in the degree to which they can professionalize because of the role conflict generated by professional and business values. The professional orientation is developed by educational training in scientific research and in laboratory techniques required by hospitals, schools, and pharmaceutical companies. The extensive training in specialized schools promotes what public acceptance there is of professionalization. The business orientation is developed by the expectation of students that most will become independent proprietors. The two orientations are "fused" with varying degrees of success but always with role conflict occurring.[72]

Examining prescription violations of retail pharmacists, Earl Quinney found that an individual's adaptation to this role conflict depends to a great extent on the degree of "differential social organization."[73] This thesis suggests that in heteronomous structures (pharmacy as both business and professionally oriented), inconsistent standards of conduct will be experienced—in other words, prescriptions will be filled illegally. Quinney hypothesizes that rates of prescription violation will vary depending on the individual's mode of adaptation to the role conflict. Persons with a professional role orientation have the least number of prescription violations, while those with a combined professional-business orientation commit a moderate number of violations. Those who are indifferent (not oriented strongly to either orientation) commit a large number of violations, and those with only a strong business orientation have the greatest number of prescription violations.[74]

This suggests that prescription violation is a matter of differential organization. It is orientation to a particular role, business or professional, that determines the degree of violation. Occupations with similar role strains are optometrist, chiropracter, osteopath, accountant, real estate agent, and psychologist in private consulting and counseling. For example, alteration of a lens prescription by a pharmacist or a secret method of procedure by an optometrist are both illegal role performances. Deviant behavior, then, reflects social structure, and the occupation itself must be studied as well as the deviant behavior within it.[75]

A study of pharmacists by Carol Kronus comes to conclusions that oppose those of previous researchers. She interviewed 53 pharmacists in a Midwestern urban area and found that *both* business-oriented and professionally oriented pharmacists had strong business *and* professional core values. The pharmacists who had a dual role orientation were least motivated by extrinsic factors (i.e., income).[76]

Hospital pharmacists, the most professionally oriented, did not manifest strong service and interpersonal values, as originally predicted. Instead, the community retail pharmacists held these values.[77]

Thus, "the portrait of pharmacists torn between conflicting values is heavily overdrawn." Also, the ideology of service to the public is used by pharmacists in highly bureaucratic as well as highly professional settings. This tends to reduce the value of the notion of service as an indicator of professionalization.[78] Most pharmacists dispense drugs but do not compound them. The latter task, involving an added degree of responsibility, has largely been taken over and automated by the pharmaceutical companies. The work of pharmacists has been deprofessionalized and their knowledge base reduced. One group of hospital pharmacists is trying to professionalize by obtaining control over the dispensing of drugs in hospitals. This group contends that nurses delegated to dispense drugs by physicians are committing too many errors. These pharmacists are beginning to move into the hospital ward and into direct contact with doctors and patients.[79] It is more a question of social control than personal or professional values that determines the degree of professionalization in pharmacy.

PARAPROFES-
SIONALS

In the late 1950s and early 1960s many subprofessional, or paraprofessional, occupations were initiated or expanded. Most of these positions are found in the human services occupations, for example, aides to teachers, to social workers, and to physicians. Other aides or assistants are found increasingly in accounting, law, and several other business and applied professions. Essentially, the recent paraprofessional movement is different from earlier subprofessional jobs in that the jobs are formally arranged into several hierarchical positions, from initiate or aide up to full professional status.[80] A combination of on-the-job training, formal education, and "life experience" credits allows people to work their way up the hierarchy to the status of professional. This permits persons from lower-income backgrounds to attain higher occupational status without having to qualify with the traditionally expensive formal education. However, in practice, very few paraprofessionals ever reach the top level of full professional or even semiprofessional. Most are trained for the aide or assistant level and remain there for the rest of their occupational lives.

Paraprofessionals have lower prestige than semiprofessionals. Many paraprofessionals work under the authority of semiprofessional workers such as social workers and teachers, making for an intense conflict of roles. For example, physicians' assistants insist that they are of higher status than nurses, but nurses and M.D.s feel that the assistants are of lower status than nurses.[81]

Paraprofessional workers have increased their numbers to relieve manpower shortages in the professions, to relieve professionals of boring and repetitive tasks, and to provide employment for the poor.[82] Some view the paraprofessions as a way to coopt the poor by incorporating their more able people into the elite occupations or at least to give them the feeling that they have the opportunity to enter the professions by climbing the paraprofessional rungs of the mobility ladder. One of the main hopes of those behind the paraprofessional movement is to create better services for the poor and near poor by developing innovating programs. However, the effect of these programs has been circumscribed. Limited mobility and power have prevented the paraprofessional movement from acting as a significant mechanism for social change.

PROTECTIVE
SERVICE WORK-
ERS: THE CASE
OF THE POLICE

Protective service workers are classified among "other service workers" in the occupational classification system of the U.S. Census Bureau. However, they earn relatively high salaries compared to most other service workers, they are likely to be unionized, they have training periods equal to technical workers and, in a few cases, they are attempting to professionalize. For these reasons, they are discussed in this chapter. The occupation of police officer best fits these characteristics. For more than a decade, but especially in the 1960s, the police have been the most maligned of all protective service workers. A stable and well-paid occupation in the 1930s and 1940s, many middle-class people chose it over a career in law or teaching or an equally prestigious occupation. During this time, technological improvements led to new methods for tracing criminals: radar, electronic listening devices, and computers. These factors helped to contribute to the professionalization of the police.[83] However, the new police officers, coming in with special technical skills and college degrees, are faced with the criticism of "being soft on criminals," enunciated by the "traditionalists," who have less education (usually a high school diploma) and who come from the working class. These attributes of the traditionalist, plus an average intelligence, a strong physical constitution, and a "cautious" personality, are considered to be the ideal characteristics of the police officer. They are what is needed for the rough and often dangerous world of crime.[84]

These characteristics do not make for a professionalized occupation. The work situation of police officers is one of pragmatism, of a "get tough and lock em up" policy. In the precinct, they are measured by their arrest record, not by how well they maintain their ethics regarding civil rights for all. It is an attitude of cynicism instead of commitment. Even when the police attempt to professionalize, the public will often not accept it. It does not allow for the graft, for the rule breaking that many see to be a privilege. After about 5 years on the force, the average police officer has had time to see enough of this "compromising" to become cynical.[85] Right or wrong, they are stereotyped as rough-spoken, crude, and unintelligent, and very clannish.[86]

Dealing with Uncertainty

In the police department the amount of discretion (judgment) used increases as one moves down the hierarchy to patrolman. This is just the opposite of the task content of most organizations, where the most routine tasks are performed at the lowest ranks. This judgment comes into play when police officers must decide whether to enforce the law or to maintain order. In the latter case they must only "keep the peace" and not make an arrest, to "handle the situation" and not become involved.[87]

To take a specific example, what do police officers do when confronted with a possibly mentally ill person? They can take legal steps to initiate the process of confinement to a psychiatric hospital if they feel that the person is mentally ill and "is likely to injure himself or others if not immediately hospitalized." However, when Egon Bittner interviewed and observed policemen at work in a large city, he found there were many reasons why the police rarely referred cases to hospitals.[88] They feared the possibility of being exploited by lawyers or psychiatrists contesting the correctness of their decision to bring an ill person to the psychiatric hospital. They are in continual contact with assorted disoriented, unhappy, and incompetent people in the community who nevertheless manage to get along on their own or with minimal help. Bringing in a mental case does not have the same prestige attached to it as the arrest of a known criminal. It does not involve any of the skills and courage known to be a part of the police officer's character and effort. Also, the processing of a mentally ill person can be a long, tedious, and boring affair.

Therefore, the conditions must be severe before the officer will make such an emergency apprehension. Because of these pressures, police officers will in many cases not make the formal *(de jure)* apprehension even if the person is mentally ill. Instead, they will act informally *(de facto* apprehension) by offering their assistance to relations or friends who feel they cannot bring the ill person to the hospital on their own. The officer is usually the only person at the scene who listens attentively to the patient and, as a result, gains the patient's trust. Another informal method is for the police officer to bring the person to a medical emergency service so that the attending physician can make the diagnosis. This lets the police officer off the hook.[89]

However, most persons are not referred to agencies and, consequently, police officers act as remedial agents. They try to find competent persons who will be able to care for patients or return them to their normal habitat, which usually calms them enough to enable management of everyday affairs. The officers are especially competent at performing these functions because they stand in the midst of an informal neighborhood or community referral structure, which includes neighbors, hotel clerks, bartenders, cabbies, and the like, who usually know the person. Usually, someone can be found to take custody of the patient.[90]

Bittner emphasizes that we know very little about these informal systems, especially in the more blighted areas of the city. The police officer is often the only social agent who can work inside this system for the protection and aid of its members. Social workers, teachers, and others mostly are unaware of are unable to gain access to these networks. Police officers are unique in this network because they can use their powers of coercion, yet they normally do not have to because they are insiders. They can find alternatives to the hospitalization of mentally ill persons. They give "psychiatric first aid."[91]

Thus it is that in some cases where officers comply with the law (i.e., bring a mentally ill person to the psychiatric hospital), they may be considered by fellow officers as incompetent practitioners of the craft. They have not handled the situation according to certain uncodified norms that depend on personal ingenuity and reason. Instead of enforcing the law, they must "keep the peace" through methodically organized routines with certain procedures, skills, and standards. They must meet certain tacit public understandings.[92]

These and other kinds of actions on the part of police take place in un-countable numbers every day. In their decision making they work around the complex set of bureaucratic rules and procedures that they technically must follow. The police can very easily subvert the entire law enforcement process by "working to the rules," that is, by following rules to the letter, enforcing the law and provoking dysfunctional actions.[93]   One example is the U.S. "blue flu," the phenomenon of calling in sick in large numbers. In this way, rules can be used as a bargaining factor with upper-echelon administrators. It draws together segments of an occupation into "acting units," into "flexible alliances" that counter some of the more repressive elements of bureaucratic rules.[94]

This is a form of colleagueship that is "professional," not in the sense of abstract theories, a code of ethics, and the like, but in the sense of power, that is, in "the potential for corruption and malfeasance and for en-abling a degree of coping with relatively impredictable events in a routine fashion."[95]

The Black Police Officer

On the basis of interviews with 41 black police officers in 1965, Nicholas Alex has written an extensive analysis of the special problems of this minority work group.[96] He notes that the black officer's reason for joining the police force is less because of identification with the police role (more prestige, satis-fies one's interest in community and youth work) than with the civil service role (higher income, opportunity for advancement, economic security). All police officers find their autonomy severely limited by civilian review boards and by general public criticism of armed paramilitary organizations.[97]

Police officers suffer because of their role as a buffer between the middle and upper classes and the lower class and minority groups in the city. These two groups are separated geographically and culturally, but both come together in the metropolitan community. The former try to isolate themselves from the latter and expect the police to keep crime and lawlessness away from them and their property. The police experience low prestige because of this peculiar position in American society. They usually come from an immigrant parental background, and they are criticized by members of their own ethnic group for not providing enough order and protection. They are looked down on by the upper middle class and upper class as being in a working class occupation, and they are vilified by many in the lower class as a tool of the establishment.

Added to this are the additional problems of black police officers. They are blacks protecting white society. They are used as a "vehicle of pressure" on the black population and are rejected by their own community. Also, as members of a highly visible minority, they are considered of an "inferior" race, even by members of their own occupation. However, for some blacks they represent success in the job market. The police occupation gives a black a secure, well-paying position at the generally highest levels open to the great majority of blacks—the semiprofessions.[98]

Police have an ideology of service to the public, of "the management of violence as a career." Black police officers consider themselves professionals through training, tests, and schooling, but they are not recognized as such by the public (they are "Uncle Toms") or by the police (they ethically support the law against illegal search, which contradicts the informal laws of the police). Thus they are not "cooperative" or "supportive" of fellow police officers.[99]

There are numerous on-the-job role conflicts that the black police officer must face. There is the contradiction of a uniform that signifies authority and color of skin that does not. Alex relates the following story of a respondent.

There is an emergency call. A nurse lived in the East 80's. Four radio cars respond. That means sixteen patrolmen. There are fifteen white patrolmen and one Negro, me. My car caught the call, and my partner and I dash into the apartment. The woman is in a nightgown. She is hysterical. But when she sees me she goes into complete shock! Ironically, I had to get all the information from her because we got the call. Things were running through my mind that the assailant was a Negro and this was why she responded to me, but he was white. She almost screamed again when she saw me. There I am with my brass buttons and my shield. It's obvious I'm a policeman but she goes back into shock. I keep telling her I'm a policeman. I actually ran downstairs and told my partner that I didn't want to have anything to do with the case. But I went back up. I have dozens of such incidents.[100]

Black police not in uniform face a series of different problems. Many are afraid of arresting someone because a white police officer happening by might think that the black officer is the criminal. Also, a white perpetrator might refuse to believe that the black arresting officer is a police officer. Black detectives don't go on "prowler runs" for fear that a white officer might kill them in a "shoot first, ask questions later" policy. Black police officers find it more difficult to arrest in white neighborhoods. Consequently, they make more arrests in black neighborhoods, further tarnishing their reputation in the black community.[101]

Alex concludes that blacks were hired onto police forces not because of increased opportunities to racial minorities, but because they were black and could help to cool down the racial tensions in the cities during the 1960s. Discrimination still existed. A recruitment quota was maintained through the mechanism of character investigation, in which minor violations of law could be found if one looked hard enough. Blacks on the force were often denied radio car patrol duty and were denied entry into certain police divisions such as homicide, fraud, and burglary squad detectives.[102]

White police see the black officer as contributing to the lowering of their status as an occupation. Blacks are associated mostly with secondary labor market occupations, and so any occupation with a large number of these minority group members will suffer a reduction in prestige and power. Also, as Alex points out, the promotion of blacks to higher police positions is an encroachment on a formerly all-white preserve of privilege within the occupation. Black police officers have received the economic rewards of their newfound social mobility, but they have more than paid for it through their position of double marginality.[103]

SUMMARY AND CONCLUSIONS

On the basis of this review of semiprofessions, it can be said that all semiprofessions are attempting to professionalize. By definition, they are extremely limited in this attempt—they have a dependent relationship to established professions in that they apply knowledge derived from them. None of the occupations discussed are developing their own knowledge base, with the possible exception of social work.

This is in general agreement with the conclusions of William Goode, who suggests that social work, marital counseling, and perhaps city planning will achieve full professional status over the next generation. Those that will not are public school teaching, nursing, chiropractic, podiatry, pharmacy, business management, librarianship, public relations, and advertising. Those who fail to professionalize will be those who will not be able to develop and control a body of knowledge, control being granted by a mandate from the governmental authorities for exclusive use of the knowledge.[104] This mandate is given because the occupation has convinced society that it alone should control this knowledge. Once it has gained this control, it translates it into power.

Management has no driving need to professionalize. Its power is attained through control over a different resource than knowledge—capital or property. Experience and daring (the latter a quality of entrepreneurship) are what count in good management more than a body of knowledge, although the latter is considered more important in certain technical areas.

Librarians, Goode points out, do believe that there is a body of scientific knowledge that they possess and that they are performing and are committed to an important public service. However, neither the public nor the granting authorities believe their skills to be esoteric. The occupation is considered unable to be harmful if its work is not carried out properly.[105] It is not functionally indispensable. Witness the effects of the recent massive budget cuts in several cities across the United States. Among the first organizations to be affected were libraries. Shorter library hours, restrictions on book purchases, and reduced library staff size were common.

To some degree, the semiprofessions will not professionalize further because they are female dominated. The problems of male nurses and schoolteachers highlight the subservient position of these "female" occupations. This situation will be difficult to overcome because of culturally prescribed male and female values about these jobs.

Finally, most semiprofessions operate in large bureaucratic settings that are the source of various role conflicts of their members: whether to be a "bedside" nurse or a professional nurse; whether to emphasize casework or social welfare; whether to be business oriented or professionally oriented; and so forth. One of the inherent threats of bureaucratization is the degree of rationalization of the occupation's body of knowledge. As knowledge becomes more certain and as standardized procedures are developed for handling clients, the monopoly of the professional group is weakened, labor is divided among the workers, and the power of the occupation shifts to the managers.[106]

There are more optimistic views of the future of the semiprofessions. As pointed out in Chapter 8, one school feels that bureaucracy is on the decline in advanced industrial societies because it is not fitted for the more creative jobs of the new services occupations (including the protective services) and professions that operate in a setting of constant change. Indeed, as one critic of the professions says, "It may not be inappropriate to consider professionalization to be a major social movement of the twentieth century."[107]

There are many, including an increasingly large segment of the public, who take the point of view best articulated by Peter Berger that today we "project an image" of our work, our occupation and, in many cases, it allows us to reap rewards. It is a game of "one-upmanship." Occupations form various "defense organizations" and "propaganda agencies" to further their individual causes. It becomes a Veblenesque world of hundreds of occupational organizations engaged in the big con. It is most explicit in the process of professionalism, "the state of affairs when an occupation is out to convince the public that it is now entitled to the status of the older respected professions." "Characteristics" of professionalization are manufactured, and a bamboozled public acquiesces to give the occupation license over another area of work.[108] Some who take this view believe that we will not be long in waiting for a "revolt of the client."[109]

The other view is that occupations are not a zero-sum game in the long run. Over the longer period, the professionalizing of a semiprofession will not mean that power, wealth, or prestige will have to be taken away from some other occupation. The status can be earned independently, through efforts that contribute more to society. New jobs are created. All benefit, not just the occupation.[110]

Regardless of which view one takes, it is well to remember that in some of these occupations the majority of the workers are part of the secondary labor force. They are poorly paid, poorly treated, and have short job tenure. Any collective gains that they are able to achieve can be welcomed as a further step toward a more equalitarian society. Whether the work of these occupations is "worth" what they receive in salaries, wages, and benefits raises the question of equality of opportunity versus the equality of results, a topic to be discussed in Chapter 17.

FOOTNOTES FOR CHAPTER 12
SEMI-PROFESSIONALS AND PROTECTIVE SERVICE WORKERS

[1] Richard L. Simpson and Ida Harper Simpson, "Women and Bureaucracy in the Semi-Professions," in Amitai Etzioni (ed.), *The Semi-Professions and Their Organization* (New York: The Free Press, 1969), p. 236.

[2] Amitai Etzioni, Preface to *The Semi-Professions...*, p. viii.

[3] Thorstein Veblen, *The Theory of the Leisure Class* (New York: Random House, Modern Library Edition, 1934), p. 13. First published in 1899 by The Macmillan Company.

[4] Simpson and Simpson, "Women and Bureaucracy in the Semi-Professions," pp. 197-198.

[5] Etzioni, Preface to *The Semi-Professions...*, p. xv.

[6] Etzioni, Preface to *The Semi-Professions...*, p. xv.

[7] Simpson and Simpson, "Women and Bureaucracy in the Semi-Professions," p. 221. C. Wright Mills discussed how the semiprofessions in the business world developed to the point where middle-management jobs became rationalized into separate occupations of personnel directors, public relations directors, and the like. See his *White Collar* (New York: Oxford University Press, 1951), p. 141.

[8] Simpson and Simpson, "Women and Bureaucracy in the Semi-Professions," pp. 199, 203-209, 233-234.

[9] Athena Theodore, "The Professional Woman: Trends and Prospects," in Athena Theodore (ed.), *The Professional Woman* (Cambridge, Mass.: Schenkman Publishing Co., 1971), p. 6.

[10] Rodney F. White, "Female Identity and Career Choice: The Nursing Case," in Theodore (ed.), *The Professional Woman*, p. 281.

[11] W. C. Blankenship, "Head Librarians: How Many Men? How Many Women?" in Theodore (ed.), *The Professional Woman*, p. 525.

[12] John E. Tropman, "The Married Professional Social Worker," in Theodore (ed.), *The Professional Woman*, p. 547.

[13] George Devereux and Florence R. Weiner, "The Occupational Status of Nurses," *American Sociological Review, 15* (October 1950), 629-634.

[14] Devereux and Weiner, "The Occupational Status of Nurses."

[15] Fred E. Katz, "Nurses," in Etzioni (ed.), *The Semi-Professions...*, pp. 55-56.

[16] Katz, "Nurses," pp. 58-60.

[17] Erving Goffman, "The Nature of Deference and Demeanor," *The American Anthropologist, 58* (1956), 473-502. The example is taken from William A. Rushing, "Social Influence and the Social Psychological Function of Deference: A Study of Psychiatric Nursing," in Theodore (ed.), *The Professional Woman*, pp. 182-194.

[18] Katz, "Nurses," p. 60.

[19] Katz, "Nurses," p. 70.

[20] Ronald G. Corwin, "The Professional Employee: A Study of Conflict in Nursing Roles," *American Journal of Sociology, 66* (May 1961), 610. The original typology was constructed by Leonard Reissman, "A Study of Role Conceptions in Bureaucracy," *Social Forces, 27* (March 1949), 305-310. He named them as: (1) functional bureaucrat, (2) specialist bureaucrat, (3) service bureaucrat, and (4) job bureaucrat.

[21] In a comparative analysis of nurses and optometrists, it was found that the more marginal the profession, the greater the discrepancy between claimed prestige (professionals' ideas about what deference they should receive) and assigned and perceived prestige (deference given by society and professionals' perceptions of deference they are accorded). Louis H. Orzack, "Professionalization and Prestige Deficits," *Sociological Focus, 4* (Spring 1971), 63-71.

[22] Corwin, "The Professional Employee," pp. 610-615.

[23] Except where otherwise noted, the information in this section is based on the essay by Anselm Strauss, "Structure and Ideology of the Nursing Profession," in Fred Davis (ed.), *The Nursing Profession* (New York: John Wiley and Sons, Inc., 1966), pp. 60-104.

[24] Robert A. Habenstein and Edwin A. Christ, *Professionalizer, Traditionalizer, and Utilizer* (Columbia, Mo.: University of Missouri Press, 1955), p. 29. As quoted by Katz, "Nurses," p. 68.

[25] Katz, "Nurses," p. 74.

[26] R. A. Hudson Rosen et al., "Health Professionals' Attitudes Toward Abortion," *Public Opinion Quarterly, 38* (Summer 1974), 171.

[27] Anne J. Davis, "Self-Concept, Occupational Role Expectations, and Occupational Choice in Nursing and Social Work," in Theodore (ed.), *The Professional Woman*, p. 375.

[28] Everett C. Hughes, "Studying the Nurse's Work," *The Sociological Eye* (Chicago: Aldine-Atherton, 1971), p. 315.

[29] Hudson Rosen et al., "Health Professionals' Attitudes Toward Abortion," p. 171. Personality characteristics of social workers are also listed by Davis, "Self-Concept . . . ," p. 375.

[30] Fred E. Katz and Harry M. Martin, "Career Choice Processes," in Theodore (ed.), *The Professional Woman*, p. 293.

[31] Strauss, "Structure and Ideology of the Nursing Profession," pp. 65-67. Physicians also sit on the licensing boards for nursing and medical technicians.

[32] The information in this section is based on an article by Bernard E. Segal, "Male Nurses: A Case Study in Status Contradiction and Prestige Loss," *Social Forces, 41* (October 1962), 31-38.

[33] Louis H. Orzack, "Work as a 'Central Life Interest' of Professionals," *Social Problems, 7* (Fall 1959), 125-132.

[34] Robert Dubin, "Industrial Workers' Worlds: A Study of 'Central Life Interests' of Industrial Workers," *Social Problems, 3* (Fall 1956), 132-142.

[35] Orzack, "Work as a 'Central Life Interest' of Professionals," p. 136.

[36] Orzack, "Work as a 'Central Life Interest' of Professionals," p. 134.

[37] John and Barbara Ehrenreich, "Hospital Workers: A Case Study in the 'New Working Class,'" *Monthly Review, 24* (January 1973), 17.

[38] Elliott A. Krause, *The Sociology of Occupations* (Boston: Little, Brown & Co., 1971), pp. 62, 79.

[39] Nina Toren, *Social Work: The Case of a Semi-Profession* (Beverly Hills, Calif.: Sage Publications, 1972).

[40] Brian J. Heraud, "Professionalism, Radicalism and Social Change," in Paul Halmos (ed.), *Professionalisation and Social Change*, The Sociological Review Monograph No. 20 (Staffordshire, England: University of Keele,

December 1973), pp. 94-95. Also, Paul Halmos, *The Personal Service Society* (London: Constable, 1970).

[41] W. Richard Scott, "Professional Employees in a Bureaucratic Structure: Social Work," in Etzioni (ed.), *The Semi-Professions,* pp. 130-133.

[42] Sheryl K. Ruzek, "Making Social Work Accountable," in Eliot Freidson (ed.), *The Professions and Their Prospects* (Beverly Hills, Calif.: Sage Publications, 1973), p. 218.

[43] Toren, *Social Work,* pp. 20-27.

[44] Ruzek, "Making Social Work Accountable," p. 233.

[45] Toren, *Social Work,* p. 58.

[46] W. Richard Scott, "Reactions to Supervision in a Heteronomous Profesfesional Organization," *Administrative Science Quarterly, 20* (June 1965), 65-81. An autonomous professional organization is one in which a professional group governs its own administrative and professional behavior. Examples are large law firms and large public accounting firms.

[47] Andrew Billingsly, "Bureaucratic and Professional Orientation Patterns in Social Casework," *The Social Service Review, 38* (December 1964), 44-107. Role orientations of British social workers are similar. See Peter Leonard, "Professionalization, Community Action and Social Service Bureaucracies," in Halmos (ed.), *Professionalisation and Social Change,* pp. 108-109. Scott also has constructed a four-fold typology: see Scott, "Professional Employees in a Bureaucratic Structure," in Etzioni (ed.), *The Semi-Professions . . . ,* p. 90.

[48] Toren, *Social Work,* p. 57.

[49] Toren, *Social Work,* pp. 57, 73, 136, 150, 229-230.

[50] Dawn Day, "White Social Workers and the Adoption of Black Children," paper presented at the annual meetings of the American Sociological Association, August 27, 1973, New York City.

[51] Peter M. Blau, *The Dynamics of Bureaucracy,* Rev. Ed. (Chicago: University of Chicago Press, 1955), Chapter 3; Peter M. Blau, Wolf V. Heydebrand, and Robert E. Stauffer, "The Structure of Small Bureaucracies," *American Sociological Review, 31* (April 1966), p. 185.

[52] Dan C. Lortie, "The Balance of Control and Autonomy in Elementary School Teaching," in Etzioni (ed.), *The Semi-Professions . . . ,* pp. 19, 24.

[53] Wesley A. Wildman, "Teachers and Collective Negotiations," in Albert

A. Blum et al., (eds.), *White-Collar Workers* (New York: Random House, 1971), p. 126.

[54] Wildman, "Teachers and Collective Negotiations, pp. 151-156.

[55] Philip M. Marcus, "Schoolteachers and Militant Conservatism," in Freidson (ed.), *The Professions and Their Prospects*, p. 200.

[56] Harmon Ziegler, "Male and Female: Differing Perceptions of the Teaching Experience," in Theodore (ed.), *The Professional Woman*, pp. 74-76.

[57] Ziegler, "Male and Female," p. 76.

[58] Howard S. Becker, "The Career of the Chicago Public School Teacher," *American Journal of Sociology, 57* (March 1952), 470-477.

[59] Becker, "The Career of the Chicago Public School Teacher."

[60] Catherine B. Silver, *Black Teachers in Urban Schools: The Case of Washington, D. C.* (New York: Praeger Publishers, 1973).

[61] Silver, *Black Teachers in Urban Schools.*

[62] Kenneth Henry, *The Large Corporation Public Relations Manager: Emerging Professional in a Bureaucracy?* (New Haven: College and University Press, 1972).

[63] Henry, *The Large Corporation Public Relations Manager.*

[64] Henry, *The Large Corporation Public Relations Manager.*

[65] Henry, *The Large Corporation Public Relations Manager.*

[66] Walter I. Wardwell, "A Marginal Professional Role: The Chiropracter," *Social Forces, 30* (March 1952), 339-348.

[67] Lee Braude, *Work and Workers: A Sociological Analysis* (New York: Praeger Publishers, 1975), p. 122.

[68] Wardwell, "A Marginal Professional Role: The Chiropracter."

[69] A large percentage (40 percent) of the body's nerve pathways cannot in any way be affected by spinal manipulation, which is the basic area of chiropractic manipulation. One medical study claims that the remaining 60 percent of nerve pathways, all located in the spinal cord, cannot be affected in any way by manipulation of the vertebrae.

[70] Joseph R. Botta, "Chiropracters: Healers or Quacks?—Part II," *Consumer Reports, 40* (October 1975), 610.

[71] Botta, "Chiropracters," p. 610.

[72] Thelma H. McCormak, "The Druggists' Dilemma: Problems of a Marginal Occupation," *American Journal of Sociology, 61* (January 1956), 308-315.

[73] Earl R. Quinney "Occupational Structure and Criminal Behavior: Prescription Violation by Retail Pharmacists," *Social Problems, 11* (Fall 1963), 179-185.

[74] Quinney, "Occupational Structure and Criminal Behavior."

[75] Quinney, "Occupational Structure and Criminal Behavior," pp. 184-185.

[76] Carol Kronus, "Occupational Values, Role Orientations, and Work Settings: The Case of Pharmacy," *The Sociological Quarterly, 16* (Spring 1975), 179. This outcome occurred using a modified version of indices developed by another researcher who studied pharmacists (see Earl Quinney, above) and whose findings supported differing core values for professionally and business-oriented pharmacists.

[77] Kronus, "Occupational Values," p. 180. This outcome occurred using a modified version of Rosenberg's questions. See Morris Rosenberg, *Occupations and Values* (New York: The Free Press, 1957).

[78] Kronus, "Occupational Values," p. 132.

[79] Norman K. Denzin, with the Assistance of Curtis J. Mettlin, "Incomplete Professionalization: The Case of Pharmacy," *Social Forces, 46* (March 1968), 375-381.

[80] Arthur Pearl and Frank Riessman, *New Careers for the Poor: The Nonprofessional in Human Service* (New York: The Free Press, 1965).

[81] Gloria V. Engel, "Social Factors Affecting Work Satisfaction of the Physician's Assistant: A Preliminary Report," in Halmos (ed.), *Professionalisation and Social Change*, pp. 256-257.

[82] Joseph Katan, "The Attitudes of Professionals Towards the Employment of Indigenous Nonprofessionals in Human Service Organizations," in Halmos (ed.), *Professionalisation and Social Change*, pp. 231-233.

[83] Arthur Niederhoffer, *Behind the Shield: The Police in Urban Society* (Garden City, N.Y.: Doubleday, 1967).

[84] Niederhoffer, *Behind the Shield.*

[85] Niederhoffer, *Behind the Shield.*

[86] David H. Bayley and Harold Mendelsohn, *Minorities and the Police* (New York: The Free Press, 1969), p. 54.

[87] James Q. Wilson, *Varieties of Police Behavior* (Cambridge, Mass.: Harvard University Press, 1968), pp. 7, 16-33.

[88] Egon Bittner, "Police Discretion in Energency Apprehension of Mentally Ill Persons," *Social Problems, 14* (Winter 1967), 278-292.

[89] Bittner, "Police Discretion...," p. 285.

[90] Bittner, "Police Discretion...," p. 286.

[91] Bittner, "Police Discretion...," pp. 227-228.

[92] Bittner, "Police Discretion...," pp. 291-292.

[93] Peter K. Manning, "Rules, Colleagues and Situationally Justified Actions," in Ralph Blankenship (ed.), *Colleagues in Organization: The Social Construction of Professional Work* (New York: John Wiley & Sons, Inc., in press).

[94] Manning, "Rules, Colleagues and Situationally Justified Actions."

[95] Nicholas Alex, *Black in Blue: A Study of the Negro Policeman* (New York: Appleton-Century-Crofts, 1969).

[96] Alex, *Black in Blue,* pp. 36-38.

[97] Alex, *Black in Blue,* pp. 6, 13.

[98] Alex, *Black in Blue,* pp. 14, 174-178.

[99] Alex, *Black in Blue,* p. 61.

[100] Alex, *Black in Blue,* pp. 178-179.

[101] Alex, *Black in Blue,* pp. 182-196.

[102] Alex, *Black in Blue,* p. 201.

[103] Alex, *Black in Blue,* pp. 204-210. Alex's portrait of the black police officer has been contested in a more recent study by Michael Wubnig, "Black Police Attitudes in the New York City Police Department: An Exploratory Study," unpublished Ph.D. thesis, The City University of New York, 1975.

[104] William J. Goode, "The Theoretical Limitations of Professionalization," in Etzioni (ed.), *The Semi-Professions,* pp. 280-281, 287.

[105] Goode, "The Theoretical Limits of Professionalization," pp. 286, 296.

[106] Collins points out that this is true of engineers and technicians. Randall Collins, *Conflict Sociology: Toward an Explanatory Science* (New York: Academic Press, 1975), p. 345.

[107] Eliot Freidson (ed.), *The Professions and Their Prospects*, p. 35.

[108] Peter L. Berger, "Some General Observations on the Problem of Work," in Peter L. Berger, *The Human Shape of Work* (New York: Macmillan Co., 1964), pp. 216, 230.

[109] Marie R. Haug and Marvin B. Sussman, "Professional Autonomy and the Revolt of the Client," *Social Problems, 17* (Fall 1969), 153-160.

[110] Goode, "The Theoretical Limits of Professionalization," pp. 269-270.

13 CLERICAL AND SALES WORKERS

Clerical and sales workers comprise the large majority of lower white-collar positions in the American labor force. Retail sales people number over 3 million workers; secretaries, 2½ million; bookkeepers, 1 million; and wholesale trades people, ½ million (see Table 2.7). Nearly one-quarter of the labor force is included in the two occupational groups that are the focus of this chapter (see Table 2.5).

Four major patterns have characterized the evolution of clerical and sales occupations over the past century.

1. The enormous increase in the number of employees.
2. The progressive femininization of the two groups.
3. The mechanization and scientific organization of work tasks.
4. The deterioration of the economic status (and, consequently, social status) of the two groups in comparison to blue-collar workers—they are now nearly equal in economic status but still superior in social status.[1]

Each pattern is covered in this chapter.

Most of the increase has been in the clerical occupations. This is where expansion in the industrial labor force was needed for new large-scale organizations to collect information, to communicate it, to record it properly, and to store and retrieve it. As I shall point out, most of the occupations in the sales and clerical occupational groups are not part of the decision-making process of the organization, even less so than the semiprofessions. However, they work in close proximity to the elite groups and, as a result, gain prestige by associating directly with the organizational leaders.

WOMEN IN CLERICAL AND SALES OCCU-PATIONS

One in every three working women is in a clerical occupation. Comparing women to men in various industries by occupation, the differences from 1940 to 1970 are striking.[2] Service industries, comprising medical, legal, and educational services, and business, personal, and hotel services, are the principal employers of women. For women, there was a large increase in clerical workers created by demand in the health and educational services industries. For example, in health care services, 8 out of every 10 employees are women. These services are extensions of the work women do in the home: teaching children, nursing the sick, and preparing food.

In examining all major industry groups (see Chart 13.1), researchers found that women are clustered into fewer occupational groups than men.[3] In the service industries in 1970 most women are still employed in the same three occupational groups as in 1940: professional and technical, clerical and sales, and service. In the trade industries women were found predominantly in the clerical and sales occupations and continued to increase their proportion in it. These jobs are located mostly in general merchandising and include titles such as sales clerks, bookkeepers, cashiers, secretaries, typists, and office machine operators. Among the manufacturing industries there has been an increase in female clerical and sales workers and a decrease in operatives (assemblers, checkers, inspectors, and sewers and stitchers).[4]

Full-time, year-round working women earn only about 60 percent of what males earn (as measured by median annual earnings). This is not so much because they are not receiving equal pay for equal work as it is because discrimination in hiring and upgrading and the kinds of jobs women perform. For example, from a sample of 18 banks in six large American cities, it was found that 73 percent of clerical and office jobs were held by women, whereas only 15 percent of the managerial positions were held by women. These figures do not vary significantly by size of bank, size of city, or percent of women in the labor force. Most important, these bank training programs gave little hope of any improvement in the future in this breakdown between males and females.[5]

CHART 13.1 OCCUPATIONAL DISTRIBUTION OF WAGE AND SALARY WORKERS, SELECTED INDUSTRIES, 1940 AND 1970

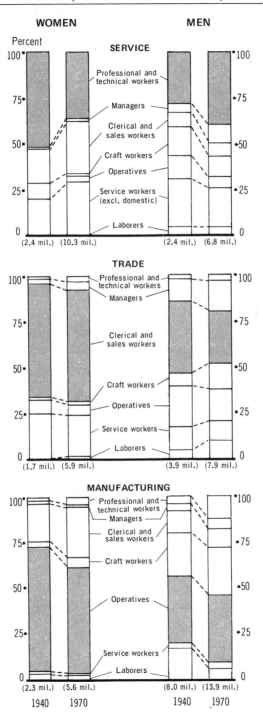

WOMEN   MEN

SERVICE

Professional and technical workers
Managers
Clerical and sales workers
Craft workers
Operatives
Service workers (excl. domestic)
Laborers

(2.4 mil.) (10.3 mil.)   (2.4 mil.) (6.8 mil.)

TRADE

Professional and technical workers
Managers
Clerical and sales workers
Craft workers
Operatives
Service workers
Laborers

(1.7 mil.) (5.9 mil.)   (3.9 mil.) (7.9 mil.)

MANUFACTURING

Professional and technical workers
Managers
Clerical and sales workers
Craft workers
Operatives
Service workers
Laborers

(2.3 mil.) (5.6 mil.)   (8.0 mil.) (13.9 mil.)

1940   1970   1940   1970

Source. Elizabeth Waldman and Beverly J. McEaddy, "Where Women Work—An Analysis by Industry and Occupation," *Monthly Labor Review, 97* (May 1974), 8.

THE MODERN
OFFICE AS A
FEMALE
GHETTO

Concentrating on the occupation of the secretary, Mary Kathleen Benét contends that the modern office is a female ghetto.[6] Historically, the secretarial position developed as a haven for unattached, middle-class women. At the beginning of the twentieth century, the traditional "genteel" occupations of governess, dressmaker, teacher and nurse were quite limited in income and prestige. Office work was seen as an acceptable occupation for these women, especially in light of the increased demand for office workers brought on by the tremendous increase in clerical work. Between 1890 and 1905 the percentage of women in clerical jobs increased from 15 to 33 percent.[7]

As usually happens, men saw the movement of women into the clerical occupations as a threat to their status and began to move out in droves. Some (e.g., accountants, personnel managers, and office managers) started to specialize and to limit entrance into their specialty by licensing and testing. Women were prevented from entering these "professionalizing" occupations by means of covert discriminatory practices.[8]

This discrimination against women in office work continues practically unabated. Women tend to receive the same amount of office space in proportion to their salary differences with men—about 20 to 50 percent less. Likewise, Benét states that the higher the concentration of women in any part of the office, the more inferior the standard of the interior decor.[9]

The secretary's work role is grossly undervalued, sharply differentiated from male sex roles, and has status gradations based on age and sex. It is, in effect, a mirror image of family life. The office is a family in that the secretary acts as wife, mistress, and maid to the manager at different stages in her career. Her work is the business equivalent of the housework of the maid. She types letters, which in many cases could be sent out in written form by her boss. Filing is like washing the dishes—it is never-ending. Both typing and filing are largely time-fillers for boring and unnecessary work. As a mother, she protects her boss form his subordinates. As a wife, she listens to his domestic problems. As a mistress, she supplies a young and sexy atmosphere.[10]

In her occupational role as "mother" and "wife" the secretary becomes an important part of the organizational efficiency. Her reliability, discreetness, and intelligence must be of a high order to carry out many of the functions of her office successfully. She must know how to handle the client before the client sees the boss. She must know how to brief the boss on new clients, appointments, threatening competitors, and the like. In many cases she is as indispensable to the manager or executive as the nurse is to the physician.

SALESPEOPLE

There are nearly 5 million salespeople in the labor force. They range from the wholesale salesperson for a major manufacturing company in steel to the clerk behind the counter of the local five-and-dime store, the local newsboy, and hucksters and peddlers. Only a few types have been studied sufficiently to review here.

Retail and Industrial Goods Salespeople

Interviews with 66 salespeople in retail and industrial goods in New York City showed the salesperson as needing both technical and psychological know-how.[11] Regarding the former, most salespeople felt that having the right kind of general selling ability was most important. The satisfaction of overcoming a great amount of uncertainty in getting the customer to buy was stated by most as being the key. It is "psychic income." The actual money is not made for its own sake or even so much for what it will buy. Salespeople are expressively oriented. Making the sale itself gratifies their egos.[12]

The technical aspect is also considered important because salespeople must constantly read in order to update themselves in a fast-changing technology. They must also present themselves very carefully—they should not overdress or underdress, but they should dress similarly to the client. They must be likable but must not overwhelm the customer with compliments. They must be literate, tactful, and look trustworthy. They must be prepared to take rebuffs and rudeness.[13]

Salespeople want to professionalize because they feel that the public usually associates them with the behind-the-counter retail salesclerk. However, since most are located in large organizations, they are ambivalent about professionalizing—the bureaucratized organizations have given them more prestige over the years. However, this prestige comes at the cost of personal autonomy as work relationships become highly routinized in the bureaucratic organization. The salesperson is no longer the individual proprietor going out into the unknown to overcome uncertainty.[14]

Mills elaborates on this point. Through rationalization, salespeople on the road are reduced as a power threat to the firm. They no longer can hold their customers as ransom for higher salaries because customers no longer depend on their services. Advertising has now taken over three important beginning sales steps: (1) making the initial contacts, (2) arousing interest, and (3) creating preference. Now salespeople only make the specific proposal and close the order. Salespeople become "objects of standardization" as their work is centralized and rationalized. They lose their autonomy—they no longer price articles or select products. Even personality is rationalized. They must sell themselves; that is, they must be friendly, courteous, and show genuine interest even if they are actually uninterested.[15]

New-Car Salespeople

Today's new-car salespeople are generally pictured as employees of an agency, who operate in a more restrained manner than the entrepreneurial wheeler-dealer of the past. As such, they are viewed as persons who generally adhere to the prescribed patterns of behavior set forth by the agency. However, in reality there is a great deal of unpredictable behavior that takes place in the interaction between customer and salesperson.

In a symbolic interactionist approach, Stephen Miller describes "the sales transaction as interaction" as operating in three distinct phases: the "contact," the "pitch," and the "close."[16] The emphasis is placed on the course of the interaction on the salesperson's behavior instead of on the influence of normative patterns of the sales agency. In the contact there are two ways in which salesperson and customer come together—randomly and soliciting through a friend. The latter method is the one preferred by the salesperson. It is known as the "bird dog" system and places the seller-buyer relationship on a more personal basis. The salesperson receives information from a friend (the "bird dog") in order to control the relationship.[17]

In the pitch salespeople try to find out why customers want to buy a car and gear their sales talk to provide the most favorable outcome. They adjust their role to the symbols and cues presented by the buyer. They attempt to control the situation by making the customers talk and reveal their wishes. The close occurs when the customer accepts one of the offers of the salesperson. The close may involve a "cooling out" period when the victim is made to feel like a shrewd buyer who has gotten the best of the deal. Salespeople do this in order to keep a steady customer. If the car is a real "lemon," to continue to keep the customer happy the salesperson makes sure that the service manager keeps "cooling him out."[18]

Salespeople must present themselves as performers with an audience. They have a "routine" that they go through, and they must adjust their timing in response to the customer's cues. They must treat themselves as "serviceable instruments" at all times.[19]

Used-Car Salespeople

The role relationship of used-car salespeople to their customers is quite different from that of new-car salespeople. In another symbolic interactionist interpretation, using participant observation of Boston salespeople, Joy Browne depicts the relationship between the used-car salesperson and customer as a game with fairly standard rules, but the interaction can vary greatly from one transaction to another. "The entire situation is one of compromise and change." Customers come to the used-car dealer expecting dishonesty. The salespeople know the customers feel this way. The customers expect that the salespeople are the experts, and the salespeople know they are not. Both the customer and the salespeople have their own self-image to maintain. This is the bargaining situation. Neither party has control of the situation, and each person depends on the actions of the other before determining how to proceed.[20]

In the process of bargaining, the relationships between customer, salesperson, and "the house" (the owner or manager of the used-car lot) are constantly changing. The salespeople will use the house as the bad guy with whom they will have to plead to accept an unusually low price which, in most cases, is actually not even rock bottom. However, salespeople usually do not know the bottom price, the price for which the lot manager bought the car. The house keeps the price secret, assuming that the salespeople will try harder to get a better price from the customer if they do not know what the actual price of the car was. Salespeople's commission is usually based on how many cars they have sold during the month, not on the difference between the purchase price and the sales price. They do not know the condition of the car, the price paid by the car lot, the income they will earn on the sale, or the level at which the house will let them bargain down to. Yet they have to maintain a "front" or a "face" strong enough to complete a long and often tedious interaction process. They are engaged in the management of impressions. Neither they nor the customers are aware of the "actual" price of the used car; thus both are free to bargain the price. The first one to convince the other that the rock bottom price has been reached usually determines the final price.[21]

The closing of a deal is seldom reached on the first visit, and much bargaining takes place on subsequent visits. An additional complication is the trade-in of the customer's old car. Often, one price is jacked up to compensate for the other, thus making the customers feel like they are driving a hard bargain. For example:

> *If a guy thinks his car is worth [$]300 and it's worth 100, then you add another 100 onto the price of the car you're selling him and then you can offer him 200 for his car even though it's only worth 100.*[22]

Then, the salesperson has techniques for pricing the customer's car.

> *When you go out to his car with him, run your hand over the fender; let him know that the dent is there, but don't mention it. Get down on your hands and knees like you are really interested. The customer will volunteer information as you walk around; he will assist you. Then he will be willing to take less money on his vechicle. Be complete. Open up the trunk, the speedometer, the hood; have an appraisal sheet and explain to the customer that you want to give him a fair price.*[23]

Buying a used car is different from buying a new car. New car dealers know the price of the car can vary only by the differences in dealer's overhead and by freight distance from the factory. In buying a used car, the price is not known by either party. The customer also finds a unique object— no two used cars are in the same condition or have the same mileage. It is the salesperson's job to make customers feel that this particular car is exactly what they have been looking for.[24]

TELEPHONE OPERATORS

The occupation of telephone operator is a low-wage job filled mostly by women high school graduates. In 1970, 95 percent of all operators were women, three-quarters of whom had 12 years of school completed, earning a median annual wage of $4241.[25] It is a job in which training is quick—usually lasting not longer than a week—and turnover is high. Approximately ½-million persons are telephone operators.

Customer's Service Representatives[26]

Elinor Langer tells of her personal experiences as a telephone company customer's service representative. Upon joining the telephone company, she found herself in a large office of about 100 women, five representitives assigned to a women supervisor, four supervisors to one male manager, and three managers to one male district supervisor in an executive suite, the top post in the office. Along with four other district supervisors in four other offices, the district manager is also subordinate to a division chief, and division chiefs are subordinate to still higher executives in the vast AT&T hierarchy. Women are very rarely found above the supervisor level.

The job of the customer's service representative (the job Langer was trained for) is highly routinized. The position is interchangeable with any other representative in any part of the country. The same course of instruction is given at all phone company offices. Every task is broken down into its simplest parts and analyzed in order to find its most rational (i.e., most efficient and productive) operation. The representative *must* use this particular behavior pattern. This almost always results in completely dehumanized interaction. A set of rules has been made up to fit all possible situations into a small set of outcomes. For example, the first rule is to obtain control of the situation by saying: "Hello, this is Miss Jones. May I help you?" The second rule is to indicate your willingness to help and indicate the need for further investigation, possibly by another representative or supervisor. While this transaction is taking place, the representative must always write down the information on a customer card. Often a single customer call, of which there are about 50 a day, can require four or five different forms to be filled out by the representative. In some cases, service calls require a long period of time to complete (10 minutes or more), and representatives must call back the customer later because they have to be "on call" for regular service calls during specified times. All this places a tremendous pressure on representatives to complete their work within the allotted time. Penalties are assessed for failure to keep within time limits. In addition, monthly sales quotas are assigned to each representative for Trimline phones, Princess extensions, and so forth.

Some effects of this boring, low-paying job are discussed by Langer. She notes that wearing wigs is very popular among the representatives, as if by drastically changing their physical appearance almost daily they will compensate for the drab routine of the work. The women are also heavily consumer oriented. Langer feels they are trying to express their individuality through the products they purchase and endlessly talk about at work, again to compensate for their work alienation. This atmosphere of consumerism is also fostered by the telephone company, which gives each woman a Christmas present and periodically distributes other small gifts. That particular year the Christmas gift was a wooden doll with a sign proclaiming "Extensions in Color."

Telephone Switchboard Operators

The job of the telephone switchboard operator is one of the less desirable white-collar jobs because the switchboards must be operated around the clock, 7 days a week. Therefore shifts are required, very uncommon for white-collar workers, as is the close supervision of their work. Supervisors are constantly monitoring the work of the operators, to the extent that the discipline is often compared to that found on the assembly line. Pay is also low by community standards.[27]

Thus the switchboard operator is unable to enjoy the usual prerogatives of the average white-collar worker: close proximity to management, one's own desk, absence of supervision, regular work hours, and freedom to move around the office. Many persons view telephone operators as falling somewhere between white-collar and blue-collar work. The job content is blue-collar, but the social outlook of the workers and some employers is that it is white-collar.[28]

Some operators expressed liking for the job because of dealing with the public.[29] Dotty Neal, who worked for the telephone company for 23 years, explains how she still likes being an "information" operator best.

I love talking to people and each call is a challenge. It's sometimes hard to understand people and get out of them what they really want. Foreign accents can be hard to handle at first, when you're a new operator, but you learn to catch on pretty fast.... You have to have a good ear. And you can't have rabbit ears—a lot of people, especially Italians, get real angry if you can't understand them.[30]

However, as the interviewer noted, "She [Dottie Neal] can count on the fingers of one hand the number of calls that have been out of the ordinary [over the past 23 years]." She answers about 75 calls an hour, 600 calls a day. After 30 years' service—which almost no operator reaches—you receive free use of your private home phone and $15 a month toward long-distance calls.[31]

GROCERY CLERKS: DIRTY WHITE COL-LARS

Grocery clerks probably have more in common with the semiskilled blue-collar workers than with white-collar workers. They rarely wait on customers and spend most of their time stocking shelves, sweeping floors, bagging groceries, and running various errands—in other words, manual labor that does not require a high degree of skill. Some blue-collar jobs, such as warehouse stockroom worker, actually involve less physical exertion and better general working conditions. The grocery clerk's job is "dirty white-collar."[32]

In the larger supermarkets the job of the grocery clerk is divided into specialized tasks so that some clerks are engaged in stocking shelves most of the time unless there is a rush at the check-out counters, others are working only on produce, and still others are food baggers except when activity at the check-out counters is very slow. "Baggers," as they are known, have perhaps the most boring job in the store. Their only task is to pick up the grocery items as they roll down the conveyer belt from the cash register and pack them into paper bags. Cans on the bottom, paper goods, eggs, and produce on top. Keep the meat away from the soap—to eliminate possible odor contamination. Spread the heavy goods between bags to balance the weight of the bags. Approximate training time—10 minutes.

It doesn't take long to become bored with this kind of work—only an hour or two at the most, as the customers' faces become a blur of nonentities in the late afternoon rush. Cash registers whirring and clicking, the background of Musak, mixed with several hundred voices and the clinking of glass and rattle of shopping carts and bags. Discussion with fellow baggers working at other cash registers is limited to a few words after each bagging—if another happens to finish at the same time you do. Otherwise, talking is forbidden. This is strictly enforced by the manager, who walks the line of check-out counters, keeping the customers happy and the baggers frustrated.

After a while, one begins to fantasize in order to break the monotony. The bagging becomes a game. What is the record time in which one can bag one full shopping cart? Two full shopping carts? What are the least number of bags in which the groceries will all fit? The last item, usually a watermelon slice, or a carton of eggs, one fantasizes as a time bomb that will go off unless it is bagged by the time the second hand on the clock in the back of the store reaches 12. Plans are made for the groceries of people waiting in line. If any shoppers are waiting with two carts of mostly soft goods and other hard-to-bag items, you suddenly slow down in the hope that they will get tired of waiting and switch to another faster-moving line.

Some persons do adjust to this work and come to enjoy it to some extent. These are persons with stability in performance,[33] persons who are psychologically stable, perseverant, calm, submissive, and of moderate intelligence. However, the question is whether these phlegmatic workers are born stable or whether the environmental factors of social class, education, and the work itself are conducive to the development of these personality types. In the remaining chapters it will be argued that the environmental factors are the important influences on worker performance.

The grocery clerk's advancement opportunities are very limited. Supermarket chains have "flat" organizational structures. There are very few steps between the lowest position and the highest—five at the most between the beginning clerk and the store manager. Level three (the experienced clerk) can be reached in most cases in less than a year. But there is no movement after that unless the clerk can obtain the one post of assistant store manager. The average supermarket has many clerks and only one manager and one asisstant manager, severely limiting upward mobility at this level. Also, store managers have little hope of advancement to middle or top management positions at the food chain's central offices. These higher-level positions need a different type of expertise and experience from that gained by working up through the occupational structure of the store.[34]

WORK ALIENA-TION

In a review of major studies of job satisfaction over the past 40 years, George Strauss concludes that in all types of work organizations the large majority of workers are satisfied with their jobs. A Gallup poll taken in 1973 supports the findings: 3 of every 4 workers are satisfied with their work, and only 1 in every 10 is dissatisfied. These rates tend to vary only slightly by age, sex, race, and occupation.[35]

These findings are in substantial disagreement with a 1971 national survey conducted by the University of Michigan Survey Research Center which, when it asked the question: "What type of work would you try to get into if you could start all over again?" received responses by only 43 percent of white-collar workers and 24 percent of blue-collar workers that they would continue in their present occupation.[36] This type of question probably gives a more accurate answer to people's true feelings about alienation from their work.

Job dissatisfaction varies by industry. Jobs with shorter cycles, those that lack autonomy and control over the work process, and those that do not offer a challenge tend to be less satisfying. The Gallup poll found that the most frequently chosen reason for job dissatisfaction was "poor wages." "Boring work" was the second most frequent choice, not the first. This extrinsic choice may reflect the economic cycle, the intrinsic choice of boring work being more popular in times of general prosperity.[37]

CHART 13.2 MEASURES OF WORK INVOLVEMENT, BY WORKER ORIENTATION AND TYPE OF WORK

		Type of Work (What the Work Gives)	
		Nonchallenging	Challenging
Worker Orientation (What I Want from the Job)	Expressive	(3)	(1)
	Instrumental	(4)	(2)

Source: George Strauss, "Workers: Attitudes and Adjustments," in Jerome M. Rosow (ed.), *The Worker and the Job: Coping with Change*, p. 87. Copyright © 1974 by Prentice-Hall, Inc. Reprinted by permission of the publisher.

Strauss presents a scheme for discussing job dissatisfaction in a two-dimensional relationship (see Chart 13.2).[38] One dimension measures the workers' orientation toward work, that is, their expectations regarding the degree of self-actualization and their need to achieve. Persons with expressive orientations tend to have their needs to achieve satisfied. Work becomes an end in itself. Persons with instrumental orientations view their jobs as only a means to another end. The second dimension measures the degree of challenge in the workers' jobs. Does it supply variety, autonomy, and opportunity to participate in major decisions? Is it intrinsically rewarding or not? The two dimensions relate what the workers want from the job to what they give to it. Four possible types emerge:

1. The highly satisfied worker. These workers seek self-fulfillment on the job and are fortunate enough to find jobs that fill this requirement.
2. These workers hold jobs too demanding for their desires and capabilities.

They feel overpressured by constant changes and uncertainty, receiving more challenge than they desire. These people are the "underachievers." Many will, if they can, move to cell 4 by changing jobs or, less likely, to cell 1 by changing aspirations.

3. The highly dissatisfied. The overtrained are often found here, for example, college graduates in clerical jobs. Some keep this job and turn to nonwork activities within the family or the community in order to find self-fulfillment. Others become depressed, lower their job expectations, and move to cell 4.

4. The work is nonchallenging, and no intrinsic rewards are expected from it. It is "a job," "a living," providing the money necessary for "the good things in life." Management provides the necessary hygienic conditions, that is, acceptable wages and benefits and decent supervision. Workers are not motivated. They are apathetic but not necessarily dissatisfied.[39]

Regarding cell 4, a Marxist interpretation would be that the workers have been given a hygienic work setting in terms of pay, security, and working conditions but nevertheless are not motivated through responsibility and challenge. Because they are alienated (Marx's definition of alienation as work that serves as a means for other ends only and not as a satisfying activity in itself), the worker cannot accept challenging work. When workers sell their labor on the market, they also sell their control over the work process. "In his work he [the worker] does not belong to himself but to another person." The fruit of one's productivity is the "surplus value" of the organization, that is, the savings to the owner or manager of private property over and above the cost of production plus wages. Thus, what workers do (their work in capitalist society) alienates them.[40]

Strauss concludes, however, that his reading of the evidence of studies in social science is that for all groups of workers, including professional and managerial, the lack of challenge is not as oppressive as the lack of income.[41] Marx emphasized both money and meaningfulness as important—money for physical needs and meaningfulness for personal and social needs. However, as unemployment increases and the number of the working poor increases, income again is taking precedence.

Alienation of the Office Worker

In a study of seven Parisian insurance companies from 1956 to 1960, Michel Crozier asked office workers in interviews whether they considered themselves members of an exploited class (a Marxist orientation) or as "non-manual" workers, that is, not related to a social class antagonistic to its employers.[42] Six occupations were studied: insurance claims adjusters, policy writers, clerks, typists, keypunchers, and filers. He found that:

- The more professional the occupation, the more interested the incumbents are in their work and the more they tend to complain about their position.
- Those who are most dissatisfied with their position have parents with the highest level of education and more prestigious occupations.
- Persons in the lower-level occupations are satified with their positions because they have job security, something they have been taught and experience as important.
- Persons in the higher-level occupations feel a revolution of rising expectations; they are willing to take the risk of complaining because they are higher in the hierarchy. They feel that they have some power, that they have some say in decision making. They are more satisfied with their work but less loyal to their company and less happy—they feel their position does not carry much prestige.[43]

Office workers have ambivalent attitudes. They feel themselves as both exploited workers and as participants in directing the work of others, specifically, blue-collar workers. What really differentiates office workers from blue-collar workers is that they are on the promotional ladder to the top of the organization, even though they are at the bottom of that ladder. They are aware that they or their children might possibly climb this ladder, and they know what they must do in advance to move upward. They engage in what Robert Merton called anticipatory socialization—they prepare for the next higher position by taking on the values and attitudes of those in that position. They tend to maintain these values even if they become downwardly mobile, even into blue-collar occupations.[44]

This reference group orientation indicates that structural characteristics of the organization in which workers are located are very significant regarding involvement in work. In a study of a large electronics manufacturing plant, J. M. Pennings found that white-collar workers in lower-prestige occupations who have jobs with a prospect of promotion show a value system that is consistent with the role of the social position that they hope to attain. They are expressively oriented (see Chart 13.2), whereas those low white-collar workers who see little chance for social mobility have an instrumental attitude toward work. Therefore, the white-collar "class" is not homogeneous, as C. Wright Mills and others contend. The differences in their value systems created by the structural factor of promotion or demotion cause them to view themselves as either middle class or working class.[45]

Thus, the labor market is stratified, but by balkanizing it instead of creating social classes. Crozier believes that because there are no real social class differences, balkanization by management is necessary in order to motivate employees to participate actively and efficiently in the organization. Organizations are homogeneous enough to maintain participation, yet stratified enough to foster rejection of those persons who are different. People are now differentiated on the basis of several ambiguous roles.[46]

The rational life of modern organizations permits a fairly cheap and efficient way for everyone to play the games they like. There are the games of conflict and cooperation, in which risk is limited but nevertheless always present.[47] If there were no uncertainty to life, no ambiguity and contradiction, life would be fully predictable, one-dimensional. As a result, there is an embourgeoisement of blue-collar workers instead of a proletarianization of the white-collar worker.[48] It is a level consciousness instead of a class consciousness that predominates.

However, everyone does not play these games with equal amounts of risk. Workers in the more professionalized occupations (nonoffice workers) feel freer to act. They desire more participation in decision making, are more critical of the company, and have successfully fought the strict paternalism of the French culture. Office workers, on the other hand, generally cannot cope with highly tolerant situations. They tend to fall back into formality and obedience when faced with ambiguous situations.[49] Since alienation is nothing but the "necessary counterpart" of the increased participation of people in organizations, those persons in the least professionalized occupations are most easily alienated from their work, and those at the top of the scale of professionalization are most easily involved.[50] As previously mentioned, whether they are involved depends to a considerable extent on the structural characteristics of the organization in which they work.

The Marxist View

The Marxist scholar would argue that job satisfaction can be high, as indicated earlier in this chapter, and at the same time job alienation can be high among the same individuals. Harry Braverman has defined alienation by referring to the original meaning of the verb, "to alienate." To alienate is "to transfer ownership to another." The lack of the following, then, are alienating features of capitalist society.

- Ownership of the tools and instruments of production.
- Ownership of the product.
- Ownership of the proceeds from the sale of the product.
- Ownership of the process of production.[51]

The wage becomes the sole equity of the worker in production. Thus, production in capitalist society is carried on by a mass of hostile or, at most, indifferent workers who have no stake in the outcome. Perhaps they are satisfied with salary and working conditions this year as compared to last, but they are alienated from their work.

Braverman then expands this into a labor market theory.[52] The purpose of capitalism is to create surplus capital, which is extracted from the process of production. This is accomplished by reducing the cost of labor power by breaking down complex work processes into simple tasks. The workers needed for simplified tasks are not well educated, require only brief job training, and possess easily replaceable and interchangeable skills.

As this process of the reduction of the costs of labor continues, more and more skilled jobs become less-skilled secondary market jobs. This is accomplished for the most part by the transferral of jobs from the primary labor market to the secondary labor market. Primary market jobs are found mostly in the goods-producing sector of the economy, and this sector's jobs are decreasing.[53] Jobs in the service-producing sector, which is expanding, are mostly secondary market jobs. Thus, a majority of jobs in the economy are now transformed into meaningless tasks, into jobs once considered as second jobs or as "pin money" jobs, but that now must be taken to support a family at or near the subsistence level.[54] The percentage of change in output and employment in U. S. industries between 1947 and 1964 reflects this overall trend.

INDUSTRY	PERCENT OF INCREASE IN OUTPUT	PERCENT OF EMPLOYMENT
Textiles	40	–33
Petroleum	84	+25
Construction	100	+50
Electrical machinery	300	–50
Motor freight	300	–70
Aluminum	400	–100
Air transport	800	–133

In no case does the increase in employment equal the increase in output. In some cases employment *decreases* as output increases. The rapid growth in employment has come in the clerical and service occupations, but it has not been enough to absorb the decrease in employment in other occupational groups and industries.

Braverman concludes that the federal government is performing a cover-up operation of these unemployed by manipulating the statistics and by accepting higher unemployment rates. In 1949 an unemployment rate of 6 percent was considered recessionary; in 1975 a 7 percent rate would be considered an acceptable recovery from the 1974 to 1975 recession. In February 1975, the

Bureau of the Census stated that unemployment had fallen by ½ million persons from January 1975. However, during that same period, the number of persons who had "dropped out of the labor force" between January and February was 600,000. "Dropped out of the labor force" means that these 600,000 people had given up "actively seeking employment." They then became uncounted persons or nonpersons as far as the Bureau of the Census was concerned. They fall into the increasing group of welfare recipients—that pauperized mass of about 15 million persons.

From Braverman's analysis one can conclude that most people in clerical jobs are highly alienated. The "office mentality," that is, the belief of the office worker that no matter how trivial his work or lowly his position he is part of management, is no longer a powerful motivation. For example, once the work of secretaries becomes rationalized into an office pool, they no longer have the close contact with management or the ability to control small areas of information. The secretarial pool has been likened to the tasks of factory production workers. These white-collar workers have "jobs" instead of "careers."[55] As Mills described them, these new white-collar workers are workers without property and are in constant fear of unemployment. They are "increasingly subject to wage-worker conditions." They have no "plan of life." "The absence of any order of belief has left them morally defenseless as individuals and politically impotent as a group.... White-collar man has no culture to lean upon except the contents of a mass society that has shaped him and seeks to manipulate him to its alien ends." Theirs is a Kafkaesque world of paper routine.[56]

AUTOMATION AND ALIENA-TION

Automation can be simply defined as "a production process which uses electronic or other mechanical means to control the quality and quantity of a product."[57] In office work there are four technological levels of production; only the fourth level is truly automated:

1. *Office work as a craft.* Work is done by hand; for example, paperwork is processed and organized by persons without any mechanical aids. Examples are bookkeepers, with pen, ledger, and their ability to compute arithmetically; and secretaries, who act only as receptionists and message-takers for their employers.
2. *Office work as machine-tending.* Special-purpose machines are used to process information. Control still resides with the operator, who must feed the proper data cards to the machine. An example is simple mechanization: typewriters, adding machines, and dictating machines, which aid the work of the office clerk.

3. *Office work as assembly line.* The worker still has some control over
the information that is given to the system but not the speed at which
it is given. Punched data cards are used in discrete (uncoordinated)
machines. An example is punched-card data processing. Punched
cards run through machines with electronic sensors, and results are
printed up. Separate tasks are involved in using key punch machines,
programmed computers, and the like.

4. *Office work as fully automated.* The materials-handling process becomes fully integrated and controlled by machines. The computer
program controls all processes, and adjustments are made on the basis
of internal "feedback" systems built into the program. The process
is entirely controlled by the computer from start to finish. "Technology responds independently of man's actions." An example is electronic data processing. Programmed instructions on handling of data
and feedback mechanisms allow internal operation of computer without
human intervention. Integration and control are automated.[58]

Often, studies of the effects of automation on office workers fail to clarify
the stage of control and integration of technology and, as a result, come to
contradictory conclusions.[59] Shepard deals with these factors. His first analysis covered five insurance companies, a large bank, and an oil refinery. In the
refinery, machine maintenance craftsmen (nonmechanized) and the machine
monitors (automated) were much less alienated and more involved in their
work than machine operators (mechanized). The maintenance craftsmen had
a number of diverse and ever-changing tasks and in each case had to exercise
their skills in performing their jobs.[60]

In the insurance companies, the introduction of computers increased the
number of higher-level clerical jobs and reduced the number of boring jobs.
Jobs were generally upgraded. Job specialization increased when moving from
a craft operation to punched-card data. For example, the bookkeeper's functions of collecting and recording are now split into several parts with a job and
a machine for each part. With the advent of electronic data processing, these
separate jobs are again integrated into one, with much of the craft clerk's
boring tasks being eliminated. Now an "account control clerk" examines his
sets of computer tapes for overall output, forgeries, new accounts, overdrafts,
and so forth. Contacts are made with branch managers to rectify errors
found. The new occupation of "computer operator" is established to oversee
the running of a complex set of integrated computers, which handle what was
once the work of as many as a score or more persons in several occupations.
They are paid managerial-level salaries but are considered clericals from the point
view of the origin of their tasks. They have a great deal of flexibility in developing their programs.[61]

The prediction that office and factory work are becoming indistinguishable can only be analyzed, says Shepard, if one compares both groups in terms of their current levels of technology. He points out that workers in semiautomated offices and factories felt they had less responsibility[62] than workers in a chemical plant and a steel plant, which were fully automated.[63] Shepard's own research indicates basically the same lower degree of alienation among office computer operators and oil refinery control room operators. Although white-collar workers are generally less alienated than blue-collar workers, the level of technology may change the entire relationship. Office and factory are *not* becoming alike in the kinds of work done. There are too many variations from one industry to another and from one firm to another. The degree of control and integration is a better measure of the impact of automation on industry.[64]

In a review of studies of the effect of computer installations in insurance companies, an airline ticket reservation system, and an EDP inventory control system in a shoe company, Mann and Williams came to essentially the same conclusion as Shepard: the overall impact on employee alienation depends mostly on the degree of mechanization in the organization prior to changeover.[65] However, they disagree in that generally, the less mechanized the organization or department, the more alienated the workers will become when automation is introduced. In the accounting departments there was about an 80 percent change in jobs, many of them eliminated, and an overall 50 percent reduction in clerical jobs.[66] Although many routine jobs were eliminated, there was no substantial upgrading of jobs in general, and decision making became highly centralized. Also, many middle-level supervisory positions were eliminated, which meant less opportunity for advancement for the office worker. EDP created the need for a double shift in the shoe corporation to utilize the machine better. This caused greater visibility of people's mistakes because of its accuracy.[67]

One expert on computerization estimates that if computers were to disappear from insurance companies they would need an increase of 60 percent more clerical workers, 9 percent more supervisors, and 2 percent more managers.[68] Those who do remain in higher-level jobs are still in highly routinized, nonsupervisory work (e.g., Shepard's computer operators). According to Whisler, the resulting hierarchy is one of fewer levels instead of more levels. This emphasizes the largely unbridgeable gap between clericals and management[69] and means the death of the office mentality.

Automation is a very definite threat to many occupations. When such threats are received, an occupation will attempt to protect itself by preventing the rationalizing of its body of knowledge. An example of this protective reaction in a clerical occupation is presented by Bernard Karsh and Jack Siegman in their analysis of the reactions of tabulating machine operators to the

installation of a new computer.[70] The purpose of this computer was to combine many of the operations formerly completed by the tabulating operators.
The only persons who knew how to run the computer and coordinate operations for it were the newly hired programmers who came with the computer.
Top management had little idea of what kind of knowledge was required by
the computer for most efficient operation.

The programmers, higher in authority than the tabulators, were given only
information that they requested for the computer. No information was volun-
teered that would increase computer efficiency. This withholding of knowledge from the programmers gave the tabulators power over the areas of knowledge that they still controlled. The programmers insisted that management
institute rules and procedures in the various departments that would "extend
to all relevant operations the logical structure and needs of the computer."
This would be functional for the organization because it would provide the
needed information for efficient operation. Yet it would be dysfunctional for
the tabulators and all other departments whose secret knowledge would be
made "public" by ,the disclosure of information. They would literally be
programmed out of existence.

Thus, for awhile, subordinates held power over superordinates. "The object
of the game is to keep the occupant of the formally superior status sufficiently
ignorant to preclude the possibility that the ignorant one may eventually be
able to perform the act himself." Formal organizations are thus viewed as
structures of knowledge and ignorance.[71] They are places where social control is contested, where power relations are legalized but not necessarily legitimated in the eyes of workers.[72]

Joan Greenbaum[73] has documented the most recent changes in computer
occupations, showing that in the late 1960s rationalization of work tasks took
place very rapidly as new generations of computers allowed management to
create a strict division of labor between computer operators and computer
programmers. Programmers were no longer allowed in the computer room,
which reduced contact with operators (now called machine attendants) and
prevented any opportunity for the exchange of ideas and the development of
an integrated knowledge and control base. Furthermore, as programming
languages became simplified into "preplanned applications," programmers have
lost their monopoly on their expertise. Concurrently, the systems analyst, a
management-level position, became the person to decide on methods for solving
business problems. As the systems approach was pushed to full development
by management, skills were gradually removed from computer occupations and
a rigid hierarchy instituted.

SUMMARY AND
CONCLUSIONS

Clerical and sales occupations are the lower-prestige white-collar occupations. Following earlier observations that women and minorities are found in disproportionately large numbers in lower-prestige, lower-paid occupations, it is not surprising that most clerical positions of low rank are female dominated. Examples dealt with in this chapter are secretaries and telephone operators. Sales occupations present a slightly different story. They often require aggressive, dominant persons to operate in highly competitive and risky situations. These are defined as male work characteristics in U.S. culture and, consequently, females are less equally represented in sales positions—excepting the lowest-level jobs in department and variety stores.

Studies of work alienation in these lower white-collar occupations vary depending on the definition used. "Job satisfaction" research generally shows the average clerical or sales worker to be satisfied with his or her work. It is not so much the lack of challenge as it is the lack of income that reduces job satisfaction. However, "alienation" research (of the Marxist variety) emphasizes that income or wages is only one factor in the total measurement process, that the lack of worker equity in any part of the productive process prevents any intrinsic value from being assigned to one's work. By definition, work in a capitalist system is alienating.

Clerical workers are becoming more like blue-collar semiskilled workers in terms of income and working conditions. Although enough research evidence is not yet collected and some of the results are contradictory, studies of the effects of automation on worker involvement indicate that involvement will vary by the level of technology. The highest degree of technological control and integration (i.e., automation) tends to increase job satisfaction. Yet others contend that it also increases alienation in a capitalist economy because it reduces the last areas of uncertainty or control of the "lower participants" in the organization. Examples were given of transfer of secretaries to "pools," of computer programmers displacing tabulating machine operators, and of the balkanization of workers in the computer field.

There are many interpretations that can be made from this summary. Most of them seem to confirm the Marxist or conflict approach. Secondary market jobs are increasing and primary market jobs are decreasing. Clerical occupations are among those being most affected by this change in the occupational structure. Automation, which tends to produce higher incomes for a small group of the clerical workers, does not aid in increasing involvement in one's work, because the worker in the continuous process industry is still a propertyless worker, still unmotivated intrinsically because there is no real stake in the outcome of production.[74] Some of the most recent research in highly automated occupations (e.g., the computer field) indicates that these jobs are highly routinized and the very few that are integrated are converted to managerial-level positions.

The gradual dissolution of the office mentality, the belief of clericals that they or their children will be upwardly mobile, and the long-range effects of automation indicate more clearly than ever the diversity of views of white-collar workers. Level consciousness becomes more predominant among the upper-level white-collar workers and class consciousness among the lower-level white-collar workers.

FOOTNOTES FOR CHAPTER 13
CLERICAL AND SALES WORKERS

[1] Michel Crozier, *The World of the Office Worker* (Chicago: The University of Chicago Press, 1971), pp. 8-19.

[2] Elizabeth Waldman and Beverly J. McEaddy, "Where Women Work—An Analysis by Industry and Occupation," *Monthly Labor Review, 97* (May 1974), 3-13. For a list of industries see Table 3.4.

[3] Waldman and McEaddy, "Where Women Work," p. 5.

[4] Waldman and McEaddy, "Where Women Work," pp. 7-8.

[5] Rodney Alexander and Elizabeth Sapery, *The Shortchanged: Women and Minorities in Banking* (New York: Dunellen Publishing Co., 1973).

[6] Mary Kathleen Benét, *The Secretarial Ghetto* (New York: McGraw-Hill, 1972).

[7] Benét, *The Secretarial Ghetto*, pp. 33-38.

[8] Benét, *The Secretarial Ghetto*, pp. 42-43.

[9] Benét, *The Secretarial Ghetto*, pp. 64-65.

[10] Benét, *The Secretarial Ghetto*, pp. 42-43, 64-65, 68-74, 79.

[11] F. William Howton and Bernard Rosenberg, "The Salesman: Ideology and Self-Imagery in a Prototypical Occupation," *Social Research, 32* (Autumn 1965), 283.

[12] Howton and Rosenberg, "The Salesman," p. 283.

[13] Howton and Rosenberg, "The Salesman," pp. 280, 284.

[14] Howton and Rosenberg, "The Salesman," pp. 295-296.

[15] C. Wright Mills, *White Collar* (New York: Oxford University Press, 1951), pp. 180-181.

[16] Stephen J. Miller, "The Social Base of Sales Behavior," *Social Problems, 12* (Summer 1964), 15-23.

[17] Miller, "The Social Base of Sales Behavior."

[18] Miller, "The Social Base of Sales Behavior."

[19] Howton and Rosenberg, "The Salesman," pp. 296-297.

[20] Joy Browne, *The Used-Car Game: A Sociology of the Bargain* (Lexington, Mass.: D.C. Heath & Co., 1973), pp. xiv, 5.

[21] Browne, *The Used-Car Game*, pp. 66-69. 78. 95.

[22] Browne, *The Used-Car Game*, p. 105.

[23] Browne, *The Used-Car Game*, p. 48.

[24] Browne, *The Used-Car Game*, p. 9.

[25] Dixie Sommers, "Occupational Rankings for Men and Women by Earnings," *Monthly Labor Review, 97* (August 1974), Table 2, p. 45.

[26] Information in this section is based on the experiences of Elinor Langer, as she describes them in her "The Women of the Telephone Company," *The New York Review of Books, 14* (March 12 and March 26, 1970), 16-24, 14-22.

[27] Joel Seidman et al., "Telephone Workers," in Sigmund Nosow and William H. Form (eds.), *Man, Work, and Society* (New York: Basic Books, 1962), pp. 494, 499.

[28] Seidman, et al., "Telephone Workers," p. 498.

[29] Seidman, et al., "Telephone Workers," p. 499.

[30] Kenneth Lasson, "The Telephone Worker," in Kenneth Lasson (ed.), *The Workers* (New York: Bantam Books, 1972), p. 223.

[31] Lasson, "The Telephone Worker," pp. 228, 234.

[32] Martin Estey, "The Retail Clerks," in Albert A. Blum et al., (eds.), *White-Collar Workers* (New York: Random House, 1971), p. 65.

[33] German psychologists of the 1920s studied performance and coined the terms *Übungsfähigkeit* (ability in performance) and *Übungfestigkeit* (stabi-

lity in performance). These studies are reviewed by Georges Friedmann, *Industrial Society* (New York: The Free Press, 1955), pp. 134-136, 167-168.

[34] Estey, "The Retail Clerks," pp. 65-67.

[35] George Strauss, "Workers: Attitudes and Adjustments," in Jerome M. Rosow (ed.), *The Worker and the Job: Coping with Change* (Englewood Cliffs, N.J.: Prentice-Hall, 1974), pp. 74-75.

[36] *Work in America,* Report of a Special Task Force to the Secretary of Health, Education, and Welfare (Cambridge, Mass.: The MIT Press, 1973), pp. 14-15.

[37] Strauss, "Workers: Attitudes and Adjustments," pp. 75, 89.

[38] Strauss, "Workers: Attitudes and Adjustments," pp. 86-89.

[39] Strauss, "The Worker: Attitudes and Adjustments."

[40] Karl Marx, *Economic and Philosophic Manuscripts of 1844* (Moscow: Foreign Languages Publishing House, 1961), pp. 69-72.

[41] Strauss, "The Worker: Attitudes and Adjustments," p. 97.

[42] Michel Crozier, *The World of the Office Worker.*

[43] Crozier, *The World of the Office Worker,* pp. 97-104, 144-146, 182-183, 200.

[44] Crozier, *The World of the Office Worker,* p. 35.

[45] J. M. Pennings, "Work-Value Systems of White-Collar Workers," *Administrative Science Quarterly, 15* (December 1970), 397-406.

[46] Crozier, *The World of the Office Worker,* pp. 160, 213.

[47] The lower participants of an organization can wield considerable power outside their formally defined positions by controlling access to persons, information, and technology. Secretaries can gain some control by taking charge of parking stickers for their organization. The ward physician is often dependent on the attendant because the latter can refuse to give important information concerning the patient or refuse to administer certain drugs. For further discussion and examples, see David Mechanic, "Sources of Power of Lower Participants in Complex Organizations," *Administrative Science Quarterly, 7* (December 1962), 349-364.

[48] Crozier, *The World of the Office Worker,* pp. x-xi, 38.

[49] Crozier, *The World of the Office Worker,* pp. 133, 155.

[50] Crozier, *The World of the Office Worker*, pp. 210, 213.

[51] Harry Braverman, "Work and Unemployment," *Monthly Review, 27* (June 1975), p. 20.

[52] Braverman, "Work and Unemployment," pp. 18-32.

[53] The analysis and statistics for this development are found in Chapters 3 and 4.

[54] The average earnings of nonsupervisory workers in the first quarter of 1973 ($7292 annually) do not even meet the Bureau of Labor Statistics' low-income adequacy budget for that year. Leonard Woodcock, "We Can Have Full Employment," *Social Policy, 5* (July-August 1974), 5.

[55] "A career is something you want to do while a job is something you have to do.... If there is one attitude that clearly separates New Classmen from workers it is a sense of importance and involvement the professionals find in their careers, the sense that they are doing something 'worthwhile.' " Robert M. Cook, "Review Essay: A View from an I-Beam," *American Journal of Sociology, 79* (September 1973), 452.

[56] C. Wright Mills, *White Collar* (New York: Oxford University Press, 1951), pp. xv-xvi.

[57] Dean J. Champion, "Some Impacts of Office Automation upon Status, Role Change, and Depersonalization," *The Sociological Quarterly, 8* (Winter 1967), 72.

[58] Jon M. Shepard, *Automation and Alienation: A Study of Office and Factory Workers* (Cambridge, Mass.: The MIT Press, 1971), Appendix B. Shepard combines levels 2 and 3, calling it the level of "mechanized production." However, from his discussion I have separated them in order to follow Robert Blauner's scheme of the four forms of production. See his *Alienation and Freedom: The Factory Worker and His Industry* (Chicago: The University of Chicago Press, 1964), p. 7.

[59] An example of results of automation indicating an increase in job satisfaction is E. H. Jacobson et al., "Employee Attitudes Toward Technological Change in a Medium-Sized Insurance Company," *Journal of Applied Psychology, 43* (1959), 349-354. Examples of results indicating a decrease in job satisfaction are: Ida R. Hoos, "The Impact of Automation on Office Workers," *International Labour Review, 82* (1960), 363-388; Champion, "Some Impacts of Office Automation." Champion does take into account the factor of time by doing a longitudinal study.

[60] Shepard, *Automation and Alienation*, p. 30.

[61] Shepard, *Automation and Alienation*, pp. 48-49, 60-62.

[62] Charles R. Walker, *Toward the Automatic Factory* (New Haven: Yale University Press, 1957); William A. Faunce, "Automation in the Automobile Industry: Some Consequences for In-Plant Social Structure," *American Sociological Review*, 23 (August 1958), 401-409; Ida R. Hoos, *Automation in the Office* (Washington, D.C.: Public Affairs Press, 1961).

[63] Blauner, *Alienation and Freedom*, Floyd C. Mann and L. Richard Hoffman, *Automation and the Worker* (New York: Henry Holt, 1960).

[64] Shepard, *Automation and Alienation*, pp. 100, 106-107. Since Shepard's studies were completed, rapid changes have occurred in the computer occupations, leading to a greater degree of rationalization and a more rigid hierarchy of authority. See the discussion on computer programmers and attendants later in this section.

[65] Floyd C. Mann and Lawrence K. Williams, "Organizational Impact of White-Collar Automation," in William A. Faunce (ed.), *Readings in Industrial Sociology* (New York: Appleton-Century-Crofts, 1967), p. 197.

[66] Mann and Williams, "Organizational Impact of White-Collar Workers." Another study found that ultimately several levels of clerical jobs were eliminated when automation took place. Champion, "Some Impacts of Office Automation."

[67] Mann and Williams, "Organizational Impact of White-Collar Automation," p. 202.

[68] Thomas L. Whisler, *The Impact of Computers on Organizations* (New York: Praeger Publishing Co., 1970), p. 63.

[69] Albert A. Blum et al., "The Office Employee," in Albert A. Blum et al. (eds.), *White-Collar Workers* (New York: Random House, 1971), pp. 18-19. It remains a question whether this gap is caused more by office reorganization and centralization trends than by automation.

[70] Bernard Karsh and Jack Siegman, "Functions of Ignorance in Introducing Automation," *Social Problems*, 12 (Fall 1964), 141-150.

[71] Karsh and Siegman, "Functions of Ignorance in Introducing Automation," quotes on pp. 149, 150.

[72] Walter Buckley, *Sociology and Modern Systems Theory* (Englewood Cliffs, N.J.: Prentice-Hall, 1967), pp. 196-201.

[73] Joan Greenbaum, "Division of Labor in the Computer Field," *Monthly Review*, 28 (July-August 1976), 27-36.

[74] Braverman, "Work and Unemployment," p. 24, emphasizes that advanced technology in the capitalist system does not truly integrate the worker holistically into the mode of production, even though it may integrate some operations. Workers are still performing alienated labor; they are propertyless.

14 SKILLED AND SEMISKILLED WORKERS: THE WORKING CLASS

The working class has been defined in several different ways. In its broader sense, it includes all occupations that are not white-collar, that is, occupations in which persons work with their hands, where some sort of manual labor is required. Often the term "blue-collar" is used to describe these occupations, blue-collar workers comprising the skilled, semiskilled, and unskilled workers. This is a more limited definition, since it leaves out service workers.

Different writers have used these terms in different ways. Eli Ginzberg includes non-household service workers and nonfarm laborers as part of the blue-collar labor force.[1] Others separate working-class from lower-class workers, the latter comprising those with wages too low to support a working-class life-style, for example, private household servants, day laborers, shoeshiners, and other low-wage jobs.

These definitions have their limits. Some clerical and sales occupations are working class (manual), for example, post office employees, supermarket stock clerks, file clerks, messengers, bill collectors, auctioneers, peddlars, office machine operators, telephone operators, typists, and other low-paying, low-status jobs. If these occupations are included, at least three-fifths of the labor force is working class.[2] The best way to solve this definitional problem would be to adopt a method of categorizing occupations on the basis of structural characteristics along the lines of Freedman's labor market model, described in Chapter 4. Factors such as amount of time worked, whether salary or wages are paid, degree of industry concentration, and extent of licensing and collective bargaining would better organize occupations into like groups based on occupational autonomy instead of on traditional proximity to management and prestige derived from such association. Such analysis will be possible when research on occupations begins to follow this kind of model. Until then, we must work with what we have and interpolate where possible for labor market analysis.

For definitional purposes and because so much of the literature deals in this way with the working class, only skilled and semiskilled workers will be emphasized in this chapter. However, other occupational groups that fit the various definitions will be mentioned in passing.

THE WORKING-
CLASS SUBCUL-
TURE

For sociologists an important factor distinguishing occupational categories and groups is life-style. In some cases the earnings of two workers may be the same, but how they use their incomes to direct their respective lives is very different. Sociological analysis has shown that working-class people have a distinctive life-style and cultural patterns that constitute a subsociety or "subculture." This subsociety ". . . contains both sexes, all ages, and family groups, and parallels the larger society in that it provides for a network of groups and institutions extending throughout the individual's entire life cycle."[3]

Working-class people are seen as traditional, old-fashioned, patriarchal, materialistic, and superstitious. They like discipline, structure, strong leadership, and they strive for stability and security. They are concerned with strength and ruggedness, espousing an eye-for-an-eye philosophy. They are radical on some economic issues and conservative on civil liberty issues. They are not well educated. Consequently, they are poor readers, poorly informed in major issues of the day, and suspicious of new ideas and "too much talk."[4]

In a participant observation study of South Chicago steelworkers, William Kornblum noted that these workers confine their social experience to corner taverns, churches, and union halls.[5] They tend to settle in ethnic enclaves within the working-class section of town. Degree of participation in community organizations (voluntarism) varies by ethnic group. In South Chicago, Serbians are much more active than Poles. Kinship patterns are important both in the community and in the factory. Voluntarism is engaged in largely to protect and preserve the ethnic and kinship basis of the local community.[6]

Randall Collins emphasizes that working-class people do not give orders to anyone in the organization in which they work, so they do not identify with the organization, but often against it. Working-class culture is localistic, cynical, and oriented toward the immediate present. Because they are manipulated and cannot themselves manipulate, the working class view of the world tends to be personalized and aggressive. They confine relationships to family and long-time neighborhood friends. They approve of the characteristics of physical toughness and loyalty to friends. Life is seen as hard and unpredictable. One therefore should enjoy life when and where one is able to, since life is short and times change rapidly. Working-class people are sexist, with a dual standard for women, and are emotionally uninhibited.[7]

When comparing blue-collar workers to white-collar workers, Arthur Shostak finds that blue-collar workers are less geographically mobile, are in poorer mental health, and are characterized by a high degree of ethnicity and toughness to prove to themselves and others that they will not accept white-collar attitudes, which they feel are unreal or out of touch.[8] Suburban American blue-collarites are found not to be organization men, active churchgoers, or political conservatives. They do not take on the life-style of the middle class.[9]

There are even differences found between more skilled and less skilled workers. The skilled are closer to the semiskilled in their attitudes and behavior than they are to the middle class. They also resemble the semiskilled in their level of organizational affiliation, union membership, religious involvement, media behavior, politics, attitude toward education, and attitude toward foreign affairs.[10] The lower skilled occupations rely heavily on brawn and highly routine manual dexterity. The highest skilled require a considerable amount of intellective capacity and extensive on-the-job training. The latter's work is not repetitive and requires innovative ideas.[11] The medium skilled are the operatives, where only rudimentary mental skills are needed for routine labor such as assembly-line worker or truck driver.[12]

THE WORKING CLASS: AN OCCUPATIONAL PROFILE

There are over 10 million skilled workers. One-and-a half million of them (15 percent) are foremen. The majority of skilled workers are mechanics and repairmen (3 million) and construction craft workers (approximately 3 million—see Chart 14.1). Two occupations have more than 800,000 workers each—carpenters and automobile mechanics (see Chart 14.2). Many skilled occupations have fewer than 20,000 workers each—watch repairers, glaziers, and paperhangers.[13]

Ninety percent of all skilled workers are employed by private organizations. The rest are self-employed or work for governmental organizations. Most of the self-employed are in the building trades, working for subcontractors.[14] Skilled workers are concentrated in the highly industrialized states, especially New York, Pennsylvania, Ohio, New Jersey, Indiana, Illinois, and California.

CHART 14.1 PERCENT DISTRIBUTION OF SKILLED WORKERS, 1970

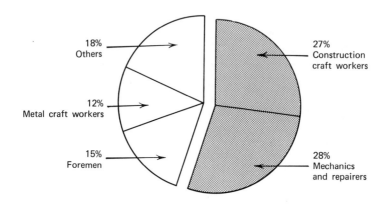

Source: U.S. Department of Labor, Bureau of Labor Statistics, *Occupational Outlook Handbook,* 1972-1973 Ed. (Washington, D.C.: U.S. Government Printing Office, 1972), p. 366.

CHART 14.2 SELECTED SKILLED OCCUPATIONS WITH MORE THAN 100,000 WORKERS, 1970

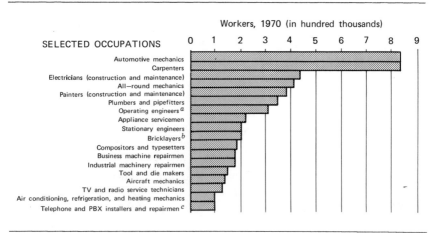

[a]Excavating grading, and road machinery operators.
[b]Including tile setters, stonemasons, and marble setters.
[c]Including central office craft workers.
Source. U.S. Department of Labor, Bureau of Labor Statistics, *Occupational Outlook Handbook,* 1972-1973 Ed. (Washington, D.C.: U.S. Government Printing Office, 1972), p. 367.

Only 3 percent of skilled workers are women. Only 1 percent of women who work are skilled workers—a rate relatively unchanged during this century (see Table 6.2).

Semiskilled workers (operatives) comprise the single largest occupational group in the labor force. Nine million of these people are in manufacturing industries, most of them engaged in producing automobiles and industrial machinery, processing food, and making textiles. The largest occupations outside manufacturing include truckdrivers, gas station attendants, bus drivers, and laundry and drycleaning workers. Thirty percent of all semiskilled workers are women—their members being swelled by women in the clothing, textile, and food processing industries.[15]

THE BUILDING INDUSTRY TRADES

Unlike the worker in the large organization, the skilled craft worker in the building industry functions as an independent unit in the labor market according to personal contacts, preferences, and schedules. Building projects are of a relatively brief duration, and usually a new labor force is assembled for each contracted job. Therefore, people in the trades are constantly engaged in new job negotiations.[16]

Trades foremen almost always do the hiring and firing of workers. Since these tradespeople have to work in close coordination, foremen try to pick people who, besides being the best they can find in technical abilities, are compatible in work and interpersonal relations with fellow workers and foremen, and who have "good judgment." The foreman has the power to hire and fire, but workers are members of the same union as the foreman and can effectively bring grievances. Also, with small contractors and subcontractors, even a slowdown or absenteeism can hurt where profit margins are narrow.[17]

The foreman carries a notebook of names of 20 to 25 craft workers, about half of whom are top-rated. These workers are often phoned or visited during evenings to maintain good relations and ask about their availability. Frequently, workers will reciprocate with a visit to the foreman in order to maintain the relationship, especially during a slow season. In some cases, particularly in highly interdependent work crews (e.g., structural steel workers or carpentry finishing crews), workers will refuse to work if one of the members is absent, fearing mistakes and poorer quality by a substitute.[18]

Compared to work in large-scale organizations, construction workers are much more autonomous, handling most of the planning of production from initial selection of raw materials and selection of tools, to scheduling of task movements in working on the goods-in-process, and to inspection of work completed. Arthur Stinchcombe has pointed out that in mass production industries all this planning is done in advance by persons not on the work crew.[19] Bureaucratic administration is dependent on the stability of the work flow over the long term. The construction industry is faced with the immediate problems of instability and flexibility in product mix, composition of the work crews, and local market conditions. Therefore, it cannot maintain a complex communications system with a clerical staff. Bureaucratic officials are appointed permanently, subcontractors only temporarily. The career of the bureaucratic worker is structured by administrative regulation, that of the construction worker by his status in the labor market.[20] The work orientation of the construction worker is *occupational*, not organizational.

Theodore Caplow explains that this situation implies two different labor markets, an industrial labor market and a crafts labor market. In the industrial labor market wages are regulated by the willingness of employers to pay within the limits of minimum wage laws and the going rates of competing industries. Within this range employers usually make a judgment on the basis of personal inclination and not on the basis of rational considerations. They are, of course, bound by labor bargaining, the current supply of labor, and the geographical closeness of competing employers.[21]

The crafts labor market presents a different case. In it there is a fixed labor supply and a highly variable demand. In addition, clients are numerous and economically weak. Therefore, workers identify with their craft and not with the particular job. The craft's work process is standardized, but the rationalization of the occupations is slowed down by keeping the ancient guild-like arrangement of master and apprentice, where the master worker is often the manager or the subcontractor of the job. Wages are standardized by members of the occupation because employers (who are the clients) are not able to organize for purposes of bargaining; they are too dispersed. Also, bargaining left to individual workers would create insecurity in the ranks because individual craft workers would undercut one another in their contract bidding.[22]

In the construction industry there is little direct supervision because work tasks are broken up into highly discrete units and cannot be constantly supervised during production. The supervisor is limited to inspection *after* the product is completed. As a result, the workers retain autonomy on the job.[23] Collins concludes that "a high level of task uncertainty and the absence of reciprocal dependence of work units on each other's [worker's] operations, gives very few power resources to a centralized hierarchy and results in a decentralized structure."[24]

RAILROAD ENGINEERS

Railroad engineers protect their skill (i.e., maintained task uncertainty) by controlling the training of student engineers. Only the minimum supply of persons is kept in reserve for peak work periods. Those who are on the reserve list are dropped from the list whenever those on regular train assignments are reduced during a 2-week period. Since the skill of the engineer can be learned only on the job, the skill is limited. As Cottrell says, the proper judgment involved in starting and stopping from two or three up to 10,000 tons of rolling stock, moving at rates up to 120 miles per hour, can only be learned through work experience on the job.[25]

Also, seniority is strictly enforced through the process of "bumping." If new runs are scheduled or new positions open up, the applicants with seniority always get the job. They "bump" all the others. In turn, the others apply for the vacated jobs and those with seniority from that group get them. Then their jobs open up, and the process continues down the line in a whole series of bumps.[26]

GENERAL CONTRACTING: THE LAYPERSON AS ENTREPRENEUR

In the building trades many of the jobs on which tradespeople work are organized and directed by general contractors who are strangers to the business. This is particularly true in the home building industry, where prospective homeowners decide to build their own homes and employ a series of subcontractors to hire and supervise craft workers in building the house.

Barney Glaser has made a thorough study of the complex relations between the homeowner—the layperson or "patsy"—and the subcontractors—the experts.[27] He notes that the typical expert-layman relationship is a totally asymmetrical power relationship. The experts have the power and the clients follow their directives. However, the subcontractor-patsy relationship is different in that the balance of power is nearly symmetrical—they are constantly contending with one another for control of work planning and the work process.

By analyzing the relationship of "generalling" patsies as they interrelate with the experts (the subcontractors) in constructing a house, Glaser offers a beginning theory of expert-layman relations. The "generalling" is done by the person who acts as the general contractor for the entire job (in this case it is the layman or "patsy"). Generalling involves: (1) comparatively bidding the subcontractors' offers; (2) administering the timing of the various jobs in their proper sequence (e.g., making sure the plumbing is installed before putting up the walls); and (3) inspecting and evaluating, that is, controlling the quality of the work.[28]

Glaser was the patsy in his participant observation study. He found that most of the activity in the expert-layman relationship can be explained by utilizing what happens in the subcontractor-patsy relationship. Three core variables exist: (1) choosing the subcontractors, (2) balancing the power symmetry, and (3) "elsewhereism." In choosing the subcontractors the patsy contacts a number of them and asks them to bid on the job to be performed. In this way the patsy maintains some control over the price of the job by seeing what services are generally offered at the "going rate." This also warns the subcontractor that price gouging will not work in this case. Choosing gives the layman power in the symmetrical power relationship.

Further balancing of the power symmetry in favor of the layperson occurs while the work is being done by the subcontractors. The patsy must maintain constant pressure regarding quality control. The subcontractor is the judge regarding technical matters, but the patsy has to make sure that the specialty items are completed according to plan and that no corners are cut in order to save on materials or labor. This Glaser calls "keeping the edge in power symmetry."[29]

"Elsewhereism" is a function of the expert's power—having to be "elsewhere" with another client at some time during his contractual relationship with the patsy. Anxious to see the work completed, the patsy is often pressured into compromises by a subcontractor's excuses (often legitimate, sometimes not) that other jobs are waiting.[30]

In the professional-client relationship the articulation of these three variables is very different. The layman or client does not choose the professional through a process of bidding. The professional has to be accepted *carte blanche* on the basis of trust alone. It is impossible to compare professionals, however, without a system of bidding and comparison. The process of information gathering in the bidding system "undermines the myth of secrecy of the professional's affairs and skills, thus eroding trust in the magic of the expert." The only form of control that laypersons have over this power asymmetry is through withdrawal as a client and by lay-referral systems, both weak or ineffectual devices when put against the power of the expert's control.

Power symmetry occurs only in those situations where laypersons "yield enough control while limiting domination although they are out of their own bailiwick." Moves toward this balance are evidenced in minority demands for better medical care and in increasing malpractice suits.[31]

FACTORY WORKERS

The large majority of factory workers are semiskilled workers, persons who operate a multitude of different machines. There are filers, polishers, sanders, buffers, punch and stamp press operatives, welders, drill press operatives, lathe and milling machine operatives, textile operatives, grinders and winders, automobile assembly-line workers, rubber, chemical, and paper plant workers, food workers, shoe factory workers, and many hundred more. As emphasized in the description of building industry trades, operatives in factories are very closely supervised, their labor is divided into miniscule parts, each worker being responsible for completing only one or a few of these parts, and worker productivity is carefully measured, with expectations that it should meet a preset standard of productivity.

In a series of reports, Donald Roy describes the life of the factory machine operative. He points out that restriction in quotas of goods produced is a common and accepted practice of workers. It is regularly practiced in order to keep high the price paid them for each piece of work produced.[32] If more items are produced than the standard per hour or per day, management will lower the price earned per unit by the worker. The worker will then have to produce more to earn the same amount. Thus, as much as 3 to 4 hours a day are "wasted" by working slowly or by "making out," that is, doing a day's work in 4 hours and relaxing or "killing time" in the other 4 hours. This was especially true at night when the foremen or management were not around.[33]

Groups as well as individuals were in collusion with one another to manipulate production. Even groups from different departments worked together. In Roy's study two groups from production worked with four groups from services. The foremen were also in on the arrangement to restrict production. As much as management tried to stamp out this collusion, it could not succeed New rules were almost immediately subverted. In many cases the new rules *reduced* productivity, but the workers managed to overcome this and "get the work out."[34]

This shop "syndicate" of cooperating workers contradicts the human relations school, which states that the problem of productivity lies in poor communication between a logical management and nonlogical work groups. The problem seems to be just the opposite: communicating between a nonlogical management and logical workers.[35]

How do workers manage to keep up their good spirits in jobs that tend to be boring and monotonous? In a participant observation analysis of workers operating "clicking machines" (machines that shape pieces of material for clothing), Roy describes how they develop a "game of work" by making variations in the timing of their simple work task such as going for coffee or food or to the john. For them it was not a "fun" kind of game, but they were "clinging to the remnants of joy in work."[36]

In Roy's particular work group there was a special time every day or every few days for a break in the monotony of work. There was "coffee time," "peach time," "banana time," "coke time," "fish time," "lunch time," "window time," and "pickup time." These activities all had themes, that is, a verbal interplay of certain types occurred. There were kidding themes—the banana was always eaten by one particular member of the group to the consternation of the owner. The interaction never varied. There were serious themes, for example, a story concerning a professor, who was a relative of one of the workers. This story was always accorded respect and was retold in reverential tones.

This type of communication between workers is "consummatory communication." It is aimless social intercourse that relieves job tensions. (Instrumental communication is communication with an intended purpose to facilitate production.) The work group had a pecking order, a hierarchy of status set up and stabilized by means of this "gaming" procedure.[37]

Another example of how rules constrict the factory worker is the case of the gypsum factory workers studied by Alvin Gouldner.[38] The gypsum plant was located next to the mine and was run by the same company that owned the plant. In the plant there was a highly bureaucratized system of rules, but in the mine there was a less developed hierarchy and set of rules. The miners behaved as if there were no formal authority in the mine. When miners needed help, they would ask whomever they preferred to ask. If repairs were needed, often the miner would make them instead of waiting for a maintenance crew. Work obligations in the mine were diffuse. There were no specific rules to follow regarding absenteeism, the amount of gypsum to be mined during a given time, or how long the men were to work.[39] The miners' strong system of beliefs and superstitions prevented a bureaucratic setting from developing.

In the gypsum plant, which manufactured gypsum wall board from the raw material received from the mine, close supervision created a vicious cycle regarding employee performance. The superior perceived workers to be unmotivated, so this meant that they had to be observed carefully to make sure that they were doing their job. Consequently, the workers became angry because they were being pushed around; they felt they were not being treated reasonably by the supervisor, who tried to control everything "by the book" and only became a nuisance.[40]

In the mines there was a lack of bureaucratic rules. The work situation was not rationalized and the workers controlled the pace of work, giving them considerable autonomy. Conversely, in the plant, workers were subjected to a broad set of rules, especially after the succession of Peele, the new plant manager. This permitted a high degree of control over the worker's production. The belief system and informal solidarity of the miners was much stronger than that of the factory workers, giving the miners the power to resist bureaucracy.[41]

The effects of denying workers participation in planning and ownership is to have them turn away from their work. A survey of several Midwestern factories disclosed that 90 percent of the workers preferred their primary interactions to be off the job; only 10 percent perceived their most valued social experiences to take place at work. "The workplace . . . cannot even evoke significant sentiments and emotions in its occupations."[42]

ASSEMBLY-LINE WORKERS

The assembly line is an innovation in the ordering of materials and construction of the product. The principle of the assembly line is mass production, which involves the use of the techniques of standardization and interchangeability in order to have: (1) an orderly progression of the product through the shop in a series of planned operations arranged so that the right part arrives at the right place at the right time; (2) the mechanical delivery of parts; and (3) operations segmented into the simplest constituent motions.[43] Most assembly-line workers are semiskilled operatives working in factories.

In one of the early studies of the effects of the assembly line on human behavior, 180 interviews with assembly-line workers were conducted by Charles Walker and Robert Guest in 1949. They confirmed the belief that the majority of assembly-line jobs required a continuous high degree of mental attention without corresponding mental absorption. In jobs previous to their assembly-line work, workers were more satisfied with many aspects such as mechanical pacing of work, degree of repetitiveness, skill requirement, predetermination of use of tools, and surface mental attention.[44]

Most workers who said they liked assembly-line work gave pay and security as the two major reasons. Workers disliked most the mechanical pacing and the repetitive nature of the work. Those who were able to "build a bank" by working their way "back up the line" (i.e., getting ahead of the line by completing operations before the product reaches their station) were more satisfied with their work because they could pace themselves to some extent.[45] Another method practiced in the new General Motors Lordstown plant is to "double up." One worker will do the tasks of two for a short time while the other relaxes or goes to visit a friend down the line. Then the other will reciprocate by taking over both tasks. To do the work of two persons on the assembly line is extremely tiring and difficult, but workers accept this method over others because the monotony of the job is so overwhelming.[46]

There are many levels of job classification in the automobile assembly plant, but mostly they involve horizontal moves from one department to another. Vertical mobility is very low. There are only a few slight differences in job status and pay—only four levels and a 12-cent difference in pay rates between them.[47]

The unrelieved and unchanging tempo of the line generates a very high degree of tension. A cheer goes up whenever the line breaks down. Yet, in many cases, workers refuse to change jobs and often say they enjoy their work. However, as Chinoy points out, this does not necessarily mean that workers are satisfied with what they are doing. Instead, they just do not want to bother learning a new job, especially if it offers no promise of improved working conditions and if there are good social relations with fellow workers and supervisors on the present job.[48]

However, on most lines, the turnover is rapid, and close personal relations cannot be established. Nor can workers look forward to a career in the sense of positions of increasing responsbility and income and meaning to one's work.[49] No line job takes more than half an hour to learn. The management of General Motors has been able to rationalize the jobs into a few simple movements. The speedup of the line has resulted in having mostly young people working on it—they are the only ones able to keep up with the grueling pace without dropping out or suffering an extraordinarily high mental illness rate.[50] This is ironic in view of the report of the factory owner who, during the desperate shortage of workers in World War II, hired retarded mental patients to work on his assembly line and found them to be extremely efficient and well suited to the jobs.[51]

AUTOMATION: THE AMERICAN EXPERIENCE

In one of the first studies of the effects of automation on workers, Charles Walker interviewed the workers and management in a newly automated steel plant in 1949. The workers were transferred from the old nonautomated factory to the new factory. Walker found that the number of job levels was reduced (from 17 to 8) and that there was dissatisfaction with the leveling of status differences between members of the work groups. However, there was higher job satisfaction, and primary work groups remained cohesive and strong.[52]

In 1964, Robert Blauner summarized a large number of studies of workers' attitudes toward their work and concluded that up to a point the more highly developed the production technology, the *less* alienated workers are. Automation is that point at which workers become *more* committed to their work. The work environment is cleaner, the spread of occupations from unskilled through skilled is broader, work operations are decentralized, and previously segmented tasks are integrated.[53] Other studies, however, do not agree with Blauner's conclusions.[54]

In his review of the effects of automation on blue-collar workers, James Taylor notes that the reason for so many conflicting results in different studies is that they are based on different levels of technology. Taylor solved this problem by examining companies that were at different levels of development. This included an insurance company, a petroleum refinery, a glass products factory, a continuous-process plastics producer, and a metal products manufacturer. The results of analysis confirmed the hypothesis that, overall, modern technology supports a stronger democratic organization and management of work. Except for the insurance company, there was greater democracy, that is, more participation of workers in high-technology groups than in low-technology groups, both before and after new technology was introduced.[55]

It is interesting that Taylor's analysis included only one service-producing industry—insurance—and that here a more negative trend developed. In a study of the effects of automation on several of the major insurance companies in the United States, Thomas Whisler came up with mixed results. The level of worker skills increased, but clerical jobs became more routinized. There was more creative decision making, but only at the top levels of management. There was a reduction of the clerical labor force and an increase in specialists, but the level of interpersonal communications declined. An increasing number of people continued their educations to the professional level, but they entered more centralized firms, which grant little job autonomy.[56]

Whisler forsees the ultimate decentralization of firms when automation reaches its upper stages. This will provide the basis for a better integrated management system, but it also will mean less autonomy for the worker. In the latter stages of automation, control is built into the integrated operation, and the worker merely "watches" the process.[57]

There is a question as to how much "watching" is necessary if electronic and mechanical sensing devices can be used to monitor the processes. The only working-class people needed then would be personal services workers to cater to managers and machine engineers. The current personnel practice of not replacing workers when they retire has reduced some unions to shadows of their former size. This union-supported practice is an indicator of how automation has affected several industries, especially printing, oil, chemicals, rubber, and steel. This is a far cry from the early optimism that labor would be professionalized by retraining and placement into transformed regroupings, with "dial-watching" engineers, and a grievance procedure serving as a code of ethics for both management and labor.[58]

TAXICAB DRIVERS

One of every five semiskilled workers is engaged in operating transport equipment. This segment is so large (over 3 million workers in 1970) that in 1970 the Bureau of the Census established it as one of the two major segments of the semiskilled occupational group. Approximately 160,000 of these operatives are taxicab drivers.

The majority of nonmanufacturing operatives work in small organizations or work in situations that allow considerable autonomy, even though they are in large organizations. Prime examples are truck drivers, cabdrivers, deliverymen, butchers, and the like. These people have considerable freedom to vary their work pattern from hour to hour and often from job to job.

The work of cabdrivers is unusual because, unlike most occupations, they have no "steady" clientele with whom they can maintain contact to build up a relationship such as schoolteacher and students, waitress and regular diners, or janitor and tenants. Contacts are random and singular. Cabbies are "practitioners without a reputation." They are often treated as nonpersons by riders. Riders converse on personal matters as if the driver did not exist.[59]

Because the tip makes up a large part of cabdrivers' wages, it is usually of prime concern to them. They cannot predict the size of the tip until the interaction is near its end. This uncertainty leads many cabdrivers to "type" their fares in an attempt to anticipate the size of the tip. The Sport is "the young man on the town," who will generally give a generous tip. The Blowhard is the person imitating The Sport, and he will usually give a very small tip. The Businessman, the cabbie's daily bread, can be counted on for a moderate tip. The Live Ones—the drunkards, convention revelers, and the like— may or may not give a big tip. They are unreliable. The Stiff is the person who fails to give a tip and is passionately disliked. There are also techniques developed that attempt to manipulate the size of the tip. "Making change"— fumbling for change to embarrass the rider into leaving the small amount with the cabbie is one ploy. Another is the familiar hard-luck story of the cabbie's hungry wife and kids or the poor starving mother.[60] The cabbie's livelihood depends to a considerable extent on accurately "sizing up" the ability of potential customers to pay for the requested destination.[61]

In sum, the relationship between cabdriver and rider is random, short, and nonrenewable, which severely limits the socially integrative features of the practitioner-client common to the service occupations. This lack of homogeneity of clientele seriously limits this occupation's ability to professionalize.

BUTCHERS AND TRUCKERS: OCCUPATIONAL CULTURE VERSUS OCCUPATIONAL COMMUNITY

In many of the semiskilled and lower-skilled occupations dirty work becomes an issue with which the members of occupations must deal. The work of the butcher, considered semiskilled, is a good example. Having to handle the bodies of dead animals and cut them up and become soiled by the blood of these creatures is considered dirty work. Butchers attempt to overcome this stigma by emphasizing the skills necessary to cut meats properly, to make fancy cuts, and to use hand saws and band saws.

In addition, an elaborate occupational culture is developed. Hanna Meara points out that within the meat-cutting trade great honor is attached to the product worked on—meat.[62] Butchers recognize that they have access to a scarce commodity and emphasize this fact among themselves. Also, butchers maintain a calculated disregard for the cold temperatures in which they must work. Walk-in refrigerators are where most of the meat is cut and where speed is essential; nevertheless, heavy clothing is rejected as a hindrance to job efficiency. Those who do wear heavy clothing are considered "weak" or inexperienced. On the other hand, there is dishonor in having to wait on customers because the customer has to be satisfied about the smallest complaints. Most important, the customer takes precedence and must be waited on, creating an interruption in what the butcher considers to be the more important work of cutting.[63]

In short, butchers find honor in those aspects of their work that develop personal autonomy and judgment. The occupational culture is the mechanism for developing honor, especially in cases where dirty work is a significant factor in the work of the occupation.

The occupational culture includes the specialized knowledge, the lore, the secrets, beliefs, rituals, and ceremonies of an occupation. In a word, it is the *Weltanschauung* that it develops and presents to the world.[64] This allows the individual to identify with the occupation. Mechanisms such as songs, gestures, uniforms, and other symbols of status unify the occupation. It is part of the occupational ideology.

The occupational culture is quite well developed in lower-skilled as well as higher-skilled occupations. In order to be a member of the occupation a member must "know" the culture; otherwise membership can be difficult to attain. Jargon eliminates outsiders who cannot converse easily with those in the know. It also serves as a socializing mechanism into the occupation. John Runcie describes how truck drivers' songs transmit a set of values. They are portrayed in song as "the knights of the road" who want to come home to their women but, because of their peculiar work schedules, are prevented from doing so for long periods of time.[65] The owner-operator in steel trucking is seen as an outcast, the person everybody in the industry looks down on, the scapegoat, the low man on the totem pole, by the workers at the steel mills where the truckers pick up their orders of steel for delivery. These truckers call themselves gypsies or sailors. "We sail out on the highways." The long-distance hauler is gone for a week or two, picking up a load at one port, delivering it at another port.[66]

An *occupational community* differs from the occupational culture. An occupational community, as Goode points out, has a common identity and a common set of values.[67] In addition to this, Graeme Salaman adds that members of the community view themselves in terms of their occupational roles and not their leisure roles, that they prefer to associate with other persons *within* the occupation, and that they carry work activities and interests into their nonwork lives. It is an "integrated system of social life."[68]

Salaman emphasizes that occupational communities are highly involved in their work—work is their central life interest. Those occupations that are not highly involved are not occupational communities, for example, affluent blue-collar workers. They are more interested in life away from work and with others than their workmates. Involvement in work, then, is "the essential determinant" of occupational community. Involvement is defined as an attitude of meaningfulness toward one's work. Not only must the members of the occupation see their work as meaningful, but so must others outside the occupation.[69]

Thus, meat cutters have an occupational culture, but only surgeons have an occupational community. Truckers have a developed occupational culture, but only airline pilots have an occupational community. Surgeons are involved in dirty work, but their work is irreplaceable in the short run as well as being central to society. They have stricter control over their body of knowledge through training, licensing, and the like. Airline pilots, like truckdrivers, are gypsies of sorts, but they maintain strict entry requirements to their profession and are affected considerably by the governmental mediation role.

It is difficult to say whether only professions have community, especially since many low-prestige occupations are highly integrated, such as circus performers, seamen, railroaders, and dockworkers.[70] It is likely that these workers are bound together because they have to be and not because they want to be. Few outsiders will or can associate closely with them because of their low prestige and unusual work schedules.

IS THERE A WORKING CLASS?

A question frequently asked of modern Western society is whether a working-class subculture any longer exists. That is, instead of a development toward strengthening the working class as a *social class* in the Marxist sense, the trend is toward its disintegration as a *stratum* with its own life-style, values, and goals into the large "middle class" or stratum of the population.[71] Specifically, the argument is that there is less stress and more job satisfaction in the workplace as the physically more strenuous jobs become automated and as segmented jobs become integrated. There are fewer, more cohesive, workers in charge of automated operations, which in the unautomated past required many separated, disciplined workers.[72] It is further argued that during the past century the majority of youth in the United States has risen from a "culture of poverty" into at least the lower echelons of the white-collar class. The American system, says Thernstrom, has allowed "substantial privilege for the privileged and extensive opportunity for the underprivileged to coexist simultaneously."[73]

However, a study of the English working class by John Goldthorpe and a group of researchers found strong evidence that there is no tendency toward an assimilation of the working class into the middle class.[74] In fact, it appears there are more changes of nonmanual workers to manual workers through the development of office mechanization and automation. This process of rationalization has reduced the decision-making functions of many white-collar occupations (e.g., accountants, office machine operators—see Chapter 13 for examples). It has reduced the degree of career mobility to that attained by blue-collar workers. "Manual" white-collar workers are now in a position to accept working-class values. In other words, the white-collar worker is becoming proletarianized even more than the blue-collarites are becoming bourgeoisified.[75]

Recent evidence from social mobility studies does not support the view that equal opportunity exists to make assimilation possible. Blau and Duncan have estimated that if a worker's first job has no effect on where he or she will end up in the occupational structure, 52 percent of those who started as manual laborers would become white-collar. Only 30 percent actually did.[76] Blue-collar upward mobility is often only temporary. For example, each year a sizable number of blue-collar workers leave their occupation and strike out as small business entrepreneurs. During the first 2 years, 60 percent of these businesses fail, and most others have only limited success.[77] In addition, many of the white-collar jobs entered by the former blue-collarites are very low-paying, secondary market jobs such as office machine operators, counter clerks, and the like.

In his review of the literature, James Rinehart concludes that there are substantial differences between manual and nonmanual workers in earnings, market situations, life-styles, working conditions, and politics.[78] Regardless of the money and commodities that can be attained by blue-collar workers, the conditions of their work are what make them different from white-collar workers. What convergence will occur is limited to office workers proletarianized by the bureaucratization of firms instead of the embourgeoisement of the skilled workers by earnings and commodities.[79] The attitude of one blue-collar worker sums this up well:

> We often look back after a day's work with pride and satisfaction with what we have accomplished. But at bottom we know we are working because someone else is making money off our labors on this job. We are merely tools of a social system in which production for profit is the ultimate morality . . . . The harder we work, the more we make for them. It's not often talked about, but once we were standing around and everyone nodded assent to the story about a plumber who worked for the same company for 50 years and was "kind of proud of it." When he was about to retire and expressed his pride, the owner of the company told him: "You got paid for every minute of it, didn't you?" . . . Someone said, "The longer I'm in this business the more I hate management."[80]

A middle-of-the-road view is expressed by William Gomberg. He notes that the most secure blue-collar workers (in terms of income and job tenure) are not sympathetic to the middle class when it is not in their interests. They do not support teachers when teachers strike for higher wages in a blue-collar community. But neither are they sympathetic to the lower class. For example, they are not in favor of organizing less secure hospital workers when hospital fringe benefits are denied by the employer because hospital workers' wages push up the costs of hospitalization insurance. We seem to be moving into an organizational society where every occupational group acts as a private interest group and bargains with every other occupational group. In this scenario, the working class is neither the agent of world revolutionary change nor the victim of oppression.[81]

IS THE WORK-
ING CLASS A
SOCIAL CLASS?

According to most social analysts, the working class is not a *social* class.[82] The most critical interpretation is the radical interpretation, perhaps best summarized by Stanley Aronowitz.[83] Workers come to preceive their labor as a commodity like all other commodities—something to be bought and sold on the market. Thus, labor is identified with one's consumption style. The mediating institutions of family, school, religion, and mass culture formerly conferred individuality, but they are now instruments for socializing workers into "commodity fetishism." For example, the automobile assumes value beyond its practical utility—it takes on importance by becoming a measure of social status and economic achievement.

The system is perpetuated through various ideologies. The ideology of meritocracy says that the person who achieves credentials will be highly socially mobile. But, in fact, school personnel evaluate students on the basis of class criteria (whether students are of middle-class or working-class origin) and race criteria as determined by biased test scores of intelligence and achievement (see Chapter 17). Yet it is the individuals themselves who are blamed for lack of success—they have not made a great enough effort or they are not intelligent enough. These people are then trained for secondary labor market jobs.

Thus, educational institutions, the mass media, sports, music, and the like, are a "cultural colonialism" that prepares the individual to accept his or her role in the authority structure. Historically, this was accomplished by management's ability to increase the dependence of the worker on the organization through the institution of a refined, artificial authority structure. This hierarchical social division of labor was based on presumed skill differences, especially between mental and manual, and in the latter between skilled and unskilled.[84] In addition, machine technology was used to replace skilled labor. This is what Robert Heilbroner has called the "intellectual degradation of labor."[85]

Present labor force categories are divided by type of occupation or industry instead of by class or authority relations. White-collar and blue-collar presuppose a basic difference between factory and office, between physical and mental labor. Office work—staff administration of the distribution of goods— is assumed to be of higher status that the production of goods. But workers are dominated in both white-collar and blue-collar jobs. In the lower-paying, lower-skilled blue- and white-collar occupations, there are few if any differences in the general environment of work. The noise, discipline, and rationalization of tasks of a key punching room or a business machine room are little different from those in a machine shop. The division of labor, standardization, and rigidity of work patterns are reminiscent of industrial systems. In fact, there is even more stratification (more levels of jobs) in office occupations than in factory jobs. Furthermore, the unwillingness of office workers to maintain high productivity requires a high proportion of managers and supervisors to clerical personnel.

The term "white-collar" expresses an ideology of privilege based on type of work and status. The term "working class" expresses an ideology of privilege (or lack of it) based on social power in a hierarchical system of authority. Thus, for example, post office work is categorized by some workers as white-collar or service, but other workers see it as a variant of blue-collar work in terms of power. A convergence of mental and manual labor is occurring in many occupations through the mechanization of the office (the clerk becomes a machine operator) and the automation of factory work (technicians in the production lines).

When these groups perceive that their individual positions of powerlessness can only be overcome by collective action, then a true working class (i.e., a social class) will have an opportunity to form. But it will also have to overcome the cultural colonialism (a form of covert repression called "dependent participation" by radical postindustrial theorists—see Chapter 3) maintained by the capitalist elite. With our present mass culture of commodity fetishism, overt repression hardly seems necessary.

Presently, in the service-producing industries (which include many professionals and semiprofessionals as well as service occupations), workers are beginning to realize that although they may come home at the end of the day a little less exhausted and dirty, they are still caught up in a highly routinized system where self-sulfillment is at a minimum. Their discontent is exacerbated by their expectation that they should have achieved self-fulfillment, since they have attained high educational credentials.

Taking a phrase from the Ehrenreichs, "The new working class, like the old, is not *either* potentially revolutionary *or* potentially bourgeoisified. It is *both*."[86]

WORK
ALIENATION

There are two opposing views of the kind of involvement of the working class in its work. One view is that most workers, middle class as well as working class, would work even if they didn't have to. Work is an end in itself and is important to the large majority of workers. In a national sample of 400 employed men in 1954, Morse and Weiss found that the working-class person said he worked to occupy his time, his mind, and his hands. Work is "having something to do." The middle-class worker said he received a sense of accomplishment from his work. He said the content of his work was important; he expressed himself in his work; it had meaning.[87]

In a recent study of West End working-class residents in Boston, Massachusetts, Marc Fried discovered that these people are highly satisfied with the *effects* of their jobs, that is, the income from their occupations allows them to support their families.[88] In interviews with English factory workers, Ferdinand

Zweig found the same emphasis on what the job can buy: security, leisure commodities, and other family provisions. The workers are more contented with themselves but are not necessarily happier than their fathers were. They have developed a "compensatory mechanism" by accepting the job for what it is and making the best of it.[89]

There have also been many optimistic reports on the success of integrating the extremely simplified divided tasks of the assembly line into "enlarged" jobs, notably in Sweden at the Volvo and Saab factories and in Amsterdam at the I.B.M. typewriter plant. Yet preliminary studies from these plants indicate that problems of absenteeism and turnover have not been significantly reduced. And, as recent events at American automobile factories indicate, job enlargement is not a very popular concept with management; it often causes a decrease in productivity.

The predominant view of working-class involvement is that workers are negatively involved; they are alienated. Absenteeism has doubled in American plants from 1968 to 1974 in those plants *without* assembly lines as well as those with.[90] The daily grind of the average blue-collar worker has improved somewhat during the past 50 years, but the sweat and dirt, the drudgery, and the sense of restriction still exist. The average worker puts in an 8-hour day, 5 days a week, but one-quarter of all workers are on the job more than 48 hours a week. They may occasionally work a shift cycle, working nights 1 week out of three. There is a half-hour break for lunch and two 10-minute coffee breaks, but no pleasant lunchroom in which to relax. The noise and dirt in the typical factory are incredible. Department of Labor hearings in 1975 disclosed that it would cost $13.5 billion for the 19 major American industries to reduce their noise levels to 90 decibels or lower, the absolute maximum noise level before serious physiological and psychological harm is sustained.[91]

Industrial health and safety of the American working class is notoriously poor. In American industry each year there are 14,000 deaths due to accidents and 10,000 caused by chronic exposure to the more than 25,000 poisonous substances handled by workers.[92] Close to 100,000 workers per year suffer *permanent* impairment as a result of industrial accidents, and over 2 million per year suffer total but temporary disability.[93] A report of the Department of Labor estimates that over *25 million* serious injuries go unreported each year. Enforcement is rendered almost totally ineffective by the small number of inspectors assigned to enforce minimal laws. There are 500 inspectors to cover 4.1 million places of employment.[94]

The highest rate of occupational injuries is in organizations with 100 to 249 employees.[95] This is due partly to the large number of organizations in the construction and manufacturing industries, a large proportion of which fall into the smaller 100 to 249 size. They also contain some of the most hazardous occupations: gypsum and asbestos workers, glass workers, veneer and plywood workers, blast furnace workers, and workers in aluminum and copper plants.

The working class is less healthy, both physically and mentally, than the middle class. Blue-collar workers on shiftwork are more fatigued, have less of an appetite, have more difficulty sleeping, and are generally less healthy.[96] They are more hesitant to accept the sick role because it means time reduced at work and thus a smaller paycheck. Often blue-collar workers are found sick at work when they should be at home. They have a lower knowledge of illness, are less oriented to preventive medical treatment, and are more skeptical of the effectiveness of medical care.[97] They often seek out chiropracters instead of M.D.s, since they are less expensive and more readily available in blue-collar neighborhoods. Moreover, chiropracty is clear-cut and certain in diagnoses (all illness is considered traceable to spinal nerves), treatment is simple and direct (no surgery or drugs are used), and healing is usually quick (manipulation of the spinal column can bring quick relief for several types of injury).[98]

Blue-collar workers have shorter vacations than white-collar workers, have fewer paid holidays, and have less medical insurance and sick leave coverage.[99] In 1966, almost one-sixth of the labor force was disabled for a period of longer than 6 months. As a consequence, many households with a disabled head are poor—more than 50 percent in 1966.[100] Because a larger proportion of the poor are nonwhite, a correspondingly large proportion of nonwhites are disabled. In 1971, the days of disability per person for whites was 15.4 percent and for nonwhites was 18 percent. Poor whites received 14 percent more hospital insurance benefits than poor nonwhites.[101]

The feelings of powerlessness, insecurity, and deprivation increase the working-class person's probability of mental instability.[102] Studies in New Haven, Connecticut on the relation between social class and mental illness showed that the lower the social class, the greater the incidence of mental illness.[103] A follow-up study tends to confirm this finding.[104]

All this considered, it would be surprising if the working class had any reservoir of good will at all. When Ferdinand Zweig asked English blue-collar workers whether they would continue in their jobs if they became rich enough to retire, very few said they would remain.[105] Two-thirds of a sample of American blue-collar workers also said they would not want to remain in their present jobs.[106] Sheppard and Herrick found that young American blue-collar workers are more dissatisfied with their work, more oriented to change, and have higher job expectations than their elders. A majority of the sample of workers said that, given the choice, they would rather concentrate on interesting work than on salary or fringe benefits. Both management and labor leaders recognize there is a problem, but neither recognize workers' change in emphasis from economic to noneconomic goals.[107]

Lathe operators can earn more money, but schoolteachers have more personal autonomy at work. They have more freedom to control their schedules and to work directly with "clients." Richard Sennett and Jonathan Cobb contend that the major problem is that working-class people now feel that they should have this freedom. They should have the responsibility to control their own lives, even though there is no real possibility to do this in industrial America. People feel that they must choose certain "prestige" occupations and thus find themselves doing things they may not even enjoy. *Yet the individual feels that he is responsible for not being satisfied. He takes responsibility for his own alienation.* "Class is his personal responsibility, despite the fact he never had a chance. . . . The lower a man defines himself in society in relation to other people, the more it seems his fault."[108]

In a cross-cultural study of blue-collar workers of four different industrial nations, William Form measures their degree of "societal normlessness."[109] He interprets responses to questions that measure social anomie as cognitive data. These data explain how the social relationships among different social strata of workers affect these workers' "*beliefs* about the amount of societal anomie instead of determining who [personally] feels most deviant, rejected, or anomic."[110] He examines "the actual system of involvements of different strata and how these may affect beliefs about societal anomie."[111]

In a series of studies carried out between 1962 and 1967, Form shows that patterns of social system involvement of different hierarchies of skills of automobile assembly workers in the four countries (United States, Argentina, Italy, India) relate closely to the anomie these workers say they observe. He hypothesizes that the less industrialized the nation, the higher the level of observed anomie, and the more industrialized, the nation the lower the level of observed anomie. He also hypothesized that skilled workers would measure lower (less anomic) than unskilled workers in these relationships.

On the basis of these hypotheses the expected direction of increasing anomie is: United States—Italy—Argentina—India. However, there are many exceptions. In the factories of all four nations, skilled workers received about 50 percent higher wages than the semiskilled and unskilled, but only in the United States did a substantially larger proportion of the skilled see their society as not anomic. The same finding occurred when job satisfaction and interaction with workmates were controlled. In all countries skilled workers who viewed society as anomic were predominantly radical, and the less skilled were more conservative—again with the exception of the United States.

Individual factors did not affect the amount of anomie believed to exist in society. Such factors include: socio-economic background, job socialization, occupational mobility, unemployment, degree of monotony of work, and social isolation (extent of involvement in political affairs and involvement in family, neighborhood, community, and national groups). Technology was also not an important explanatory factor. The technological differences between the Fiat plant in Italy and the Oldsmobile plant in the United States were minute, yet the differences in workers' beliefs about societal anomie between the two plants were very large.

Form concludes that there are many varied causal factors of societal anomie. Among the most important are the local history of the factory as an employer, the system of social stratification in the country, and the political problems of the country.[112] The problems, then, are rooted in history, politics, and structure. This is a broader view than most American sociologists take.[113]

SUMMARY AND CONCLUSIONS

The occupations claimed to be working class differ according to the definition given of the working class. If it is defined as a subculture, then skilled and semiskilled workers are its total population. If it is defined by dual labor market standards, then it cuts across occupational categories and groups. Inclusion will be determined by degree of job stability (as determined by extent of licensing and collective bargaining, degree of unionization, etc.) and amount of wages. Those earning poverty-level wages or below are considered lower-class.

Following the latter definition, many skilled workers and transport equipment operatives and some service workers are properly placed in the primary labor force, although they may remain culturally working class. There are significant subcultural differences between manual and nonmanual workers, but these seem to have little effect on which labor market the worker will enter. This brings us to another definition of the working class as ". . . composed of those engaged in the production and distribution of goods and services who do not own or control the object of their labor or its uses."[114] The autonomy of the worker is extremely limited by a social division of labor and a rigid hierarchy of authority imposed from above. Technological change is limited by the social organization of work.

Whereas in many skilled occupations workers are highly autonomous in their work roles, in the semiskilled occupations they are much less so. Among skilled construction workers and railroad engineers, there is a fixed supply of labor and a variable labor demand, which makes for high autonomy. However, among semiskilled factory workers, especially assembly-line workers, the work is highly rationalized and closely supervised. The informal social organization at work is used to alleviate the boredom of standardized, simplified work patterns.

Alienation increases the size of this powerless, ownerless group, but a social class is not formed because of the overpowering force of commodity fetishism. However, researchers of another persuasion (mostly functionalist) have concluded that alienation increases only up to the point of assembly-line technology, and that the fully automated factory job integration takes place and workers feel more responsible. Work takes on more meaning as technology reaches the stage of continuous-process production. In this interpretation technology determines the social organization of work. Automation creates mostly self-directed jobs.

FOOTNOTES FOR CHAPTER 14— CRAFT WORKERS, OPERATIVES LABORERS AND SERVICE WORKERS

[1] Eli Ginzberg, "The Long View," in Sar A. Levitan (ed.), *Blue-Collar Workers* (New York: McGraw-Hill, 1971), pp. 20-46.

[2] Andrew Levison, *The Working-Class Majority* (New York: Coward, McCann & Geoghegan, 1974), p. 25.

[3] Milton M. Gordon, *Assimilation in American Life* (New York: Oxford University Press, 1964), p. 39. The distinction of white collar versus blue collar on the basis of prestige practically disappears when the 1947 and 1963 NORC occupational scales are statistically examined by using regression analysis. However, distinctions may exist on the basis of life-styles and economic security. See Norval D. Glenn, "The Contribution of White Collars to Occupational Prestige," *The Sociological Quarterly, 16* (Spring 1975), 184-189.

[4] S. M. Miller and Frank Riessman, "The Working-Class Subculture: A New View," *Social Problems, 9* (Summer 1961), 90-91. The debate over working-class authoritarianism still continues. Seymour M. Lipset presented the initial argument for authoritarianism in his "Democracy and Working-Class Authoritarianism," *American Sociological Review, 24* (August 1959), 482-501. Counterarguments are made by S. M. Miller and Frank Riessman, "Working Class Authoritarianism; A Critique of Lipset," *British Journal of Sociology, 12* (1961), 263-276; Richard Hamilton, *Class and Politics in the United States* (New York: John Wiley & Sons, 1972); Sidney Peck, "Current Trends in the American Labor Movement," *The Insurgent Sociologist, 5* (Winter 1975), 23-29. Robert Dubin and Joseph E. Champoux, "Workers' Central Life Interests and Job Performance," *Sociology of Work and Occupations, 1* (August 1974), 324, throw an interesting light on the debate. Blue-collar workers with central life interests (CLI) outside their jobs are highly adaptable, whereas those with CLI oriented to their jobs are highly conservative when it comes to technological and other work-related changes.

[5] William Kornblum, *Blue Collar Community* (Chicago: The University of Chicago Press, 1974), p. 209.

[6] Kornblum, *Blue Collar Community*, pp. 211, 214.

[7] Randall Collins, *Conflict Sociology: Toward an Explanatory Science* (New York: Academic Press, 1975), pp. 71-72.

[8] Arthur B. Shostak, *Blue-Collar Life* (New York: Random House, 1969), p. 108.

[9] Bennett M. Berger, *Working-Class Suburb: A Study of Auto Workers in Suburbia* (Berkeley, Calif.: University of California Press, 1960); Albert K. Cohen and Harold M. Hodges, Jr., "Characteristics of Lower Blue-Collar Class," *Social Problems, 11* (Spring 1963), 303-333.

[10] Richard F. Hamilton, "The Behavior and Values of Skilled Workers," in Arthur B. Shostak and William Gomberg (eds.), *Blue-Collar World* (Englewood Cliffs, N.J.: Prentice-Hall, 1964), pp. 42-57.

[11] Shostak, *Blue-Collar Life*, p. 39.

[12] Shostak, *Blue-Collar Life*, pp. 39-40.

[13] U.S. Department of Labor, Bureau of Labor Statistics, *Occupational Outlook Handbook*, 1972-1973 Ed. (Washington, D.C.: U.S. Government Printing Office, 1972), p. 366.

[14] *Occupational Outlook Handbook*, p. 366.

[15] *Occupational Outlook Handbook*, p. 367.

[16] Richard R. Myers, "Inter-Personal Relations in the Building Industry," *Applied Anthropology, 5* (Spring 1946), 1-7.

[17] Myers, "Inter-Personal Relations in the Building Industry."

[18] Myers, "Inter-Personal Relations in the Building Industry."

[19] Arthur L. Stinchcombe, "Bureaucratic and Craft Administration of Production: A Comparative Study," *Administrative Science Quarterly, 4* (September 1959), 168-187. In Braverman's terms, workers are "propertyless;" they are alienated. See Chapter 14 above, section on "Work Alienation."

[20] Stinchcombe, "Bureaucratic and Craft Administration of Production," p. 185.

[21] Theodore Caplow, *The Sociology of Work* (Minneapolis: University of Minnesota Press, 1954), pp. 158-160.

[22] Caplow, *The Sociology of Work*, pp. 166-167.

[23] Collins, *Conflict Sociology*, p. 321.

[24] Collins, *Conflict Sociology*, p. 321.

[25] W. Fred Cottrell, *The Railroader* (Stanford, Calif.: Stanford University Press, 1940), p. 14.

[26] Cottrell, *The Railroader*, pp. 15-19.

[27] Barney G. Glaser, *The Patsy and the Subcontractor: A Study of the Expert-Layman Relationship* (Mill Valley, Calif.: The Sociology Press, 1973).

[28] Glaser, *The Patsy and the Subcontractor*.

[29] Glaser, *The Patsy and the Subcontractor*, pp. 131-133.

[30] Glaser, *The Patsy and the Subcontractor*, pp. 166-167.

[31] Glaser, *The Patsy and the Subcontractor*, pp. 160-172. Quote is on p. 163.

[32] Donald F. Roy, "Quota Restriction and Goldbricking in a Machine Shop," *American Journal of Sociology*, 57 (March 1952), 427-442.

[33] Roy, "Quota Restriction and Goldbricking."

[34] Donald F. Roy, "Efficiency and 'The Fix'" Informal Intergroup Relations in a Piecework Machine Shop," *American Journal of Sociology*, 60 (November 1954), 255-266.

[35] Roy, "Efficiency and 'The Fix.'"

[36] Donald F. Roy, "'Banana Time': Job Satisfaction and Informal Interaction," *Human Organization*, 18 (Winter 1959-1960), 158-168.

[37] Roy, "'Banana Time,'" p. 166.

[38] Alvin W. Gouldner, *Patterns of Industrial Bureaucracy* (New York: The Free Press, 1954).

[39] Gouldner, *Patterns of Industrial Bureaucracy*, pp. 108-110.

[40] Gouldner, *Patterns of Industrial Bureaucracy*, pp. 160-161.

[41] Gouldner, *Patterns of Industrial Bureaucracy*, pp. 236-237.

[42] Robert Dubin, "Industrial Workers' Worlds: A Study of the 'Central Life Interests' of Industrial Workers," *Social Problems*, 3 (January 1956), 131-142.

[43] Charles R. Walker and Robert H. Guest, *The Man on the Assembly Line* (Cambridge, Mass.: Harvard University Press, 1952), pp. 10, 62-64.

[44] Walker and Guest, *The Man on the Assembly Line*, pp. 39, 146-147.

[45] Walker and Guest, *The Man on the Assembly Line.*

[46] Stanley Aronowitz, *False Promises: The Shaping of American Working Class Consciousness* (New York: McGraw-Hill, 1973), p. 23.

[47] Walker and Guest, *The Man on the Assembly Line*, pp. 157-161.

[48] Eli Chinoy, "Manning the Machines—The Assembly-Line Worker," in Peter L. Berger (ed.), *The Human Shape of Work* (New York: Macmillan, 1964), p. 70.

[49] Chinoy, "Manning the Machines," pp. 72-75.

[50] Aronowitz, *False Promises*, pp. 26, 33.

[51] Niall Brennan, *The Making of a Moron* (New York: Sheed and Ward, 1953), p. 14.

[52] Charles R. Walker, *Toward the Automated Factory* (New Haven: Yale University Press, 1957).

[53] Robert Blauner, *Alienation and Freedom: The Factory Worker and His Industry* (Chicago: The University of Chicago Press, 1964), pp. 167-173. Joan Woodward, *Industrial Organization: Theory and Practice* (London: Oxford University Press, 1965), agrees that workers are more autonomous and satisfied with their work when changing to automation, and emphasizes that organizations become more flexible and open.

[54] Tom Bevins and George M. Stalker, *The Management of Innovation* (London: Tavistock Publications, 1961), and Robert Dubin et al., (eds.), *Leadership and Productivity* (San Francisco: Chandler Publishing Co., 1965), indicate opposite findings, that organizations become more centralized and have closer supervision. For a review of these studies, see James C. Taylor et al., *Technology and Planned Organizational Change* (Ann Arbor, Mich.: Institute for Social Research, University of Michigan, 1971). For an earlier review, see Bernard Karsh, "Work and Automation," in Howard B. Jacobson and Joseph S. Roucek (eds.), *Automation and Society* (New York: Philosophical Library, 1959), pp. 379-393.

[55] Taylor, *Technology and Planned Organizational Change*, p. 123.

[56] Thomas L. Whisler, *The Impact of Computers on Organizations* (New York: Praeger Publishers, 1970).

[57] Martin Meissner, *Technology and the Worker: Technical Demands and Social Processes in Industry* (San Francisco: Chandler Publishing Co., 1969), p. 245.

[58] Nelson N. Foote, "The Professionalization of Labor in Detroit," *American Journal of Sociology, 58* (January 1953), 371-380.

[59] Fred Davis, "The Cabdriver and His Fare: Facets of a Fleeting Relationship," *American Journal of Sociology, 65* (September 1959), 159.

[60] Davis, "The Cabdriver and His Fare," p. 160-164.

[61] James M. Henslin, "Trust and the Cabdriver," in Marcello Truzzi (ed.), *Sociology and Everyday Life* (Englewood Cliffs, N.J.: Prentice-Hall, 1968), pp. 138-158.

[62] Hannah Meara, "Honor in Dirty Work: The Case of American Meat Cutters and Turkish Butchers," *Sociology of Work and Occupations, 1* (August 1974), 259-283.

[63] Meara, "Honor in Dirty Work."

[64] Lee Braude, *Work and Workers: A Sociological Analysis* (New York: Praeger Publishers, 1975), pp. 83-85.

[65] John F. Runcie, "Occupational Communication as Boundary Mechanism," *Sociology of Work and Occupations, 1* (November 1974), 420, 434, 437.

[66] Studs Terkel, *Working* (New York: Pantheon, 1974), p. 206. See also S. Kirson Weinberg and Henry Arond, "The Occupational Culture of the Boxer," *American Journal of Sociology, 57* (March 1952), 460-469.

[67] Graeme Salaman, *Community and Occupation* (New York: Cambridge University Press, 1974), pp. 21, 125.

[68] William J. Goode, "Community within a Community: The Professions," *American Sociological Review, 22* (April 1957), 194-200.

[69] Salaman, *Community and Occupation,* pp. 116-120.

[70] Julius A. Roth, "Professionalism: The Sociologists's Decoy," *Sociology of Work and Occupations, 1* (February 1974), p. 11.

[71] Clark Kerr et al., *Industrialism and Industrial Man* (Cambridge, Mass.: Harvard University Press, 1960).

[72] Blauner, *Alienation and Freedom.*

[73] Stephen Thernstrom, *The Other Bostonians: Poverty and Progress in the American Metropolis, 1880-1970* (Cambridge, Mass.: Harvard University Press, 1973), pp. 249, 258.

[74] John H. Goldthorpe et al., *The Affluent Worker in the Class Structure* (New York: Cambridge University Press, 1969), pp. 22-25.

[75] Goldthorpe et al., *The Affluent Worker in the Class Structure*, p. 26. In Chapter 2 above, Marx's basic thesis has been presented that with the maturity of capitalism a proletariat of the working class will develop, with a consciousness of kind and with organized power to overthrow its oppressors, the capitalist class (the bourgeoisie). The thesis has been modified, with the argument that Marx's historical thesis would ultimately occur, but that repressive or ideological systems such as nationalism, colonialism, militarism, and the like, will delay the inevitable. Others have argued that this transformation will be evolutionary rather than revolutionary, that in the process of change, the working class will be integrated into the social structure of capitalism, the latter becoming slightly modified in the process. Theories that would support this latter view are found in the works of Eduard Bernstein, Theodor Geiger, T. H. Marshall, and Ralf Dahrendorf.

[76] Peter M. Blau and Otis Dudley Duncan, *The American Occupational Structure* (New York: John Wiley & Sons, 1967), Chapter 6.

[77] Kurt B. Mayer and Sidney Goldstein, "Manual Workers as Small Businessmen," in Shostak and Gomberg (eds.), *Blue-Collar World*, pp. 537-550.

[78] James W. Rinehart, "Affluence and the Embourgeoisement of the Working Class: A Critical Look," *Social Problems, 19* (Fall 1971), 149.

[79] Rinehart, "Affluence and the Embourgeoisement," pp. 158-159. A recent empirical study supports this view: James De Fronzo, "Embourgeoisement in Indianapolis?" *Social Problems, 21* (Fall 1973), 269-283. Also, see Joan Talbot Dalie and Avery M. Guest, "Embourgeoisement among Blue-Collar Workers?" *The Sociological Quarterly, 16* (Summer 1975), 291-304. Theodore Caplow, *The Sociology of Work* (Minneapolis: University of Minnesota Press, 1954), p. 44, states: "In the long run the relative prestige of office jobs, set over against shop jobs, is based on the potential upward mobility of the white-collar worker."

[80] Robert M. Cook, "Review Essay: A View from an I-Beam," *American Journal of Sociology, 79* (September 1973), 455.

[81] William Gomberg, review essay of the blue-collar worker in *Contemporary Sociology, 3* (May 1974), 206-210.

[82] That is, not only do members of a social class have a common socioeconomic status but also a formal ideology, a national organization, and a willingness to act.

[83] Stanley Aronowitz, *False Promises: The Shaping of American Working Class Consciousness* (New York: McGraw-Hill, 1973). The discussion in the remainder of this section is based on his book.

[84] "Intentionally, hierarchy organizes the behavior of members so that the behavior is appropriate to the organization's purposes. Intentionally or not, hierarchy also arranges and systematizes members' satisfactions and dissatisfactions, motivation, and adjustment." Arnold S. Tannenbaum et al., *Hierarchy in Organizations* (San Francisco: Jossey-Bass, 1974), p. 186.

[85] Robert L. Heilbroner, "Men at Work," *The New York Review of Books*, January 23, 1975, p. 8.

[86] John and Barbara Ehrenreich, "Hospital Workers: A Case Study in the 'New Working Class,'" *Monthly Review, 24* (January 1973), 27.

[87] Nancy C. Morse and Robert S. Weiss, "The Function and Meaning of Work and the Job," *American Sociological Review, 30* (April 1955), 191-198.

[88] Marc Fried, *The World of the Urban Working Class* (Cambridge, Mass: Harvard University Press, 1973), p. 227.

[89] Ferdinand Zweig, *The Worker in an Affluent Society* (New York: The Free Press, 1961), pp. 191, 205-212.

[90] Leonard Woodcock, "There's Still a Car in Your Future," *Challenge, 17* (May-June 1974), 30.

[91] *The New York Times*, June 29, 1975, p. 5E. Descriptions of the typical blue-collar work-day can be found in Patricia Cayo Sexton and Brendan Sexton, *Blue-Collars and Hard Hats* (New York: Random House, 1971), pp. 131-133; and Andrew Levison, *The Working-Class Majority* (New York: Coward, McCann & Geoghegan, 1974), pp. 59-68.

[92] Jeanne Stellman and Susan Daum, *Work Is Dangerous to Your Health* (New York: Vintage, 1974).

[93] Sexton and Sexton, *Blue-Collars and Hard Hats*, p. 103.

[94] Stellman and Daum, *Work Is Dangerous to Your Health*, p. 8.

[95] U.S. Department of Labor, Bureau of Labor Statistics, *News*, May 2, 1974.

[96] Arthur B. Shostak, *Blue-Collar Life* (New York: Random House, 1969), p. 72.

[97] Daniel Rosenblatt and Edward A. Suchman, "Blue-Collar Attitudes and Information Toward Health and Illness," in Arthur B. Shostak and William Gomberg (eds.), *Blue-Collar World* (Englewood Cliffs, N.J.: Prentice-Hall, 1964), pp. 327-329.

[98] Shostak, *Blue-Collar Life*, p. 238.

[99] Shostak, *Blue-Collar Life*, p. 68.

[100] Howard M. Wachtel, "Capitalism and Poverty in America: Paradox or Contradiction?" *Monthly Review*, 24 (June 1972), 55.

[101] U.S. Department of Commerce, Bureau of the Census, *The Social and Economic Status of the Black Population in the United States, 1972* Series P-23, No. 46 (July, 1973), pp. 93-94.

[102] Claude C. Bowman, "Mental Health in the Worker's World," in Shostak and Gomberg (eds.), *Blue-Collar World*, p. 378. See also Arthur Kornhauser, *Mental Health of the Industrial Worker* (New York: John Wiley & Sons, 1965). An interesting psycho-history of working-class pressures is the work of Michael Lesy, *Wisconsin Death Trip* (New York: Random House, 1973).

[103] August B. Hollingshead and Frederick C. Redlich, *Social Class and Mental Illness* (New York: John Wiley & Sons, 1958); Jerome K. Myers and Bertram H. Roberts, *Family and Class Dynamics in Mental Illness* (New York: John Wiley & Sons, 1959).

[104] Lee J. Bean, Jerome K. Myers, and Max P. Pepper, "Social Class and Schizophrenia: A Ten-Year Follow-Up," in Shostak and Gomberg (eds.), *Blue-Collar World*, pp. 381-391.

[105] Zweig, *The Worker in an Affluent Society*, p. 77.

[106] Robert L. Kahn, "The Meaning of Work," in *The Worker in the New Industrial Environment* (Ann Arbor: Foundation for Research on Human Behavior, 1967).

[107] Harold L. Sheppard and Neal Q. Herrick, *Where Have All the Robots Gone? Worker Dissatisfaction in the '70s* (New York: The Free Press, 1972), p. 191. For a quick review of "blue-collar blues," see Stanley E. Seashore and J. Thad Barnowe, "Collar Doesn't Count," *Psychology Today*, 6 (August 1972), 53-55, 80-82.

[108] Richard Sennett and Jonathan Cobb, *The Hidden Injuries of Class* (New York: Alfred A. Knopf, 1973), pp. 36-37, 65, 95-97.

[109] William H. Form, "The Social Construction of Anomie: A Four-Nation

Study of Industrial Workers," *American Journal of Sociology*, *80* (March 1975), 1165-1191.

[110] Form, "The Social Construction of Anomie," p. 1166.

[111] Form, "The Social Construction of Anomie," p. 1173.

[112] Form, "The Social Construction of Anomie," pp. 1187-1188.

[113] For example, see Harold L. Wilensky, "Work as a Social Problem," in Howard S. Becker (ed.), *Social Problems: A Modern Approach* (New York: John Wiley & Sons, 1966), pp. 142-143; William A. Rushing, *Class, Culture, and Alienation: A Study of Farmers and Farm Workers* (Lexington, Mass.: D. C. Heath & Co., 1972), p. 13.

[114] Aronowitz, *False Promises*, pp. 11-12.

15 UNSKILLED AND SERVICE WORKERS: THE LOWER CLASS

The lower class is defined here as the working poor, that is, workers who are members of families earning less than the BLS standard of approximately $7000 yearly (in 1970 dollars). Following the dual labor market definition of the working class given in the summary of Chapter 14, the lower class is technically a subdivision of the working class. These workers also do not own or control the product of their labors. In addition, they are paid so poorly that they cannot emulate the life-style of the nonpoor working class. For example, only 16 percent of all skilled workers and 23 percent of semiskilled workers are working poor, whereas 35 percent of unskilled and service workers are (see Table 4.3).[1] Also, a large number of clerical workers (22 percent) and even 1 out of every 10 professional and managerial workers are classified as lower class. Again, given total family earnings of less than $7000, there is almost no amount of prestige or power that will make these workers part of the primary labor force.

Unskilled workers (laborers) require almost no training in order to fulfill the tasks of the job. These jobs involve mostly handling and moving materials—loading, digging, hauling, mixing. Heavy physical labor is usually required. The majority of the unskilled are employed in manufacturing and construction industries, earning an average annual income of $6082, compared to $7348 for the operatives and $8791 for the skilled. Mechanization and automation primarily are responsible for the reduction in the twentieth century in the proportion of unskilled workers in relation to the total labor force. This trend is expected to continue for the forseeable future, although the number of positions open will remain stable because of death, retirement, and transfer of present laborers to other occupational groups.[2]

Service workers are generally among the least skilled lower-class occupations and have the lowest earnings of any occupational group. The service occupations involve work tasks relating to personal and public services. The major groupings are: cleaning service workers (janitors, maids); food service workers (bartenders, waiters, dishwashers, cooks); health service workers (nursing aides, dental assistants); personal service workers (airline stewardesses, baggage attendants, barbers, elevator operators, hairdressers); protective service workers (firefighters, police officers, sanitation workers); and private household workers (servants, housekeepers, cooks).

Here again the problem of categorizing occupations is evident. A police officer has a national median annual income of $9000 (higher in large metropolitan areas) compared to that of an office messenger (white-collar clerical) at $3000.[3] Even in prestige the police officer is rated higher than the messenger. For these reasons, protective service workers have been discussed in the chapter on semiprofessions (Chapter 12).

Most unskilled labor revolves around forms of work that are better termed jobs instead of occupations. Eliot Freidson states that:

> They are merely specially constituted tasks in a division of labor created, coordinated, and controlled by management. Those jobs are created, dissolved, and reconstituted by management on the basis of changing production goals or needs, changing technology, or further rationalization for the end of greater productivity or lower cost. They have no social or economic foundation for their persistence beyond the plants, agencies or firms in which they exist.[4]

MIGRANT FARM WORKERS

One group of such temporary, low-wage, unskilled jobs is the migrant farm workers. Working as a participant observer, Dorothy Nelkin traced the daily lives of a group of Southern black migrant farm workers on upstate New York farms.[5] They function as temporary work groups, ranging in size from about 30 to 130 persons. Each group is organized by a crew leader who acts as an old-style foreman. These crew leaders recruit workers in the South in the spring and transport them North, usually by bus. The worker has contact only with the crew leader who, in turn, negotiates deals for services with the managers or owners of farms.

The crew leaders are omnipotent. They serve as contractor, recruiter, camp manager, work supervisor, police officer, and banker. They also purchase the food and drink and provide transportation. Migrant workers have literally no control over their own lives. Piecework rates are negotiated with management by the crew leader. The weather determines whether and how they will work. Uncertainty and disorder pervade their experience. They are even isolated from the local community, living in camps on the farms. There may be no work for long periods of time. Closed up together in these camps, violence often results among the workers in the form of fights. Gambling is popular. These deviant activities seem to have the sole purpose of breaking up the monotony for the frequently idle workers.[6]

An increasing proportion of unskilled farm labor consists of children. In the Pacific Northwest states there is no minimum wage legislation for children under 16 years old. Most of the berry crop in these states is picked by them during the summer months. At least 15 percent of the wage earners in the strawberry fields in the state of Washington are less than 12 years old.

WAITRESSES

The job of the waitress is unusual because she has to work in an organization—the restaurant—that deals in both production and services. She must deal with the services end (the customer) and the production end (the kitchen staff). At times the food is not ready when the waitress needs it, and the result is lower tips (which she depends on for more than half her wages). At times the customers can unnerve the waitress. They may become dissatisfied if the kitchen runs out of a favorite food, or they may not order for a long time, creating problems of scheduling them into the waitress' work pattern.[7]

There are five possible solutions to her problem: (1) talk back to the customers; (2) yell at the kitchen workers; (3) cry; (4) control the customer and thus take pressure off herself; or (5) blow off steam by talking about one's problems to the supervisor. The best solution is number 4. However, there are always many customers who are not controllable. Therefore, in many instances, the waitress ends up crying, frustrated at being unable to complete her duties properly in this situation.[8]

The cocktail waitress faces a different but equally difficult situation. Her environment fosters role degradation. She works for tips, too. As a result, she must treat the client deferentially, even though the client (usually male) often does not treat her with respect. She has little control over the formal work situation, since she is subservient to management, bartender, and customer. The customer frequently is unhappy or upset and tries to degrade the waitress by acting superior to her, thus relieving his own tensions.[9]

The young male waiter in a college sorority, known as a "hasher," is another case of the difficult role of personal service workers. The hasher is a college man with above average intelligence, manners that are middle class or higher, a man-of-the-world attitude, and the expectation of holding a white-collar position in the near future. In his occupational role as hasher he is not allowed to date the girls he serves nor even to speak to them. The image is fostered of menial or "dirty" work, of low prestige, and lack of sophistication. The hasher has a middle-class background or, if not, is pushing in that direction, but he is performing a working-class job.[10]

To relieve the tension of this role conflict, hashers resort to many tactics. They insult the girls, thus implying that the girls are no better status-wise than the hashers. Or they play a "game," an activity with a theme that mimics the girls. These serve as tension-relieving activities and, at the same time, provide a basis for social cohesion among hashers. That the status ranking is evident to all is indicated by the yearly "turnabout" day when the girls serve meals to the hashers.[11]

JANITORS

Janitors play two major roles in their work: (1) as entrepreneurs they run the building without direct supervision and are responsible for its safety and for the safety of the tenants; and (2) as master mechanics they run a cash business by servicing the tenants' needs.[12]

These roles do not fit the stereotype of the tenants, who view the janitor's work as low-status, dirty work. In addition, where janitors are unionized, they sometimes earn more than the tenants. Tenants become very disturbed about this seeming inequity. The janitor's new automobile parked in front of the apartment building produces many disgruntled tenants.[13] They feel that janitors are undeserving of their wages, much in the same way college professors feel about the wages of sanitation workers.

Janitors perceive themselves as acting professionally when they are in a position to "protect the client's secrets." They are often questioned about tenants by police, insurance agents, and other officials. They also compare their 24-hour job to the physician's. They are on call at all hours. Often they meet the physician in the hall in the middle of the night while both are on emergency calls.

However, these highlights of janitors' work are counterbalanced by the dirty work—the removal of garbage. This is the most important factor contributing to their low status. Also, they are required to be available 7 days a week for emergencies, and they must do chores 7 days a week. The furnace and hot water boilers must be checked several times daily. The routine and monotony become overpowering, so that janitors need to get away. Since there is so little time between their watchguard rounds and chores, their most common diversion is the local corner tavern. While they are gone, there is no one to watch their buildings, unless a nearby janitor can be persuaded to check them occasionally. They consider themselves the guardians of the building and its occupants.[14]

Even though janitors are free of direct supervision, they almost never are free from their responsibility for the safety of the building and its tenants. What is most aggravating is that tenants do not appreciate the importance and difficulties of this work. Janitors feel that their status should be much higher than the tenants' perception of it.

PRIVATE
HOUSEHOLD
WORKERS

There are approximately 1½ million private household workers in the United States today. Only 75 thousand live in their employers' homes. The proportion of domestics as a percentage of the labor force has gradually decreased from 5 percent in 1900 to less than 2 percent in 1970 (see Table 2.5). The higher cost of domestic work caused by minimum wage laws and the development of new housecleaning and cooking aids have together created a decline in these services.

Domestic service is a working-class occupation in terms of income and social status but with middle-class pretensions. The type of labor that domestics offer has much in common with other occupations where personal deference is practiced, for example, sales clerks in luxury stores. The "style" in which one serves one's employer is as important as the technical skills applied.[15]

Domestic work has traditionally served as an escape for minority group members who could not or did not want to enter the main labor force occupations. This was acceptable to many, even though they were highly exploited. Domestics are expected to be loyal to the employer and to perform a wide range of duties in all areas of housework.[16]

However, there are many aspects of the work that lead to job dissatisfaction. Most work as the single domestic in the household; consequently, they lack any fellowship with members of their own occupation. There are no objective criteria for measuring performance of their duties. The measure of success is how much they please the employer from one day to the next; there is a lack of privacy;[17] and the median annual earnings are low, the lowest of any occupational group: $1712 for men and $981 for women.[18]

Some particular problems have developed as a result of the reduction of live-in domestics. Living away from the employer requires that the domestic worker travel long distances to his place of work. Usually a ghetto resident, he must travel to the suburbs, which are as far away from the ghetto as the middle class can get. Also, more work is part-time, lowering the wages of the domestic. Part-time work also permits more middle-class homes to acquire services. As a result, there are more employers with no experience in relating to domestic workers.[19]

JAZZ MUSI-
CIANS: A
DEVIANT
OCCUPATION[20]

Deviant people are those who are placed in a personally discreditable position because they have not followed the normative prescriptions of the group in power. Deviance is caused by what a person is or does. It is a matter of degree rather than an either-or proposition.[21]

A deviant occupation is one in which its members are viewed as deviant if:

1. Its activities are illegal (it continually breaks the laws of the society).
2. It violates what is considered "morally correct behavior toward one's fellow man" by the society that defines what is morally correct.
3. It is not considered "a proper and fitting occupation."[22]

This is a form of "labelling theory," which says that we must accept as deviant what people see as deviant. Those who break laws, violate moral standards, and harm individuals and groups, but who are able to hide these actions or deflect labeling, are not deviant.[23] American business executives engaged in price fixing and illegal political contributions are a good case in point. On the other hand, many persons can be violated by a system that denies them decent jobs or consigns them to life in a ghetto. A great many "deviants" are located in these categories. As Nanette Davis indicates, emphasis in deviance studies has been placed on "deviant categories rather than on the authority structures which generate deviant types."[24] Present deviance theory says nothing about the behavior of the power-holders in determining who and what is deviant and *for what purposes these determinations are made.*

From this analysis Alexander Liazos argues that if sociologists accept currently successful definitions of what is deviant as the only ones worthy of their attention, they will perpetuate the very notions that they think they debunk.[25] The following analysis, which considers jazz musicians as a deviant occupation merely because our society defines it as deviant, could then be accused of this failure to debunk. "Labeling tends to deny the intrinsic evil [or the intrinsic good—PDM] in some human acts."[26] Thus, labeling could not support the view that music is inherently good or that slavery or genocide is inherently bad but only what society presently defines as good or bad.

I will give two responses to this criticism. First, it is part of the work of sociology to examine "those persons whom the members of a society see as deviant."[27] Second, an explicit purpose of this book is to analyze critically the multitude of theories and conceptualizations regarding occupations so that we, as sociologists, can help to develop a better understanding of how others develop, maintain, and discard their images.

In the service occupations clients come into direct and personal contact with workers—doctors with patients, social workers with clients, and musicians with their audience. The client at times will attempt to influence the work of the worker. Then a great deal of conflict and hostility is manifested.

In most cases jazz musicians find it difficult to obtain a steady job where they can play the music they prefer all the time—jazz. Outsiders (clients) tell them what to play—most nonjazz. The degree to which the clients affect their work will determine how musicians define themselves. If there is little or no influence, musicians play the music they want. Jazz musicians fit this description. If they play music to satisfy the public, they are "commercial musicians."[28]

The dilemma of jazz musicians is that they must perform their work in a fashion that disagrees with what they want to perform. Becker drives home this point with an example.

> *I was playing solo for one night over at the Y___ on ___rd Street. What a drag! The second set, I was playing* Sunny Side, *I played the melody for one chorus, then I played a little jazz. All of a sudden the boss leaned over the side of the bar and hollered, "I'll kiss your ass if anybody in this place knows what tune you're playing!" And everybody in the place heard him, too. What a big square! What could I do? I didn't say anything, just kept playing. Sure was a drag.*[29]

People's work is extremely important in shaping their personal identities. When they commit themselves to a particular occupation, persons assume others' perceptions of that occupation and its members. They try to shape a favorable image of their occupation. If they cannot, they will turn inward and will temporarily disregard the outside world's perceptions of their work.

The jazz musicians Becker studied adjusted themselves to their dilemma by physically isolating themselves. They used their instruments—the piano and the drums—to form a barricade between themselves and the audience. They psychologically isolated themselves by using their own jargon and by not looking at or talking to "the squares" (the audience).[30]

The music form of jazz itself tends to produce an in-group attitude. The jazz musician selects sound patterns as different as possible from the melody, yet he will stay within a pattern consistent and recognizable to other jazz musicians. The music is unique and abstract, and recognizable to the expert only. It is difficult for anyone, no less a jazz musician, to verbalize this phenomenon. Jazz players know they can communicate their aims and methods to one another and to a few elite outsiders, but they believe that the rest of humanity is hopelessly ignorant of what they are doing.[31]

Jazz musicians must play in the "square" world to earn a living, but it is the jam session, the after-hours get-together, for which the true jazz musician really lives. The rules for playing at this session are many and very limiting.

One must know the right keys, the right tunes, and the right ways of playing them. The improvisations within the chordal harmonics and basic rhythm mark the uniqueness of each jazz player.

Dance musicians play primarily for the enjoyment of the client. They also enjoy the music they play. The music is most always prearranged; that is, all notes, chord structures, and tempos are written out in the musical scores and the musician is left to decide on the more minor details of speed of tempo and noise level. The music is played "straight."

Having been a "Saturday-night" dance band musician myself, I would suggest adding another type of musician, one who is somewhere between a jazz musician and a dance musician. These people find themselves part-deviant. (This emphasizes the fact that there are degrees of deviance.) These variations begin when a dance or jazz musician's particular style is copied during parts of the score. One will hear a bit of Harry James or Miles Davis in the musician's rendition. The typical workplace for this hybrid musician is the small, intimate nightclub or the fashionable bar.

Jazz musicians and their audience are a "semicommunity"[32] in that they all share an interest in jazz and participate in the occupation's ideology.[33] It is an ingrown culture because of its isolation. The profession is isolated because its members are associated with crime and deviance, black spirituals, and other religious fervor, and because whites saw it as a black creation and thus a threat to white culture.[34] Additionally, the musician must spend much time practicing and must work at night when others are at their leisure. The public is scorned because it doesn't accept jazz as a serious art form.[35]

Edward Harvey disagrees with the conclusions of Cameron and Becker, who studied jazz musicians in the early 1950s. He questions their ability to obtain fairly representative samples and indicates that he random sampled 118 musicians, jazz and nonjazz, from union lists to conduct interviews and engage in participant observation. He found that social backgrounds and recruitment patterns of the young (35 or less) and old musicians are different.[35]

For the younger, the occupation was seen by the aspirants and their parents to be a legitimate one, a respectable one to enter. The younger hopefuls tend to come from white-collar backgrounds and older blue-collar backgrounds. The trend is from a "lower-class deviant" occupation to a "middle-class artist" occupation.[37]

Jazz musicians are no longer hostile toward their audiences because of the latter's lack of understanding of jazz. There are more jazz clubs, jazz associations in several major cities, jazz "hot lines" to obtain recorded information on daily jazz concerts and events, and jazz radio stations. They feel more responsible to their occupation and to the society as a whole because of this; they no longer try to flaunt accepted behavioral norms.

There is less ethnic and racial tolerance among jazz musicians than expected. They seem to be growing more like the general public in their attitudes toward others with whom they work. They have a highly controlled on-the-job organization, contrary to Becker's implication that social control of members is weak. Finally, the younger musicians are less isolated from the community.

There is the tendency to professionalize jazz. Younger members are attempting to routinize and formalize standards of competence within the occupation. The jazz school is one way in which this is being accomplished. Occupational change is instigated by the public's changing attitude toward the occupation. The old occupational role strain has been pretty well eliminated as a consequence, but a new strain, how to live up to the new image, has emerged as a result.[38]

Harvey's analysis implies that because jazz musicians no longer consider themselves deviant and no longer act deviant, it will not be long before the public also legitimates jazz as a professional service occupation.

An entirely different analysis of the development of jazz as an occupation is given by Frank Kofsky, who sees the structural and historical factors of society as the keys to explaining the current position of jazz musicians.[39] Basing his analysis on Marx's statement in *The German Ideology* that the literature, art, and philosophy of a people come out of the material conditions of their existence, Kofsky traces the development of black music from the 1930s. "Be bop" became popular in the 1930s along with the attempt at integration with white society. Duke Ellington's symphonic jazz is another example. The 1940s witnessed a drastic change. Overt discrimination in the armed services during World War II and the white takeover and cash-in of black swing music while blacks were left out were a serious blow to black hopes for equality. Their change to the angry music of the 1950s and 1960s is reflected in historical circumstances.[40]

Our society failed to establish jazz as an acceptable form of music during the early period of optimism; it failed to give it recognition. Instead, white critics of black music suggested bourgeois theories such as the biological one that "Negroes as a race have a rhythmic genius that is not like that of other races and ... that [their] genius has found unique expression in the United States."[41] Establishing jazz schools, introducing jazz in public school programs, and offering prizes and scholarships all would have helped to remove jazz from its "unwholesome atmosphere" of one-night stands in drab neighborhood nightclubs and of resulting financial and family insecurity. Fundamental to this change would be to end discrimination against minority people in this occupation and in the cultural areas and educational institutions that support it.[42]

THE "NEW WORKING CLASS"

The working and living conditions of people in lower-class jobs are poor enough that they are aware of their alienation to a greater extent than any other working group. Add to this those workers who experience relative deprivation (e.g., those in professional, managerial, semiprofessional, and sales occupations who feel they are not given autonomy appropriate to their position), and we have the basis of a new working-class movement. Many variations of this basic structure of the working class have been cited throughout this book.

It seems to be left to the minority groups in the United States to create the impetus for a significant workers' movement. Signs were seen of a strong women's coalition of labor unions in the founding in 1974 of the international Coalition of Labor Union Women. It was the largest labor union convention in the history of the United States. Over 3200 delegates registered from 58 different unions.[43] Blacks have established a strong base in industrial unions, with a majority in the Laborers Union and increasing memberships in the AFL-CIO and the Teamsters. Government actions through federal civil rights legislation have pressured corporate management to enforce civil rights laws. Corporations potentially have much more power than unions in combatting segregation. They can threaten to use economic sanctions that affect everyone in a community, for example, the threat of moving away.[44]

But the unions, as the organizers of labor, must take the role of leadership in creating a better work world. So far they haven't. The typical union stance is to respond to planned or unplanned change instead of innovating change. Paul Jacobs has commented on this situation.

If unions are going to survive and grow in the coming period, they have to break with their old patterns. First of all, they have to break with their pattern of not thinking about work, *the nature of work, their relationship to work, and what they can do about work. What do we do about work now? Well, we say we're going to fix the wages, we're going to try to establish what we think ought to be minimal working conditions, we're going to slow down the line, we're going to argue about the speed of the line. But do we ever say: Hey, the whole concept of production of an automobile on a line stinks; the whole thing is wrong. what we ought to be doing is figuring out new ways of looking at the problem of work? No, these are questions from which every union withdraws.*

I heard the vice-president of Kaiser explain their new agreement with the Steelworkers Union, and he was asked what the union would have to say about the nature of work processes in the plant. "Nothing," he said. "My goodness, the steelworkers Union wouldn't ever dream of venturing into this area....[45]

A true industrial democracy is far off for the United States as well as for other countries that have experimented with worker participation plans. None offer workers the right to decide the kinds of goods they will produce or to redirect the economy in any significant way. Perhaps a step in this direction is to require all workers to spend some time periodically doing physical labor in fields related to their own. Agronomists would work in the fields 1 year out of every 3 years, as they presently do in China.[46] Executives would work on the assembly line. As one worker said to Walker during his early study of the automated steel factory, "I'm not saying that they should not have engineers, but I'm saying that the engineers should spend a lot of time as millmen themselves."[47]

SUMMARY AND
CONCLUSIONS

Lower-class workers have the most unstable, poorest paying jobs in the labor force. Viewed from the traditional occupational groups of the Bureau of the Census, the unskilled and service occupations contain the largest proportion of these jobs. However, as dual labor market analysis has enabled us to see, these jobs are found in all occupational categories and groups. The primary and secondary labor market categories cut across the Bureau of the Census categories to show the degree of worker autonomy in terms of control over the work process and workers' rights instead of degree of occupational skill or prestige. Both are "ideological" ways of viewing the labor force. Both have been presented to give the reader a broad view of labor market analysis in the context of occupational sociology.

Most sociological literature on lower-class occupations is in the area of the personal service jobs. A review of the positions of waitress, janitor, and private household worker indicates a high degree of role conflict among these jobs. Conflict arises when janitors pretend to be professionals, when waitresses are caught between the demands of the customer and the kitchen staff, and when private household workers have pretentions to the middle class.

Some occupations are viewed as deviant by members of society. Jazz musicians are one of these occupations. The struggle of jazz musicians is to overcome the "client control" of the listener in order to play more jazz. Most of the time, however, they are playing music that they do not particularly like but that satisfies the client.

The present state of these "have-not" occupations regarding their struggle to attain a better position, that is, more wealth, prestige, and power in proportion to "have" occupations, is one of underdevelopment. There are signs that changes may be in store. For example, there is the increasing unionization of blacks and women in the lower class and of the human service occupations at all occupational levels. However, the distance to full work equality and full worker participation is great and must overcome many tremendous hurdles yet to be solved by any political economy.

FOOTNOTES FOR CHAPTER 15
UNSKILLED AND SERVICE WORKERS: THE LOWER CLASS

[1] These statistics agree with other estimates. See Charles T. Stewart, Jr., *Low Wage Workers in an Affluent Society* (Chicago: Nelson-Hall, 1974), p. 71; Andrew Levison, *The Working Class Majority* (New York: Coward, McCann & Geoghegan, Inc., 1974), p. 32. There is also a positive relationship between the low-wage primary income earner and the wages of a secondary income earner in the family. See Elizabeth Waldman, "Marital and Family Characteristics of Workers, March 1966," *Monthly Labor Review, 91* (April 1968), 35.

[2] U.S. Department of Labor, Bureau of Labor Statistics, *Occupational Outlook Handbook*, 1972-1973 Ed. (Washington, D.C.: U.S. Government Printing Office, 1972), pp. 368-369.

[3] U.S. Department of Commerce, Bureau of the Census, *Occupational Characteristics: 1970 Census of the Population* (Washington, D.C.: U.S. Government Printing Office, 1973), Table 1, pp. 4, 10-11.

[4] Eliot Freidson, "Professionalization and the Organization of Labor in Post-Industrial Society," in Paul Halmos (ed.), *Professionalization and Social Change*, The Sociological Review Monograph No. 20 (Staffordshire, England: University of Keele, September 1973), p. 54.

[5] Dorothy Nelkin, "Unpredictability and Life Style in a Migrant Labor Camp," *Social Problems, 17* (Spring 1970), 472-486.

[6] Nelkin, "Unpredictability and Life Style."

[7] William Foote Whyte "When Workers and Customers Meet," Chapter 7 of *Industry and Society* (New York: McGraw-Hill, 1946), pp. 123-147.

[8] Whyte, "When Workers and Customers Meet."

[9] H. L. Hearn and Patricia Stoll, "Continuance Commitment in Low-Status Occupations: The Cocktail Waitress," *The Sociological Quarterly, 16* (Winter 1975), 105-114.

[10] Louis A. Zurcher, Jr., David W. Sonenschein, and Eric L. Metzner, "The Hasher: A Study of Role Conflict," *Social Forces, 44* (June 1966), 505-514.

[11] Zurcher, Sonenschein, and Metzner, "The Hasher."

[12] Ray Gold, "Janitor Versus Tenant: A Status-Income Dilemma," *American Journal of Sociology, 57* (March 1952), 486-493.

[13] Gold, "Janitor Versus Tenant."

[14] Raymond L. Gold, "In the Basement—The Apartment-Building Janitor," in Peter L. Berger (ed.), *The Human Shape of Work* (New York: Macmillan Company, 1964), p. 10.

[15] David Chaplin, "Domestic Service and the Negro," in Shostak and Gomberg (eds.), *Blue-Collar World*, p. 528.

[16] Chaplin, "Domestic Service and the Negro," pp. 527, 530.

[17] *Occupational Characteristics*, p. 11.

[18] Chaplin, "Domestic Service and the Negro," pp. 531-532.

[19] Chaplin, "Domestic Service and the Negro," p. 533.

[20] Since deviant occupations generally confer low prestige (e.g., poolroom hustlers, prostitutes, strippers, pickpockets, burglers) and often a majority of their members are found in low-income categories, the discussion of jazz musicians is placed in this chapter, even though many are not low-income workers.

[21] Edward Sagarin, *Deviants and Deviance* (New York: Praeger Publishers, 1975), p. 9.

[22] Ned Polsky, *Hustlers, Beats, and Others* (Chicago: Aldine Publishing Co., 1967), p. 41.

[23] Alexander Liazos, "The Poverty of the Sociology of Deviance: Nuts, Sluts, and Perverts," *Social Problems, 20* (Summer 1972), 109. A good example of lawbreaking that is overlooked by supervisors is the situation at aircraft manufacturing plants, where an illegal tool is openly used by workers. See Joseph Bensman and Israel Gerver, "Crime and Punishment in the Factory: The Function of Deviancy in Maintaining the Social System," *American Sociological Review, 28* (August 1963), 588-598.

[24] Nanette J. Davis, *Sociological Constructions of Deviance* (Dubuque, Iowa: Wm. C. Brown Co., 1975), p. 11.

[25] Liazos, "The Poverty of the Sociology of Deviance," pp. 110-111. Two sociologists, Kitsuse and Spector, argue that Robert Merton's statement that "The sociologist does not impose his values upon others when he undertakes to *supply knowledge* about latent social problems," does not recognize the question of whether sociologists impose their own values in

identifying conditions as "latent" problems in the first place. Because they define latency, sociologists thereby determine what will become manifest, since something cannot become manifest unless it is first defined as latent. According to this argument, members of society must accept the sociologist's definition of a latent problem. John I. Kitsuse and Malcolm Spector, "Toward a Sociology of Social Problems: Social Conditions, Value-Judgments, and Social Problems," *Social Problems, 20* (Spring 1973), 407-418.

[26] Sagarin, *Deviants and Deviance*, p. 134.

[27] Sagarin, *Deviants and Deviance*, p. 135. Sagarin distinguishes this from "that which is evil," that is, a moral and personal judgment of what or who is deviant.

[28] Howard S. Becker, "The Professional Dance Musician and His Audience," *American Journal of Sociology, 57* (September 1951), 136.

[29] Becker, "The Professional Dance Musician," p. 141.

[30] Becker, "The Professional Dance Musician," p. 141.

[31] William Bruce Cameron, "Sociological Notes on the Jam Session," *Social Forces, 33* (December 1954), 177-181.

[32] Robert A. Stebbins, "A Theory of the Jazz Community," *The Sociological Quarterly, 9* (Summer 1968), 331.

[33] Alan P. Merriam and Raymond W. Mack, "The Jazz Community," *Social Forces, 38* (March 1960), 211. The audience is made up of adolescents, intellectuals, and blacks, who are against standardization and commercialism and for individuality and artistic spontaneity. Another study indicated that politically liberal college students are more likely to enjoy jazz than conservatives. William S. Fox and James D. Williams, "Political Orientation and Music Preferences Among College Students," *Public Opinion Quarterly, 38* (Fall 1974), 367-368.

[34] Monroe Berger, "Jazz: Resistance to the Diffusion of a Cultural Pattern," *Journal of Negro History, 32* (October 1947), 461-497.

[35] Merriam and Mack, "The Jazz Community."

[36] Edward Harvey, "Social Change and the Jazz Musician," *Social Forces, 46* (September 1967), 34-42.

[37] Harvey, "Social Change and the Jazz Musician," pp. 36-37.

[38] Harvey, "Social Change and the Jazz Musician," pp. 40-41.

[39] Frank Kofsky, "The Jazz Tradition: Black Music and Its White Critics," *Journal of Black Studies, 1* (June 1971), 403-434.

[40] Kofsky, "The Jazz Tradition," pp. 415-416.

[41] Martin Williams, *The Jazz Tradition* (New York: Oxford University Press, 1970), p. 8.

[42] Kofsky, "The Jazz Tradition," pp. 421-422.

[43] Patricia Cayo Sexton, "Workers (Female) Arise!" *Dissent, 21* (Summer 1974), 381.

[44] Examples are given by Theodore V. Purcell and Gerald F. Cavanagh, *Blacks in the Industrial World* (New York: The Free Press, 1972), pp. 34-35.

[45] Paul Jacobs, *Labor Looks at Labor* (Santa Barbara, Calif: Center for the Study of Democratic Institutions, 1963), pp. 14-15.

[46] Even though experience shows that, when compared to American methods, technological development and productivity are slowed by this practice, it might be considered worthwhile from the human point of view. Food production in China is able to support its immense population and may even produce a surpluss by 1978. See the reports in *RF Illustrated,* (Rockefeller Foundation) Vol. 2, No. 2 (March 1975), and *The New York Times* (December 27, 1975).

[47] Charles R. Walker, *Toward the Automated Factory* (New Haven: Yale University Press, 1957), p. 215.

PART 3

OCCUPATIONS
AND INSTITUTIONS

In the relation between occupations and institutions, the family and education raise a large number of important issues. In studying the family in Chapter 16, some of the questions examined are: how it socializes its members for work roles; the effect of the father's occupation on family life-style, aspirations of children, and community relations; the relationship between work patterns and income in the family; and the role of working mothers.

The relationship of education to occupation is an important and most pressing issue today. Recent court tests at all levels of government stress the significance of the underlying arguments for and against the role of education in attaining occupational success. Among the issues examined in Chapter 17 are: the relation of education to occupation and income by race and sex; the effects of family background (in terms of both occupation and education) on occupation; the genetic factor; man-power utilization; and the role of the family and the school in supporting the dual-labor market.

These remaining chapters show how the occupational structure, in terms of markets and shelters, conditions the changes in education and the family, even though the latter do have some independent effects on one another and on the occupational order.

16 OCCUPATIONS, THE FAMILY, AND THE INDIVIDUAL

Because occupations are instrumental in conferring social status and personal identity on individuals, there is no question that occupations will significantly influence the life-style and internal cohesion of the family. The family, in turn, has an effect on one's occupational destination, as shown in Chapters 6 and 7. Both family and occupation influence a person's work role; they also influence nonwork activities. This chapter explores the various interconnections among occupations, the family, and the individual.

THE EFFECT OF FAMILY ON OCCUPATIONS

In their milestone study on inequality, Christopher Jencks and his associates conclude at one point that family background is not an important determinant of a person's status.[1] This result does not agree with a considerable body of sociological research, however. Family values and family structure play an important role in shaping a person's occupational destination and thus his social status.

There are certain economic costs of starting and maintaining a family. Treiman and Terrel estimate that the cost of being married for a woman is $252 a year. That is, single women capitalize on their occupational attainment more than married women. There are several possible reasons for this occurrence. One is the overt or covert discrimination against married women by employers. They are afraid a woman will leave soon after she marries in order to have children and become a full-time house- wife. Then there is the problem of finding a job in one's specialty within rea- sonable commuting distance so that children can be cared for shortly after school lets out.[2]

Until child labor laws were passed in the 1920s, children were wage earn- ers in factories and fields or were unpaid labor working for the family enter- prise. But no economic gain comes from having children in the modern nu- clear family. Parents today have an ambivalent attitude toward their children because they know that they suffer occupational handicaps because of them. For example, the family is less mobile if children are established in school and have friends. The family has a lower standard of living created by the cost of supporting children, sometimes through an expensive college education. In turn, children may resent their parents if they are placed in a lower socio-eco- nomic status because their parents have not achieved occupational success.[3]

Families are sometimes very important as the sole means of support for persons preparing for and entering certain occupations. In a study of Ameri- can composers, Dennison Nash found that successful composers had strong family support for their serious interest in music. The family gave moral sup- port to the fledgling artist working in a hostile or indifferent social environ- ment. In the creative arts family support can often make the difference be- tween success and failure.[4]

Other occupations are in direct conflict with the values of the family. Alvin Gouldner describes how the work norms of the "progressive" male trade union leader are in direct contradiction to those dominant in our society. They eschew individual competitive aggressiveness in order to work for ideals, and they belittle personal success. Marriage tends to aggravate the situation. Wives expect husbands home in the evening, but union leaders must spend evenings organizing meetings. Wives expect a middle-class life, but their husbands' salary will not support it.[5]

The Influence of the Working Mother

A young married woman's employment status (working or not) most direct- ly depends on her immediate family circumstances, that is, economic pressures and the number of children in the family. Also important is the factor of whether or not her mother worked. Neither of the two parents' attempted encouragements seem to have had much direct effect on their children's aspira- tions. Having had an employed mother improves a married woman's employ- ment status.[6] Lane also found that the greater the dominance of the wo- man's father in the family, the higher her career commitment. But, in turn, it also means she has more traditional sex-role viewpoints.[7]

Research conducted in Great Britain, France, and the United States shows that children of mothers who work perform better at school than those whose mothers stay at home. Also, children of working mothers do not have higher rates of sickness, are as well adjusted, and are no more delinquent than children of nonworking mothers.[8]

In 1970, 4 out of every 10 women in the labor force were mothers. Of these, 36 percent had children under the age of six. Work time lost because of illness or injury was 5.6 days per person per year for women and 5.3 days per person per year for men.[9]

These facts support the present increase in the proportion of working mothers in the labor force.

In the United States and many other Western countries the traditional ways of rearing children have created a bimodal employment curve for women. The first peak occurs at ages 20 to 24; then there is a dip for marriage and maternity; then a second peak occurs at around ages 35 to 40, depending on the country. Work is interrupted for childrearing, and women suffer by having to enter the labor force twice. This is not so much of a problem for women in socialist societies, who take short maternity leaves and who place infants in state supervised nurseries in order to return to their original jobs.[10]

The trend toward maternity leaves is beginning to catch on in American industry. As of 1973, Connecticut made it an unfair labor practice for an employer to terminate employment because of pregnancy, to refuse to grant a reasonable leave of absence for pregnancy, or to deny benefits covered by an established disability plan. Other states are conducting studies in preparation for legislation on women's rights.[11] Day care programs are becoming established as part of the expected services for working women.

Broken Families

In 1973, 13 percent of all families were one-parent families headed by a woman. Approximately two-thirds of these families (5 million families) had no other income earners in the family than the woman head.[12] The percentage of one-parent families has been on the increase in the United States, caused primarily by the continued increase in divorce rates.[13] It is known that men living with their spouses have a higher socio-economic status than divorced or separated men. About half the status difference between these two groups of men is caused by the variables of family background, educational attainment, and status of first job. The family background factor of marriage disruption is one of the significant variables affecting occupational achievement.[14]

Among the family background factors greatly influencing a young person's educational preparation for entry into the labor force are number of siblings, head of household's education, head of household's occupation, and stability of the husband-wife relationships.[15] Since the higher the education, the higher the occupational achievement (see Chapter 17), it is important to note the results of Duncan's analysis. She discovered that:

- An increase in occupational status of ten points for the head of the family resulted in .3 years of additional schooling for the child.
- Intact families had children with .6 to 1.0 more years of schooling than broken families.
- An increase in the family head's education by one year increased the child's education by .2 year.
- A decrease in the number of siblings by one increased a child's education by .2 year.[16]

One can safely conclude that being raised in a broken family is disadvantageous for occupational attainment.

THE EFFECT OF OCCUPATION ON FAMILY

In a broad national study of the relationship between values and social class, Melvin Kohn found that social class, as measured by the occupational dimensions of self-direction and conformity, greatly affects family values. Kohn documents how middle-class parents are more likely to value their children's self-direction, whereas working-class parents value conformity to external authority.[17] *Self-direction* focuses on one's internal standards for behavior, on one's being tuned into one's own and others' internal dynamics. *Conformity*, on the other hand, focuses on obedience to authority figures and adherence to externally imposed rules. It implies rigidity, isolation, or insensitivity to others. This relationship of social class (i.e., socio-economic status as measured by occupation) to family values is so strong that it overrides other factors influencing values, such as race, religion, national background, region of country, size of community, and size of family.[18]

Kohn also found that middle-class parents are more likely to punish their children on the basis of the child's motivation. Working-class parents are more likely to punish their children on the basis of the immediate consequences of the child's behavior. This does not mean that the values of working-class parents are "present-oriented" only. It does mean that the two classes act on the basis of different goals for different values. What is unacceptable to working-class parents is acceptable to middle-class parents, and vice versa.[19]

Another study verifies Kohn's findings. Comparing the values of the sons of professionals and businessmen to their fathers' values, Mortimer found that they were similar for both occupations. When the business occupations were separated into those that worked with people (managers, salespersons) versus those that worked with data or things (accountants, engineers), sons of fathers in the data-oriented occupations were more extrinsically motivated, and those in the people-oriented occupations were more intrinsically motivated.[20]

Occupations and the Nuclear Family

There is a major dilemma between the modern nuclear family and the occupations of its members. Family status is determined by age, sex, and biological affiliation, whereas occupational status is determined by objective standards of performance. Occupations emphasize competition, which is rational, continuous, and unlimited, a value that the family does not hold.[21]

Caplow has explained how the importance of the family in the modern West has declined as rational values take over. The increasing size of formal groups (aggregation), the diversification of their functions (differentiation), and the increasing formal control of human behavior (rationalization) have, as manifested in occupations, "destroyed the continuity of the individual's life history."[22] There is a shift from a status system based on one's family background and personal ambition and achievement to occupational function, that is, the general status of the occupation in which one works. People are adjusted to the job (administrative authority) instead of being able to develop their jobs according to their personal capabilities and insights (occupational authority).[23]

However, as I pointed out in Part 1, the occupational structure does not operate rationally in many cases. The evaluation of workers is often based on affective elements. Competition is not always continuous. The early stages of a career are more highly competitive than the later stages. In addition, competition is not unlimited. Status attained on the basis of occupational achievement is severely limited for minority groups.[24]

Whatever the degree of affective judgment, occupations are important determinants of family life. Udry explains how the husband's occupation, through its income, determines the standard of living of the family and its stability. Everything from family life-style, aspirations of children, family recreation, friends, and area of the community in which they live is affected by occupation.[25]

The family is organized around the breadwinner's job. Whether the spouse works, where the family lives, and countless other factors stem from the worker's job and earnings. The structure of the family has become predominantly nuclear as the extended family, with its close-knit network of relatives, found it difficult to pick up and follow the worker searching for a job. People moved with the increasing movement of industries, with the invasion of undesired ethnic groups into their neighborhoods, and when they were forced into smaller living units in urban redevelopment apartments.

In blue-collar families the relationship between husband and wife has become closer. They now tend to share the same friends instead of maintaining separate friendships. Conjugal roles are less segregated. There also is greater mutuality of sexual relations and a greater psychic investment in each child.[26]

However, others have found that the low wages of many blue-collar workers cause economic strains that seriously inhibit companionship between husband and wife. A wife's employment does not normally diminish shared companionship. In fact, the higher socio-economic status engendered by an extra wage in the family leads to a better adjustment to marriage.[27]

Some occupational roles are more compatible with family life and others are not. Traveling salesmen and musicians experience a low degree of marital happiness, whereas college professors and ministers experience a high degree.[28] Those persons involved in shift work also have more family problems than those with regular nine to five hours. Persons who are under strict supervision, such as factory workers, tend to bring home their aggravations and vent them on their families.[29]

Interviews with wives in major metropolitan areas of the United States disclosed that if a married woman is in the labor market only because of the economic needs of the family, there is a decrease in happiness of both husband and wife. The wife is unhappy because of decreased sociability with her husband—she doesn't get to see him as much. The husband is unhappy because he sees his role as provider threatened. This is true of husbands in occupations with lower socio-economic standing.[30]

If the wife is free to choose whether or not to work, there is no detectable strain in the husband-wife relationship. In fact, the relations tend to improve, with less tension for men and more sociability for women. The wife feels good about contributing to the family income in meaningful ways and by creating improved leisure time activity by using her income for it.[31]

Working Married Women

Over 23 million married women worked in 1972. This comprises more than one of every four persons in the work force and three of every five working women. Half of all married women worked at some time in 1972; nearly all of these (42.7 percent of all married women) worked year-round full-time. Twenty percent (4,600,000 women) had children under 3 years old and worked year-round full-time. This increases to 35 percent for those with children 3 to 5 years old.[32]

For nonwhite married women work force participation is higher for all categories. Fifty-one percent of all married nonwhite women worked full-time for the entire year, one of every three had children under 3 years of age, and one of every two had children 3 to 5 years old.[33] The greater participation of nonwhite women is larger in families where the husband is not present because lower average family incomes press the woman into obtaining work.

The married woman who works increases family income by about 25 percent, which achieves middle-class status for many lower middle-class families. In 1970, two-thirds of all working women had husbands who earned less than $7000 annually. Thus, two out of every three women worked to help support a family and were not working just for pin money.

Many of these jobs became available as the occupational structure grew in the number of simplified, unskilled, and semiskilled occupations. Women's occupations were developed both in manufacturing and service industries. Caplow's theory of aggregation, differentiation, and rationalization continues to explain the decline of the family as occupational status gains in significance.

The Life-Cycle Squeeze

There is a "life-cycle squeeze" for families when the breadwinner does not have enough earnings to supply the family adequately. This is the case for most blue-collar families and many middle-level and lower-level white-collar occupations. Maximum earnings are not reached at the same time maximum family needs are experienced. As a consequence, married women enter the labor market.[34]

There are two major time periods when a family's economic needs are greatest: early in marriage when a home is purchased, and when children reach adolescence. Taking the median earnings by age for each specific occupation, Oppenheimer uncovered distinctive patterns in which each occupation peaked regarding its median earnings. In higher-income occupations (professional and technical, and managers and administrators) earnings are low for the young, rise rapidly from age group to age group, peak later in one's career, and stay high. In lower-income groups (lower white-collar and working class) peak median earnings occur at a young age (at about 35 to 44) and do not come close to the increase in earnings of the upper-income occupations. Earnings then drop off during later work life.[35]

Since heavy child-care expenses occur for families when the male head is between the late thirties and the mid-fifties, the occupational life-cycle (in terms of earnings) overlaps with the family life-cycle (in terms of needs) only for upper-income occupations. On the other hand, for three out of the seven lower-income blue-collar occupations, the median earnings at age 45 to 55 were actually *less* than the median earnings at age 25 to 34. Also, now that the children of blue-collar workers are attending school for longer periods of time, they face a more serious life-cycle squeeze than white-collar workers. Strong pressures for an additional income are exerted and undoubtedly account for the high labor-force participation of married women in their forties and fifties.[36]

This life-cycle squeeze is important enough that one sociologist found it to be one of the three primary reasons for job alienation among a sample of over 1300 workers from various occupational groups.[37] The economist, Kenneth

Boulding, suggests that the ideal pattern for human life would be the late peak, that is, "a constantly rising level of status and income as long as bodily and mental vigor are maintained."[38]

CAREERS

There is a constant tension maintained between career and family roles. These tensions will vary in intensity, depending on both the husband's and wife's occupation.

The two most important factors determining a married woman's performance in her career role are her husband's attitude toward her employment and the amount of education and specialized training she receives before she marries.[39] If her husband does not pressure her to stay in her expressive role of homemaker and mother, she has more freedom to develop a career.

For single women, the situation is different. They do not "choose" a career. They wait for signals from approving others, especially eligible males. Athena Theodore concludes that a woman does not normally choose an organization for the career opportunities it affords (e.g., money, promotions, and research opportunities), but for the opportunity to find a mate. This attitude results in her not wanting to continue her education if it would jeopardize marriage, thus bringing another shift in career pattern.[40]

Women have a cultural mandate to give priority to their families, men to give priority to their occupations. For women, this means that they derive their social prestige from their husbands. A woman's occupation is secondary. Hence, most women's jobs are considered "fill-ins," work to be taken at times when the occupational system becomes overloaded. Acceptance of a career means a high probability of conflict of allegiance for the married woman. If she were highly committed to her work, then she would be giving less attention to her family and thus would not be fulfilling her mandate.[41]

Consequently, married women with or without children are more likely to be found in lower-ranking positions in occupations than men and unmarried women. They are discriminated against because of their family position. As discussed in Chapter 6, employers fear that the husband's job may require her to move or that children will require her to leave the firm permanently.

A major cultural value of Americans is that to be a good provider one must be a good husband and a good father. Men justify being away from the family for long periods of time because it is essential to their careers and, in the long run, is to the benefit of the family. Women, on the other hand, are considered to work at the expense of the family instead of for the sake of the family. "Frequently, the working mother is asked how she could *leave* her children to go to work, while no one ever considers raising the same issue to the working father."[42]

Having wives at home permits men to devote more time to their work.

Men do not feel obliged to share in the household work, cooking, and care of children. In addition, the employer is excused from any responsibility to provide day-care facilities, and employee time off for family emergencies is reduced because the housewife can handle them.[43] A nonworking wife even serves as a status symbol of the husband's success—she can afford to stay home. Only about 20 percent of the wives of the established professions are employed, which is less than half the national average.[44]

Thus, if women are married, with or without children, it is detrimental to their occupation. Yet, if they remain single, they are considered deviant because they are seen as unable to attract a husband. It is a "damned-if-you-do, damned-if-you-don't" situation.

Frequently, both the instrumental and expressive roles are assumed by a parent in his or her relationship to children. This becomes a dilemma, especially for parents in upper middle-class occupations, because work demands so much of their time. Whether to spend time with the children (expressive role) at the expense of one's career (instrumental role) is a continual problem. The emphasis on the expressive role may lead to the lowering of one's status because the expectation in U.S. society is to place one's job ahead of all else.[45]

This expectation is qualified for women, however. Women are not expected to be as competitive. Nor do work matters always take precedence over family matters. There is a presumption on the part of employers that married women will be absent more frequently than married men. Suggestions have been made to develop careers that are less success oriented, that is, "lateral careers," where persons do not aspire to the higher levels of the occupation. This makes it easier to interrupt one's career for family reasons. Another idea is to have two persons share one job, splitting a full-time job into two part-time jobs. This has already proven effective in education, social work, and library work.[46]

DEMOGRAPHIC
TRENDS

One of the major questions facing population forecasters is whether the World War II "baby-boom" women will increase the labor supply and put older women out of work from 1970 to 2000. Valerie Oppenheimer gives three reasons why this will not occur: (1) the need for women in tertiary-sector occupations (the personal service occupations); (2) increased schooling for women; and (3) fertility has leveled off and likely will remain fairly stationary.[47] These trends will lead to a "more extensive integration of women into the economy at all points in the family life cycle. [Thus] ... women's family status may be becoming less important as a determinant of their labor force status than other factors such as economic aspirations, marketable skills, occupational commitments, and the like.[48]

The U.S. Department of Labor notes that if the present popular two-child family continues, the total population under 5 years of age will not reach the 1960 level until 1980 and following that will remain fairly constant until the year 2000. Therefore, the need for medical and health-related personnel ministering to expectant mothers, infants, and the very young can be expected to level off. On the other hand, the proportion of people 65 years old and over is expected to increase by more than 40 percent between 1970 and 2000. Thus the demand for workers in the gerontological field (psychiatry, nursing home personnel) should rise dramatically.[49]

As the age of a woman at marriage and childbirth continues to decrease, she will now be in her forties by the time all her children are out of the house.[50] At this time she could begin a full-time career, as many women are beginning to do. This may have significant consequences for the occupational structure, placing a large supply of eager women in competition for lower-income office and clerical jobs, as well as several service occupations.

There are also those who feel that the family as a social institution will become very weak in the near future. The continued decline of male dominance and patriarchal authority will lessen the rewards men receive by marrying. The continuing women's movement toward equality will leave women dissatisfied with the minor achievements of housework and child-rearing beyond infancy.[51] Whole new structures will develop to take over many of these functions, and the family's role in influencing occupations will diminish.

BUREAUCRACY AND PERSON-ALITY

A popular view among many sociologists has been that bureaucracy has an adverse effect on personality. The classic statement was made by Robert Merton in 1940, in which he described the person's high degree of conformity to rules because of the high degree of reliability necessary to operate the bureaucracy. Strict adherence to these rules resulted in a displacement of goals—rules that were originally conceived as a means became transformed as ends-in-themselves. In order to have these rules followed, the bureaucrat operated under norms of impersonality. He became methodical, disciplined, and prudent.[52] In short, people become very dull, narrow-minded, impersonal, and ritualistic in their work and in their leisure.

William F. Whyte depicted those in large organizations as developing a new ethic, the Social Ethic. As compared to the Protestant Ethic of individualism, the Social Ethic stressed the need for persons to integrate themselves into the positions demanded by bureaucratic organizations.[53] David Riesman described "other-directed" persons, who no longer looked to their own capabilities for adapting to and changing their situation, but who looked to their peers and to the mass media for guidance, where the emphasis is not on personal innovation but on adjustment to the social system.[54]

However, the notion that bureaucrats tend to perpetuate the highly bureaucratic system by displacing goals and sticking to the rules because their personalities have been profoundly affected by it is not shared by the newer interpretation, which is discussed in Chapter 8. If areas of uncertainty always exist in the bureaucratic structure, "the group which, by its position in the occupational structure can control the unregulated area, has a great strategic advantage which is naturally used in order to improve its power position and ensure a greater share of organizational rewards."[55] This is a *rational* strategy by which bureaucrats attempt to affirm and maintain their autonomy and power.[56]

Looked at from this point of view, is the nature of what is considered to be bureaucratic now changing? Is the increased rationality caused by centralization of the organization and increased specialization of technique a phenomenon of bureaucracy or merely "rational formal organization," common to both bureaucratization and professionalization? This question has been examined in various types of work organizations and occupations, and the results seem to support the latter contention. A summary of research on production organizations in both industrialized and nonindustrialized societies indicates that rational formal organization, as measured by specialization, rewards for performance, and contractual agreements, is not necessarily bureaucratic.[57] In a national sample of over 3000 men in U.S. civilian occupations, in which bureaucracy was measured by degree of hierarchy of authority, it was found that men who work in bureaucracies "tend to value, not conformity, but self-direction. They are more open-minded, have more personally responsible standards of morality, and are more receptive to change than are men who work in nonbureaucratic organizations.... They spend their leisure time in more intellectually demanding activities."[58] This finding does not vary with occupational position (white-collar versus blue-collar), sector of the economy (government versus private industry), or type of work position (entrepreneur versus bureaucrat).

What is there, then, asks Kohn, about working in a bureaucratic organization that causes this finding? Certain occupational conditions necessary for bureaucracy cause bureaucratic persons to be more self-directed, open to change, and intellectually flexible. These conditions are: first, job protections—tenure, contract agreements, retirement security, and the like, which have most benefit for blue-collar workers; second, higher income, which tends to give employees the feeling that they are sufficiently in control of their lives to give them a sense of self-direction; and third, substantively more complex work than that found among persons in nonbureaucratic organizations with a comparable educational level (this has most impact with white-collar workers).[59]

Arthur Stinchcombe examined steel plant administrations in Chile, Argentina, and Venezuela, following the Weberian notion that rationality is a variable, a property of a system instead of a property of an individual's psyche. Stinchcombe holds that rationality in a system cannot be achieved without constant and substantial innovation. "The fundamental characteristic of a rational industrial administration is that it innovates constantly...."[60] What, then, is the set of processes that determines the rate of innovation? Stinchcombe says it is *bureaucracy*, specifically the system of abstract rules, and not so much the hierarchy of authority. The process is more intellectual ("adequacy of cognition") than it is motivational ("adequacy of motivation"). For example, staff persons spend much more time working on innovations than either entrepreneurs or executives.[61] These innovations attempt to reduce uncertainty rather than extend it (see Chart 8.1).

The superior innovativeness of bureaucracy arises from its *structural* arrangements for thinking and planning and not because some people are more strongly motivated to do well in occupational roles. Bureaucrats are recruited, step by step, into their positions through a series of promotions in a hierarchy of authority. These job ladders place only the more experienced persons into positions of authority. Upward job mobility depends on the ability of individuals to increase productivity through innovation. The basis for movement on the occupational ladder is performance, and not kinship or morality. Individuals see their jobs as careers to the extent that they see their present position as the result of past occupational performance.[62]

In a study of corporate counsel lawyers it has been found that technical competence is not seen by these lawyers to be bureaucratic. What this seems to signify is that professionals, at least some professionals, perceive their technical expertise as rational knowledge but not of a bureaucratic nature.[63] In some cases the work may be taken out of the hands of the bureaucrat and given to the professional person, and that professional will call the work professional. But it is still bureaucratic by definition. This is true of many professionalizing occupations, especially in the middle-level white-collar occupations of management, engineering, and the like. As pointed out in Chapter 8, the bureaucratic authority of administrative office has many factors in common with professional authority.

OCCUPATION AND PERSON- ALITY

Does a person's occupation affect his personality; that is, does it play an important role in shaping and reshaping personal characteristics? Or does personality largely determine the ultimate occupational position a person will occupy? Most theories see the relation operating in one direction—personality affects occupation. However, recent evidence from a national sample of over 3000 men representative of all men employed in civilian occupations in the United States in 1964 shows that the reverse is true: the job affects the man considerably more than the man affects the job.[64] The job is measured in terms of its structural imperatives, most important, the substantive complexity of the work, including closeness of supervision and routinization of the work. Personality is measured in terms of psychological functioning (e.g., occupational commitment, job satisfaction, self-esteem, and intellectual flexibility). When factors such as age, race, urbanicity, religious background, and national background are statistically controlled, the relation is not appreciably reduced.

Not only does occupation affect personality, but it significantly affects social structure. In a person's work "the central fact of occupational life today is not ownership of the means of production; nor is it status, income, or interpersonal relationships. Instead, it is the opportunity to use initiative, thought, and independent judgment in one's work—to direct one's own occupational activities."[65] This opportunity tends to be found in bureaucratic structures, Kohn notes elsewhere.[66] It is therefore the ability to influence the means of production through one's occupation that is important to the worker. And it is the occupation in which workers experience similar conditions of life. As social structure, it shapes the everyday realities of the individual and thus exerts psychological impact.[67]

WORK
ALIENATION

Closely tied to the discussion of the relation of personality to organization and occupation is the concept of worker alienation. Those who lean toward the negative view of the effects of bureaucracy on personality readily interpret persons in all types of occupations as highly alienated in their work or leisure (see Chapter 10). Critical theorists generally support this view. One of its major spokesmen, Herbert Marcuse, states that capitalist society has made humanity one-dimensional.[68] People are unable to see beyond the technical rationality built up by the systems analysts. Our high degree of material consumption is bred and fed by constant technological improvements and changes. The material comforts of this society blind us to the new type of "unacknowledged domination"[69] by a small elite and its technical experts, who repress the second dimension, the dimension of the opposite, the antithesis, which produces conflict and change.

Others have seen the degree of a person's work commitment as a measure of the degree of alienation in modern occupations. A commitment to a career is, with the exception of those occupations with a "mission" or a "calling," a passive experience in which the person looks for the security of stages of a career. Thus, persons who are socialized to escape freedom, to reject free choice, are unwilling to take risks.[70]   If an occupation has within it enough individuals of this type, then it will face almost certain atrophy, especially if it will not innovate but wishes only to keep its knowledge "mysterious" and indeterminate.

The more optimistic writers see the new forms of organization and occupational specialization as the panaceas of modern life, eliminating much of the alienation experienced by people in their work. One recent book[71] suggests that bigness produces decentralization of decision making because the number of decisions being made is far greater as a result of that bigness. Some of these decisions are passed down to middle management. Furthermore, centralized data now allow the small unit to have access to information on its own in order to make organization-wide decisions. There is a centralizing of objectives in order to decentralize decision making. This, plus increased specialization, has led to the development of temporary work teams and the need for bringing in outside expert consultants. This kind of temporizing leads Berkley to the conclusion that "What is good for the nation increasingly tends to be good for business and vice-versa."[72] This almost exactly parallels the famous comment of Charles E. Wilson, President Eisenhower's Secretary of Labor, that whatever was good for business was good for the country—including ecological destruction and discriminatory practices, although these were not mentioned. Neither does Berkley mention them in his organizational analysis. He also failed to mention that the creation of centralized information allows for control over the construction and dissemination of knowledge derived from that information. Automation serves as the mechanism for control here because the performance of all persons must fit into the EDP program. "The risks of delegation and decentralization are thus further minimized with these procedures."[73]

SUMMARY AND
CONCLUSIONS

Family values are a significant factor affecting a person's occupational choice. The family also serves as the most important economic source for preparing for the job market. Working mothers have been found to have a positive effect on their children, and broken families have a negative effect.

Occupational values have greatly changed the structure and role of the family in modern industrial society. The rationalization of the work process in large-scale organizations has reshaped people's values and goals to fit the occupation and not the family. One interpretation is that half of an individual's waking hours is spent at a job that is boring, monotonous, and lacks autonomy. The results are brought home in the form of low pay (one out of every five families is working poor), physical and mental illness, tiredness, anger, and self-estrangement. The effect on family life can be devastating. Various degrees of marital discord and divorce are the outcome.

However, the majority of families do manage to make some arrangement in the conflict of values between occupation and family. Men are becoming more willing to share in housework and child-rearing, helping their mates to find occupational fulfillment. For working-class wives the situation is different. They *have* to go to work to help support the family, and the jobs they obtain are mostly low-wage women's occupations: secretarial and other clerical jobs or service jobs.

In addition, women are expected to give first priority to their families. The job comes second, and women are not expected to be competitive in pursuing their careers. This puts them at a distinct disadvantage with respect to men. With rare exceptions, men are expected to pursue their work to the exclusion of all family matters.

It is in the study of the relationship between occupations, the family, and the individual that one finds that a more complex connection than previously depicted exists between the bureaucratic organization and innovating people. Examination of the effect of the family on its children shows that working-class parents tend to stress conformity. Therefore one could surmise that the children will be more tolerant of administrative authority, will more easily adapt to highly bureaucratized structures, and consequently will be well prepared for their positions in the secondary labor market. On the other hand, middle-class children, being more self-directed, will demand the professional authority of less bureaucratized organizations and thus would better fit into primary labor market occupations.

However, Kohn found evidence that those persons who work in bureaucratic organizations are highly self-directed, regardless of occupational category. Furthermore, Stinchcombe concludes that *rationality* in bureaucratic systems is tied to *innovation*. Job mobility that is produced in a carefully calibrated hierarchy of authority stimulates productivity. Innovation is characterized by discipline and a technical orientation to work—innovation by rationalization rather than innovation by extension, as depicted in Chapter 8. These findings indicate that there are areas of uncertainty extensive enough to permit the exercise of considerable worker autonomy, again showing that rationalization is not a simple, one-way process.

FOOTNOTES FOR CHAPTER 16
OCCUPATIONS, THE FAMILY, AND THE INDIVIDUAL

[1] Christopher Jencks et al., *Inequality: A Reassessment of The Effect of Family and Schooling in America* (New York: Harper Colophon, 1972),

p. 179. This conclusion is reached by assuming that intergenerational mobility over three or four generations is minimal. Assuming a father passes on half of his occupational advantage or disadvantage to his son, his effect on his grandson will be only 25 percent, his great grandson 12½ percent, and so forth. This linear interpretation plus the differences in brothers' statuses are evidence given for their conclusion.

2 Donald J. Treiman and Kermit Terrell, "Sex and the Process of Status Attainment: A Comparison of Working Women and Men," *American Sociological Review, 40* (April 1975), 190.

3 Theodore Caplow, *The Sociology of Work* (Minneapolis: University of Minnesota Press, 1954), p. 273.

4 Dennison J. Nash, "The Socialization of an Artist: The American Composer," *Social Forces, 35* (May 1957), 307-313.

5 Alvin W. Gouldner, "Attitudes of 'Progressive' Trade Union Leaders," *American Journal of Sociology, 52* (March 1947), 389-392.

6 Angela Lane, "The Effect of Family of Origin on Female College Graduates' Career Commitment and Full-Time Employment," paper presented at the Seminar on Theoretical and Methodological Issues in Sex Stratification, Social Science Research Council, New York, November 16, 1974.

7 Lane, "The Effect of Family of Origin."

8 Evelyne Sullerot, *Woman, Society and Change* (New York: McGraw-Hill Book Co., 1971), pp. 89, 106. Also, Alice Rossi, "Equality Between the Sexes: An Immodest Proposal," *Daedalus, 93* (Spring 1964), 273.

9 *Work in America* (Cambridge, Mass.: The MIT Press, 1973), p. 59.

10 David A. Levy, "State Labor Legislation Enacted in 1973," *Monthly Labor Review, 97* (January 1974), 26.

11 Sullerot, *Woman, Society and Change*, pp. 96-97.

12 Elizabeth Waldman and Robert Whitmore, "Children of Working Mothers, March 1973," *Monthly Labor Review, 97* (May 1974), 50.

13 Waldman and Whitmore, "Children of Working Mothers," p. 51.

14 Otis Dudley Duncan, David L. Featherman, and Beverly Duncan, *Socioeconomic Background and Achievement* (New York: Seminar Press, 1972), pp. 235-236.

15 Beverly Duncan, *Family Factors and School Dropout, 1920-1960* (Ann Arbor, Mich.: University of Michigan Press, 1965).

[16] Duncan, *Family Factors and School Dropout.*

[17] Melvin L. Kohn, *Class and Conformity: A Study in Values* (Homewood, Ill.: Dorsey Press, 1969).

[18] Kohn, *Class and Conformity*, pp. 34-36, 72.

[19] Kohn, *Class and Conformity*, pp. 104-105.

[20] Jeylan T. Mortimer, "Occupational Value Socialization in Business and Professional Families," *Sociology of Work and Occupations*, 2 (February 1975), 29-54.

[21] Caplow, *The Sociology of Work*, pp. 255-259.

[22] Caplow, *The Sociology of Work*, pp. 19, 31.

[23] Caplow, *The Sociology of Work*, p. 25.

[24] Caplow, *The Sociology of Work*, pp. 258-259.

[25] J. Richard Udry, *The Social Context of Marriage*, 2nd Ed. (Philadelphia: Lippincott, 1971), p. 343.

[26] Lee Rainwater and Gerald Handel, "Changing Family Roles in the Working Class," in Arthur Shostak and William Gomberg (eds.), *Blue-Collar World* (Englewood Cliffs, N.J.: Prentice-Hall, 1964), pp. 70-76. For a different view, see Mirra Komorovsky, *Blue-Collar Marriage* (New York: Vintage Books, 1967).

[27] Marc Fried, *The World of the Urban Working Class* (Cambridge, Mass.: Harvard University Press, 1973), pp. 139-143.

[28] Udry, *The Social Context of Marriage*, p. 344.

[29] Ferdynand Zweig, *The Worker in an Affluent Society* (New York: The Free Press, 1961), pp. 56-58, 85.

[30] Susan R. Orden and Norman M. Bradburn, "Working Wives and Marriage Happiness," *American Journal of Sociology*, 74 (January 1969), 392-407.

[31] Orden and Bradburn, "Working Wives and Marriage Happiness."

[32] U.S. Department of Labor, Bureau of Labor Statistics, *Work Experience of the Population in March, 1972*, Special Labor Force Report No. 162, (Washington, D.C.: U.S. Government Printing Office, 1974), Table 4, p. 54.

[33] *Work Experience of the Population in March, 1972*, p. 54. See also, U.S. Department of Labor, Bureau of Labor Statistics, *Children of*

Working Mothers, March 1974, Special Labor Force Report, September 1974.

[34] Valerie Kincade Oppenheimer, "The Life-Cycle Squeeze: The Interaction of Men's Occupational and Family Life Cycles," *Demography, 11* (May 1974), 227-246.

[35] Oppenheimer, "The Life-Cycle Squeeze."

[36] Oppenheimer, "The Life-Cycle Squeeze."

[37] Harold L. Wilensky, "Work as a Social Problem," in Howard S. Becker (ed.), *Social Problems: A Modern Approach* (New York: John Wiley and Sons, 1966), p. 143.

[38] Kenneth Boulding, "The Shadow of the Stationary State," *Daedalus, 102* (Fall 1973), 94.

[39] Mildred W. Weil, "An Analysis of the Factors Influencing Married Women's Actual or Planned Work Participation," *American Sociological Review, 26* (February 1961), 91-96.

[40] Athena Theodore, "The Professional Woman: Trends and Prospects," in Athena Theodore (ed.), *The Professional Woman* (Cambridge, Mass.: Schenkman Publishing Co., 1971), pp. 14-17. Thus, for many women it may not in fact be a career as defined in this book, lacking a graduated sequence of ever-increasing responsibilities and recognition.

[41] Rose Laub Coser and Gerald Rokoff, "Women in the Occupational World: Social Disruption and Conflict," *Social Problems, 18* (Spring 1971), 535-553.

[42] Jane Prather, "Why Can't Women Be More Like Men?" *American Behavioral Scientist, 15* (November-December 1971), 180-181.

[43] Mary Huff Stevenson, "Determinants of Low Wages for Women Workers," unpublished Ph.D. dissertation, University of Michigan, 1974, p. 71.

[44] Alice S. Rossi, "Women in Science: Why So Few?" *Science,* Vol. 148, No. 3674 (1965), p. 1198.

[45] David A. Schulz, *The Changing Family* (Englewood Cliffs, N.J.: Prentice-Hall, 1972), p. 339.

[46] Martha S. White, "Psychological and Social Barriers to Women in Science," *Science, 170* (October 23, 1970), 413-416.

[47] Valerie Kincade Oppenheimer, "Demographic Influence on Female Employment and the Status of Women," *American Journal of Sociology, 78* (January 1973), 951-952.

[48] Oppenheimer, "Demographic Influence on Female Employment," p. 960.

[49] U.S. Department of Labor, Bureau of Manpower Administration, *Manpower Report of the President, 1973* (Washington, D.C.: U.S. Government Printing Office, 1974), p. 78.

[50] Suzanne Keller, "Does the Family Have a Future," *Journal of Comparative Family Studies* (Spring 1971), 6.

[51] Keller, "Does the Family Have a Future?" p. 8.

[52] Robert K. Merton, "Bureaucratic Structure and Personality," *Social Forces, 18* (May 1940), 560-568.

[53] William F. Whyte, *The Organization Man* (New York: Simon and Schuster, 1956).

[54] David Riesman, Nathan Glazer, and Reuel Denney, *The Lonely Crowd* (New Haven: Yale University Press, 1950).

[55] Nicos P. Mouzelis, *Organisation and Bureaucracy* (Chicago: Aldine Publishing Co., 1968), p. 161.

[56] Mouzelis, *Organisation and Bureaucracy*, p. 162.

[57] Peter M. Blau and W. Richard Scott, *Formal Organizations* (San Francisco: Chandler Publishing Co., 1962), pp. 246-247.

[58] Melvin L. Kohn, "Bureaucratic Man: A Portrait and an Interpretation," *American Sociological Review, 36* (June 1971), 465.

[59] Kohn, "Bureaucratic Man: A Portrait and an Interpretation."

[60] Arthur L. Stinchcombe, *Creating Efficient Industrial Administrations* (New York: Academic Press, 1974), pp. 34-35.

[61] Stinchcombe, *Creating Efficient Industrial Administrations*, Chapter 2.

[62] Stinchcombe, *Creating Efficient Industrial Administrations*, pp. 36, 116-118, 129.

[63] Erwin O. Smigel, unpublished manuscript, 1972.

[64] Melvin L. Kohn and Carmi Schooler, "Occupational Experience and Psychological Functioning: An Assessment of Reciprocal Effects," *American Sociological Review, 38* (February 1973), 97-118. Also, Joseph Bensman and Robert Lilienfeld, *Craft and Consciousness: Occupational Technique and the Development of World Images* (New York: John Wiley & Sons, 1973).

[65] Kohn and Schooler, "Occupational Experience and Psychological Functioning...," p. 117.

[66] Kohn, "Bureaucratic Man: A Portrait and an Interpretation."

[67] Kohn and Schooler, "Occupational Experience and Psychological Functioning," p. 117.

[68] Herbert Marcuse, *One-Dimensional Man* (Boston: Beacon Press, 1964).

[69] Jürgen Habermas, *Toward A Rational Society* (Boston: Beacon Press, 1970), p. 82.

[70] Elliott A. Krause, *The Sociology of Occupations* (Boston: Little, Brown & Co., 1971), p. 56.

[71] George E. Berkley, *The Administrative Revolution* (Englewood Cliffs, N.J.: Prentice-Hall, 1971).

[72] Berkley, *The Administrative Revolution*, p. 163.

[73] Richard H. Hall, *Organizations: Structure and Process* (Englewood Cliffs, N.J.: Prentice-Hall, 1972), p. 228.

17 OCCUPATIONS AND EDUCATION

We know that men can be turned by coercion into robots. We did not know before our own time they could cheerfully and willingly turn themselves into robots.

C. Wright Mills, Power, Politics, and People, p. 185.

Examination of the relationship between occupations and education uncovers many serious problems facing the American labor force. These problems exist at many levels: educational discrimination against minority groups, the proper utilization of manpower, planning for social mobility, and the development of a more equalitarian society. Each is analyzed in this chapter in order to focus on the complexity of the relationship between occupations and education, with its many intervening factors.

THE IMPORTANCE OF EDUCATION

Educational requirements for employment have increased at all occupational levels. From 1937 to 1967 the percent of employers requiring a high school diploma for unskilled workers rose from 1 percent to 16 percent; for semiskilled workers, from 3 percent to 24 percent; and for skilled workers, from 11 percent to 28 percent. Education increasingly tends to shape careers.[1]

In March 1974 7 out of every 10 workers in the labor force (62 million persons) had completed 4 years of high school, and 15 percent had completed at least 4 years of college (13.5 million—see Table 17.2).[2] Younger workers have more education than older workers. In 1973, in the 20 to 34 year age group, 82 percent had 4 years of high school. Of those over 34, only 63 percent had 4 years of high school.[3]

The more the education, the greater the probability that a person will be in a high-wage white-collar occupation, that is, in the professional or managerial groups (see Tables 17.1 and 17.2). Table 17.1 also indicates that the rising educational attainment of workers during the decade of the 1960s has occured in all occupational groups. Increases in high school diplomas occurred in the blue-collar, service, and farm occupations, and college increases were largest in managerial and sales groups.[4]

TABLE 17.1 PERCENT OF WORKERS 25 AND OLDER WITH 12 YEARS OF EDUCATION OR MORE, BY OCCUPATION, 1960 AND 1970

OCCUPATIONAL GROUP	PERCENT WITH 4 YEARS OF HIGH SCHOOL		PERCENT WITH 1 TO 3 YEARS OF COLLEGE		PERCENT WITH 4 YEARS OF COLLEGE OR MORE	
	1960	1970	1960	1970	1960	1970
Professional and technical	16.0	17.5	19.7	17.8	55.4	58.4
Managers and proprietors	30.4	33.8	17.2	19.2	15.7	23.8
Sales workers	33.3	39.4	15.2	17.9	9.9	13.5
Clerical workers	47.6	54.6	15.9	16.9	5.7	5.9
Craft workers	27.2	38.0	6.2	8.0	2.1	2.2
Operatives	20.3	30.4	3.2	4.1	.6	.8
Service	20.2	30.5	4.6	6.4	1.2	1.7
Laborers, except farm and mine	13.2	23.7	2.4	4.0	.6	1.2
Farmers and farm managers	20.1	31.4	5.0	6.9	2.2	3.9
Farm laborers and foremen	10.3	18.6	2.3	3.4	.8	1.8

Source. Department of Labor, Bureau of Labor Statistics, *Educational Attainment of Workers, March 1973*, Special Labor Force Report No. 161, p. 60.

TABLE 17.2 OCCUPATION OF EMPLOYED PERSONS, BY YEARS OF SCHOOL COMPLETED, MARCH 1974 (IN PERCENT)

| | | | Percent distribution by years of school completed | | | | | | | | | |
| | | | Elementary | | | | High school | | College | | | Median school years completed |
OCCUPATION	Total employed (thousands)	Total	No school years completed	1 to 4 years	5 to 7 years	8 years	1 to 3 years	4 years	1 to 3 years	4 years	5 years or more	
All occupational groups	84,878	100.0	0.3	1.5	4.3	6.5	17.2	39.4	15.2	9.2	6.3	12.5
Professional, technical, and kindred workers	12,342	100.0	—	0.1	0.2	0.6	2.2	16.1	17.9	31.5	31.4	16.4
Managers and administrators, except farm	8,862	100.0	.1	.5	1.9	3.5	9.0	36.2	20.9	17.6	10.4	13.0
Sales workers	5,399	100.0	.1	.3	1.1	3.3	16.9	41.0	20.8	13.1	3.4	12.7
Clerical and kindred workers	14,940	100.0	—	.2	.7	2.0	11.3	56.8	22.5	5.1	1.4	12.6
Craft and kindred workers	11,436	100.0	.2	1.2	5.3	9.5	20.8	47.9	12.2	2.5	.6	12.3
Operatives, except transport	10,398	100.0	.7	2.9	8.5	11.4	27.0	41.0	7.0	1.2	.3	11.9
Transport equipment operatives	3,191	100.0	.2	1.7	8.3	10.9	24.9	42.8	9.9	1.1	.2	12.1
Laborers, except farm	4,114	100.0	1.2	4.9	9.5	9.9	30.3	32.8	10.0	1.1	.3	11.4
Private household workers	1,269	100.0	.6	5.8	13.1	12.8	38.8	21.6	5.2	1.4	.6	10.4
Service workers, except private household	10,035	100.0	.4	2.1	6.8	9.3	26.9	39.0	12.5	2.5	.5	12.1
Farm workers	2,892	100.0	2.0	6.7	11.5	17.3	18.9	31.5	7.3	4.0	.8	11.0

Source. U.S. Department of Labor, Bureau of Labor Statistics, *Educational Attainment of Workers, March 1974*, Special Labor Force Report No. 175, p. 64.

411

By 1990, it is expected that four out of five workers will have completed 4 years of high school (see Chart 17.1). In the 24 to 34 year age group almost 90 percent will have completed 4 years of high school. One out of five workers will have attained 4 years of college. It is expected that the number of less educated workers will continue to decline during the 1980s.[5]

CHART 17.1 EDUCATIONAL ATTAINMENT OF THE CIVILIAN LABOR FORCE 25 YEARS OLD AND OVER, 1957–1959 AVERAGE, 1970–1972 AVERAGE, AND PROJECTED 1980 AND 1990

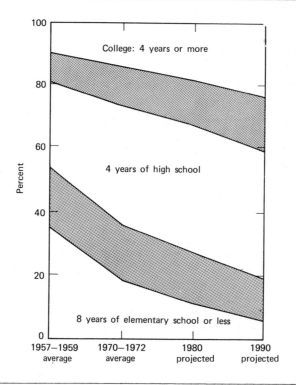

Source. U.S. Department of Labor, Bureau of Labor Statistics, *Education of Workers: Projections to 1990,* Special Labor Force Report No. 160, p. 24.

EDUCATIONAL AND OCCUPATIONAL ATTAINMENT OF NONWHITES

Comparison of the *expected* rate of educational attainment of nonwhites at each occupational level to *actual* nonwhite rates in 1960 and 1970 shows only a very slight improvement in occupational attainment, even though there is a considerable improvement in educational attainment.[6]

At *equal* levels of education, blacks earn less than whites, not so much because of wage discrimination as occupational discrimination. Blacks with the same education cannot attain the same jobs, although now young blacks in the labor force have nearly the same median education (12 years versus 12.5 years for whites in 1972).[7]

> *Blacks with professional degrees are less likely to be managers than whites with only a high school diploma; blacks with college degrees are less likely to be sales workers than whites who have not completed high school. And black males with high school diplomas are less likely to be in skilled crafts occupations than whites who have an eighth grade education or less.*[8]

In addition, blacks working in the *same* occupations as whites experience income discrimination, but education does not significantly help to modify this imbalance.[9] Despite the evidence that increased schooling has only marginal payoffs for minorities relative to whites, educational opportunity has been the government's main weapon in its fight against inequality (e.g., the War on Poverty). The effects of affirmative action have been negligible. It is estimated that without aggressive affirmative action programs, it will take blacks 60 years or more to attain equal employment rates.[10]

EDUCATIONAL AND OCCUPATIONAL ATTAINMENT OF WOMEN

Comparing occupation to level of education, a predictable pattern exists for women: the higher the educational attainment, the higher the occupational attainment (see Table 17.3). Chances are very slim (only 1 in 20) for a wo-

TABLE 17.3 OCCUPATIONAL DISTRIBUTION OF EMPLOYED FEMALES BY EDUCATIONAL ATTAINMENT, 1970 (IN PERCENT)

OCCUPATIONAL GROUP	HIGH SCHOOL LESS THAN 4 YEARS	HIGH SCHOOL, 4 YEARS	COLLEGE 1-3 YEARS	COLLEGE, 4 YEARS	COLLEGE 5 YEARS AND OVER
Total	100.0	100.0	100.0	100.0	100.0
White-Collar	26.4	68.7	82.6	94.4	98.1
Professional and technical	1.8	6.7	22.1	74.8	89.0
Managers, Officials, and Proprietors	3.4	4.7	6.7	4.4	3.0
Clerical workers	14.6	50.0	46.6	13.0	4.8
Sales workers	6.6	7.3	7.2	2.2	1.3
Blue-Collar, service, and farm workers	73.6	31.3	17.4	5.6	1.9

Source. Valerie Kincade Oppenheimer, "Rising Educational Attainment, Declining Fertility and the Inadequacies of the Female Labor Market," in Charles F. Westoff and Robert Parke, Jr. (eds.), *Demographic and Social Aspects of Population Growth,* Vol. I (Washington, D.C.: U.S. Government Printing Office, 1972), p. 314. Based on the Bureau of Labor Statistics Special Labor Force Report No. 125, *Educational Attainment of Workers, March 1969,* Table 1.

man to attain a managerial or professional position without at least a high school diploma. They do not increase much with the diploma. The college degree is necessary to increase a woman's chances to obtain one of these higher-level positions.

Women have traditionally accepted interim jobs in the labor force, filling part-time or full-time clerical and service jobs until they got married or raised children. However, women increasingly are not satisfied with these kinds of jobs because work is no longer of secondary importance. More women are now divorced and separated than ever before, and they depend entirely on their own earning capacities. Poorly paying jobs with poor advancement opportunities are no longer acceptable.[11]

Second, the rising educational attainment of women will generate a rising demand for high-level jobs. But the traditional female occupations cannot continue to supply jobs for the increasing number of graduates. Already in 1970, 80 percent of women with 4 or more years of college were in the pro-

TABLE 17.4 EDUCATIONAL ATTAINMENT OF WOMEN 25 YEARS OR OLDER: 1957–1959 AND 1970 WITH PROJECTIONS FOR 1980 AND 1985 (IN PERCENT)

EDUCATIONAL ATTAINMENT	1957-1959[a]	1970	1980	1985
Number (000 omitted)	(50,141)	(57,527)	(67,123)	(73.004)
Total	100.0	100.0	100.0	100.0
High school, less than 4 years	56.1	44.6	36.1	31.6
High school, 4 years	30.2	37.5	42.1	44.0
College, 1-3 years	7.8	9.7	11.2	12.0
College, 4 years	——	5.8	7.9	9.1
College, 5 years or more	5.9	2.4	2.9	3.4

[a] 1957 and 1959 data were averaged.

Source. Valerie Kincade Oppenheimer, "Rising Educational Attainment, Declining Fertility, and the Inadquacies of the Female Labor Market," in Charles F. Westoff and Robert Parke, Jr. (eds.), Demographic and Social Aspects of Population Growth, Vol. I (Washington, D.C.: U.S. Government Printing Office, 1972), p. 315. Based on U.S. Bureau of the Census, Current Population Reports, Series P-25, No. 390, Projections of Educational Attainment 1970-1985, March 29, 1968, Tables 1 and 2; Series P-20, No. 207, Educational Attainment, March 1970, Nov. 30, 1970, Table 2.

fessions, mostly in public school teaching. The market will not expand as fast as the supply, so there will be pressure for jobs traditionally held by men.[12]

Third, decreasing fertility rates allow more women to work. Families with fewer children mean more young married women in the labor force. There will be an immediate increase, and it will continue until the end of the century. (See Table 17.4 for projections to 1980). If rising educational attainment is added to this (see Table 17.5), the impact is very great.[13]

Assuming that the same rate of occupational growth continues through 1980, there will be an increase in the supply of women in the white-collar occupations, especially in clerical and professional areas. This will create an excess of supply over demand and will result in fewer job opportunities for women—to the tune of 2.5 million fewer in white-collar occupations alone. The alternatives are: (1) break out of traditional female jobs and increase their total share of upper-level white-collar and blue-collar occupations; (2) accept jobs at lower levels than one's education has trained one for; and (3) withdraw from the labor force early in marriage. Home and family can provide women with central life interests, whereas the jobs then available will be unrewarding and nonmeaningful.[14]

TABLE 17.5 FEMALE LABOR FORCE PARTICIPATION RATES, 1959 AND 1970, with PROJECTIONS TO 1980 (IN PERCENT)

AGE	1959	1970	1980
Total	37.4	43.8	43.8
18-64 years	41.8	50.1	50.4
18–19 years	46.4	48.4	48.4
20–24 years	45.0	57.1	57.2
25–34 years	35.4	45.6	46.6
35–44 years	43.3	51.3	51.6
45–54 years	48.5	54.4	54.8
55–64 years	36.7	43.7	45.1
65 years and over	10.4	10.3	10.9

Source. Valerie Kincade Oppenheimer, "Rising Educational Attainment, Declining Fertility and the Inadequacies of the Female Labor Market," in Charles F. Westoff and Robert Parke, Jr. (eds.), *Demographic and Social Aspects of Population Growth*, Vol. 1 (Washington, D.C.: U.S. Government Printing Office, 1972), p. 315. Based on Department of Labor, Bureau of Labor Statistics, *Educational Attainment of Workers, 1959*, Special Labor Force Report No. 1, Tables D and E; and *Educational Attainment of Workers, March 1969, 1970*, Special Labor Force Report No. 125, Tables D and E.

Oppenheimer predicts that a major problem will be in teaching, which will suffer a double blow. Declining fertility will result in more married women available for work and thus increase the supply of teachers. At the same time, it will reduce the number of children in the population and thus attending school. Demand (students) will be reduced and supply (teachers) increased simultaneously. Projections also show that if the 10 professions that account for three-quarters of all female professional workers with college education do not increase their already heavily female proportions, there will be an over-supply of 1.2 million women in the labor force by 1980.[15]

UTILIZATION
OF COLLEGE
GRADUATES

In the 1974 to 1975 recession years many college graduates experienced dif-ficulty obtaining jobs. Many complained that the jobs that were available had little or nothing to do with their fields of concentration. Although there are no figures available for 1974 or 1975, statistics from 1972 give an idea of the size of the problem. Education majors were able to find work related to their fields in 82 percent of all cases. Business majors had a rate of 61 percent. The rates for humanities majors was 50 percent and for social science majors only 30 percent.[16]

The proportion of persons receiving college degrees increased by 300 per-cent per year (271,000 to 755,000) from 1948 to 1969, whereas the popula-tion increased by 33 percent. Most evidence supports the hypothesis that job requirements of the labor market have not increased at the rate that education-al attainment has. Thus the human capital theory that educational oversupply would correct itself when wages of the more highly educated were reduced as the rates of return (i.e., profit received from employer investment in more highly educated personnel) were reduced was proved false.[17]

An examination of 450 occupations from the professional and technical group by Lane Rawlins and Lloyd Ullman indicated that the increase in educa-tional requirements made by employers for these occupations is partly a result of the increased supply of highly educated persons.[18] As Ivar Berg estimated, there were 4 million college graduates in 1950, but only 1 million were required. In 1960 there were 6 million graduates for 1.4 million jobs.[19]

Furthermore, changes in earnings in the 450 occupations were not related to changes in educational requirements of employees or of educational attain-ment of employees. Whereas professional and technical occupations experi-enced a large increase in earnings, educational requirements were not raised significantly. Craft occupations, on the other hand, experienced higher educa-tional requirements and higher incomes. Employment grew rapidly in professional occupations but remained stable in the crafts. This indicates that formal education serves U.S. employers as an inexpensive screening device.[20]

The size of today's firms is also a contributing factor toward increasing the level of education. Decentralization at the departmental level requires managers who can make decisions on important production and personnel matters. Also, the pyramidal structure permits executive training and screening at lower levels, even though in some of these jobs the educational requirements specified are not needed.[21]

Meanwhile, regardless of the increasing demand for the highly educated, there are still not enough jobs to go around. There is now a large oversupply of graduates on a shrinking market. It is estimated that the total oversupply may hit 140,000 college graduates per year in the 1980s.[22]

SOCIAL
MOBILITY

Many studies have been conducted over the past three decades to determine which variables affect occupational attainment. In their landmark study, Blau and Duncan conclude that certain ascriptive and achievement factors in combination determine the occupational attainment of the individual:[23]

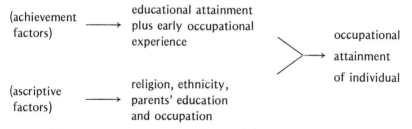

William Sewell and his associates conducted a series of studies that examined a sample of male high school graduates of Wisconsin high schools by following them over a 10-year period. The researchers lay more stress on the ascriptive factors of parents' socio-economic status and the influence of parents, teachers, and peers as being important factors in determining educational aspirations and attainment, early occupational status, and earnings.[24] This pattern negatively affects the goal of equal opportunity.[25]

Once an individual is in the labor force, once the important entry job is obtained, family background has only a marginal effect on the person's future occupational status. This happens because "family background operates through education and occupation, and these have strong effects only after a person's career is under way."[26] Chart 17.2 depicts the intricacies of these interrelationships, indicating the degree of association of variables.

CHART 17.2 DUAL CAUSAL CHAIN MODEL FOR THE SOCIO-ECO-NOMIC CAREER

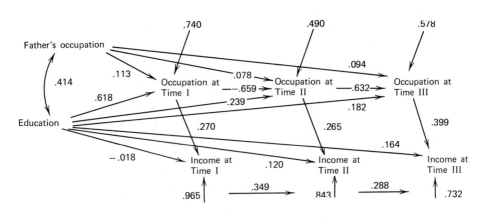

Source. Jonathan Kelley, "Causal Chain Models for the Socioeconomic Career," *American Sociological Review, 38* (August 1973), 491. Copyright © 1973 by the American Sociological Association. Reprinted by permission of the author and publisher.

Family Background and Education

Other findings indicate that family background affects career possibilities in later stages as well as earlier. The sons of professional and managerial fathers tend to follow in their fathers' footsteps more than the sons of fathers from any other occupational group. Likewise, those with higher family incomes (largely professionals and managers) can afford the cost of sending their children to college to prepare for the higher-level positions.[27]

Forty percent of poor students (family income of less than $12,000 per year) who rank between the fiftieth and seventy-fifth percentiles in aptitude tests attend college. Eighty percent of the nonpoor students with the same ranking do. The son of an elite occupation father (professional or managerial) has three times the chance as the son of a middle-class father to become elite himself and 16 times the chance as the son of a semiskilled father. The odds are amongst four out of five that you will end up in the same general type of work (either manual or nonmanual) as your father.[28]

VanZeyl disputes the argument that social mobility is strictly limited in the United States or that it is "sponsored," that is, controlled by an elite who select those who are to take their places.[29] Instead, the United States operates under "contest mobility," where candidates for occupations compete under certain basic rules. The rules of education are those of achievement, of a system open to all without any advantage given to birth. In this country, as compared to the Netherlands, for example, it is rare for families to share similar life chances over three generations, which is the time needed to build a true social class.[30] "The school is the primary formal agency of status allocation in our society" and thus is the cause of continued high social mobility in a classless society.[31]

There may be some contest mobility, but research indicates more and more that it is restricted ethnically, racially, and economically. The first section of this book addresses itself to this issue. More specifically, an analysis of patterns of educational mobility of American males over a 40-year period from 1927 to 1967 shows that sons of fathers from a lower socio-economic status have less opportunity to attain a college education than sons of fathers of higher socioeconomic status. In keeping with the high relationship between education and occupation, it is unlikely that there will be much upward occupational mobility of lower-class persons in the near future.[32] This is true *intra*generationally as well as intergenerationally.[33]

Lin and Yauger emphasize that even where educational opportunities are high, unless they are matched by equally high occupational opportunities, father's occupation becomes an important indicator of occupational success. Where occupational opportunities do not keep pace with increases in education, social unrest and occupational migrations are likely to occur in all but the most highly industrialized societies. In the latter, according to Lin and Yauger, a high achievement orientation reduces the threat of upheaval.[34] Presumably, the United States falls into this category even though an education-occupation imbalance persists.

Although education has always been considered an important variable determining occupation, there are many indications that its influence is waning. The strength of the relationship between level of educational attainment and occupation decreased during the 20-year period from 1944 to 1964, and trends indicate that it will continue to decrease.[35] In addition, it was pointed out that employers tend to use education as an excuse to hire who they prefer.

Using a national sample of high school students of the same age cohort, researchers replicated Sewell's Wisconsin high school study and found that family socio-economic origins had a "pervasive influence" on a person's occupational attainment.[37] In addition, as with the Wisconsin study, the national sample disclosed a very small relationship between education and earnings. This indicates that, contrary to human capital theory, a person's capital (i.e., education) is *not* an important factor in determining his or her earnings.[37]

I.Q. AND OC-CUPATION

Other major factors influencing occupation besides family background and education are race, degree of intactness of marriage, size of family, and I.Q.[38] However, the authors of this statement are very careful to point out that although I.Q. contributes "appreciably" to occupational attainment, "there remains a very substantial amount of variation still 'unexplained'" by genetic differences. The current difference between blacks and whites on I.Q. tests is about one standard deviation on a normal I.Q. scale—or 20 points. This does not nearly account for the occupational differences between whites and blacks. "Substantial occupational and educational disadvantages accrue to black men despite controlling for social origins, education, and I.Q. scores."[39]

The genetic determinism argument has recently been revived by psychologists Richard Herrnstein, Arthur Jensen, and Hans Eysenck.[40] They state that genetic limitations of intelligence account for those who fall to the bottom of the economic and social order. Thus, very little can be done for these people because they are genetically unequal, and this will insure low incomes.

However, present I.Q. tests measure those who are quick, retentive, and flexible. But there is no assessment of qualitative abilities. It tells us how the persons measured fit into the present educational and occupational structure. But, says Don Hager, it tells us nothing about the more enduring qualities of persons: wisdom, integrity, creativeness, courage, and humaneness. "It consistently emphasizes lower rather than upper limits of human attainment."[41]

There is a long argument over what percent of the variance in I.Q. scores is explained by genetic factors. The amount has ranged from 30 to 80 percent. If I.Q. did explain so much of the distribution of occupations and income, there would be very little inequality of wages in a given occupation. This, of course, is not the situation. Blacks are not paid at least 25 percent less than whites for the same work because of gene deficiencies. Also, the fact that black family income as a proportion of white family income improved in the 1960s was not a result of improved genetic intellectual capacity but, instead, a result of political pressures and economic expansion.[42]

Jencks and his associates have argued that neither desegregation, nor preschool programs, nor money spent on schools, nor class size have much affected people's cognitive skills, that is, the ability to work with words and numbers, to absorb information, and to make logical inferences. Therefore, the assumption of educational reformers that family background and education are the major indicants of one's earning power is incorrect. Three-quarters of all variations in income within a given occupation is caused by variances in luck and personality. Genetic differences account for very little.[43]

One recent study disagrees with Jencks's findings. An analysis of a sample of public school districts in Colorado in 1970 shows that student academic achievement is affected by (1) a well-qualified staff of teachers with a reasonable student-teacher ratio (size of school does not affect achievement if the ratio remains unchanged), and (2) adequate school district revenues to support the necessary teachers and resources.[44]

Most studies have concluded that achievement is not affected by the amount of financial resources utilized. However, the Colorado study takes into consideration environmental and organizational factors such as school district size, fiscal resources, percent of low-income students, parental education, percent of nonwhites, pupil-teacher ratios, administrative intensity, the professional staff-teacher ratio, and the percent of staff certified. The authors conclude that the formal organization of schooling *is* important for student academic attainment.

Jencks's argument presupposes a reason why luck and personality are the two most important factors determining a person's income. His example of luck is "chance acquaintances who steer you to one line of work rather than another." His example of personality is "the ability to look a man in the eye without seeming to stare."[45] However, the chance acquaintances one would meet at Choate and Harvard are quite different from chance acquaintances in Los Angeles public schools and a California community college, especially regarding the consequences of those meetings. These factors of luck and personality are attributes developed in one's social class milieu, for example, ways of maintaining one's cool, speech mannerisms, personal contacts, and the like. In other words, these attributes are highly dependent on family background and, in turn, quality of schooling, the latter to a great extent depending on the former.[46]

In a carefully devised attack on the I.Q. theorists, Samuel Bowles and Herbert Gintis point out that when correlated with I.Q., both socio-economic background and educational attainment are causal factors of economic (occupational) success. Therefore, schooling affects one's chances of occupational success predominantly by the noncognitive traits that it generates—specifically, parents' occupation and education.[47]

In addition, Bowles and Gintis emphasize that when children with different social class backgrounds but equal I.Q.s are compared later in life, they show little or no social mobility. Those who started in the lower class remained in lower-class occupations. Those who started in the upper class (and with I.Q.s equal to those in the lower class) stayed in the upper class. They conclude that "The beliefs surrounding I.Q. betray its true functioning—that of legitimating the social institutions underpinning the stratification system itself." This necessitates a hierarchical division of labor and level consciousness.[48]

In support of Bowles and Gintis, Allan King found in a study of 1960 census data that persons from wealthier families choose occupations involving greater monetary risks than those from less wealthy families. Risk is defined as "the certainty of income success in an occupation. The less certain the income success the more risky an occupation."

Thus, contrary to human capital theory, family income and not individual ability is a more important determinant of occupational success. Family background affects occupational choice independent of market forces.[49]

Stanley Masters has summed up the argument regarding the reasons for I.Q. differences between blacks and whites:

1. Present discrimination in schools.
2. Differences in family background resulting in part from past discrimination.
3. The effects of discrimination on the child's aspirations and educational performance.
4. Cultural biases in the tests.[50]

The Meritocratic Principle

A meritocratic society requires that I.Q. plus effort be the basic measures for occupational placement. This fits well with the human capital theory of a free labor market, in which employers will hire those persons willing and qualified to perform the required tasks and in which employees will perform those tasks for any employer willing to pay for their training and experience, the price to be determined by the market for such talent. Their achieved qualifications (achievement always depending on innate abilities) will determine their income level and occupational level, and these in turn determine social position and status. If everyone in the society has equal opportunity to attain status, then the meritocratic system is universalistic. The majority of U.S. sociologists see our society as evolving toward a universalistic system.[51] The functional theory of social stratification (inequality) adds one final statement—that the most important positions are filled by the most qualified people, qualified in terms of ability and effort.

The great majority of American people accept this principle. The American ideology that supports this principle contains the following beliefs.

- There is equal opportunity to learn a trade, skill, or profession because public schooling is available to all.
- A job can be found if one looks hard enough because there are always jobs that need doing.
- A person who works hard will get ahead. One who doesn't is lazy or stupid or both.
- Hard work is rewarded through money and property.
- Unequal rewards are necessary because they stimulate high achievement.
- The economic marketplace is the chief instrument through which individual self-seeking will lead to the greatest good for the greatest number.
- The value placed on individualism in this manner closely relates it to a major goal of capitalism: "self-realization in the sense of fulfillment of

the self-interest of the individual person, and the resultant moral and *material* progress of the society."

- If rewards become unfairly distributed then the people can vote to change the system of distribution by electing representatives who will protect individual achievement.[52]

The Rebuttal

This dominant ideology places the worker in a difficult position. The majority of blue-collar workers are not aware of the biases in tests of I.Q. and ability and, as a result, they feel that they have no right to complain if they are unsuccessful. The better trained have the authority, as legitimated by the lesser trained, to govern others and to enforce the rules. The working-class male must attain whatever dignity he can by being aggressive, by acting highly sexual, and by fostering the cult of masculinity. As a result, he limits his career development to jobs in which these traits are acceptable.[53] As an example, gang behavior often travels from community to workplace.[54]

The average person sees poverty as caused by wrong attitudes, values, and personality characteristics. The poor are seen to be less competitive. It is their own fault for being poor, or they are born into a culture of poverty.[55] However, an increasing number of studies indicate that the poor have as high aspirations as the nonpoor (see Chapter 6). It has also been found that although aspirations are high, the poor lack the confidence to act in order to fulfill these aspirations.[56] They are aware of the extreme limits on their chances because of discriminatory practices. Once a baggage handler, always a baggage handler, and the chances of being fired or laid off are very high compared to most high-status occupations. In such situations aspirations are of no help in maintaining occupational stability.

Functionalists argue that inequality is necessary to the survival of a society because it unconsciously insures that the most important positions are filled by the most qualified people. The principle of "equal access to the information resources of the society"[57] provides the equality necessary for proper functioning of the system. However, those who inherit wealth use it to buy educational privilege, which in turn affects I.Q. level. I.Q. then justifies class inequality.

But who is to say that a $50,000-a-year CPA is more important to society than a $15,000-a-year social worker? Also, do positions with more importance to society have to be rewarded more highly in order to get them filled?[58] The functionalist argument ends up in a bizarre logic. Those who have more deserve to keep it and to maintain more, because they are superior people indispensable to society, while those who have less deserve less, because they are inferior people and are dispensable, possibly even dangerous to the well-being of society.[59]

Peter Blau argues that:

The basic premise of the functional theory of stratification is tautological. The social rewards offered by others for a certain service are the operational criterion that defines its functional importance, which therefore cannot be an independent cause of these rewards....[60]

The functional importance of the services in terms of training and talent needed determines social rewards and thus social status. But on the other hand, social rewards (and resulting status) will also determine functional importance. For example, wealth can be inherited, and power can be institutionalized. The power of a given university can go far in enhancing the rewards and status of any given faculty member, whether he is a good scholar or not. As Blau says, the problem of the tautology is that it permits functional theory to assume that "resources have no effect on the ability to obtain rewards."[61]

With regard to education, Huber and Form systematically sampled an urban area in the Midwest and found that there was downward income mobility for the poor and middle-income groups but not for the rich. This was true even though 50 percent of the poor experienced significant upward generational educational mobility.[62] Other studies have shown that in general increased education actually increases the differences between the average earnings of low-wage minority workers (women and blacks) and the rest of the labor force.[63] This raises a serious question of the validity of the economic (and occupational) payoff in a system of high educational mobility.

THE RADICAL CRITIQUE OF EDUCATION

There are two basic models of education: the functional model, which attempts to maximize the growth of technological knowledge, and the liberal model, which attempts to minimize the distance between the most and least educated. Radical theorists criticize both models.

The functional model has already been partially described. There are other more specific hypotheses and assumptions, however, that need elucidation. The functional model states that educational growth creates educational equality. As talent becomes more important in the labor market, opportunities increase for the less educated as well as the better educated because productivity increases as the investment in machinery and training at higher levels increases.[64]

Schooling is a liberating (civilizing) force. To participate in a national and worldwide program of material and moral advancement, there must be a rational and objective means to select those individuals who are most capable of governing the social, political, and economic functions of the society. This means is education. Schooling operates according to the meritocratic principle.

Schooling is a productive force for development as long as it produces more human capital to be used in the productive process. As a result, increased schooling leads to increased per capita income. Also, countries with high-er levels of schooling are more likely to have western-style democratic governments.[65]

Feinberg criticizes this theory through an examination of the occupational structure, pointing out (as this book has in Part 2) that manual and clerical tasks are rationalized and simplified while managerial tasks are integrated and expanded. There is no lessening of inequality. The job of schooling is to gloss over this reality by teaching future workers to accept passively the situation and not to offer any perspective by which to evaluate the system. Consequently, those nations with the greatest educational growth have the greatest educational inequality, as measured by the number of occupational levels between the most and least educated.[66]

The liberal theory, based on the idea that increasing the level of education and other social services across the board will equitably redistribute income and status, is not supported by research. There has been no significant decrease in income inequality in the United States in the twentieth century.[67] Nor is there any clear evidence to support the theory that education contributes to economic development (and, consequently, changes in occupational structure) beyond the provisions of mass literacy.[68] Not even a political democracy will necessarily change this relationship.[69] Stinchcombe has taken an example from his South American research to explain the dominance of structural economic factors and not culture (i.e., education) as causes of modernization and occupational change.

If a man's education and luck have put him into a high position in a part of the economy which is not organized bureaucratically and not expand-ing rapidly, he will not see himself as having an organized career. If the same education and luck put him in a position in an expanding steel bureaucracy, he will see himself as having an organized career.

This finding is of profound significance for the theory of motivation of economic effort in poorer countries. It implies that the strength of moti-vation to work toward the modernization of the economy is not deter-mined by the culture of a country, but rather by the structure of its economy.[70]

Further support for this conclusion is presented by Orlando Rodriguez, who shows that during the 1960s only 25 percent of the increase in education was caused by shifts in the labor force from occupations requiring less education to occupations requiring more education.[71]

The Academic Tracking System

Schooling in America tends to weed out those students who perform poorly. Those who cannot afford higher (and even secondary) education are also forced to drop out. The graduates are those from the higher-class families. Education maintains the hierarchical structure and income distribution of the system.[72]

The most effective weeding-out system in the schools is tracking. James Rosenbaum measured achievement differences by I.Q. of college-bound versus vocational groups in a homogeneous, white, working-class community (thus controlling for structural factors of race and social class). The students were questioned in the eight grade and then 2 years later in the tenth grade. Rosenbaum concludes that tracking produces a highly rigid stratification system much like that of a caste structure. People in the college group seemed to be more self-directed and those in the noncollege group seemed more conforming, following Kohn's findings (see Chapter 16).[73]

In an examination of the City University of New York, which contains a graduate center, senior colleges, and community (junior) colleges, Ellen Trimberger finds three tracks: (1) elite preprofessional, (2) social services, and (3) clerical and vocational. Tracks 1 and 2 are working toward academic diplomas; track 3 is working toward general and vocational degrees in the community colleges.[74]

The trend toward tracking minority groups into the community colleges is unmistakable. In 1969, two out of every three community college students were white. By 1973, the ratio was one out of every two.[75] In the senior colleges there has been an *increase* in minority group students from 18 percent of total enrollment in 1969 to 33 percent in 1973.[76] However, the dropout rate is the significant factor in this case. Dropout rates are highest among the open enrollment students, among whom are many minority-group students. Within the City University of New York rates range from 30 to 40 percent, as compared to 10 to 15 percent for non-open enrollment students.[77]

The immediate value of open enrollment, says Trimberger is that the dropouts reinforce the ideology of equal opportunity. They believe that they have been given a fair chance to succeed and blame themselves for their failure to stay in school, and they then lower their aspirations. This is especially important in a labor market that is expanding at a *decreasing* rate and where the standard of living remains stationary. Formerly, where sons and daughters remained in the same social class position as their parents and received more schooling, they did experience a higher standard of living. General economic prosperity and an expanding labor force permitted those with higher levels of education to fill the better positions that opened up.

But now youth have expectations of going beyond their parents' level.

However, there is no room for them because economic expansion has leveled off and graduate schools are not expanding to meet the "inflation" of college degrees. Youth are more often ending up with the same standard of living as their parents.[78]

This is where the community colleges step in, according to the radical critique by Pincus. The unpublicized goals of the community college are to train a paraprofessional labor force, to "cool out" students who have unrealistic occupational aspirations, to serve as custodians to keep youth out of the labor market, and to screen those few who will be sent to 4-year colleges.[79]

It was found that test scores of community college students are lower than those of 4-year college students. It is also true that the higher the student's social class, the higher the test scores, and that the 4-year schools have higher socio-economic student populations. Blacks and Latinos are highly underrepresented in the 4-year schools and slightly underrepresented in community colleges, nationally. Low income and black students are more likely to be in programs that terminate with the community college degree.[80]

On the basis of these studies one can conclude that there is a definite patterning of social class and a system of racial tracking within public higher education. Those areas of the country with the most developed system of community colleges have the *lowest* proportion of students who ultimately attain a bachelor's degree. Community colleges are part of the problem of class and ethnic inequality instead of part of the solution. The community college system has been strongly encouraged and aided by the leaders of industry, who find a reserve pool of labor trained free of charge.[81]

Therefore, Pincus concludes, the inequality at community colleges will last as long as economic inequality lasts. The capitalist class has control over these schools (through boards and more informal arrangements) and will not relinquish it voluntarily.[82]

International Educational Colonialism

Educational colonialism between nations works much in the same way as within nations. The colonized schools in developing countries teach the ideals, values, and beliefs of the colonizer. Children are alienated from their own culture, and the society is not able to define itself.[83]

Some theorists say there are some positive effects of formal schooling, that because education is inherently liberating that the educated would turn against their oppressors once they became conscious of their situation. However, Carnoy believes that schooling has developed new leaders who are trained in the politics and economics of Western thought. As a result, newly independent countries are likely to follow these standards of conduct and remain heavily dependent on the colonizer.[84] This theory differs greatly from earlier political theories of the inevitable "communization" of developing countries.

Summary

The broadest critique of the American educational system is made by Bowles and Gintis.[85] They list four "undemocratic" elements of the capitalist system that structure work roles: (1) bureaucratic organization, (2) hierarchical lines of authority, which promote control from the top, (3) job fragmentation, and (4) an unequal reward structure. In order to maintain these elements unchanged the capitalist class controls occupational status by first requiring a pattern of noncognitive personality traits (e.g., learning to accept discipline, to be methodical, predictable, and persevering); second, by discriminating in their choice of certain ascriptive characteristics of workers (the race, sex, and age factors discussed in Part 1 of this book); and third, by requiring certain acquired credentials such as educational degrees or seniority.

Personality and motivation to attain credentials are acquired through the family. The values of self-direction or conformity will vary by socio-economic status of the family. The school will perpetuate these values and further prepare workers for their role in industry. "The social relations of schooling are structured similarly to the social relations of production...." The school has a bureaucratic order with a hierarchy of authority and an orientation to rules. It also has a system of external incentives, that is, grades, which are promises of "promotion." And it has stratification by age and "ability" (i.e., tracking). The authors note that students are graded according to "personality traits associated with discipline, subordinacy and rule-following quite independently of the level of cognitive achievement."[86]

Herman and Julia Schwendinger state that the family and the school are the two most important institutions in the development of the secondary labor market. Of the two, education is the most important, because the family "is forced to regulate productive relations according to the meritocratic and technical standards exerted by the school." In turn, the schools are run according to the needs of the industrial economy—they supply the needs of hierarchical structures with a reserve army of labor. Student behavior is standardized according to the behavior required by the managers of industry.[87]

The Equality of Results Debate

The philosopher, John Rawls, has emphasized the necessity of going beyond the idea of the equality of opportunity. The principle of equality of opportunity merely perpetuates the status quo system of inequality: it is the equality of opportunity *to be unequal*. Rawls suggests that there be an equality of results instead. He states in his argument that the inequalities of birth and natural endowment are undeserved. Therefore, in order to compensate for them, that is, to treat all persons equally, we must "redress the bias of contingencies in the direction of equality." For example, we must spend more money on education of the less intelligent instead of the more intelligent—an equality of result. "Those who have been favored by nature thus may gain from their good fortune only on terms that improve the situation of those who have lost out."[88]

This "difference principle" that there shall be no difference between people regarding social position, income, property, and the like controverts the tenets of *classical liberalism.* The latter states that unencumbered individuals are to be rewarded on the basis of their effort and risk in order to maximize their own satisfaction. Now, in *social liberalism* (or liberal socialism), it is not individual satisfaction that is the measure of social good but, instead, the "redress of the disadvantaged" that must take precedence.[89]

A major criticism of Rawls's thesis is that only a strong centralized state has the power to maintain effectively the difference principle that there shall be no inequality of "social primary goods" unless it can be shown that these differences benefit the less advantaged people.[90] Related to this issue is the problem raised by Frank Parkin: "A political system which guarantees constitutional rights for groups to organize in defence of their interests is almost bound to favor the privileged at the expense of the disprivileged." The dominant class has greater capacity to organize and mobilize to protect its interests because it has greater access to the means of social control. Thus, "the pluralist or democratic political structure always works to the advantage of the dominant class." The egalitarian society therefore requires a strong (centralized?) state in order to moderate the power of social and occupational groups.[91]

SUMMARY AND CONCLUSIONS

Education tends to shape careers. It is listed as an important factor in practically all studies of occupational attainment and social mobility. It is considered by some to be the most important attribute in determining one's occupational destination.

However, despite equal educational backgrounds, minority groups in America do not attain as high an occupational status as white males. Women, in particular, face the problem of an increase in their proportion of the labor force with a corresponding decrease in the growth of the labor force. Unless some drastic inroads can be made into traditionally male-dominated occupations, women will suffer extraordinarily high unemployment and subemployment rates.

The relation of the family to education is an important one. A person's family background is a significant factor affecting his or her occupational chances. Also, in another context, the family is important in transmitting the values, beliefs, and norms of the society to its children.

Two major questions revolving around the relationship between occupation and education are: (1) How do persons achieve, and (2) Why do they achieve? Human capital or functional theory (and the theory of the merito-cracy) attempt to answer the first question by examining I.Q. scores, educa-tion, and personal effort. These are seen as the key factors in several research studies.

The radical critique of functional theory attempts to answer the second question: Why do people attempt to achieve occupational success in the way they do, especially if the entire educational system has been shown to be highly inequalitarian? Their answer is that the majority of Americans are suf-fering under a false consciousness; that the American ideology of individualism, as perpetuated by the family and the school, keeps people "in their place." Minority groups do not fit the dominant group's ascriptive requirements (age, sex, and race) and are kept subservient by means of discriminatory ("non-cognitive") selection standards of personality and educational credentials. Be-cause of the castelike structure of educational tracking, most self-directed people are college trained and in the primary labor market.

Thus, argue the radicals, education is both a weapon used by the dominant class to train the soldiers of the reserve army of laborers and an excuse for selecting "suitable" candidates to replace themselves.

A radical *theory* of schooling is lacking, although the principle of "equal results," instead of equal opportunity, has presented the basis for such a begin-ning.

FOOTNOTES FOR CHAPTER 17
OCCUPATIONS AND EDUCATION

[1] Randall Collins, "Functional and Conflict Theories of Educational Stratifi-cation," *American Sociological Review, 36* (December 1971), 1003-1004.

[2] U.S. Department of Labor, Bureau of Labor Statistics, *Educational Attain-ment of Workers, March 1974,* Special Labor Report No. 175, p. 64.

[3] U.S. Department of Labor, Bureau of Labor Statistics, *Educational Attain-ment of Workers, March 1973,* Special Labor Report No. 161, p. 60.

[4] *Educational Attainment of Workers, March 1973,* p. 60.

[5] U.S. Department of Labor, Bureau fo Labor Statistics, *Education of Work-ers: Projections to 1990,* Special Labor Force Report No. 160, p. 24. For other factors related to age see Chapter 7 above.

[6] Brigitte Mach Erbe, "Black Occupational Change and Education," *Socio-logy of Work and Occupations, 2* (May 1975), 156-158. Also, George W. Dowdall, "White Gains From Black Subordination in 1960 and 1970," *Social Problems, 22* (December 1974), 162-183. The expected rate of

educational attainment is derived by comparing it to occupation by education level of the total labor force.

[7] Charles T. Stewart, Jr., *Low Wages in an Affluent Society* (Chicago: Nelson-Hall, 1974).

[8] Erbe, "Black Occupational Change and Education," p. 166.

[9] Ross M. Stolzenberg, "Education, Occupation, and Wage Differences between White and Black Men," *American Journal of Sociology, 81* (September 1975), 299-323.

[10] Theodore Purcell and Gerald F. Cavanagh, *Blacks in the Industrial World* (New York: The Free Press, 1972), p. 172.

[11] Valerie Kincade Oppenheimer, "A Sociologist's Skepticism," in Eli Ginzberg and Alice M. Yohalem (eds.), *Corporate Lib: Women's Challenge to Management* (Baltimore: The Johns Hopkins University Press, 1973).

[12] Oppenheimer, "A Sociologist's Skepticism."

[13] Valerie Kincade Oppenheimer, "Rising Educational Attainment, Declining Fertility and the Inadequacies of the Female Labor Market," in Charles F. Westoff and Robert Parke, Jr. (eds.), *Demographic and Social Aspects of Population Growth*, Vol. I (Washington, D.C.: The Commission on Population Growth and the American Future, U.S. Government Printing Office, 1972), pp. 309-327.

[14] Oppenheimer, "Rising Educational Attainment."

[15] Oppenheimer, "Rising Educational Attainment."

[16] U.S. Department of Labor, Bureau of Labor Statistics, *Employment of Recent College Graduates, October 1972,* Special Labor Force Report No. 169, pp. 34-35.

[17] V. Lane Rawlins and Lloyd Ullman, "The Utilization of College-Trained Manpower in the United States," in Margaret S. Gordon (ed.), *Higher Education and the Labor Market* (New York: The Carnegie Foundation for the Advancement of Teaching, 1974), p. 195.

[18] Rawlins and Ullman, "The Utilization of College-Trained Manpower," p. 201.

[19] Ivar Berg, *Education and Jobs: The Great Training Robbery* (New York: Praeger Publishers, 1970), p. 46.

[20] Rawlins and Ullman, "The Utilization of College-Trained Manpower," p. 208.

[21] Rawlins and Ullman, "The Utilization of College-Trained Manpower," pp. 216-218.

[22] News release of the U.S. Department of Labor, Office of Information, December 11, 1973.

[23] Peter M. Blau and Otis Dudley Duncan, *The American Occupational Structure* (New York: John Wiley & Sons, 1967).

[24] William H. Sewell, Archibald O. Haller, and Alejandre Portes, "The Educational and Early Occupational Attainment Process," *American Sociological Review, 34* (February 1969), 82-92; and William H. Sewell, Archibald O. Haller, and George W. Ohlendorf, "The Educational and Early Occupational Status Attainment Process: Replication and Revision," *American Sociological Review, 35* (December 1970), 1014-1027. The entire study is summarized in William H. Sewell and Robert M. Hauser, *Education, Occupation, and Earnings* (New York: Academic Press, 1975). For similar findings see also Alan C. Kerckhoff, *Ambition and Attainment* (Washington, D.C.: American Sociological Association, 1974).

[25] Sewell and Hauser, *Education, Occupation, and Earnings,* p. 185. See also Sally Hillsman Baker and Bernard Levenson, "Job Opportunities of Black and White Working-Class Women," *Social Problems, 22* (April 1975), 510-533.

[26] Jonathan Kelley, "Causal Chain Models for the Socioeconomic Career," *American Sociological Review, 38* (August 1973), 491. Also, S.M. Lipset and F.T. Malm, "First Jobs and Career Patterns," *American Journal of Economics and Sociology, 14* (1955), 247-261.

[27] Frank Ackerman et al., "The Extent of Income Inequality in the United States," in Richard C. Edwards, Michael Reich, and Thomas E. Weisskopf (eds.), *The Capitalist System: A Radical Analysis of American Society* (Englewood Cliffs, N.J.: Prentice-Hall, 1973), p. 21.

[28] Arthur B. Shostak, Jon Van Til, and Sally Bould Van Til, *Privilege in America: An End to Inequality?* (Englewood Cliffs, N.J.: Prentice-Hall, 1973), p. 21.

[29] Cornelis J. Van Zeyl, *Ambition and Social Structure* (Lexington, Mass.: D. C. Heath & Co., 1974).

[30] Van Zeyl, *Ambition and Social Structure,* pp. 20-21.

[31] Van Zeyl, *Ambition and Social Structure,* p. 27.

[32] William G. Spady, "Educational Mobility and Access: Growth and

Paradoxes," *American Journal of Sociology, 72* (November 1967), 273-286.

[33] Otis Dudley Duncan, David Featherman, and Beverly Duncan, *Socioeconomic Background and Achievement* (New York: Seminar Press, 1972).

[34] Nan Lin and Daniel Yauger, "The Process of Occupational Status Achievement: A Preliminary Cross-national Comparison," *American Journal of Sociology, 81* (November 1975), 557.

[35] John K. Folger and Charles B. Nam, "Trends in Education in Relation to the Occupational Structure," *Sociology of Education, 38* (Fall 1964), 19-33.

[36] Karl L. Alexander, Bruce K. Eckland, and Larry J. Griffin, "The Wisconsin Model of Socioeconomic Achievement: A Replication," *American Journal of Sociology, 81* (September 1975), 324-342. Also, in the same issue, Kenneth L. Wilson and Alejandro Portes, "The Educational Attainment Process: Results from a National Sample," pp. 343-363, examine a national sample of more recent high school graduates (1970) and come to the same conclusion.

[37] Alexander, Eckland, and Griffin, "The Wisconsin Model of Socioeconomic Achievement," pp. 339-340.

[38] Duncan, Featherman, and Duncan, *Socioeconomic Background and Achievement.*

[39] Duncan, Featherman, and Duncan, *Socioeconomic Background and Achievement,* p. 106.

[40] Richard J. Hernnstein, *I.Q. in the Meritocracy* (Boston: Little, Brown, 1972); Hans J. Eysenck, *The I.Q. Argument: Race, Intelligence, and Education* (New York: Library Press, 1971).

[41] Don J. Hager, review of Richard J. Hernnstein, "I.Q. in the Meritocracy," in *Contemporary Sociology, 3* (March 1974), 118.

[42] S. M. Miller and Ronnie Ratner, "The American Resignation: The New Assault on Equality," *Social Policy, 3* (May-June 1972), 7.

[43] Christopher Jencks et al., *Inequality: A Reassessment of the Effect of Family and Schooling in America* (New York: Basic Books, 1972).

[44] Charles E. Bidwell and John D. Kasarda, "School District Organization and Student Achievement," *American Sociological Review, 40* (February 1975), 55-70.

[45] Jencks et al., *Inequality*, p. 227.

[46] As Wilson and Portes, "The Educational Attainment Process," p. 359, say: "Socioeconomic background not only provides a context for different interpersonal influences but also makes available the means to buy or gain entry into educational institutions and to support longer periods of full-time enrollment."

[47] Samuel Bowles and Herbert Gintis, "I.Q. in the U.S. Class Structure," *Social Policy, 3* (November-December 1972 to January-February 1973), 65-96.

[48] Bowles and Gintis, "I.Q. in the U.S. Class Structure."

[49] Allan G. King, "Occupational Choice, Risk Aversion, and Wealth," *Industrial and Labor Relations Review, 27* (July 1974), 586-596.

[50] Stanley H. Masters, *Black-White Income Differentials* (New York: Academic Press, 1975), p. 41.

[51] For an excellent summary, see Judah Matras, *Social Inequality, Stratification, and Mobility* (Englewood Cliffs, N.J.: Prentice-Hall, 1975), pp. 283-284.

[52] Summarized from Joan Huber and William H. Form, *Income and Ideology: An Analysis of the American Political Formula* (New York: The Free Press, 1973), p. 4; and Kenneth M. Dolbeare and Patricia Dolbeare, *American Ideologies* (Chicago: Rand McNally, 1973), pp. 27-35.

[53] Richard Sennett and Jonathan Cobb, *The Hidden Injuries of Class* (New York: Alfred A. Knopf, 1973).

[54] William Kornblum, *Blue Collar Community* (Chicago: The University of Chicago Press, 1974).

[55] Huber and Form, *Income and Ideology*, pp. x-xi.

[56] Dennis P. Sobin, *The Working Poor* (Port Washington, N.Y.: Kennikat Press, 1973), p. 76.

[57] Edwin B. Parker, "Implications of New Information Technology," *Public Opinion Quarterly, 37* (Winter 1973-1974), 559.

[58] Charles H. Anderson, *The Political Economy of Social Class* (Englewood Cliffs, N.J.: Prentice-Hall, 1974), pp. 81-88. Special monetary rewards are not necessary to recruit managers with heavy responsibilities in kibbutzim. See Arnold S. Tannenbaum, *Hierarchy in Organizations* (San Francisco: Jossey-Boss, 1974), pp. 120-121.

[59] Anderson, *The Political Economy of Social Class*, p. 88.

[60] Peter M. Blau, *The Organization of Academic Work* (New York: John Wiley & Sons, 1973), pp. 276-277.

[61] Blau, *The Organization of Academic Work*, p. 277.

[62] Huber and Form, Income and Ideology, pp. 189-191.

[63] Barry Bluestone, William M. Murphy, and Mary Stevenson, *Low Wages and the Working Poor* (Ann Arbor, Mich.: Institute of Labor and Industrial Relations, The University of Michigan and Wayne State University, 1973), pp. 137-138.

[64] From a critique by Walter Feinberg, "Educational Equality Under Two Conflicting Models of Educational Development," *Theory and Society, 2* (Summer 1975), 187.

[65] From a critique by Martin Carnoy, *Education as Cultural Imperialism* (New York: David McKay Co., 1974), pp. 2-5, 344.

[66] Feinberg, "Educational Equality," pp. 190-194. For a more detailed analysis see his *Reason and Rhetoric: The Intellectual Foundations of Twentieth Century Educational Policy* (New York: John Wiley & Sons, 1975).

[67] Carnoy, *Education as Cultural Imperialism*, p. 261; Herman P. Miller, "A Profile of the Blue-Collar American," in Sar Levitan (ed.), *Blue-Collar Workers* (New York: McGraw-Hill, 1971), p. 59; Frank Parkin, *Class Inequality and Political Order* (New York: Praeger Publishers, 1971), p. 119.

[68] Randall Collins, "Functional and Conflict Theories of Educational Stratification," pp. 1005-1006. Many studies show that better educated employees are often *less* productive.

[69] Robert W. Jackman, "Political Democracy and Social Equality: A Comparative Analysis," *American Sociological Review, 39* (February 1974), 38.

[70] Arthur L. Stinchcombe, *Creating Efficient Industrial Administrations* (New York: Academic Press, 1974), p. 141. Another writer comes to the opposite conclusion that in the long run schooling provides a "cultural climate" favorable to new technologies in a developing nation. C. Arnold Anderson, "The Impact of the Educational System on Technological Change and Modernization," in Bert F. Hoselitz and Wilbert E. Moore (eds.), *Industrialization and Society* (Mouton: UNESCO, 1966), pp. 259-278.

[71] Orlando Rodriguez, "Occupational Shifts and Educational Upgrading in the American Labor Force between 1950 and 1970," paper read at the Annual Meetings of the American Sociological Association, New York City, August 1976, p. 11. This figure has increased from an estimated 15 percent for 1940 to 1960. See Folger and Nam, "Trends in Education . . .," p. 29.

[72] Carnoy, *Education as Cultural Imperialism*, p. 322.

[73] James E. Rosenbaum, "The Stratification of Socialization Processes," *American Sociological Review, 40* (February 1975), 48-54.

[74] Ellen Kay Trimberger, "Open Admissions: A New Form of Tracking?" *The Insurgent Sociologist, 4* (Fall 1973), 35-36.

[75] As computed from figures in *The CUNY Courier* (May 9, 1974), 4.

[76] *The CUNY Courier* (May 9, 1974), 4.

[77] Trimberger, "Open Admissions," p. 39.

[78] Trimberger, "Open Admissions," pp. 39-40.

[79] Fred Pincus, "Tracking in Community Colleges," *The Insurgent Sociologist, 4* (Spring 1974), 19-35. For a detailed analysis of the City University of New York see *Crisis at CUNY* (New York: The Newt Davidson Collective, 1974).

[80] Pincus, "Tracking in Community Colleges." However, it is possible that in a depressed job market vocationally trained 2-year graduates are often able to obtain entry jobs with wages or salaries equal to or better than those acquired by liberally trained 4-year graduates. A unionized paraprofessional may command a higher wage than a bank teller, a computer programmer a higher salary than an office assistant with a B.A. in English.

[81] Pincus, "Tracking in Community Colleges."

[82] Pincus, "Tracking in Community Colleges."

[83] Carnoy, *Education as Cultural Imperialism*, pp. 71-72.

[84] Carnoy, *Education as Cultural Imperialism*, p. 143.

[85] Bowles and Gintis, "I.Q. in the U. S. Class Structure."

[86] Bowles and Gintis, "I.Q. in the U. S. Class Structure."

[87] Herman Schwendinger and Julia R. Schwendinger, *Delinquency and the Collective Varieties of Youth*, unpublished manuscript, Chapter 2. It is

interesting that Kohn, not a radical theorist, states that the family is the major agent perpetuating the values and beliefs of inequality. Education aids in countering this influence, but only to a very small degree. Melvin L. Kohn, *Class and Conformity: A Study in Values* (Homewood, Ill.: Dorsey Press, 1969), p. 201.

[88] John Rawls, *A Theory of Justice* (Cambridge, Mass.: Harvard University Press, 1971).

[89] Rawls, *A Theory of Justice*, 65-76, 107-108.

[90] Robert A. Nisbet, "The New Despotism," *Commentary*, *59* (June 1975), 38.

[91] Frank Parkin, *Class, Inequality and Political Order* (New York: Praeger Publishers, 1971), pp. 181-183.

AUTHOR INDEX

Ackerman, Frank, 156, 433
Aiken, Michael, 241, 243
Aldrich, Howard, 275
Alex, Nicholas, 297-299, 307
Alexander, Karl L., 434
Alexander, Rodney, 330
Anderson, C. Arnold, 436
Anderson, Charles H., 8, 95, 122, 164, 211,
    218, 435-436
Antonovsky, Aaron, 164
Argyris, Chris, 251, 270
Arond, Henry, 365
Aronowitz, Stanley, 250, 270, 355, 364, 367,
    369
Athanasiou, Robert, 41, 46, 135, 145
Azumi, Koya, 171, 189

Back, Kurt W., 230, 241
Baker, Frank, 241
Baker, Sally Hillsman, 433
Bakke, E. Wight, 91
Baldridge, J. Victor, 180
Barber, Bernard, 265-266, 275-276
Barnard, Chester I., 248, 269
Barnowe, J. Thad, 368
Baron, Harold, 91
Barringer, Richard E., 92
Barton, Allen H., 276
Bayley, David H., 306
Bealer, R. C., 164
Bean, Lee J., 368
Becker, Gary S., 91
Becker, Howard S., 204, 215-217, 289, 305,
    369, 377-379, 384, 406
Beckman, Linda, 239
Beer, Samuel H., 92
Beer, William R., 124
Bell, Caroline Shaw, 132, 144
Bell, Daniel, 49-52, 54, 57-58, 62-63, 171, 189,
    276

Bell, Richard, 124, 215
Ben-David, Joseph, 218
Bendix, Reinhard, 45-46, 163-164, 218
Benét, Mary Kathleen, 312, 330
Bensman, Joseph, 115, 123-124, 194, 210,
    218, 383, 407
Berg, Ivar, 122, 417, 432
Berger, Alan S., 165
Berger, Bennett M., 362
Berger, Brigitte, 164
Berger, Morroe, 384
Berger, Peter L., 300, 308, 383
Berquist, Virginia A., 271
Berkley, George E., 191, 402, 408
Bernard, Jessie, 134, 145, 240
Bernstein, Eduard, 2, 366
Bernstein, Marver H., 271
Betsey, Charles, 77-78, 94
Bevins, Tom, 364
Bidwell, Charles E., 434
Billingsly, Andrew, 287, 304
Bird, Caroline, 144
Birnbaum, Norman, 57, 63
Bittner, Egon, 295-296, 307
Blankenship, Ralph L., 216, 301, 307
Blau, Peter M., 121-122, 156-158, 162-163,
    181, 190, 192, 209, 216, 304, 353, 366,
    407, 418, 425, 433, 436
Blauner, Robert, 190, 333-334, 349, 364-
    365
Bluestone, Barry, 76, 93-95, 436
Blum, Albert A., 305, 331, 334
Bock, E. Wilbur, 228, 240
Bogan, Forrest A., 163
Boggs, Michael D., 120
Bok, Derek C., 270-271
Bonacich, Edna, 96
Borow, Henry, 241
Botta, Joseph R., 305
Boudon, Raymond, 123
Boulding, Kenneth, 184, 193, 396, 406
Bowen, William G., 162
Bowles, Samuel, 93, 145, 422, 429, 435,
    437
Bowman, Claude C., 368
Bradburn, Norman M., 405
Braude, Lee, 305, 365
Braverman, Harry, 74, 93, 211, 219, 323-
    325, 333, 335, 362
Brawer, Milton J., 143

Brennan, Niall, 364
Brookfield, Cornelia, 8
Broom, Leonard, 20, 194, 215
Browne, Joy, 314, 331
Bucher, Rue, 218, 274
Buckley, Walter, 334
Burkett, Gary, 215
Burns, Tom, 180, 189
Burrage, Michael, 183, 193-194

Cameron, William Bruce, 378, 384
Cantor, Muriel G., 179, 191-192, 217, 244
Capdeville, Patricia, 93
Caplow, Theodore, 44, 93, 216, 223, 238,
    342, 362-363, 366, 393, 395, 404-405
Carnoy, Martin, 428, 436-437
Carr-Saunders, Alexander, 213
Casey, M. Claire, 22
Cavanaugh, Gerald F., 385, 432
Centers, Richard, 45, 209, 218
Champion, Dean J., 333
Champoux, Joseph E., 361
Chaplin, David, 383
Chinoy, Eli, 348, 364
Christ, Edwin A., 284, 302
Cicourel, Aaron V., 273
Clark, Shirley Merritt, 238
Clarke, Alfred C., 123, 242
Coates, Charles H., 270
Cobb, Jonathan, 359, 368, 435
Cohen, Albert K., 362
Cohen, Eliot E., 162
Cohen, Louise, 165
Cohen, Percy, 244
Coker, Robert E., Jr., 238
Collins, Randall, 8, 133, 144, 307, 338,
    342, 362-363, 431, 436
Conyers, James E., 240
Cook, Fred, 163
Cook, Robert M., 333
Corwin, Ronald G., 217, 232-233, 242,
    282, 287, 302
Coser, Rose Laub, 406
Cottrell, Leonard S., Jr., 194, 215
Cottrell, W. Fred, 343, 363
Crowley, Michael F., 44-45
Crozier, Michel, 182, 192, 215, 236, 244,
    321-322, 330, 332-333

Dahrendorf, Ralf, 366

Dalie, Joan Talbot, 366
Dalton, Melville, 273
Daniels, Arlene Kaplan, 179, 191, 200-201, 214
D'Antonio, William V., 123
Daum, Susan, 367
David, Deborah, 135, 145, 224, 239
Davis, Anne J., 303
Davis, Fred, 302, 365
Davis, Kingsley, 45, 106
Davis, Miles, 378
Davis, Nanette, x, 376, 383
Day, Dawn, 288, 304
DeFleur, Lois B., 123
DeFleur, Melvin L., 123
De Fronzo, James, 366
De Jong, Peter, 143
Denney, Reuel, 407
Denzin, Norman K., 306
Devereux, George, 302
Dobb, Maurice, 93
Dodge, Norton, 146
Doeringer, Peter B., 67, 91-92
Domhoff, G. William, 92, 209, 256, 270, 272
Dorn, Dean S., 214
Dowdall, George W., 431
Draper, Ann, 95
Drucker, Peter F., 272-273, 276
Dubin, Robert, 303, 361, 363-364
Duncan, Beverly, 392, 404-405, 434
Duncan, Otis Dudley, 31, 35, 45-46, 121-122, 156-158, 163, 209, 353, 366, 404, 418, 433-434
Duncan, Robert, 180
Dunlap, John T., 270-271
Durkheim, Émile, 3, 8

Eckland, Bruce K., 434
Edwards, Alba M., 19, 44
Edwards, Richard, 156, 433
Eells, Kenneth, 46
Ehrenreich, Barbara, 70, 92, 303, 356, 367
Ehrenreich, John, 70, 92, 303, 356, 367
Eiduson, Bernice, 239
Eky, Kermit, 274
Ellington, Duke, 379
Elliott, Philip, 194, 216, 218
Engel, Gloria V., 192, 306
Engels, Friedrich, 122

Epstein, Cynthia Fuchs, 143, 145
Epstein, Irwin, 243
Epstein, Jason, 94
Erbe, Brigitte Mach, 431-432
Estey, Martin, 331-332
Etheridge, Carolyn F., 193
Etzioni, Amitai, 176, 190, 241, 279, 301, 304, 307
Eysenck, Hans J., 421, 434

Fanon, Frantz, 229-230
Faulkner, Robert, 205-206, 216
Faunce, William A., 44, 334
Fava, Sylvia F., 239
Featherman, David L., 82, 94, 163, 404, 434
Feinberg, Walter, 426, 436
Feld, Sheila, 232, 242
Ference, Thomas P., 241
Finch, Henry A., 189
Finegan, T. A., 162
Finn, David, 270
Flacks, Richard, 211, 218
Flexner, Abraham, 213
Foley, Eugene P., 275
Folger, John D., 434
Foote, Nelson N., 365
Form, William H., 44, 172, 190, 213, 331, 359, 368-369, 425, 435-436
Fox, William S., 384
Frazier, E. Franklin, 229-230, 267
Freedman, Marcia, 79, 81, 94, 177, 191, 337
Freidson, Eliot, 190-191, 193, 208, 213-214, 217-218, 234, 243-245, 304-305, 308, 372, 382
Fried, Marc, 356, 367, 405
Friedmann, Georges, 332
Fuguitt, Glenn V., 121

Gagala, Ken, 91
Galbraith, John Kenneth, 63
Galway, Kathleen, 238
Garland, T. Neal, 225, 239
Gartner, Alan, 55-56, 62-63, 210, 218
Geiger, Theodore, 366
Gerstl, Joel E., 239
Gerth, Hans H., 45, 189, 242
Gerver, Israel, 383
Gillespie, David F., 192

Gilroy, Curtis L., 122
Gintis, Herbert, 93, 145, 422, 429, 435, 437
Ginzberg, Eli, 92, 143-144, 162-163, 337, 361, 432
Glaser, Barney, 215, 343-344, 363
Glazer, Nathan, 407
Glenn, Norval D., 361
Goffman, Erving, 163, 282, 302
Gold, David A., 272
Gold, Ray, 383
Goldman, Daniel R., 277
Goldner, Fred H., 241
Goldstein, Sidney, 275, 366
Goldthorpe, John H., 353, 366
Gomberg, William, 240, 354, 362, 366, 368, 383, 405
Goode, William J., 144-145, 182, 192-193, 199, 201, 213-214, 217, 299, 307-308, 352, 365
Goodwin, Leonard, 165
Gordon, David M., 88, 90-91, 93, 95-96
Gordon, Margaret S., 432
Gordon, Milton M., 361
Goss, Mary E. W., 181, 192
Gouldner, Alvin W., 273, 346, 363, 390, 404
Graham, Patricia Albjerg, 238
Greenbaum, Joan, 328, 334
Greenwood, Ernest, 213-214
Griffin, Larry J., 434
Gross, Bertram, 95
Gross, Edward, 136, 144-145
Gross, Llewellyn, 123
Grusky, Oscar, 273
Guest, Avery M., 366
Guest, Robert H., 262, 274, 347, 364
Gursslin, Orville, 123
Guttman, Louis, 39, 46, 274

Habenstein, Robert A., 284, 302
Habermas, Jürgen, 408
Hage, Jerald, 171-189, 241, 243
Hager, Don J., 421, 434
Hagstrom, Warren O., 191
Hall, Richard H., 44, 190-192, 202, 213-215, 269, 408
Haller, Archibald O., 123, 433
Halmos, Paul, 191, 219, 244-245, 303-304, 306, 382

Halpern, Richard S., 262, 275
Hamilton, Charles V., 123
Hamilton, Richard F., 361-362
Handel, Gerald, 405
Hare, Nathan, 122
Harrington, Michael, 67, 211, 219
Harris, Joan R., 240
Harrison, Bennett, 91, 93, 95, 115-116, 120, 123
Harvey, Edward, 378-379, 384
Harwood, Edwin, 44
Hatt, Paul D., 35, 38, 45-46
Haug, Marie, 190, 194, 217, 308
Hauser, Robert M., 82, 94, 163, 433
Havighurst, Robert J., 241
Head, Kendra B., 41, 46, 135, 145
Hearn, H. L., 382
Heer, David M., 47
Heilbroner, Robert, 53-54, 63, 355, 367
Heller, Celia S., 46
Helson, Ravena, 239
Henderson, A. M., 8
Henning, Dale A., 272
Henry, Kenneth, 43, 259, 273, 290-291, 305
Henry, William E., 250-251, 270
Henslin, James M., 365
Hentoff, Nat, 150, 162
Heraud, Brian J., 303
Herrick, Neal Q., 358, 368
Herrnstein, Richard, 421, 434
Heydebrand, Wolf V., 170-171, 188-189, 192, 243, 304
Hill, Richard, 63
Hirsch, Walter, 244
Hodge, Claire C., 44
Hodge, Robert W., 46
Hodges, Harold M., Jr., 362
Hoffman, L. Richard, 334
Holbeck, Jonny, 180
Hollingshead, August B., 209, 218, 368
Holmstrom, Linda Lytle, 239
Holzner, Burkhart, 217
Hoos, Ida R., 333-334
Hoppock, Robert, 163
Hoselitz, Bert F., 436
Howard, David H., 230, 241
Howard, John R., 243
Howard, Mary D., 243
Howton, F. William, 330-331

Huber, Joan, 425, 435-436
Hudson, Rosen R. A., 303
Hughes, Everett C., 45, 186, 190, 192-195, 203-204, 212, 215, 284, 303
Hughes, Helen MacGill, 238
Hunt, William C., 19
Hyman, Herbert H., 164
Hymer, Bennet, 91

Irelan, Lola M., 164
Israel, Joachim, 230, 241

Jackman, Mary R., 118, 124
Jackman, Robert W., 118, 124, 436
Jackson, J. A., 193
Jacobs, Paul, 163, 380, 385
Jacobson, E. H., 333, 364
James, Harry, 378
Jamous, H., 193
Jencks, Christopher, 389, 403, 421-422, 434-435
Jenson, Arthur, 421
Johnson, Elmer, H., 272
Jones, F. Lancaster, 20
Jourard, Sidney M., 145

Kagan, Jerome, 145
Kahn, E. J., Jr., 144
Kahn, Robert L., 368
Kalleberg, Arne L., 93
Kammerer, Gladys M., 257, 273
Kaplan, H. Roy, 22, 164
Kaplan, Norman, 273
Kapp, Eli E., 165
Kapp, Louise, 162
Karsh, Bernard, 327, 334, 364
Kasarda, John D., 434
Katan, Joseph, 306
Katz, Fred E., 282, 302-303
Keller, Suzanne, 407
Kelley, Jonathan, 164, 419, 433
Kelman, Mark, 243
Kendall, Patricia L., 213
Kerckhoff, Alan C., 433
Kerr, Clark, 67, 91, 365
Kidder, Alice H., 163
Kimbrough, Emory, Jr., 272
King, Allan G., 422, 435
Kitsuse, John I., 383-384
Klepp, Susan, 47

Klineberg, Benjamin S., 62
Knafl, Kathleen, 215
Kofsky, Frank, 379, 385
Kohn, Melvin, 392, 399, 401, 403, 405, 407-408, 427, 438
Komorovsky, Mirra, 405
Kornblum, William, 338, 362, 435
Kornhauser, William, 191, 254, 271
Kosa, John, 238
Krause, Elliott A., 92, 190, 303, 408
Kreps, Juanita, 144
Kronus, Carol, 293, 306
Kuhn, Thomas S., 243-244
Kuvesky, W. P., 164

Lampman, Robert J., 92
Lane, Angela, 404
Lane, Robert E., 31, 45
Langer, Elinor, 316-317, 331
Lanham, Frank, 163
LaSorte, Michael A., 238
Lasson, Kenneth, 331
Lasswell, Thomas E., 45-46, 121
Laumann, Edward O., 46
Lazarsfeld, Paul F., 185, 193
Lebergott, Stanley, 113, 122
Leggett, John, 117, 124
Leiter, Robert, 260, 274
Lenin, V. I., 2
Lenski, Gerhard, 45
Leonard, Peter, 304
Lerner, Melvin J., 164
Lesy, Michael, 368
Levenson, Bernard, 433
Levison, Andrew, 122, 361, 367, 382
Levitan, Sar A., 92, 361, 436
Levy, David A., 162, 404
Lewis, Edwin C., 143
Lewis, Lionel S., 201, 214
Liazos, Alexander, 376, 383
Lieberson, Stanley, 121
Lillienfeld, Robert, 124, 194, 210, 218, 407
Lin, Nan, 420, 434
Lipset, Seymour M., 44-46, 163-164, 253, 271, 361, 433
Litwak, Eugene, 181, 192
Lo, Clarence Y. H., 272
Long, Gary L., 214
Lopata, Helena Z., 132, 144

Lopate, Carole, 133, 144
Lortie, Dan C., 304
Lowell, Ruth Fabricant, 94, 164
Lunt, Paul S., 218
Lynch, Richard M., 274
Lynd, Helen Merrell, 209, 218
Lynd, Robert S., 209, 218

MacDonald, Lois, 271
Mack, Raymond W., 384
Malm, F. T., 433
Mann, Floyd C., 327, 334
Mannheim, Karl, 171, 189, 213
Manning, Peter K., 307
Marcus, Philip M., 271, 305
Marcuse, Herbert, 401, 408
Marglin, Stephen A., 270
Marshall, T. H., 366
Martin, Harry M., 303
Marx, Karl, 2-3, 8, 37, 72, 96, 114, 122,
    124, 167, 171, 232, 242, 321, 332, 366,
    379
Masters, Stanley H., 423, 435
Matras, Judah, 435
Mayer, Kurt B., 275, 366
McCarthy, John D., 243
McCormak, Thelma H., 306
McEaddy, Beverly J., 311, 330
McEwan, Peter J. M., 241
McGee, Reece J., 216, 223, 238
McKeefery, Virginia, 124, 215
Meara, Hannah, 351, 365
Mechanic, David, 332
Meeker, Marchia, 46
Meissner, Martin, 365
Mendelsohn, Harold, 306
Mennerick, Lewis A., 191
Merriam, Alan P., 384
Merton, Robert K., 193, 198, 210, 213,
    215, 218, 322, 383, 398, 407
Mettlin, Curtis J., 306
Metzner, Eric L., 382
Miller, Ann R., 47
Miller, Delbert C., 172, 190
Miller, Gale, 124, 215
Miller, George A., 242, 277
Miller, Herman P., 95, 436
Miller, Ron, 218
Miller, S. M., 121, 165, 361, 434
Miller, Stephen J., 314, 331

Mills, C. Wright, 45, 189, 209, 242, 253,
    260, 269, 271, 274, 301, 313, 322, 325,
    331-332, 409
Mills, Donald L., 180, 217, 239
Mitchell, Joyce M., 238
Mitchell, William C., 271
Mok, Albert L., 233, 243
Montagna, Paul D., 192-193, 215, 274
Montoya, Joseph, 43
Moore, Wilbert E., 21, 44-45, 106, 163,
    199, 213, 436
Morris, Richard T., 38, 46
Morrissey, Elizabeth, 192
Morse, Nancy C., 367
Mortimer, Jeylan T., 392, 405
Moseley, Roger L., 272
Moses, Stanley, 95
Mouzelis, Nicos P., 407
Moy, Joyanna, 92
Murphy, Raymond J., 38, 46
Murphy, William M., 76, 93-94, 436
Myers, Jerome K., 368
Myers, Richard R., 362

Nam, Charles B., 46, 434
Nash, Dennison, 390, 404
Neef, Arthur, 93
Nelkin, Dorothy, 372, 382
Niederhoffer, Arthur, 306
Nisbet, Robert A., 40, 46, 438
Noell, James J., 170-171, 188-189, 192,
    243
North, Cecil C., 35, 45-46
Nosow, Sigmund, 331

Ohlendorf, George W., 433
Oppenheimer, Martin, 96, 122, 219
Oppenheimer, Valerie Kincade, 126-127,
    143, 153, 162, 395, 397, 406-407, 414-
    417, 432
Orden, Susan R., 405
Orzack, Louis H., 302-303
Otero, J. F., 120

Park, Rosemary, 127, 143
Parke, Robert, Jr., 143, 414-416, 432
Parker, Edwin B., 435
Parkin, Frank, 430, 436, 438
Parnes, Herbert S., 122
Parsons, Carole W., 46

Parsons, Talcott, 3, 8-9, 188, 195, 210, 212, 218
Pavalko, Ronald M., 164
Pearl, Arthur, 306
Peck, Sidney, 361
Pellegrin, Roland J., 270
Peloille, B., 193
Pennings, J. M., 322, 332
Pepper, Max P., 368
Perlman, Selig, 9
Perrella, Vera C., 163
Perrow, Charles, 190
Perrucci, Robert, 164, 238, 273
Peterson, James, 121-122
Peterson, Richard A., 185, 193
Phillips, Derek L., 200, 214
Pichler, Joseph A., 214
Piker, Jeffry, 123, 162-163
Pincus, Fred, 428, 437
Piore, Michael J., 67-70, 91-92
Podhoretz, Norman, 145
Poloma, Margaret M., 225, 239
Polsky, Ned, 383
Poole, Michael J. F., 275
Porter, James N., 122
Porter, Sylvia, 131
Portes, Alejandre, 433-435
Powers, Mary G., 46
Prather, Jane, 126, 142-143, 238, 406
Preston, Samuel H., 121
Purcell, Theodore V., 385, 432
Purvin, George, 145

Quinney, Earl R., 292, 306

Rainwater, Lee, 67, 405
Ratner, Ronnie S., 121, 434
Rawlins, V. Lane, 417, 432-433
Rawls, John, 429-430, 438
Reader, George, 213
Reavic, Larry E., 164
Redlich, Frederick C., 368
Reich, Michael, 156, 433
Reiss, Albert J., Jr., 35, 45-46, 275
Reissman, Leonard, 302
Remmling, Gunther W., 9
Reuschemeyer, Dietrich, 214
Richard, Michel P., 229, 240-241
Riesman, David, 398, 407
Riessman, Frank, 55-56, 62-63,

210, 218, 306, 361
Rinehart, James W., 354, 366
Ritti, R. Richard, 241, 258, 273
Ritzer, George, 124, 190, 197-198, 202, 206, 213, 215-217, 244, 273
Roach, Jack L., 123
Roberts, Bertram H., 368
Robie, Edward A., 143
Robin, Stanley S., 143
Robinson, John P., 41, 46, 135, 145
Rodriguez, Orlando, 426, 436
Rogoff, Natalie, 213
Rokoff, Gerald, 406
Rose, Arnold M., 255, 272
Rose, Barbara, 124
Rosenbaum, James E., 437
Rosenberg, Bernard, 330-331
Rosenberg, Morris, 144, 224, 239, 306
Rosenblatt, Daniel, 368
Rosenblum, Gerald W., 213
Rosow, Jerome M., 332
Ross, Arthur M., 162
Rossi, Alice S., 224, 238-239, 404, 406
Rossi, Peter H., 46
Roth, Gunther, 8
Roth, Julius A., 214, 217, 365
Roucek, Joseph S., 364
Roy, Donald F., 345-346, 363
Ruderman, Florence, 145
Runcie, John F., 352, 365
Rushing, William A., 302, 369
Ruzek, Sheryl K., 304

Safilios-Rothschild, Constantina, 146
Sagarin, Edward, 243, 383-384
Salaman, Graeme, 352, 365
St. Simon, Henri, 2, 36
Sapery, Elizabeth, 330
Sayles, Leonard R., 275
Scammon, Richard M., 145
Schaff, Adam, 8
Schooler, Carmi, 407-408
Schulz, David A., 406
Schwendinger, Herman, 429, 437
Schwendinger, Julia, 429, 437
Scott, W. Richard, 180, 190, 287, 304, 407
Seashore, Stanley E., 368
Segal, Bernard E., 303
Seider, Maynard, 265-266, 276
Seidman, Joel, 331

Sennett, Richard, 359, 368, 435
Sewell, William H., 123, 418, 420, 433
Sexton, Brendan, 367
Sexton, Patricia Cayo, 271, 367, 385
Seymour, F. J. C., 217
Sheldon, Alan, 241
Shepard, Jon M., 326-327, 333-334
Sheppard, Harold L., 123, 358, 368
Shils, Edward A., 189
Shostak, Arthur B., 275, 339, 362, 366-368, 383, 405, 433
Siegel, Jacob S., 47
Siegel, Paul M., 46
Siegelman, Louis, 276
Siegman, Jack, 327, 334
Silver, Catherine Bodard, 290, 305
Silverman, Bertram, 8, 91
Simon, Rita James, 238
Simon, William, 165
Simpson, George, 8
Simpson, Ida Harper, 230, 241, 301
Simpson, Richard L., 171, 189, 301
Singell, Larry, 163
Smelser, Neil, 44, 163
Smigel, Erwin O., 191-192, 212, 274, 407
Smith, Peter B., 273
Sobin, Dennis P., 435
Sommers, Dixie, 331
Sonnenschein, David W., 382
Sørensen, Aage B., 93
Sorrentino, Constance, 92
Spady, William G., 433
Spector, Malcolm, 383-384
Spencer, Milton, 276
Spring, William, 93, 95, 123
Stalker, George M., 180, 189, 364
Starr, Rachel R., 238
Stauffer, Robert E., 304
Stebbins, Robert A., 384
Steinberg, Stephen, 123, 275
Stellman, Jeanne, 367
Stevenson, Gloria, 275
Stevenson, Mary, 76, 93-94, 140, 145-146, 406, 436
Stewart, Charles T., Jr., 382, 432
Stewart, Phyllis, L., 179, 191-192, 217, 244
Stinchcombe, Arthur, 342, 362, 400, 403, 407, 426, 436
Stoll, Patricia, 382
Stolzenberg, Ross M., 432

Stone, Katherine, 249, 270
Stover, Ed, 146
Strauss, Anselm, 215-218, 226, 240, 302-303
Strauss, George, 192, 275-276, 319-321, 332
Strauss, Murray A., 123
Stub, Holger, 116, 123
Suchman, Edward A., 368
Sullerot, Evelyne, 129, 142, 404
Sussman, Marvin B., 190, 194, 217, 308
Sutton, Francis X., 266, 270, 276
Swanstrom, Thomas E., 163
Sweezy, Paul M., 95
Sylvester, Sawyer F., Jr., 243

Tannenbaum, Arnold S., 191, 216, 367, 435
Tate, Will D., 230, 241
Tausky, Curt, 164
Tawney, R. H., 3, 8
Taylor, David P., 122
Taylor, James C., 349, 364
Taylor, Lee, 190
Terkel, Studs, 365
Terrebury, Shirley, 185, 193
Terrell, Kermit, 78, 94, 389, 404
Theodore, Athena, 237, 239, 301-303, 305, 396, 406
Thernstrom, Steven, 353, 365
Thielens, Wagner, Jr., 213
Thompson, James D., 170
Thurow, Lester C., 91-92
Tinker, Irene, 240
Tiryakian, Edward A., 275
Toennies, Ferdinand, 2
Toren, Nina, 242, 286, 303-304
Touraine, Alain, 52-53, 57, 62-63, 124, 211, 219
Treas, Judith, 143
Treiman, Donald J., 78, 94, 389, 404
Trice, Harrison M., 273
Trilling, Lionel, vii, x
Trimberger, Ellen Kay, 427, 437
Tropman, John E., 302
Trow, Donald B., 272
Trow, Martin, 276
Truzzi, Marcello, 365
Tsuchigane, Robert, 146
Tumin, Melvin, 121

Turner, Arthur N., 262, 274
Tyree, Andrea, 143

Udry, J. Richard, 393, 405
Udy, Stanley H., 188
Ullman, Lloyd, 417, 432-433

VanFossen, Beth, 46
Van Til, Jon, 433
Van Til, Sally Bould, 433
Van Tine, Warren R., 271
VanZeyl, Cornelis J., 419, 433
Veblen, Thorstein, 279, 301
Veroff, Joseph, 232, 242
Vidich, Arthur, 115, 123
Vietorisz, Thomas, 93, 95
Vollmer, Howard M., 180, 217, 239

Wachtel, Howard M., 77-78, 87, 93-95, 368
Waldman, Elizabeth, 311, 330, 382, 404
Walker, Charles R., 262, 274, 334, 347-348,
    364, 381, 385
Wallace, Phyllis A., 143-144
Wallerstein, Immanual, 56
Wardwell, Walter I., 305
Warner, W. Lloyd, 30, 45-46, 209, 218,
    270-271
Wattenberg, Ben J., 145
Weber, Max, ix, 3, 8, 45, 51, 171, 189,
    242
Weil, Mildred W., 406
Weinberg, S. Kirson, 365
Weiner, Florence R., 302
Weiss, Robert S., 367
Weisskopf, Thomas E., 156, 433
Westoff, Charles F., 143, 414-416, 432
Whisler, Thomas L., 334, 349, 364
White, Martha S., 406

White, Rodney F., 301
Whitmore, Robert, 404
Whyte, William Foote, 261, 273-275, 382,
    398, 407
Wildman, Wesley A., 304-305
Wilensky, Harold L., 92, 145, 235, 241-243,
    259, 271, 274, 369, 406
Wiley, Norbert, 267, 277
Williams, James D., 384
Williams, Lawrence K., 327, 334
Williams, Martin, 385
Willner, Barry, 274
Wilson, Alan B., 123
Wilson, Charles E., 402
Wilson, James Q., 307
Wilson, Kenneth L., 434-435
Wilson, P. A., 213
Winick, Charles, 218
Wispé, Lauren, 240
Wittich, Claus, 8
Wolfbein, Seymour, 15
Woodcock, Leonard, 333, 367
Woodward, Joan, 364
Wray, Donald E., 274
Wright, Erik Olin, 272
Wubnig, Michael, 307

Yanowitch, Murray, 8, 91
Yauger, Daniel, 420, 434
Yohalem, Alice M., 143-144, 432

Zald, Meyer, 243, 274
Zaltman, Gerald, 180
Ziegler, Harmon, 305
Zollschan, George K., 244
Zurcher, Louis A., 382
Zweig, Ferdinand, 357-358, 367-368,
    405

SUBJECT INDEX

Academic tracking, 427-428
Administrative authority, 177, 188, 237, 249-250, 258, 268, 280, 342, 393, 400
Alienation, of administrators, defined, 230-231, 323
  and involvement, 357
  and job autonomy, 268. *See also* Work alienation
  and job satisfaction, 242
  of office workers, 321-323
  and professionalization, 231, 323
  of professionals, 268
  and rationalization, 231
Anticipatory socialization, 322
Antiprofessionalism, 187
Ascribed status, 118
Aspirations, *see* Occupational aspirations
Assembly line workers, 347-348
Attributes, of an occupation, 197
  of a profession, 196-198, 201
Automation, and alienation, 325-328
  and blue-collar workers, 349
  and decentralization, 349
  defined, 325
  and office workers, 326
  and professionalization, 350
  and technology, 327-328, 361
  and working class, 348-350
Autonomous professional organization, 304
Autonomy, defined, 9. *See also* Worker autonomy

Balkanization of labor force, 67, 73, 75, 88, 211, 322
Bilateral labor market, 75
Black labor union leaders, 254-255
Black professionals, 227-230
Blue-collar workers, 117, 353, 357
Body of knowledge, 71
Bourgeoisie, 8, 117, 366
Building industry trades, 341-342
Bureaucracy, defined, 172
  and innovation, 400
  iron cage of, ix, 171

and personality, 398-400
  typology of, 282, 302
Bureaucrat, 398
Bureaucratic rules, 346
Bureaucratization, 172-174, 179
  and professionalization, 174
  and rationalization, 300
Bureau of Labor Statistics, 13, 42
Bureau of the Census, 13
Business executives, 250-251
Business ideologies, 265-266
Businessmen, values of, 392
Butchers, 351-353

Capitalism, and alienation, 329
  Marxist theory of, 2
  and poverty, 72
  and wage labor, 72, 324
Career, commitment to, 401
  defined, 14, 71, 197, 204-206
  and family, 396-397
  functionalist view, 198
  interactionist view, 204
  lateral careers, 397
  of managers, 268
  and risk-taking, 401-402
Career agents, 155
Career choice, 224
Career education program, 151
Career pattern, 69, 81-82, 88
Carnegie Commission on Higher Education, 24
Census undercount, 42
Centralization, 327, 349
Central life interest, see Work, as a central life interest
Ceramic engineering, 186
Certified public accountants, 184-185
Child labor, 150, 373, 390
Chiropracters, 291-292, 358
City managers, 257
City University of New York, 43, 427
Class, for itself, 118
  in itself, 72, 118
Class action, 117, 119
Class consciousness, 40, 73, 211, 323, 330
  by race, 117
  and unions, 175
Class discrimination, 116
Clergy, 37

Client advocacy, 187
Client influence, 175, 377
Client patronage, 234
Client revolt, 187, 300
Cocktail waitress, 373
Colleagial authority, 174, 179
Colleague control, 201
College graduates, 24, 417
  employment problems, 151
Commodity fetishism, 167, 355-356, 360
Community colleges, educational level of, 428
Computer programers, 328
Computers and social control, 185
Contest mobility, 115
Cooling out process, 206, 314, 428
Cosmopolitan identity, 178
Crafts labor market, 342
Critical analysis, viii, 2, 376
Cult of individualism, 1
Cultural colonialism, 355-356
Culture of poverty, 84-85, 160, 353, 423

Dance musicians, 378
Deprofessionalization, 187, 233, 293
Deviance, 376
Deviant occupation, 376
Dictionary of Occupational Titles, 25, 43, 135
Dirty work, 203-204, 351-352, 374
Division of labor, 177, 249, 355
Domestic workers, 375
Dual career families, 224-225
Dual labor market, 1, 4
  and goods producing sector, 324
  and licensing, 81
  lower tier, 68-69
  primary sector, 1, 68-69. See also Primary labor market
  and racial discrimination, 106
  secondary sector, 1, 68-69. See also Secondary labor market
  and service producing sector, 324
  upper tier, 68-69
  and working class, 6
Dual labor market theory, 68-69, 88, 324
Duncan Socio-Economic Index, 37, 82, 209

Education, and earnings of nonwhites, 103-105

and occupation, 410-411
and occupational attainment, of nonwhites, 413
 of women, 413-417
and social mobility, 420
and socioeconomic status, 115
Educational colonialism, 428
Educational inequality, 426
Educational opportunities, 420
Elected public officials, 252
Embourgeoisement, of blue-collar
 workers, 323, 353-354
 of labor union leaders, 253
 of lower-middle class, 57
Engineers, 224, 258, 268
Employed poor, 72-75, 107, 114
 and dual labor market, 109
 by race, 107-109
 see also Working poor
Entry jobs, 106, 154-155
 and discrimination, 155
 and socioeconomic background, 155,
 159, 418
Equality, of opportunity, 78, 429
 of results, 429-430
Executives, 248-256
 as elites, 248-249
 female, 131
 functions of, 248
 male, 132
 social background, 250
Experts, 236, 258-260
 and power, 343
External labor market, 67-68

Factory workers, 345-347
False consciousness, 167, 329, 431
Family background and occupational
 achievement, 391-392
Farmer's daughter effect, 228-229
Federal executives, 251-252
Female labor union leaders, 254-255
Female occupations, 81, 137-140,
 153, 235, 255, 280, 300, 310-
 311
Foremen, 260-263, 341

General contractors, 343-344
Goods producing industries, 49
Grocery clerks, 318-319

Hashers, 373
Health service professions, 183
Heteronomous organization, 287, 292
Hierarchy of authority, 73, 249, 367, 399-
 400
 levels of, 179
 and size, 191
Hierarchy fetishism, 73
Hockey players, 205-206
Homemaker, 131-133
 defined, 132
 neo-Freudian interpretation of, 133
 neo-Marxist interpretation of, 133
 social role of, 132
Hospital bureaucracy, 227
Hospital workers, 70
Housewife, see Homemaker
Human capital theory, 66-67, 71, 75, 77-78,
 115-116, 137, 140, 142, 209, 417,
 420, 422-423
Human relations school, 345
Human services, 55

Ideal type, 172
Index of sexual segregation, 136, 140-141
Index of Status Characteristics, 37
Industrial labor market, 342
Innovation, 170, 233-234, 403
Instrumental occupations, 126
Intellectual vanguard, 114
Interest group theory, 116, 118-119
Intergenerational mobility, 106, 155-159
Internal labor market, 67
Involvement, 231, 320, 329, 352, 356-357
I.Q., and educational attainment, 422
 and occupation, 420-423
 and race, 421, 423
 and socioeconomic background, 422

Janitors, 374-375
Jazz musicians, 376-379
 as deviants, 376, 383
Job clusters, 151-153
Job description, 25
Job enlargement, 357
Job integration, 326
Job satisfaction, 320, 323, 348, 356, 358-
 359
Job segmentation, 79
Job specialization, 73, 326

Knowledge, control of, 183, 208, 236, 299
  demystification of, 7
  development of, 199, 233, 236
  as mystique, 203, 208, 235, 328, 344
  rationalization of, 6, 234

Labeling theory, 376
Labor force, size of, 14-15
Labor force participation, 17
Labor market segmentation, 80, 177, 211,
  337-338
Labor market shelters, 79, 81-82, 177
Labor market stratification theories, 4
Labor union leaders, 253-255
Leisure, 231-232
Level consciousness, 40, 73, 211, 323, 329-
  330, 422
Librarians, 183, 201, 299
Licensing, 81
Life-cycle squeeze, 395-396
Line management, 256
Local identity, 178
Lower class, 337, 371
Luck and occupational attainment, 422
Lumpen-proletariat, 8, 117

Male work values, 329, 424
Management consulting, 179-184
Managers, city managers, 257
  functions of, 256-260
  line managers, 257-258
  personnel managers, 259
  professionalization of, 299
  public relations manager, 259, 290-291
  staff managers, 256, 258-259
Mass production, 347
Material handlers, 107
Means of production, 72, 116-119
Medical students, 204-205
Men's liberation, 141-142
Meritocracy, 52, 355, 423
  and human capital, 425-426
Middle class values, 392
Migrant farm workers, 372-373
Minority groups, defined, 96
  educational discrimination, 103-106
  income discrimination, 103-106
  wages of, 76
Minority owned businesses, 263-
  265

Neoclassical economic theory, 65-67, 86, 88
New working class, 36, 74, 89, 211, 380-
  381
NORC Scale, 31-35, 209
Nurses, 227, 281-286
  bureaucratization of, 283
  functional indispensability of, 285
  hierarchy of authority, 283
  male nurses, 285
  and occupational choice, 285
  professionalization of, 282-284
  role of, 281-282, 284
  role conflict, 282
  work alienation, 285
Nurturant occupations, 126, 135, 222
Nurturant role, 225

Occupation, defined, 14
  function of, 106
  and personality, 400-401
  and social class, 115-116
  as social structure, 401
Occupational achievement, see Occupational
  attainment
Occupational aspirations, 115, 159-161, 423,
  427-428
Occupational attainment, 78, 115, 136,
  418, 420
  and luck, 422
  and personality, 422
Occupational authority, see Professional
  authority
Occupational autonomy, 172, 177, 179,
  338
  and alienation, 167
  defined, 167
  and rationalization, 234
  and uncertainty, 188
Occupational categories, types of, 19
Occupational change, 426
Occupational choice, 224, 284
  and careers, 134, 154, 159
  defined, 154
  and primary labor market, 134
  and sex typing, 134
Occupational community, 352-353, 378
Occupational culture, 116, 199, 204, 351-
  353
Occupational discrimination, 102-104
  by age, 17-18, 147, 151, 153

of blacks, 106
of black women, 18
of nonwhites, 107-112
of professional women, 130
by sex, 103, 140, 310
of women, 125-126, 130, 222-226
of young women, 153
Occupational expectations, 160-161
Occupational groups, changes in, 21
Occupational ideology, 351
Occupational injuries, 357-358
Occupational mobility, 106-107, 159
by race, 106
see also Intergenerational mobility
Occupational opportunities, 420
Occupational prestige, 30-35, 115, 209
measures of, 30, 209
Occupational rankings, 37, 209
Occupational roles and family life, 394
Occupational role typing, 131-132
Occupational sex typing, 126-130
agentic approach, 134, 141
communal approach, 135, 142
and occupational choice, 134
Occupational socialization, 183, 198-199, 204
Occupational sociology, role of, vii
Occupational status, 116
Occupational structure, 69
of nonwhites, 99-102
Occupational values, 160, 224
Occupations, and the central city, 99
and economic development, 19-21
and family values, 390, 393
and fertility rates, 153-154
versus jobs, 372
and paradigms, 244
ratio of women to men, 129-130
as social control units, 182
and suburbs, 99
Office as a family, 312
Office mentality, 325, 327
Organization, back and front regions of, 256-257
mechanistic model, 189, 257
in occupations, degree of, 233
organic model, 189, 257
Organizational structures, types of, 174-175
Organized labor, power of, 51

Orthopedic surgeons, 203-204

Paradigm, 243-244
Paradigm change, 244
Paraprofessionals, 294, 428
Pediatricians, 135-136
Personality and occupational attainment, 422
Personnel managers, 259
Petty bourgeoisie, 117
Pharmicists, 292-293
Physicians, 199, 208
black physicians, 229-230
Police officers, 295-299
black police officers, 297-299
professionalization of, 295
and uncertainty, 295-297
Political scientists, 222-223
Postcapitalist society, 53-55
Postindustrial society, 234
blue collar workers, 57-58
conflict theory perspective, 52
defined, 49-50
functionalist perspective, 51
goods producing sector, 74. *See also* Goods-producing industries
professional and technical workers, 57
service producing sector, 74. *See also* Service-producing industries
Postindustrial theories, 4
Poverty, and capitalism, 72
and education, 78
structural characteristics of, 78
structural problems of, 78, 86
Poverty level, 113-114
Bureau of the Census, 84, 107, 114
Bureau of Labor statistics, 84, 109
Power elite, 72-73
Prestige, defined, 78
Primary labor force, 82-83, 360
Primary labor market, 68, 116, 324
and men's occupations, 136-137, 139
and women's occupations, 134, 136, 139
Production, forces of, 2, 55
relations of, 2
socialist mode of, 55
Professional associations, 175
Professional authority, 176-177, 188, 203, 237, 258, 268, 280, 342, 393, 400, 403

Professional autonomy, 176, 183, 201, 207, 234
Professional bureaucracy, 178, 181, 258
Professional community, 210
Professional department, 177, 182
Professional ethics, 200
Professional ideology, 201, 207
Professionalism, 234, 300
  of business, 266
  defined, 182
  interactionist definition, 207
  and professionalization, 234
  and social change, 234
  structuralist definition, 202
Professionalization, 182, 197, 209
  and alienation, 267-268
  and bureaucratization, 232-233
  of business, 265-267
  and change, 232-236
  defined, 172
  interactionist definition, 206-207
  of jazz musicians, 379
  of paradigms, 244
  and power, 207, 232
  and rationalization, 233
  structuralist definition of, 202
Professional knowledge, 170, 189
Professional men, blacks, 229, 230
  married, 224, 225
  role ambivalence, 230
Professional mystique, 204
Professional sex typing, 221-222, 225-226
Professional women, 221-226
  blacks, 228-229
  married, 223-225, 255
  role typing, 225
Professionals and bureaucracy, 201
Professional values, 392-393
Professions, attributes of, 197-198
  Chicago School of, 195
  as coalitions, 208-209
  competition between, 184-186
  defined, 177, 195-196, 202-203
  encroachment of, 199, 244
  interactionist view, 207
  Ivy League School of, 195
  and power, 209, 297
  reasons for studying, 196
  social class approach, 196, 209-212
  as a social force, 237

  structuralist view, 196-202, 199, 201
Proletarianization, 250
  of office workers, 354
  of white collar workers, 323, 353
Proletariat, 8, 117, 366
Proprietors, 263-265
Psychiatrists, 179, 226-227
Public relations manager, 259, 290-291
Public school teachers, 288-290
  professionalism of, 290
  professionalization of, 289
  social mobility, 289

Queue theory of labor market economics,
  see Neoclassical economic theory

Race, and discrimination, 116
  and education, 77
Radical economic theory, 71-79, 86, 88-89, 119
  and women's occupations, 140
Railroad engineers, 343
Rationalization, of assembly line workers, 347
  and bureaucratization, 399
  in construction occupations, 342
  defined, 169-170, 393
  and division of labor, 249
  and dual labor market, 6
  of factory workers, 346-348
  and innovation, 400
  of knowledge, 327-328
  and power, 236
  of professional knowledge, 183
  and technology, 249
  of white collar workers, 353
Research administrators, 257-258
Reserve army of labor, 72, 74, 81, 429
Reserve labor force, see Reserve army of labor
Risk-taking, in lower class, 160
  and professionalization, 236, 323
  and socioeconomic status, 422
Rural occupations, 98-99

Salespeople, 313-316
  new car salespeople, 314
  and professionalization, 313
  and rationalization, 313
  used car salespeople, 314-316

Scientists, 135, 224, 268
  and uncertainty, 243-244
Secondary labor force, 71, 82
Secondary labor market, 68, 116, 324
  and education, 429
  occupations in, 61
  and poverty, 70
  and women's occupations, 134, 140-141
  and youth, 150, 154, 159
Secretaries, 312
Semiprofessionals, and knowledge control, 279
  relationship to professionals, 279-280
  and secondary labor market, 280, 300-301
  and sex typing, 280
  values of, 280-281
Semiskilled workers, 341
Service producing industries, 49-51
Service society, 55, 71
Service workers, 372
Sex, and income inequality, 130
  and industry, 77
  and occupation, 77
Sex role, 134
Sex typing, in occupations, see Occupational sex typing
  in professions, see Professional sex typing
Situs, 38, 78
Skilled workers, 339-341
Smallest space analysis, 39
Social class, 3, 36, 117, 209
  functional definition of, 115
  Marxist definition of, 196, 209-212
  and mental illness, 358
  and occupation, 115, 118
  and social status, 209
  and values, 392
Social control of professionals, 201
Social mobility, of black professionals, 228-230
  of blue collar workers, 353-354
  contest mobility, 419
  defined, 106
  and dual labor market, 113
  and education, 418-420
  and race, 109-113
  sponsored mobility, 419
Social problems, 383-384

Social role, of men, 140-141
  of women, 125-126
Social status, 3, 36, 209
Social stratification, conflict theory of, 4, 36
  defined, 36
  functional theory of, 4, 36, 106, 423-424
Social stratum, 3, 115, 116, 353
Social structure, 216
Social work agencies, 288
Social workers, 103, 286-288
  bureaucracy among, 287
  professionalization of, 287
Socioeconomic achievement, 82
Socioeconomic status and occupational attainment, 420
Sociologists, 223
  black, 228
Sociology of knowledge, 7
Sponsored mobility, 114-115
Staff management, 256, 258-260
Status group, 3, 51, 116, 210
Status inconsistency, 240
Status passage, 204-206
Subemployment, 116
Superstructure, 2
Surplus labor, 2
Surplus value, 88
Symphony orchestra musicians, 205-206
Systems analyst, 328

Tabulating machine operators, 327-328
Taxicab drivers, 350-351
Teachers, high school teachers, 232-233
  jail school teachers, 179, 181
  public school teachers, 179, 181
Technical knowledge, 170, 189
Technology, and alienation, 348
  and occupational control, 185, 250
  and rationalization, 249
  and work involvement, 329
  and work organization, 349
Technostructure, 57
Telephone operators, 316-318
  customer's service representatives, 316
  switchboard, 317-318
Traditional knowledge, 170, 188-189, 233
Tripartite economy, 73
Truckers, 351-353

Uncertainty, and alienation, 329
  and bureaucracy, 399
  in craft industries, 342
  and judgment, 203, 276
  and knowledge control, 184, 235
  and occupational autonomy, 188
  and risk-taking, 235, 323
Underemployment, 72, 74, 86, 88
  by race, 114
Unemployment, defined, 83, 95
  of professionals, 24
  and youth, 160
Unemployment rates, 324
  by age, 83, 147-148
  by occupation, 83-84
  professional and technical, 151
  by race, 83, 107, 118, 148-149
  by sex, 83, 140-141, 148
Union democracy, 253
Unionization, 176
Unions, 176-177
Union stewards, 262-263
Upper class, 255
Urban occupations, 98
Unskilled workers, 371-372

Wage labor, 72
Waitresses, 373-374
Women, images of, 126

Women's labor unions, 380
Women's occupations, see Female occupa-
  tions
Women's values, 134, 224
Work, 356
  as alienation, 321
  as a central life interest, 232, 268, 284
    352, 361
Work alienation, 267-268, 319-325, 356-
    360, 401-402
Worker autonomy, 349, 360
Worker productivity, 345
Worker retraining, 151
Working class, defined, 337, 360
  health of, 358
  as a social class, 354-356
  values, 392
Working-class subculture, 338-339,
    353
Working married women, 140, 389, 394,
    396
  and fertility rates, 397-398, 416
Working mothers, 390-391
Working poor, 72, 371
  by occupational group, 109
  see also Employed poor
Work involvement, see Involvement
Work roles, 134, 182
Work values, 352